1001 DAYS OUT
HISTORIC HOUSES, GARDENS
& PLACES TO VISIT

1001 DAYS OUT

HISTORIC HOUSES, GARDENS & PLACES TO VISIT

MARKS &
SPENCER

Marks and Spencer p.l.c.
PO Box 3339
Chester CH99 9QS

www.marksandspencer.com

ISBN 1-84461-284-8

Printed in Dubai

Designed by Butler and Tanner

Front cover
Penshurst Place, Kent
Frontispiece
Iford Manor, Wiltshire
Right
Hampton Court Palace, London

Acknowledgements & Picture Credits

The Publishers would like to acknowledge the important contribution the British Tourist Authority made to this publication through the use of images from its website, *www.britainonview.com*

The publishers would like to thank The National Trust, The National Trust for Scotland and English Heritage who kindly supplied photographs for use with their entries.

The publishers would also like to thank all contributors who provided information, and particularly all those who kindly supplied photographs.

Compiled, edited and designed by Butler and Tanner. Edited by Helen Burge, Julian Flanders and Dara O'Hare. Design and layout by Lyn Davies and Carole McDonald. Special thanks to Carl Luke, Arran Macdonald and Jennie Golding.

Index

1000 Newton Stewart

Galloway Red Deer Range

2 hrs   Jun–Sep

This attraction has a viewpoint near the road from which these beautiful red deer can be observed in their natural habitat. Visitors to the range can also walk among the deer, photograph them and even touch them, under supervision.

* Guided tours in summer
* See and hear roaring stags during the rutting season

Location
On A712, 3 miles SW of Clatteringshaws Loch

Opening
End of Jun–mid Sep Tue & Thu 11am–2pm Sun 11am–2.30pm

Admission
Adult £3, Child £1, Concs £2

Contact
Red Deer Range Car Park, nr Clatteringshaws, Newton Stewart, Dumfries & Galloway DG7 3SQ

t 01671 402420
w forrestry.gov.uk/ gallowayforestpark
e galloway@forestry.gsi.gov.uk

1001 Sanquhar

Sanquhar Tolbooth Museum

1 hr   Apr–Sep

Find out about Sanquhar knitting, the mines and miners of Sanquhar and Kirkconnel, the history and customs of the Royal Burgh of Sanquhar, three centuries of local literature, what life was like in Sanquhar jail and the earliest inhabitants of the area, both native and Roman.

* Housed in a fine C18 tolbooth
* Community life in times past

Location
In town centre

Opening
Apr–Sep Tue–Sat 10am–1pm 2pm–5pm Sun 2pm–5pm

Admission
Free

Contact
High Street, Sanquhar, Dumfries & Galloway DG46BN

t 01659 50186
w dumfriesmuseum.demon.co.uk
e dumfriesmuseum@dumgal.gov.uk

© Melrose Abbey

997   Melrose

Abbotsford

1 hr+   Mar–Oct

Abbotsford is the house built and lived in by Sir Walter Scott, the C19 novelist and author of timeless classics such as *Waverley*, *Rob Roy* and *Ivanhoe*. Situated on the banks of the River Tweed, the house contains an impressive collection of relics, weapons and armour.

* Rob Roy's gun and Montrose's sword
* Extensive grounds and walled garden

Location
On A6091, 2 miles from Melrose

Opening
14 Mar–30 Oct Mon–Sat 9.30am–5pm
Sun Mar–May & Oct 2pm–5pm
Sun Jun–Sep 9.30–5pm

Admission
Adult £4.75, Child £2.40

Contact
Melrose, Borders TD6 9BQ

t 01896 752043
w sirwalterscottsabbotsford.com
e sirwalterscottsabbotsford@btinter-
    net.com

998   Melrose

Melrose Abbey

½ hr   All year

Arguably the finest of Scotland's border abbeys, Melrose is a magnificent ruin on a grand scale with lavishly decorated masonry. It is thought to be the burial place of Robert the Bruce's heart, marked with a commemorative carved stone plaque within the grounds.

* Large collection of objects found during excavation
* Museum with local artefacts found in abbey ground

Location
Off A7 / A68, in Melrose

Opening
Daily; Apr–Sep 9.30am–6.30pm
Oct–Mar 9.30am–4.30pm Sun
2pm–4.30pm

Admission
Adult £3.50, Child £1.20, Concs £2.50

Contact
Abbey Street, Melrose,
Roxburghshire TD6 9LG

t 01896 822562
w historic-scotland.gov.uk

999   Melrose

Three Hills Roman Centre & Fort

4 hrs   All year

The most important Roman military complex between Hadrian's Wall and the Antonine Wall guarded and secured the crossing of the Tweed at Newstead in C1 and C2 AD. Excavations have revealed much of what was going on there.

* See millennium milestone & timber tower
* Viewing platforms and information boards

Location
1 mile E of Melrose, in Newstead

Opening
Walks 17 Mar–31 Oct Thu 1.30–5pm
Jun–Jul Tue & Thu 1.30–5pm
Exhibition 17 Mar–31 Oct
10.30am–4.30pm
1 Nov–31 Mar on request

Admission
Site free
Walks Adult £3, Child £2.50, Concs
£2.50
Exhibition £1.50, £1, £1

Contact
Ormistram, Melrose, TD6 9PN

t 01896 822651
w trimontium.net

994 Kelso

Floors' Castle

2 hrs   Apr–Oct

Boasting fine views over the river Tweed to the Cheviot Hills, the castle has been home to the Roxburghe family since it was built by WIlliam Adam in 1721. It houses superb collections of art, tapestries and antiques and is set in parkland which abounds with flora and fauna.

* Various sporting activities (golf, shooting) on offer
* Works by well-known artists, including Matisse

Location
On the edge of Kelso

Opening
Daily; Apr–Oct 10am–4.30pm

Admission
Adult £5.75, Child £3.25, Concs £4.75

Contact
Kelso, Roxburghshire TD5 7SF

t 01573 223333
w www.floorscastle.com
e marketing@floorscastle.com

995 Largs

The Viking Experience

1 hr   Feb–Nov

This multimedia journey recounts the saga of the Vikings in Scotland, from invasion to defeat at the Battle of Largs. Meet the Gods and Valkyries in Valhalla, come face to face with Odin, the Viking god of war, and walk with him into the Viking world of 700 years ago.

* Shows begin regularly
* Leisure Facilities, Soft play centre and theatre

Location
On the Largs seafront

Opening
Daily; Apr–Sep 10.30am–5.30pm
Oct & Mar 10.30am–3.30pm;
Nov & Feb Sat 12.30pm–3.30pm
Sun 10.30am–3.30pm

Admission
Adult £4, Child & Concs £3

Contact
Vikingar, Greenock Road,
Largs, Ayrshire KA30 8QL

t 01475 689777
w vikingar.co.uk
e info@vikingar.co.uk

996 Lockerbie

Carlyle's Birthplace

½ hr   May–Sep

The Arched House, in which Thomas Carlyle was born in 1795, was built by his father and uncle in 1791. Carlyle was a great writer and historian and one of the most powerful influences on C19 British thought. The house is now furnished to reflect Victorian domestic life.

* Collection of portraits
* Carlyle's belongings

Location
Off M74, on A74, in Ecclefechan,
5½ miles SE of Lockerbie

Opening
May–Sep Thu–Mon 1pm–5pm

Admission
Adult £2.50, Child & Concs £1.90

Contact
The Arched House, Ecclefechan,
Lockerbie, Dumfries & Galloway
DG11 3DG

t 01576 300666
w nts.org.uk

990 Eyemouth

Eyemouth Museum

1 hr Apr-Oct

This newly-refurbished museum has a magnificent 15 x 4ft tapestry which commemorates the great east-coast fishing disaster of 1881 in which 189 local fishermen were drowned. It also has exhibitions on fishing, farming, milling, wheelwrighting, and blacksmithing.

* 3 Star attraction

Location
In the centre of Eyemouth

Opening
Daily; Apr–Jun & Sep, Mon–Sat, 10am–5pm, Sun 12 noon–2pm; Jul–Aug, Mon–Sat, 10am–5.30pm, Sun 12 noon–2pm; Oct, Mon–Sat, 10am–4pm

Admission
Adult £3, Child free, Concs £1.50

Contact
Auld Kirk, Manse Road, Eyemouth

t 018907 50678

991 Hawick

Drumlanrig's Tower

1 hr All year

The Black Tower of Drumlanrig is an imposing landmark in the Scottish Borders town of Hawick. The tower has borne silent witness to the savage cross-border warfare and bitter inter-family feuding which marked the town's turbulent past.

* Exhibition tells the story of the house
* Display of watercolours by the artist Tom Scott

Location
Hawick High Street

Opening
Daily; Jul–Aug Mon–Sat 10am–6pm Sun 1pm–5pm
Apr–Jun & Sep–Oct Mon–Sat 10am–5pm Sun 1pm–5pm
Winter times vary, phone for details

Admission
Adult £2.50, Child free

Contact
1 Towerknowe, Hawick TD9 9EN

t 01450 373457

992 Heathhall

Dumfries & Galloway Aviation Museum

3hrs All year

Founded in 1977 by a group of aviation enthusiasts and based on a former Second World War airfield, the museum is located in and around the original 3-storey-high control tower. It is now home to engines, memorabilia and personal histories.

* 3 Star Award
* Huge collection of artefacts

Location
On the Heathhall Industrial Estate, easily accessed from A75 Dumfries bypass. From the town centre follow A701 Edinburgh road

Opening
Daily; Easter–Oct Sat–Sun 10am–5pm; Jul–Aug Wed–Fri 11am–4pm; Oct–Easter Sun only 11am–4pm

Admission
Adult £2.50, Child £1.50, Concs £1.50

Contact
Heathhall Industrial Estate
Heathhall, Dumfries DG13PH

t 01387 251623
w www.dumfriesaviationmuseum.com
e alammin@hotmail.com

993 Isle of Arran

King's Cave

2 hrs All year

This is said to be the legendary spot where Robert the Bruce, dejected and battle weary, was inspired by the tenacity of a small spider as it painstakingly spun its web. He went on to win many battles following this episode. On the cave wall are rare writings by Picts.

Location
Off A841, nr Blackwaterfoot, Isle of Arran, access by coastal path only

Opening
Daily; at any reasonable time

Admission
Free

Contact
Blackwaterfoot, Isle of Arran

t 0845 2255121
w showcaves.com

987   Caerlaverock

WWT Caerlaverock Wetlands Centre

½ day   All year

This 1,400-acre wild nature reserve is a must for bird lovers. The site has hides and observation towers linked by a network of screened approaches. The number of barnacle geese that fly from Norway to the banks of the Solway Firth each year is testament to the quality of the wetlands.

* Self-catering accommodation available
* Badger-watching & summer nature trail

Location
Located 9 miles SE of Dumfries along the Solway Coast Heritage Trail

Opening
Daily; 10am–5pm;

Admission
Adult £4.40, Child £2.70, Concs £3.60
Under-4s Free

Contact
Eastpark Farm, Caerlaverock
Dumfriesshire DG1 4RS

t 01387 770200
w wwt.org.uk
e info.caerlaverock@wwt.org.uk

989   Dumfries

Gretna Green World Famous Blacksmith's Shop

1 hr+   All year

Runaway marriages began in 1753, when it became illegal to marry under 21. However, in Scotland it was, and still is, possible to marry at 16. Gretna Green is the first village across the border that many 'elopers' came to and the Blacksmith's Shop was the centre of the marriage trade.

* Old coach collection
* Juicy stories of romance, intrigue & scandal

Location
On A74, just N of the border

Opening
Daily; Apr–Sep 9am– Early evening
Oct–Mar 9am–5pm

Admission
Exhibition Adult £2.50, Child £2

Contact
Gretna Green Group Ltd,
Headless Cross, Gretna Green,
Dumfriesshire DG16 5EA

t 01461 338441
w gretnagreen.com
e info@gretnagreen.com

988   Dumfries

Dumfries Museum & Camera Obscura

1 hr   Mar–Oct

A treasure house of the history of south west Scotland, the museum is centred on the C18 windmill tower that stands above the town. On the top floor, there is a camera obscura and on the tabletop screen visitors can see panoramic views of Dumfries and the surrounding countryside.

* Prehistoric reptile footprints
* Tools & weapons from the area's oldest people

Location
In town centre

Opening
Daily; Apr–Sep Mon–Sat 10am–5pm
Sun 2pm–5pm;
Oct & Mar Tue–Sat 10am–1pm
2pm–5pm

Admission
Museum Free
Camera Obscura Adult £1.55,
Child 80p, Concs 80p

Contact
Rotchell Road, Dumfries DG2 7SW

t 01387 253374
w dumfal.gov.uk/museums
e dumfriesmuseum2dumfal.gov.uk

984 Alloway

Burns National Heritage Park

2 hrs   All year

Now fully restored to its original state, Burns' cottage forms the heart of this attraction, offering a unique encounter with Scotland's most exceptional man. Set among the delightful scenery of historic Alloway, this is an unmatched opportunity to experience Scotland's national poet.

* Unique authentic locations & artefacts
* The world's most important Robert Burns collection

Location
On A719, south of Ayr

Opening
Daily; Apr–Oct 10am–5.30pm
Nov–Mar 10am–5pm

Admission
Adult £5, Child & Concs £2.50

Contact
Murdoch's Lone, Alloway, Ayr
KA7 4PQ

t 01292 443700
w burnsheritagepark.com
e info@burnsheritagepark.com

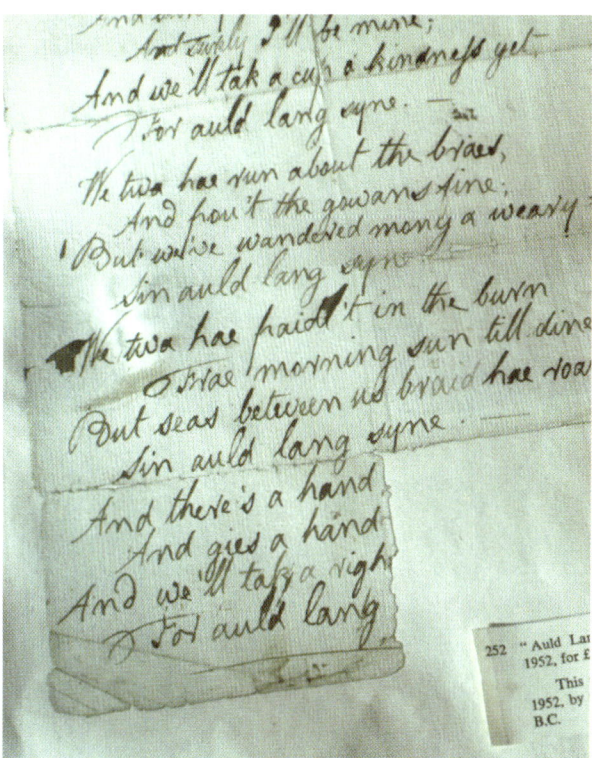

985 Ayr

Dunaskin Heritage Centre

4 hrs+   Apr–Oct

Set in a 110-acre site amid the picturesque scenery of the Doon Valley, this museum was originally an ironworks, built around 1850, and today it tells the story of the ironworks, coal mining and brickworks at Dunaskin through the eyes of the people who lived and worked there.

* Audio tours
* Guided tours

Location
Off A713, between Ayr & Castle
Douglas / Dumfries

Opening
Daily; Apr–Oct 10am–5pm

Admission
Adult £4.50, Child £2.50, Concs £3.75

Contact
Dalmellington Road, Waterside,
Waterside by Patna, Ayrshire KA6 7JF

t 01292 531144
w dunaskin.co.uk
e dunaskin@btconnect.com

986 Ayr

The Electric Brae

½ hr   All year

This is a hill with a difference. While the views are spectacular, try placing a round object, like a ball, on the ground. What direction do you think it will roll? Due to an optical illusion the ball will roll upwards; let off the hand brake for a second and the car will move uphill!

Location
A719 9 miles S of Ayr, 2 miles S of
Dunure, 1 mile N of the A719–B7023
junction, NW edge of the hamlet of
Knoweside

Opening
Daily; at any reasonable time

Admission
Free

Contact
t 01292 678100
w ayrshire-arran.com

© ArnolBlackhouse

981 Spean Bridge

Monster Activities

  2 hrs All year

From its base in the Scottish Highlands, this sports centre offers outdoor activities of all kinds, including the country's most exciting whitewater rafting. Not only does it offer instruction, hire, courses and short breaks, it also guarantees fun for the whole family.

* All kinds of outdoor activities on land & water
* All necessary equipment available

Location
On A82, between Fort William & Inverness

Opening
Daily; 9.30am–5.30pm

Admission
Depends on activity–please phone for details

Contact
Great Glen Water Park, South Laggan, Spean Bridge, Invernessshire PH34 4AE
t 01809 501340
w monsteractivities.com
e info@monsteractivities.com

982 Stornoway

The Black House Museum

  ½ hr+ All year

The site includes a traditional Lewis thatched crofter's cottage, or black house, with byre and stackyard, complete with a peat fire burning in the central hearth. There is also a restored 1920s white house and a visitor centre with fascinating information about Herbridean life.

* Green Gold Tourism award-winner
* 5 Star Scottish Tourism Award

Location
Off A858

Opening
Apr–Sep Mon–Sat 9.30am–6pm
Oct–Mar 9.30am–4pm

Admission
Adult £3, Child £1, Concs £2.30

Contact
Arnol Isle of Lewis HS2 9DB
t 01851 710395
w historic-scotland.gov.uk

983 Tain

Glenmorangie Distillery Centre

   1 hr All year

Tour the distillery in the company of one of the guides, who will explain the whisky-making process from beginning to end and introduce you to the Sixteen Men of Tain who make it, before a visit to the tasting room to sample the results of their industry and skill.

* Located in the Glen of Tranquility
* Regular distillery tours

Location
On A9, 1 hour N of Inverness

Opening
Shop Daily; Mon–Fri 9am–5pm
Sat 10am–4pm Sun 12 noon–4pm
Tours Daily; 10.30am 11.30am 2.30pm
3.30pm (prebooking advisable)

Admission
Adults £2.50

Contact
Tain, Rosshire IV19 1PZ
t 01862 892477
w glenmorangie.com
e visitors@glenmorangieplc.co.uk

977 Mull

Hebridean Whale & Dolphin Trust

  ½ hr All year

On land and sea. Mull has a greater variety and abundance of wildlife than any other Hebridean island. Go to the HWDT visitor centre in Tobermory for information on whale and dolphin watching trips, as well as a whole range of other wildlife 'safaris'.

* Huge variety of Scottish wildlife in its natural habitat
* Land & sea 'safaris'

Location
To reach Mull, take ferry from Oban to Craignure, Trust is opposite clock tower in Tobermoray

Opening
Daily; Apr–Oct 10am–5.30pm
Nov–Mar 11am–5pm

Admission
Free

Contact
28 Main Street, Tobermory, Isle of Mull, Argyll PA75 6NU
t 01688 302620
w hwdt.org
e hwdt@sol.co.uk

978 Oban

McCaig's Tower

  1 hr All year

Undoubtedly Oban's most outstanding feature, McCaig's Tower was built in 1897 by local banker John Stuart McCaig to provide work for local stonemasons and a lasting monument to his family. The steep climb from the town centre is well worth the effort.

* Breathtaking views over Oban Bay to the Atlantic islands
* Peaceful gardens inside the tower

Location
Short, steep walk from town centre

Opening
Daily

Admission
Free

Contact
Oban Tourist Information Centre, Argyll Square, Oban, Argyll
t 01631 563122
w oban.org.uk
e info@oban.org.uk

979 Oban

Scottish Sealife & Marine Sanctuary

  2½ hrs All year

Located on the shores of beautiful Loch Creran, the sanctuary is home to over 30 fascinating natural marine habitats containing everything from shrimps and starfish to sharks and stingrays. The sanctuary also cares for many sick and injured seal pups every year.

* 3 Star Marine Attraction
* New displays added regularly

Location
10 miles N of Oban on A82

Opening
Daily; Feb–Nov 10am–6pm (last admission 5pm); Dec & Jan w/e hols

Admission
Adult £7.95, Child £5.50, Concs £6.50

Contact
Sanctuary, Barcaldine
By Oban, Argyll PA37 1SE
t 01631 720386
w www.sealsanctuary.co.uk
e oban@sealife.fsbusiness.co.uk

980 Skye

Dunvegan Castle

 2 hrs All year

The north of Scotland's oldest inhabited castle is also Skye's most famous landmark, having been the seat and home of the MacLeod chiefs for 800 years. Dunvegan Castle is a fortress stronghold in an idyllic lochside setting, surrounded by dramatic scenery.

* Many fine oil paintings & great clan treasures
* Picturesque woodland garden

Location
1 mile N of Dunvegan

Opening
Daily; Mar–Oct 10am–5.30pm
Nov–Feb 11am–4pm

Admission
Summer, Adult £6.50, Child £3.50, Concs £5.50

Winter, Adult £4, Child £2.50, Concs £3.50

Contact
Isle of Skye IV55 8WF
t 01470 521206
w dunvegancastle.com

975 Lewis

Calanais Standing Stones

  1 hr All year

This is a fascinating, cross-shaped setting of 50 standing stones. The site dates to 3000 BC and the configuration is unique in Scotland (and special in Great Britain). The audio- visual presentation in the visitor centre tells their story.

* Visitor centre
* Story of the Stones exhibition

Location
Off A859, 12 miles W of Stornoway

Opening
Site **Daily**
Visitor centre **Apr–Sep Mon–Sat 10am–6pm Oct–Mar Wed–Sat 10am–4pm**

Admission
Exhibition **Adult £1.75, Child £75p, Concs £1.25**

Contact
Visitor Centre, Calanais, Isle of Lewis, Western Isles HS2 9DY

t 01851 621422
w historic-scotland.gov.uk

976 Kyle of Lochalsh

Eilean Donan Castle

  1 hr Mar–Nov

Eilean Donan is located on a small island near Dornie, Rossshire. In a superbly romantic setting amid silent, tree-clad hills, it possesses a rare and dream-like quality, but, in reality, is a fortress of solid stone and formidable defences. The Isle of Skye can be seen across the water.

* Visitor centre
* The most photographed castle in Scotland

Location
On A87, 8 miles from Kyle of Lochalsh

Opening
Daily; Easter–Oct 10am–6pm
Mar–Easter Nov 10am–5.30pm
Nov 10am–4pm

Admission
Adult £4.50, Child £3.40, Concs £3.40

Contact
Dornie, Kyle of Lochalsh IV40 8DX

t 01599 555202
w eileandonancastle.com
e info@donan.f9.co.uk

972 Glencoe

Glencoe Visitor Centre

1 hr   All year

Some of the finest climbing and walking country in the Highlands is to be found within this area of dramatic landscapes and historical fact and legend. The infamous massacre of 1692 took place throughout the glen, one of the main locations being near the new visitor centre.

* Video about the massacre
* Display on the history of mountaineering in the glen

Location
On A82, between Glasgow & Fort William

Opening
Daily; Mar 10am–4pm
Apr–Aug 9.30am–5.30pm
Sep–Oct 10am–5pm
Nov–Feb Thu–Sun 10am–4pm

Admission
Adult £4.50, Child £2.95, Concs £2.95

Contact
Ballachulish, Argyll PH49 4LA

t 01855 811307
w nts.org.uk
e sborland@nts.org.uk

973 Inverary

Inverary Castle

1 hr   Apr–Oct

Also known as the 'Fairy Tale Castle', it's easy to see why this is one of Scotland's hidden treasures. Originally the home of the Campbell clan, the castle now boasts a selection of magnificent rooms through which the visitor can trace its history.

* History of the clan Campbell
* Remains the home of the Duke of Argyll

Location
On A83, on shores of Loch Fyne

Opening
Daily; Jun–Sep Mon–Sat
10am–5.45pm, Sun 1pm–5.45pm,
Apr–May Oct Mon–Thu Sat 10am–1pm
2–5.45pm Sun 1pm–5.45pm

Admission
Adult £5.90, Child £3.90, Concs £4.90

Contact
The Factor, Argyll Estates Office,
Inverary, Argyll PA32 8XE

t 01499 302203
w inverary-castle.com
e enquiries@inveraray-castle.com

974 John o' Groats

The Last House in Scotland Museum

½ hr+   All year

Visitors to the Last House in Scotland can enjoy a pictorial history of the area and see some of the wonderful artefacts of bygone times that have been loaned to the museum by local residents of John O'Groats.

* Postcards stamped with the official 'Last House' stamp

Location
17 miles N of Wick

Opening
Daily; Jun–Sep 8am–6.30pm
Oct–May 9am–5pm
Times vary due to ferry

Admission
Free

Contact
John O' Groats KW1 4YR

t 01955 611250

969 Fort William

The Jacobite Steam Train

6 hrs   Jun–Oct

Described as one of the great railway journeys of the world, the Jacobite Steam Train leaves Fort William and travels on an 84-mile round trip. It passes Ben Nevis, then crosses the Glenfinnan Viaduct used in the *Harry Potter* films and arrives by the Atlantic Ocean in Mallaig.

* Leaves Fort William at 10.20am and returns at 4pm
* 1½ hour stopover in Mallaig

Location
Fort William station, in town centre

Opening
6 Jun–30 Jul Mon–Fri
31 Jul–28 Aug Sun–Fri
29 Aug–7 Oct Mon–Fri

Admission
Return Tickets Adult £25, Child £14.50
First Class Adult £38, Child £19

Contact
West Coast Railway Company, Warton Road, Carnforth, Lancashire LA5 9HX

t 01463 239026
w steamtrain.info

970 Fort William

Treasures of the Earth

1hr   Feb–Dec

A unique collection of minerals, fossils and precious stones from all around the world, displayed in simulated caves and caverns. There are casts of T-Rex and a sabre-toothed tiger, together with fossil fish and dinosaur bones.

Location
In Corpach by Fort William

Opening
Daily; in summer open 9.30am–7pm;
in winter 10am–5pm;
Closed Jan

Admission
Adult £3.50, Child £2, Senior £3

Contact
Corpach
Fort William
Inverness-shire PH33 7JL

t 01397 772283

971 Fort William

Vertical Descents

3 hrs+   Apr–Oct

Located at Inchree Falls, this is Scotland's first and longest canyoning descent. Canyoning involves a combination of abseiling, swimming and sliding through water flumes, plus jumping into giant rock pools, as you make your way downstream.

* No previous experience necessary
* All necessary clothing and equipment provided

Location
Off A82, 7 miles south of Fort William

Opening
Apr–mid–Oct

Admission
£35 per person (half-day canyoning)

Contact
Inchree Falls, Inchree, Onich, nr Fort William PH33 6SE

t 01855 821593
w activities-scotland.com
e verticaldescents@yahoo.com

© The National Trust for Scotland

967 Culloden Moor

Culloden Battlefield

1 hr+   Feb–Dec

No name in Scottish history evokes more emotion than Culloden, the bleak moor where, in 1746, Bonnie Prince Charlie's hopes were crushed and the Jacobite Rising was put down. The prince's forces were greatly outnumbered, but nevertheless went into battle with legendary courage.

* Permanent exhibition of weapons used in the battle
* Audio-visual programme

Location
On B9006, 5 miles E of Inverness

Opening
Daily; Apr–Oct 9am–6pm
Nov–Dec Feb–Mar 11am–4pm

Admission
Adult £5, Child £3.75 Concs £3.75

Contact
The National Trust for Scotland,
Culloden Moor, Inverness IV1 5EU

t 01463 790607
w nts.org.uk/culloden

968 Drumnadrochit

Loch Ness Monster Exhibition Centre

1 hr+   All Year

Through photographs, descriptions and film footage, this exhibition presents the evidence about the existence of the Loch Ness Monster. It also highlights the efforts of various search expeditions, by both individuals and respected institutions, such as Operation Deepscan.

* Travel round the loch, view places and meet locals
* Exhibition cinema in eight different languages

Location
On A82, W of Inverness

Opening
Daily; Apr–Oct 9am–9pm
Nov–Mar 9am–5pm

Admission
Adult £4.75, Child £3.25, Concs £3.75

Contact
Drumnadrochit, Invernesshire
IV63 6TU

t 01456 450342
w lochness-centre.com
e donald@lochness-centre.com

964 Aviemore

Cairngorm Reindeer Centre

½ hr   Feb–Dec

See Britain's only reindeer herd roaming free in the Cairngorm mountains. These extremely tame and friendly animals are a joy to all who come and meet them. Under supervision, visitors can feed and stroke the animals in this herd of about 50.

* Guided tours on the hills weather permitting
* Learn more about these fascinating creatures

Location
6 miles E of Aviemore

Opening
Daily; Feb–Apr Oct–Dec 11am
May–Sep 11am & 2.30pm

Admission
Adult £8, Child & Concs £4

Contact
Glenmore, Aviemore,
Invernesshire PH22 1QU

t 01479 861228
w reindeer-company.demon.co.uk
e info@reindeer-company.demon.
    co.uk

966 Broadford

Family's Pride II Glassbottom Boat Trips

1hr   Mar–Oct

Frequent daily sailings provide an opportunity to see the stunning coastal scenery of Skye and marine wildlife (which may include dolphins, whales and seals), both above and below the waves through unique under-sea windows, enhanced by an aquatic floodlight system.

Location
In Broadford, Isle of Skye,
8 miles from the Skye Bridge. There is
a free minibus collection at the
Information Centre if required

Opening
Daily; Mar–Oct 10.30am–4.45pm

Admission
Adult £9.50, Under-12s £4.75

Contact
5 Scullamus, Breakish
Isle of Skye IV42 8QB

t 0800 783 2175
w glassbottomboat.co.uk

965 Balmaha

Loch Lomond National Nature Reserve

3 hrs   All year

Inchailloch, one of the most accessible of Loch Lomond's 38 islands, has a long association with Christianity. Cloaked in oak woodland, with a wealth of bird life and flora, there are several woodland trails giving fantastic views of the loch.

* Wonderful camp & picnic site
* Remains of a C13 parish church

Location
Inchailloch is reached by ferry from
the Balmaha boatyard.

Opening
Daily; wardens present Apr– Sep

Admission
Free

Contact
Loch Lomond & Trossochs National
Park, Balmaha Visitor Centre

t 01389 722600

960 Dufftown

Glenfiddich Distillery

2 hrs   All year

Visit the home of the only Highland single malt Scotch whisky that is distilled, matured and bottled at its distillery. Whisky has flowed from the stills at this site since 1887. Tours of the distillery begin at the visitor centre.

* Distillery tours and shop

Location
On A941, ½ mile N of Dufftown

Opening
Daily; Easter–mid Oct
Mon–Sat 9.30am–4.30pm
Sun 12 noon–4.30pm;
Mid Oct–Easter Mon–Fri
9.30am–4.30pm

Admission
Free

Contact
Dufftown, Banffshire AB55 4DH

t 01340 820373
w glenfiddich.com

961 Ellon

Scottish Tartans Museums

1 hr+   Apr–Oct

This charming museum has over 1,000 artefacts including the famous Mauchlinware on display. There are over 700 Tartans on display in the Tartan Section including clan, family, military, district, corporate and commercial in a selection of modern designs.

* See a portrait of John Brown, commissioned by Queen Victoria
* A facsimile of the Falkirk Tartan – the oldest tartan ever found

Location
Keith town centre

Opening
Apr–Oct, Mon–Fri 11.00am–3.00pm,
Sat 11.00am–4.00pm

Admission
Adult £2.50, Child £1.50, Concs £2.00

Contact
138 Mid Street, Keith, Banffshire
AB55 5BJ

t 01542 888419
w keithcommunity.co.uk

962 Fraserburgh

The Museum of Scottish Lighthouses

2 hrs+   All year

Located in Scotland's oldest lighthouse, the museum tells the history of Scotland's lighthouses. There are multi-screen audio-visual presentations and a guided tour to the top of the fully-restored lighthouse where visitors can enjoy panoramic views of the Buchan Coast.

* Largest collection of lighthouse equipment in UK
* The 1st lighthouse built on top of a fortified castle

Location
In Fraserburgh

Opening
Daily; Apr–Oct, Mon–Sat, 11am–5pm,
Sun, 12 noon–5pm; Jul–Aug, Mon–Sat,
10am–6pm, Sun, 11am–6pm; Nov–Mar,
Mon–Sat, 11am–4pm, Sun 12 noon–
4pm

Admission
Adult £4.75, Child £2, Concs £4

Contact
Kinnaird Head, Stevenson Road,
Fraserburgh AB43 9DU

t 01346 511022
w lighthousemuseum.co.uk

963 Peterhead

Peterhead Maritime Heritage

1hr+   Jun–Aug

This heritage centre offers a historic look back at the Peterhead experience of fishing and whaling, and gives a brief insight into the oil industry.

* 3 Star Speciality Attraction

Location
Overlooking Peterhead Bay &
beside the beach and marina.
Reached via the A90 or A950

Opening
Daily; Jun–Aug 10.30am–5pm & Sun
11.30am–5pm

Admission
Please phone for details

Contact
South Road, Peterhead,
Aberdeenshire AB42 2YP

t 01779 473000

956 Aberdeen

Aberdeen Maritime Museum

1 hr+   All year

This museum tells the story of Aberdeen's long relationship with the sea. It houses a unique collection, covering shipbuilding, fast sailing ships, fishing and port history, and is the only place in the UK where you can see displays on the North Sea oil industry.

* Incorporates Provost Ross's House, built in 1593
* Offers a spectacular viewpoint over the busy harbour

Location
On the harbour

Opening
Daily; Mon–Sat 10am–5pm
Sun 12 noon–3pm

Admission
Free

Contact
Shiprow, Aberdeen AB11 5BY

t 01224 337700
w aberdeencity.gov.uk
e info@aagm.co.uk

957 Aberdeen

Beach Leisure Centre

4 hrs+   All year

This centre has a leisure pool with many water features, including waves, a fountain and rapids. There is a well-equipped fitness studio, saunas, a steam room, a hydrojet, and a double-sized sports hall, equipped for virtually every indoor game.

Location
Next to the beach at Aberdeen

Opening
Please phone for details

Admission
Facilities individualy priced

Contact
Beach Promenade
Aberdeen AB24 5NR

t 01224 647647
w www.aberdeencity.gov.uk
e info@aberdeencity.gov.uk

958 Ballater

Balmoral Castle & Estate

1 hr+   Easter–Aug

The Queen's favourite home is still a working estate. A visit provides a marvellous insight into royal heritage and the life of a large estate, that provides employment and housing, as well as working to conserve and regenerate the natural environment.

* Access to the grounds, gardens, exhibitions, shops, tearoom and ballroom

Location
Off A93, between Ballater & Braemar

Opening
Daily; Easter–Aug 10am–5pm

Admission
Adult £6, Child £1, Concs £5

Contact
Estates Office, Balmoral Estates,
Ballater, Aberdeenshire AB35 5TB

t 013397 42534
w balmoralcastle.com
e info@balmoralcastle.com

959 Braemar

Braemar Castle

2 hrs   Apr–Oct

Located in the Cairngorms on Royal Deeside, this impressive fortress was built in 1628 by the Earl of Mar and later transformed by the Farquharsons of Invercauld into a family residence. It has a fine collection of art and antiques and a military room with Highland uniforms.

* Home of the world's largest cairngorm (52 lbs)
* Curio room with interesting memorabilia

Location
½ mile NE of Braemar on A93
Aberdeen-to-Perth scenic route

Opening
Apr–Oct, Sat–Thu, 10am–6pm

Admission
Adult £3

Contact
Braemar, Aberdeenshire AB35 5XR

t 013397 41219
w braemarcastle.co.uk
e invercauld@btconnect.com

953 Stirling

Argyll's Lodging

½ hr   All year

A superb mansion built around an earlier core in about 1630 and further extended by the Earl of Argyll in the 1670s. It is the most impressive town house of its period in Scotland. The principal rooms are now restored to their 1680 state.

* Beautiful furniture and furnishings
* Magnificent restoration

Location
Near town centre

Opening
Daily; Apr–Oct 9.30am–6pm
Nov–Mar 9.30am–5pm

Admission
Adult £3.30, Child £1.20, Concs £2.50

Contact
Castle Wynd, Stirling, Stirlingshire FK8 1EG

t 01786 431319
w historic-scotland.gov.uk

954 Stirling

Bannockburn Heritage Centre

½ hr+   All year

Located at one of the most important historical sites in Scotland, this centre offers great insights into the Battle of Bannockburn, Robert the Bruce and William Wallace. Learn about the legendary battle in which Bruce and his army defeated Edward II of England.

* Wars of independence exhibition
* Audio-visual presentation of the famous battle

Location
Off M80/M9 junction 9, 2 miles S of Stirling

Opening
Daily; Feb–Mar Nov–Dec 10.30am–4pm
Apr–Oct 10am–5.30pm

Admission
Adult £3.50, Child £2.60, Concs £2.60

Contact
Glasgow Road, Whins of Milton, Stirling, Stirlingshire FK7 0LJ

t 01786 812664
w nts.org.uk

955 Stirling

Wallace Monument

1 hr   All year

This is a chance to renew your acquaintance with Scotland's national hero and the Hollywood legend, Sir William Wallace, popularly known as Braveheart, at the spectacular 220 foot (67m) National Wallace Monument, completed in 1869.

* See the mighty two-handed broadsword
* Visit the Hall of Heroes

Location
Off M9 junction 10, 1 mile NE of Stirling town centre

Opening
Daily; Mar–May Oct 10am–5pm
Jun 10am–6pm
Jul–Aug 9.30am–6.30pm
Sep 9.30am–5pm
Nov–Feb 10.30am–4pm

Admission
Adult £6, Child£4, Concs £4

Contact
Abbey Craig, Stirling, Stirlingshire FK9 5LF

t 01786 472140
w nationalwallacemonument.com
e nwm@aillst.ossian.net

949 Pitlochry

Killiecrankie Visitor Centre

½ hr+   Apr–Oct

In 1689, the Pass of Killiecrankie echoed with the sounds of battle, when a Jacobite army defeated the government forces. The spectacular gorge is tranquil now and a fine example of mixed deciduous woodland. The visitor centre exhibits battle, natural history and ranger services.

* Site of special scientific interest
* Visitors can watch birds nesting via a remote camera

Location
On B8079, 3 miles N of Pitlochry

Opening
Daily; Jul–Aug 9.30am–6pm
Apr–Oct 10am–5.30pm

Admission
Free, £2 charge for car park

Contact
nr Pitlochry, Tayside PH16 5LG

t 01796 473233
w nts.org.uk

950 St Andrews

British Golf Museum

½ hr+   All year

Using a range of exciting, interactive displays, this museum tells the story of British golf, from its origins in the Middle Ages to the present day. The players, tournaments and equipment which make golf the game it now is are explored in detail.

* Regular calendar of events
* Guided walks on the Old Course (summer only)

Location
Signed from town centre

Opening
Daily; Apr–Oct 9.30am–5.30pm
Winter times vary

Admission
Adult £4, Child £2, Concs £3

Contact
Bruce Embankment, St Andrews,
Fife KY16 9AB

t 01334 460046
w britishgolfmuseum.co.uk
e alisonwood@randagc.org

951 St Andrews

Scotland's Secret Bunker

1 hr+   Apr–Oct

Discover the twilight world of the government's Cold War headquarters. Hidden for over 40 years beneath a Scottish farmhouse, a tunnel leads to Scotland's Secret Bunker – 24,000 square feet of secret accommodation on two levels, 100 feet underground.

* Built in complete secrecy in 1950s
* Imagine life after a nuclear holocaust

Location
On B940, between St Andrews
& Anstruther

Opening
Daily; Apr–Oct 10am–6pm

Admission
Adult £7.20, Child £4.50, Concs £5.95

Contact
Crown Buildings, Troywood,
nr St Andrews, Fife KY16 8QH

t 01333 310301
w secretbunker.co.uk
e mod@secretbunker.co.uk

952 Stirling

Stirling Castle

1 hr+   All year

Without doubt one of the grandest of all Scottish castles, both in its situation on a rocky outcrop and in its architecture. The Great Hall and the gatehouse of James IV, the marvellous palace of James V, the Chapel Royal and the artillery fortifications are all of outstanding interest.

* Audio-visual presentation
* Regimental Museum of the Highlanders

Location
Off M9, in old town

Opening
Daily; Apr–Sep 9.30am–6pm
Oct–Mar 9.30am–5pm

Admission
Adult £8, Child £2, Concs £6

Contact
Esplanade, Stirling,
Stirlingshire FK8 1EJ

t 01786 450000
w historic-scotland.gov.uk

946 Perth

Scone Palace

1 hr+   Apr–Oct

In a spectacular setting above the River Tay, Scone Palace has been the seat of parliaments and the crowning place of kings. It has housed the Stone of Destiny and been immortalised in Shakespeare's *Macbeth*, and is regarded by many as the heart of Scottish history.

* One of the finest private collections of furniture in Britain
* Beautiful gardens, including Moot Hill

Location
Signed from M90/A9, between Edinburgh & the Highlands

Opening
Daily; Apr–Oct 9.30am–5.30pm

Admission
Adult £6.75, Child £3.80, Concs £5.70

Contact
The Administrator, Scone Palace, Perth, Perthshire PH2 6BD

t 01738 552300
w scone-palace.co.uk
e visits@scone-palace.co.uk

947 Pittenweem

Kellie Castle & Garden

2 hrs   All year

Now in the care of the National Trust Scotland, it contains magnificent plaster ceilings, painted panelling and furniture by Sir Robert Lorimer. New exhibition commemorating Hew Lorimer's life and work. Audio tour of garden.

* Fine example of domestic architecture
* Beautiful walled garden

Location
On B9171, 3 miles from Pittenweem

Opening
Daily; *Castle* Easter & Jun–Sep 1pm–5pm
Garden Daily; 9.30am–sunset

Admission
Castle & grounds Adult £5, Concs £3.75
Garden £2

Contact
Pittenweem, Fife, KY10 2RF

t 01333 720271
w nts.org.uk
e info@1001daysout.com

948 Pitlochry

Blair Castle

1 hr+   All year

Over 700 years of Scottish history await the visitor to Blair Castle. See displays of beautiful furniture, fine paintings, arms and armour, china, costumes, lace and embroidery, masonic regalia and Jacobite relics – all of which provide a colourful picture of Scottish life from the C16 to today.

* Spectacular setting in the Strath of Garry
* Guided tours available for parties of over 12

Location
At Blair Atholl, N of Pitlochry

Opening
Daily; Mar–Oct 9.30am–4.30pm;
Oct–Mar Tue & Sat 9.30am–12.30pm

Admission
Adult £6.90, Child £4.30, Concs £5.90

Contact
Blair Atholl, Pitlochry, Perthshire PH18 5TL

t 01796 481207
w blair-castle.co.uk
e office@blair-castle.co.uk

942 Linlithgow

Linlithgow Palace

  1 hr All year

This magnificent ruin of a great royal palace is set in its own park, beside Linlithgow Loch. It was a favoured home of the Stuart kings and queens, from James I (1406–37) onward, and building work from the eras of James I, III, IV, V and VI can be seen, including the great hall and chapel.

* Birthplace of James V and Mary Queen of Scots
* The oldest working fountain in Great Britain

Location
On A803 / M9, in town centre

Opening
Daily; Apr–Sep 9.30am–6.30pm
Oct–Mar Mon–Sat 9.30am–4.30pm
Sun 2pm–4.30pm

Admission
Adult £3, Child £1, Concs £2.30

Contact
Kirkgate, Linlithgow, West Lothian
EH49 7AL

t 01506 842896
w historic-scotland.gov.uk

943 Loch Tay

Scottish Crannog Centre

  1 hr Mar–Nov

Crannogs are a type of ancient loch dwelling found throughout Scotland and Ireland. The Scottish Crannog Centre features an authentic replica of an early Iron Age crannog, based on the underwater excavations of the 2,500-year-old Oakbank Crannog.

* Shore based exhibition with audio-visual presentation
* Tour the real thing

Location
Croft-na-Caber just S of Kenmore

Opening
Daily; Mar–Oct 10am–5.30pm;
Nov Sat & Sun 10am–4pm

Admission
Adult £4.50, Child £3, Concs £4

Contact
Kenmore, Loch Tay,
Perthshire PH15 2HY

t 01887 830 583
w crannog.co.uk
e info@crannog.co.uk

944 Newtongrange

Scottish Mining Museum

  2 hrs All year

This museum is based at one of the finest surviving examples of a Victorian colliery in Europe, the Lady Victoria Colliery at Newtongrange. A fully accessible, three-storey visitor centre allows everyone to experience the atmosphere and noise of a working pit.

* Two major exhibitions: The Story of Coal and A Race Apart
* Audio tour with 'magic helmets'

Location
On A7, 9 miles S of Edinburgh

Opening
Daily; Mar–Oct 10am–5pm
Nov–Feb 10am–4pm

Admission
Adult £4.95 ,Child & Concs £3.30

Contact
Lady Victoria Colliery, Newtongrange,
Midlothian EH22 4QN

t 0131 6637519
w scottishminingmuseum.com
e visitorservices@
   scottishminingmuseum.com

945 North Queensferry

Deep Sea World

  2 hrs+ All year

Explore the undersea world at the triple award-winning National Aquarium of Scotland. Situated on the banks of the Firth of Forth, below the Forth Railway Bridge, this spectacular attraction is a perfect day out for the whole family.

* Also known as Scotland's shark capital

Location
1 mile from M90 on N side of
Forth Road Bridge

Opening
Daily; Apr–Aug 10am–6pm
Sep–Mar Mon–Fri 10am–5pm
Sat–Sun 10am–6pm

Admission
Adult £8.25, Child £6, Concs £6.50

Contact
North Queensferry, Fife KY11 1JR

t 01383 411411
w deepseaworld.com
e info@deepseaworld.com

940 Lanark

New Lanark World Heritage Village

2 hrs+   All year

The cotton mills of New Lanark were founded over 200 years ago and the village soon became famous because of the work of mill-owner Robert Owen, who provided a decent life for the villagers. Today, New Lanark has been restored and visitors can explore this fascinating village.

* Award-winning visitor centre (accommodation available)
* See the Falls of Clyde wildlife reserve

Location
Off M74 junction 13, signed off all routes

Opening
Daily; 11am–5pm

Admission
Adult £5.95, Child & Concs £3.95

Contact
New Lanark Mills,
South Lanarkshire ML11 9DB

t 01555 661345
w newlanark.org
e trust@newlanark.org

941 Leith

The Royal Yacht *Britannia*

1 hr+   All year

Now permanently moored in Edinburgh's historic port of Leith, the *Britannia* experience begins in the new visitor centre, located in Ocean Terminal, Edinburgh's stylish new waterfront shopping and leisure development. Then step onboard for a self-led audio tour of five decks.

* See royal apartments and crews' quarters
* Children's audio tour

Location
At Leith Docks, signed from city outskirts

Opening
Daily; Apr–Sep 9.30am–4.30pm
Oct–Mar 10am–3.30pm

Admission
Adult £9, Child £5, Concs £7

Contact
Ocean Drive, Leith, Edinburgh EH6 6JJ

t 0131 5555566
w royalyachtbritannia.co.uk
e enquiries@tryb.co.uk

937 Glasgow

Tall Ship in Glasgow Harbour

1 hr+   All year

Explore the tall ship *Glenlee*, one of only five Clyde-built sailing ships that remain afloat. Built in 1896, she operated as a long haul cargo vessel before being bought by the Spanish Navy as a training ship. She has circumnavigated the globe four times.

* New exhibition tells the *Glenlee* story
* Visitor centre

Location
Off M8 junction 19, follow brown thistle signs

Opening
Daily; Mar–Nov 10am–5pm
Dec–Feb 11am–4pm

Admission
Adult £4.50, Child £2.50, Concs £3.25 (one child free with each paying adult)

Contact
100 Stobe Cross Road, Glasgow G3 8QQ

t 0141 222 2513
w thetallship.com
e info@thetallship.com

938 Kinross

Loch Leven Castle

2 hrs   Apr–Oct

The dramatic ruins of this castle stand on an island in Loch Leven. This late C14 or early C15 tower is infamous as the place where Mary Queen of Scots was imprisoned in 1567. She escaped the following year, but her ghost is alleged to haunt the castle to this day.

* The Loch is an important RSPB site

Location
Accessible by boat from Scottish Angling Academy in Kinross, signposted from A922

Opening
Daily; Apr–Sep 9.30am– 5.15pm;
Oct Mon Wed–Thu Sat–Sun 9.30am–3.15pm

Admission
Adult £3.50, Child £1.20, Concs £2.50

Contact
Kinross, Perthshire KY13 7AR

t 07778 040483
w historic-scotland.gov.uk

939 Kirriemuir

Barrie's Birthplace

½ hr   All year

J.M. Barrie, the creator of the eternal magic of *Peter Pan*, was born here in 1860. The upper floor is furnished as it was when Barrie lived there. The adjacent house, number 11, houses an exhibition about Barrie's literary and theatrical works.

* Audio programme
* Near Kirriemuir camera obscura

Location
A901/A926 in Kirriemuir, 6 miles NW of Forfar

Opening
Daily; Jul–Aug 12 noon–5pm
Sep–Jun Fri–Tue 12 noon–5pm

Admission
Adult £5, Child £3.75, Concs £3.75 (combined ticket with camera obscura)

Contact
9 Brechin Road, Kirriemuir, Angus DD8 4BX

t 01575 572 646
w nts.org.uk/barrie.html
e barriesbirthplace@nts.org.uk

934 Glasgow

Necropolis

1 hr+   All year

The Necropolis stands on a hill to the east of Glasgow Cathedral, just a short walk across the Bridge of Sighs. The monument to John Knox, which was erected in 1825, dominates the hill. This Victorian cemetery was modelled on Père-Lachaise in Paris.

* Glasgow's great architects are represented, including Thomson, Wilson, Baird, Bryce, and Hamilton

Location
nr Glasgow Cathedral

Opening
Daily; 8am–4.30pm

Admission
Free

Contact
Cemeteries and Crematoria, 1st Floor, 20 Trongate, Glasgow G1 5ES

t 0141 2873961

935 Glasgow

People's Palace

2 hrs+   All year

The People's Palace is Glasgow's social history museum and tells the story of the people and city of Glasgow from 1760 to the present. There are paintings, prints and photographs displayed alongside a wealth of historic artefacts, film and computer interactives.

* Discover how a family lived in a typical single end Glasgow tenement

Location
Short walk from city centre

Opening
Daily; Mon–Thu Sat 10am–5pm
Fri & Sun 11am–5pm

Admission
Free

Contact
Glasgow Green, Glasgow G40 1AT

t 0141 2712951
w glasgowmuseums.com

936 Glasgow

Scottish Football Museum

2 hrs+   All year

The world's first national football museum is housed at Hampden Park, the oldest continuously used international ground in the world. It is owned by Queen's Park FC, the oldest association team in Scotland (founded 1867) and one with an unrivalled history.

* The world's most impressive collection of football memorabilia, covering 140 years of football history

Location
Junction 1 off M77, onto B768 (Titwood Road), right onto B766 (Battlefield Road), then Kings Park Road, left into Kinghorn Drive

Opening
Mon–Sat 10am–5pm Sun 11am–5pm

Admission
Adult £5, Child & Concs £2.50

Contact
Hampden Park, Glasgow G42 9BA

t 0141 616 6139
w scottishfootballmuseum.org.uk
e info@scottishfootballmuseum.org.uk

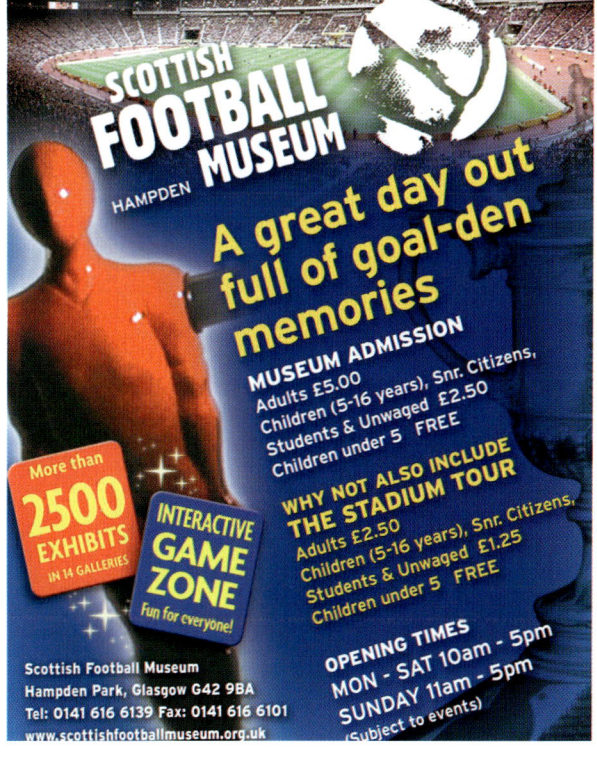

931 Glasgow

Gallery of Modern Art

½ hr   All year

GoMA is the second most visited contemporary art gallery outside London, offering a thought-provoking programme of temporary exhibitions and workshops. The focus of the gallery is on contemporary social issues, often featuring groups marginalised in today's society.

* Includes work by Bridget Riley and Scottish artists
  John Byrne and Christine Borland

Location
In city centre, off Buchanan Street, close to central station

Opening
Mon–Tue 10am–5pm Thu 10am–8pm
Fri & Sun 11am–5pm Sat 10am–5pm

Admission
Free

Contact
Queen Street, Glasgow G1 3AH

t 0141 2291996
w glasgowmuseums.com

932 Glasgow

Museum of Piping

½ hr   All year

Nothing makes a Scotsman feel more patriotic than the sound of a pipe band. This is the sound of Scotland, a haunting melody or a noise fit to lift the soul. At the Museum of Piping you can witness hundreds of years of Scottish heritage, played right before your eyes and ears.

* An outstanding collection of piping artefacts
* Study the history and origins of bagpiping

Location
In city centre, in pedestrian area

Opening
Daily; Jun–Aug Mon–Sat
9.30am–4.30pm Sun 10am–4pm;
Sep–May Mon–Sat 9.30am–4.30pm

Admission
Adult £3, Child/Concs £2

Contact
30–34 McPhater Street, Cowcaddens, Glasgow G4 0HW

t 0141 3530220
w thepipingcentre.co.uk
e reception@thepipingcentre.co.uk

933 Glasgow

Glasgow Science Centre

2 hrs+   All Year

Shake hands with yourself, make a 3D image of your face and see how you will look in years to come. Enjoy over 300 hands-on and interactive exhibits, take in a live science show, see the latest Imax fim, visit the planetarium and observe the stars.

* Imax theatre
* Space theatre with planetarium projector

Location
Opposite the Scottish Exhibition Centre & the Moat House Hotel on the Clyde

Opening
Daily; 10am–6pm

Admission
Adult £6.95 Child £4.95, Concs £4.95

Contact
50 Pacific Quay
Glasgow G51 1EA

t 0141 420 5000
w glasgowsciencecentre.org
e admin@gsc.org.uk

928 Fife

Scottish Deer Centre

2 hrs +   All year

This 55-acre park is home to over 140 deer representing 9 species. Other attractions include ranger tours, dramatic bird-of-prey demonstrations, a treetop walkway, viewing platforms, scenic pathways, and indoor and outdoor adventure play areas for children.

* Falconry displays

Location
On the outskirts of Cupar, 12 miles from St Andrews on A91

Opening
Please phone for details

Admission
Adult £4.95, Child £3.45, Conc £3.95
Under 3's are free
Family discounts available

Contact
Rankeilour Park,
Bow-of-Fife,
Cupar,
Fife KY15 4NQ

t 01337 810391
e simplythebest@ewm.co.uk

929 Glamis by Forfar

Glamis Castle

2 hrs+   Mar–Dec

Glamis Castle has a long and colourful history. It has a legendary association, at least according to Shakespeare, with the C11 Macbeth and has a place in C20 history as the childhood home of HM The Queen Mother.

* Rich variety of furnishings, tapestries and art
* Extensive estate and formal gardens

Location
On A94, between Aberdeen & Perth

Opening
Daily; Mar–Oct 10am–6pm
Nov–24 Dec 11am–3pm

Admission
Adult £7, Child £3.80, Concs £5.70

Contact
The Castle Administrator,
Estates Office, Glamis by Forfar,
Angus DD8 1RJ

t 01307 840393
w glamis-castle.co.uk
e enquiries@glamis-castle.co.uk

930 Glasgow

Burrell Collection

½ hr+   All year

When Sir William Burrell gifted his collection of over 9,000 works of art to Glasgow, the city acquired one of its greatest collections. He had been an art collector since his teens and the collection is made up of a vast array of works of all periods, from all over the world.

* Medieval art, tapestries, alabasters and stained glass
* Paintings by Degas and Cézanne

Location
5 miles S of Glasgow

Opening
Daily; Mon–Thu Sat 10am–5pm
Fri–Sun 11am–5pm

Admission
Free

Contact
Pollok Country Park,
2060 Pollokshaws Road,
Glasgow G43 1AT

t 0141 287 2550
w glasgowmuseums.com
e cls.glasgow.gov.uk

925 Edinburgh

Palace of Holyroodhouse

1 hr   All year

Originally founded in 1128 as a monastery, the Palace of Holyroodhouse in Edinburgh is the Queen's official residence in Scotland, and is no stranger to royalty, as Mary Queen of Scots, among others, lived here. In fact the palace has many associations with Scottish history.

* New Queen's gallery
* One of the finest art collections in the world

Location
At bottom of Royal Mile

Opening
Daily; Nov–Mar 9.30am–4.30pm
Apr–Oct 9.30am–6pm

Admission
Adult £8, Child £4, Concs £6.50
By timed ticket slots

Contact
Edinburgh EH8 8DX

t 0131 5565100
w royal.gov.uk
e information@royalcollection.org.uk

926 Edinburgh

St Giles' Cathedral

½ hr+   All year

This is the High Kirk of Edinburgh and it has been at the heart of the city's spiritual life for at least 900 years. A living church with an active congregation, it also welcomes visitors who come to experience the unique atmosphere of continuing worship and ages-old history.

* The mother church of Presbyterianism
* One of Scotland's most historically important buildings

Location
On Royal Mile

Opening
Daily; May–Sep Mon–Fri 9am–7pm
Sat 9am–5pm Sun 1–5pm
Oct–Apr Mon–Sat 9am–5pm
Sun 1–5pm

Admission
Free

Contact
High Street, Edinburgh EH1 1RE

t 0131 2259442
w stgiles.net
e info@stgiles.net

927 Edinburgh

Royal Botanic Garden Edinburgh

2 hrs   All year

Founded in the C17 as a 'physic garden', growing medicinal plants, the Royal Botanic is now acknowledged as one of the finest gardens in the world. It's a place to rest and relax, away from the city's hustle and bustle, and is home to unusual and beautiful plants.

* Guided and themed tours
* Rock/peat/woodland gardens, chinese plants

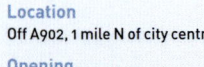   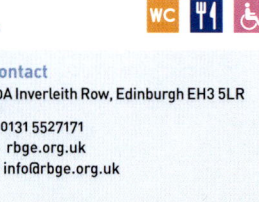

Location
Off A902, 1 mile N of city centre

Opening
Daily; Apr–Sep 10am–7pm
Mar Oct 10am–6pm
Nov–Feb 10am–4pm

Admission
Free

Contact
20A Inverleith Row, Edinburgh EH3 5LR

t 0131 5527171
w rbge.org.uk
e info@rbge.org.uk

923 Edinburgh

National Gallery of Scotland

½ - 2 hrs   All year

The gallery is home to Scotland's greatest collection of European paintings and sculpture, ranging from the Renaissance to Post-Impressionism. One of Edinburgh's major attractions, it is also one of the finest galleries of its size in the world.

* Includes masterpieces by Van Dyck and Tiepolo
* Comprehensive collection of Scottish paintings

Location
Off Princes Street

Opening
Daily; Mon–Wed Fri–Sun 10am–5pm
Thu 10am–7pm

Admission
Free, charges for some exhibitions

Contact
The Mound, Edinburgh EH2 2EL

t 0131 6246200
w nationalgalleries.org
e enquiries@nationalgalleries.org

924 Edinburgh

Our Dynamic Earth

1 hr+   All year

A fantastic journey of discovery. Travel back in time to witness the Big Bang from the deck of a space ship, then forward through the history of our planet. You'll be shaken by earthquakes, dive deep beneath the ocean, feel the chill of polar ice and even get caught in a tropical rainstorm.

* Find out if there's a monster in Loch Ness
* Live 4500 million years in a day

Location
At the foot of Arthur's Seat, adjacent to the new Scottish Parliament

Opening
Daily; Apr–Oct 10am–5pm;
Nov–Mar Wed–Sun 10am–5pm

Admission
Adult £8.95, Child & Concs £5.45

Contact
112 Holyrood Road, Edinburgh EH8 8AS

t 0131 5507800
w dynamicearth.co.uk
e enquiries@dynamicearth.co.uk

919 Edinburgh

Edinburgh Dungeon

1hr All Year

An indoor attraction depicting the darkest chapters of Scottish history. The Dungeon blends horror and humour to represent Scotland's bloody past.

* Actors bring history to life
* Horror rides

Location
Edinburgh city centre

Opening
Please phone for details

Admission
Adult £8.95, Child (10–14) £6.95, (4–9) £4.95

Contact
31 Market Street
Edinburgh EH1 1QB
t 0131 240 1000
e edinburghdungeon@merlinentertainments.biz

920 Edinburgh

Edinburgh Zoo

4 hrs All year

This is Scotland's most popular wildlife attraction, with over a thousand animals, including meerkats, pygmy hippos, tigers, giraffes and blue poison arrow frogs. Set in beautiful parkland, it has the world's biggest penguin pool, home to Europe's largest colony of penguins.

* African Plains Experience, Magic Forest
* Hilltop safari, tour and maze

Location
10 mins from city centre

Opening
Daily; Apr–Sep 9am–6pm
Oct Mar 9am–5pm
Nov–Feb 9am–4.30pm

Admission
Adult £8.50, Child £5.50, Concs £6.50

Contact
134 Corstorphine Road, Edinburgh
EH12 6TS
t 0131 3349171
w edinburghzoo.org.uk
e info@edinburghzoo.org.uk

* NB an adult (over 17) must accompany children under 14 at all times

921 Edinburgh

Museum of Scotland

2 hrs+ All year

This museum presents, for the first time, the history of Scotland – its land, its people and their achievements – through the rich national collections. The stunning series of galleries takes you from Scotland's geological beginnings through time right up to C20.

* Over 10,000 artefacts
* Same site as Royal Museum

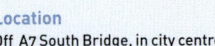

Location
Off A7 South Bridge, in city centre

Opening
Daily; Mon–Sat 10m–5pm Tue
10am–8pm Sun 12 noon–5pm

Admission
Free

Contact
Chambers Street, Edinburgh EH1 1JF
t 0131 2474422
w nms.ac.uk
e info@nms.ac.uk

922 Edinburgh

National Portrait Gallery

2 hrs All year

The gallery provides a visual history of Scotland, told through portraits of those who shaped it: royals and rebels, poets and philosophers, heroes and villains. All the portraits are of Scots by well-known masters, including Kokoschka & van Dyck.

* Works by Gainsborough, Copley and Rodin
* Unparalleled collection of Scottish portraits

Location
E end of Queen Street, Edinburgh city centre

Opening
Daily; 10am–5pm, Thu 10am–7pm;
1 Jan, 12 noon–5pm.

Admission
Free

Contact
1 Queen Street, Edinburgh EH2 1JD
t 0131 624 6200
w nationalgalleries.org
e enquiries@nationalgalleries.org

917   East Fortune

Museum of Flight

2 hrs+   All year

Two massive hangars, part of a Second World War airfield, are packed with aeroplanes, rockets, models and memorabilia – from a 100-year-old hang glider to the Blue Streak rocket, and from a Spitfire to the massive Lightning.

* Recently acquired Concorde for display Mar 2005
* Site of take-off for first east-west Atlantic flight

Location
Off A1, 20m E of Edinburgh

Opening
Summer Daily; 10am–5pm,
Winter Sat & Sun 11am–4pm

Admission
Adults £4, Child free, Concs £3

Contact
East Fortune Airfield,
East Lothian EH39 5LF

t 01620 880308
w nms.ac.uk/flight/

918   Edinburgh

Edinburgh Castle

1 hr+   All year

A majestic landmark that dominates the city's skyline, Edinburgh Castle is the most visited of Scotland's historic buildings. Perched on an extinct volcano and offering stunning views, this fortress is a powerful national symbol and part of Edinburgh's World Heritage site.

* Guided and audio tours
* The Scottish Crown Jewels and the Stone of Destiny

Location
At top of Royal Mile

Opening
Daily; Apr–Sep 9am–6pm
Oct–Mar 9am–5pm

Admission
Adult £9.50, Child £2, Concs £7

Contact
Castle Hill, Edinburgh EH1 2NG

t 0131 2259846
w historic-scotland.gov.uk

914 Dunfermline

Knockhill Racing Circuit

3 hrs   All year

Scotland's national motorsport centre features major international and national motorsport events for both cars and bikes. It's also a major venue for corporate entertainment, as visitors can drive race and rally cars, go off-road on a 4x4 course and do many other activities.

* Hands -on driving experiences
* Relaxing hospitality at race events

Location
Signposted from M90 junction 4

Opening
Daily; 9am–6.30pm

Admission
Prices vary depending on the event, please phone for details

Contact
Dunfermline, Fife KY12 9TF

t 01383 723337
w knockhill.co.uk
e enquiries@knockhill.co.uk

915 Dundee

Atholl Country Life Museum

5 hrs+   May–Sep

This museum of local life has exhibitions of rural trades, agri-cultural and domestic life. Displays cover a wide variety of subjects – road, rail and postal services, the kirk, school and smiddy, and photographs of local wild flowers.

* Gamekeeper's corner
* Display of stuffed wild animals

Location
Turn off the A9 for Blair Atholl, 7 miles north of Pitlochry

Opening
Daily; Easter & May–Sep 1.30pm–5pm; Jul & Aug from 10am on weekdays

Admission
Adult £3 , Child £1

Contact
Blair Atholl, Pitlochry, Perthshire PH18 5SP

t 01796 481232
e janet.com@virgin.net

916 Dundee

Discovery Point

1 hr+   All year

Climb aboard Captain Scott's royal research ship, *Discovery*, which was originally built in Dundee to sail to the Antarctic and is now berthed on the River Tay and open to visitors. The ship represents the city's shipbuilders' greatest achievement.

* State-of-the-art multimedia exhibitions
* Voted Scotland's best family attraction 2004

Location
City centre, opposite train station

Opening
Daily; Apr–Oct Mon–Sat 10am–6pm
Sun 11am–6pm
Nov–Mar Mon–Sat 10am–5pm
Sun 11am–5pm

Admission
Adult £6.25, Child £3.85, Concs £4.70

Contact
Discovery Quay, Dundee DD1 4XA

t 01382 201245
w rrsdiscovery.com
e info@dundeeheritage.co.uk

912 Crieff

Stuart Crystal Factory Shop

½ hr   All year

Come and see the wonderful craft of crystal at the Stuart Crystal Factory Shop. A large display of Stuart Crystal, Waterford Crystal and Wedgwood China, with factory seconds. There is also a crystal engraving service for that personalised special gift or memento.

* Souvenir gift shop
* Chip repair service

Location
Signposted from town centre

Opening
Jun–Sep daily 10am–6pm
Oct–May Mon–Sat 10am–5pm
Sun 11am–5pm

Admission
Free

Contact
Muthill Road, Crieff
Perthshire PH7 4HQ

t 01764 654 004

913 Dunfermline

Dunfermline Abbey & Palace

1 hr   All year

The elegant ruins of Dunfermline Abbey are what is left of a great Benedictine abbey founded by Queen Margaret in the C11. Robert the Bruce was buried in the choir and the royal palace next door, also partially ruined, was the birthplace of Charles I.

* Substantial parts of the abbey buildings remain
* Next to the ruin of the royal palace

Location
Off M90, in town centre

Opening
Daily; Apr–Sep 9.30am–6.30pm;
Oct–Mar Mon–Thu & Sat
9.30am–4.30pm Sun 2pm–4.30pm

Admission
Adult £2.20, Child 75p, Concs £1.60

Contact
St. Margaret Street, Dunfermline,
Fife KY12 7PE

t 01383 739 026
w historic-scotland.gov.uk

©Dunfermline Abbey & Palace

909 Crieff

Auchingarrich Wildlife Centre

2 hrs+   All Year

This award-winning centre features the Highland Cattle Centre. You can see these majestic beasts, stroke them and feed them. Other animals include wallabies, raccoons, otters, chipmunks, porcupines and Scotland's largest collection of waterfowl, ornamental and game birds.

* Over 150 species of animals and birds
* Hatchings every day from Easter to October

Location
On B827, 2 miles N of Comrie

Opening
Daily; 10am–dusk

Admission
Adult £5.50, Child & Concs £4

Contact
Glascorrie Road, Crieff, Perthshire PH6 2JS

t 01764 679469
e auchingarrich@wilton.sol.co.uk

910 Crieff

Drummond Castle Gardens

1 hr   May–Oct

Drummond Castle Gardens are thought to be Scotland's most important formal gardens and are certainly among the finest in Europe. The magnificent Italianate parterre was first laid in C17 by John Drummond and renewed in the 1950s.

* Charles I's sundial
* Gardens featured in the film *Rob Roy*

Location
Off A822, 2 miles S of Crieff

Opening
Daily; May–Oct 1pm–6pm
Also open Easter

Admission
Adults £3.50, Child £1.50, Concs £2.50

Contact
Muthill, nr Crieff, Perthshire PH5 2AA

t 01764 681257
w drummondcastlegardens.co.uk
e info@drummondcastle.sol.co.uk

911 Crieff

The Famous Grouse Experience at Glenturret Distillery

1 hr+   All year

Scotland's only five-star, Bafta award-winning interactive whisky attraction is fun for young and old alike. Crack some ice, splash in the water and do a jigsaw puzzle with your feet or fly over the wonderous beauty of Scotland on the back of a grouse.

* New style audio-visual presentation
* New on-site restaurant

Location
Off A85, 1 mile from Crieff

Opening
Daily; 9am–6pm

Admission
Adult £5.95, Child £3, Concs £4.95

Contact
Glenturret Distillery, The Hosh, Crieff, Perthshire PH7 4HA

t 01764 656565
w famousgrouse.com
e enquiries@famousgrouse.com

906 Aberfoyle

Forest Hills Watersports

½–1 day   Mar–Dec

Based on the banks of Loch Ard and accessible by motorboat, canoe, kayak and sailing boat, the centre offers a multitude of activities for all ages and abilities. Sailing, canoeing, fishing, quad biking, and off-road driving are just some of the courses on offer.

* Equipment available for hire
* Courses taught by qualified instructors

Location
Off junction 10 of M9 & junction 16 of M8. Follow the signs for Aberfoyle, then to Forest Hills Watersports, 4 miles along B829

Opening
Daily; Mar–Dec ; in summer open 9.30am–7pm; in winter open 10.30am–5pm

Admission
Activities priced individually

Contact
Kinlochard, Aberfoyle, Stirlingshire FK8 3TL
t 01877 387775
w goforth.co.uk
e info@goforth.co.uk

907 Arbroath

Arbroath Abbey

2 hrs+   All year

This was the site of the signing of the Declaration of Arbroath in 1320, when Scotland's nobles affirmed their allegiance to Robert the Bruce as their king. The recent addition of a visitor centre has reinforced its reputation as one of Scotland's most important historical places.

* Audio-visual facilities
* Displays on abbey life

Location
On A92, in town centre

Opening
Daily; Apr–Sep 9.30am-6.30pm
Oct–Mar 9.30am to 4.30pm

Admission
Adult £3.30, Child £1, Concs £2.50

Contact
Arbroath, Angus DD11 1EG
t 01241 878756
w historic-scotland.gov.uk
e hs.explorer@scotland.gsi.gov.uk

908 Cupar

Hill of Tarvit Mansion House & Garden

2 hrs   Easter–Oct

A fascinating mansion house, built in 1906, reflects the period 1870–1920, when Scotland was the industrial workshop of the world. The house is a showcase for Flemish tapestries, Chinese porcelain and bronzes, French and English furniture and paintings by many eminent artists.

* Edwardian-style interior
* Set in beautiful gardens

Location
Off A916, 2 miles S of Cupar

Opening
Easter Sat & Sun 1pm–5pm
Daily; May–Sep 1pm–5pm
Oct Sat–Sun 1pm–5pm

Admission
Please phone for details

Contact
Cupar, Fife KY15 5PB
t 01334 653 127
w nts.org.uk
e hilloftarvit@nts.org.uk

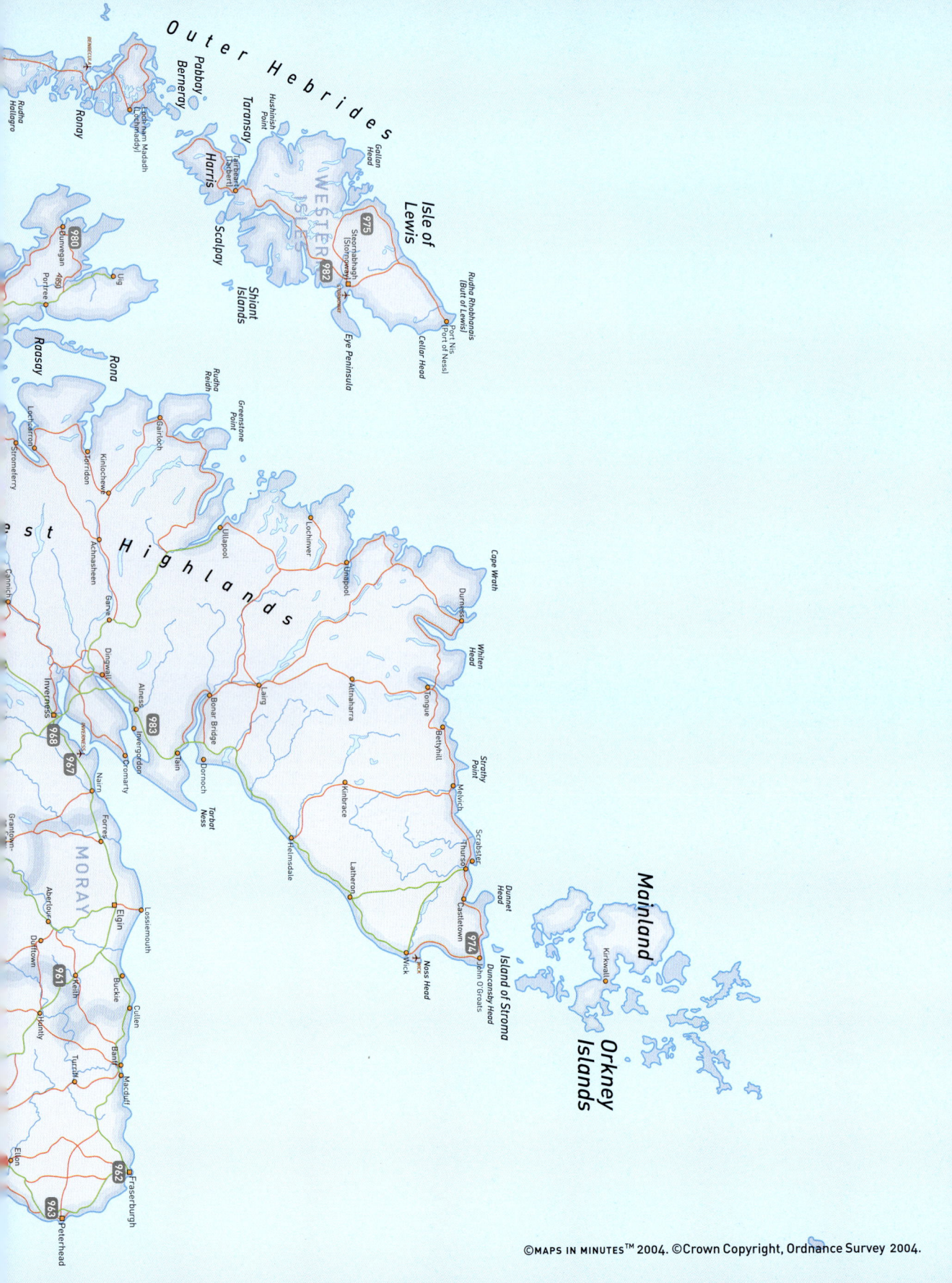

Outer Hebrides

WESTERN ISLES

Isle of Lewis

Gallan Head
Hushinish Point
Taransay
Tarbert (Tairbeart)
Harris
Scalpay
Pabbay
Berneray
Ronay
Rudha Hallagro
Lochmaddy
Lochmaddy Madadh
Shiant Islands

975
982
Steornabhagh (Stornoway)

Rudha Rhobhanais (Butt of Lewis)
Port Nis (Port of Ness)
Cellar Head
Eye Peninsula

980
Dunvegan
Portree
460
Uig
Raasay
Rona
Rudha Reidh
Greenstone Point
Gairloch
Kinlochewe
Garve
Gairdon
Lochcarron
Stromeferry
Camirch

Highlands

Ullapool
Lochinver
Durness
Cape Wrath
Whiten Head
Tongue
Bettyhill
Strathy Point
Melvich

Altnaharra
Laing
Bonar Bridge
Alness
983
Invergordon
Tain
Dingwall
Inverness
968
967
Nairn
Forres
Cromarty
Dornoch
Tarbat Ness
Kinbrace

Kildonan
Helmsdale
Latheron
Wick
Ness Head
John O'Groats
Duncansby Head
Scrabster
Thurso
Castletown
Dunnet Head
974
Island of Stroma
Mainland
Kirkwall
Orkney Islands

MORAY
Aberlour
Elgin
Lossiemouth
Buckie
Cullen
Banff
Macduff
Dufftown
961
Keith
Huntly
Turriff
Grantown-on-Spey
962
Fraserburgh
963
Peterhead
Ellon

est

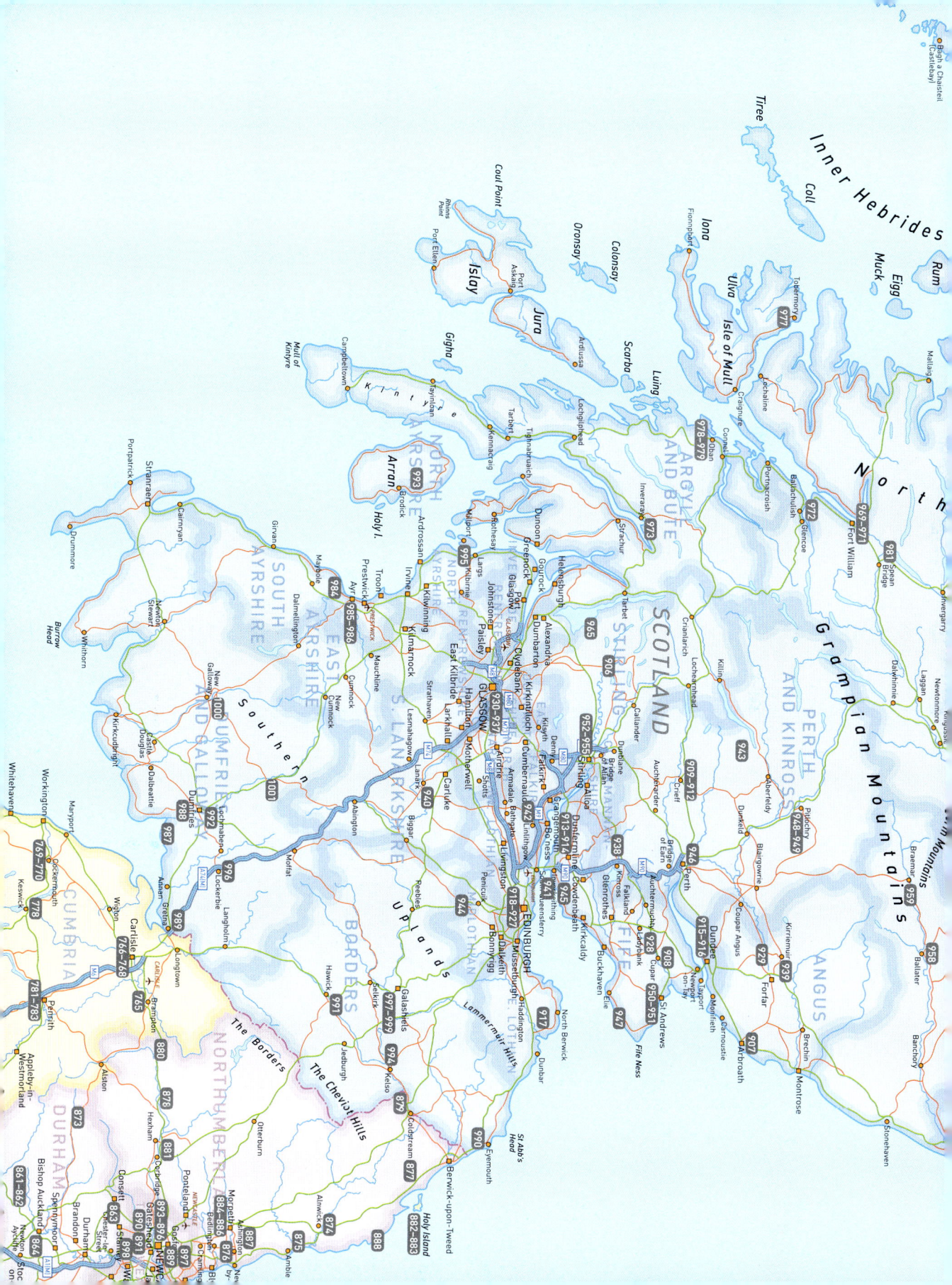

Loch Sunart, Drumbuie

Scotland

Central Scotland Grampian
Highlands and Islands Southern Scotland

903 Wallsend

Segedunum Roman Fort, Baths & Museum

2 hrs+   All year

For almost 300 years Segedunum, which means 'strong fort', was home to 600 Roman soldiers and was the last outpost of Hadrian's Wall. Today the complex combines the excavated remains with reconstructions and hands-on museum displays of life in Roman Britain.

* The most extensively excavated site in Britain
* 100 foot-high viewing tower

Location
Just 1 minute's walk from Wallsend
Metro & bus station

Opening
Daily; 10am–5pm (3.30pm 1 Nov–31 Mar)

Admission
Adult £3.50, Child £1.95, Concs £1.95

Contact
Buddle Street
Wallsend NE28 6HR

t 0191 236 9347
w twmuseums.org.uk

904 Washington

Washington Old Hall

2 hrs   Apr–Oct

From 1183 this house was the home of George Washington's direct ancestors, who took their surname from the village of Washington. The manor remained in the family until 1613. Mementoes of the American connection and the War of Independence are on display.

* Fine collection of contemporary blue and white Delft
* Jacobean-style garden

Location
5 miles W of Sunderland, well signed

Opening
House 25 Mar–30 Oct Sun–Wed
11am–5pm.
Open Good Friday

Admission
Adult £3.80, Child £2.30

Contact
The Avenue,
Washington Village NE38 7LE

t 0191 416 6879
w nationaltrust.org

905 Washington

Wildfowl & Wetlands Trust Washington

3 hrs   All year

Ideally placed to provide a stopover and wintering habitat for migratory waterbirds after their passage over the North Sea, this recreated wetland provides large flocks of curlew and redshank with a safe place to roost and herons with a place to breed.

* Nuthatch sighted in 2003 for the first time in 10 years
* See waders, kingfishers, snipe, shovelers and flamingo

Location
E of Washington, 4 miles from A1(M)

Opening
Daily; *Summer* 9.30am–5.30pm
Winter 9.30am–4pm

Admission
Adult £5.75, Child £3.75, Concs £4.75

Contact
Pattinson,
Washington NE38 8LE

t 0191 416 5454
w wwt.org.uk
e info.washington@wwt.org.uk

900   Sunderland

Souter Lighthouse

1 hr+   Feb–Nov

When it first shone its light in 1871, Souter was the most advanced lighthouse in the world, and the first purpose-built lighthouse to utilise electricity. Explore the compass room, Victorian keeper's cottage, engine room, the huge optic and enjoy the stunning views.

* When operational, light could be seen from 19 miles
* See the engine room and cramped living quarters

Location
2½ miles S of South Shields on A183

Opening
Daily; 12 Feb–27 Feb 11am–5pm
Easter–Nov 6 Sat–Thu 11am–5pm

Admission
Adult £3.50, Child £2

Contact
Coast Road, Whitburn,
Sunderland SR6 7NH
t 0191 529 3161
w nationaltrust.org.uk
e souter@nationaltrust.org.uk

© National Trust Photographic Library

901   Sunderland

Sunderland Museum & Winter Gardens

4 hrs   All year

Hands-on exhibits and interactive displays tell the story of Sunderland from its prehistoric past through to the present day. The art gallery features paintings by L.S.Lowry alongside Victorian masterpieces. The winter gardens contain over 1,500 flowers and plants.

* Good facilities for disabled visitors
* Many educational exhibits

Location
City centre on Burdon Road

Opening
Daily; Mon–Sat 10am–5pm, Sun 2pm–5pm

Admission
Free

Contact
Burdon Road,
Sunderland SR1 1PP
t 0191 553 2323
w twmuseums.org.uk/sunderland
e sunderland@twmuseums.org.uk

902   Tynemouth

Blue Reef Aquarium

1 hr+   All year

Overlooking the North Sea, the aquarium has a gigantic ocean display complete with underwater tunnel and is home to hundreds of local and tropical marine species. There's a nursery with new-born creatures, frogs, predators and an octopus that can unscrew jam-jar lids.

* Quality Assured Visitor Attraction

Location
From A19, take A1058 to the town centre & follow the brown tourist signs

Opening
Daily; Mar–Oct from 10am–5pm
Nov–Feb 10am–4pm

Admission
Adult £5.50, Child £3.75, Concs £4.95

Contact
Grand Parade,
Tynemouth NE30 4JF
t 0191 258 1031
w bluereefaquarium.co.uk
e tynemouth@bluereefaquarium.co.uk

897 North Shields

Stephenson Railway Museum

1 hr   May–Sep

Re-live the glorious days of the steam railway at the Stephenson Railway Museum. The museum is home to George Stephenson's Billy, a forerunner to the world-famous Rocket, and many other engines from the age of steam. Rides on a steam train can be taken.

* See the story of coal and electricity's impact on lives

Location
Well signed from junction of
A19/A1058

Opening
May–Sep Tue–Thu 11am–3pm
Sat, Sun & Bank Hols 11am–4pm

Admission
Free

Contact
Middle Engine Lane,
North Shields NE29 8DX

t 0191 200 7146
w twmuseums.org.uk/stephenson
e stephenson@twmuseums.org.uk

898 Rowlands Gill

Gibside

3 hrs   All year

One of the north's finest landscapes, much of which is a SSSI, a forest garden currently under restoration and embracing many miles of riverside and forest walks. There are several outstanding buildings, including a Palladian chapel and the Column of Liberty.

* Former home of Queen Mother's family
* Several buildings still under restoration

Location
6 miles SW of Gateshead on B6314

Opening
Grounds Mar–Oct Tue–Sun & Bank
Hols 10am–6pm
Nov–Feb 10am–3.30pm
Chapel Apr–Oct Tue–Sun
11am–4.30pm

Admission
Adult £3.50, Child £2

Contact
Nr Rowlands Gill,
Burnopfield NE16 6BG

t 01207 541 820
w nationaltrust.org.uk
e gibside@nationaltrust.org.uk

899 Sunderland

Monkwearmouth Station Museum

1 hr+   All year

This splendid Victorian railway station recreates a sense of rail travel in the past. Explore the ticket office as it was in Victorian times, see the guard's van and goods wagon in the railway sidings and watch today's trains zoom past the platform gallery.

* Experience Victorian rail travel
* Children's gallery

Location
On A1018. 1 minute walk from St
Peter's Metro station

Opening
Daily; Mon–Sat 10am–5pm & Sun
2pm–5pm

Admission
Free

Contact
North Bridge Street
Sunderland SR5 1AP

t 0191 232 7734
w twmuseum.org.uk

895 Newcastle-upon-Tyne

Life Science Centre

2 hrs+   All year

Discover amazing facts about life and learn to understand how DNA spells out instructions for every species. Explore where life comes from and how it works. Meet your 4-billion-year-old family, find out what makes you unique and test your brainpower.

* Open air ice rink in winter, carries a separate charge
* Enjoy the thrill of the motion simulator

Location
Near Central Station

Opening
Daily; Mon–Sat 10am–6pm, Sun 11am–6pm

Admission
Adult £6.95, Child £4.50, Concs £5.50

Contact
Times Square,
Newcastle upon Tyne NE1 4EP

t 0191 243 8223 / 243 8210
w lifesciencecentre.org.uk
e bookings@life.org.uk

896 Newcastle-upon-Tyne

The People's Museum of Memorabilia

1 hr   All year

This small but fascinating museum and shopping arcade recreates Newcastle's past in miniature with a cluster of C18 and C19 cottages, shops and alleyways. The museum houses artefacts and memorabilia from the past 200 years of the region's history.

* 16 antique & jewellery shops
* 'Wor Kate's pantry'

Location
Grainger St, Newcastle town centre

Opening
Mon–Sat 10am–5pm

Admission
Free

Contact
42 Grainger Street,
Newcastle upon Tyne NE1 5JG

t 0191 221 1688

893 Newcastle-upon-Tyne

Discovery Museum

2 hrs   All year

Discovery is the region's biggest free museum and the gateway to fun and facts about life on Tyneside. Explore Newcastle's past from Roman times to the present day, Tyneside's inventions that changed the world, a fun approach to science, and take a walk through fashion.

* See Roman, Norman and medieval Newcastle
* Find out about life along the River Tyne

Location
Short walk from Newcastle Central Station

Opening
Daily; Mon–Sat 10am–5pm Sun 2pm–5pm

Admission
Free

Contact
Blandford Square,
Newcastle upon Tyne NE1 4JA

t 0191 232 6789
w twmuseums.org.uk
e discovery@twmuseums.org.uk

894 Newcastle-upon-Tyne

Hancock Museum

2 hrs+   All year

For more than 100 years this museum has provided visitors with an insight into the animal kingdom and the powerful forces of nature. From the dinosaurs to living animals, the Hancock is home to creatures past and present and even the odd Egyptian mummy.

* Live reptiles, snakes and insects
* Always housing a blockbuster exhibition

Location
City centre nr Haymarket

Opening
Daily; Mon–Sat 10am–5pm, Sun 2pm–5pm

Admission
Prices vary please phone for details

Contact
Barras Bridge,
Newcastle upon Tyne NE2 4PT

t 0191 222 6765
w twmuseums.org.uk/hancock
e hancock.museum@ncl.ac.uk

890 Dunston

Whickham Thorns Outdoor Activity Centre

1 hr+   All year

This centre offers a wide range of activities, including climbing, skiing, boarding, mountain biking, orienteering, and archery. There are skiing and snowboarding courses for beginners, activity days and mountain bikes for hire.

* Duke of Edinburgh Award scheme
* First Boulder Park in the North-East

Location
Off A1 on the opposite side of the motorway to the MetroCentre

Opening
Daily; Mon–Fri 11am–10pm, Sat 11am–6.30pm, Sun 12 noon–3pm; Please phone for details

Admission
Free; please phone for activity prices

Contact
Market Lane,
Dunston,
Gateshead NE11 9NX

t 0191 433 5767
w gateshead.gov.uk

891 Gateshead

BALTIC

1 hr+   All year

A major new international centre for contemporary art, situated on the south bank of the River Tyne. Housed in a 1950s' grain warehouse (part of the former Baltic Flour Mills), BALTIC is a site for the production, presentation and experience of contemporary art.

* Constantly changing programme of exhibitions
* Displays of artists in residence

Location
Gateshead Quayside, 10 mins walk from town centre

Opening
Times vary please ring for details or visit our website

Admission
Free

Contact
South Shore Road,
Gateshead NE8 3BA

t 0191 4781810
w balticmill.com
e info@balticmill.com

892 Jarrow

Bede's World & St Paul's Church

3 hrs   All year

The extraordinary life of the Venerable Bede (AD 673–735) created a rich legacy that is celebrated today at Bede's World, where Bede lived and worked 1300 years ago. Stunning new museum building and site of Anglo-Saxon monastery of St Paul and medieval monastic ruins.

* Herb garden based on Anglo-Saxon & medieval plants
* Anglo-Saxon demo farm, complete with animals

Location
Near S end of Tyne tunnel, off A185

Opening
Apr–Oct Mon–Sat 10am–5.30pm
Sun 12 noon–5.30, Nov–Mar 4.30pm.
Church closed during services

Admission
Adult £4.50, Child/Concs £3

Contact
Church Bank NE32 3DY

t 0191 4892106
w bedesworld.co.uk
e visitorinfo@bedesworld.co.uk

©English Heritage Photographic Library

887 Rothbury

Brinkburn Priory

1 hr   Apr–Sep

Founded in 1135 as a house for the Augustinian canons, the church is the only complete surviving building of the monastery. In the summer season a number of choral events can be attended at this practising church.

* Adjacent manor house has open ground floor
* Lovely setting beside River Coquet

Location
4½ miles SE of Rothbury off B6344

Opening
Daily; Apr–Sep 10am–6pm

Admission
Adult £2, Child £1, Concs £1.50

Contact
Longframlinton,
Morpeth NE65 8AR

t 01665 570628
w english-heritage.org.uk

888 Seahouses

Farne islands

2½ hrs   Varies

Lying 2-3 miles off the Northumberland coast, the islands are home to a large colony of Atlantic or grey seals and the most famous sea-bird sanctuary in Britain. Visitors can see 20 different species, including puffins, eider ducks and tern.

* Views of Bamburgh Castle
* Regular ferry services

Location
The islands are 2–3 miles off the north Northumberland Coast. Take the B1340 & then a boat from Seahouses harbour

Opening
Please phone for details

Admission
Please phone for details

Contact
Seahouses

t 01665 721099
w nationaltrust.org.uk

889 Tynemouth

Tynemouth Priory & Castle

1 hr   All year

A burial place of saints and kings, this commanding castle has provided defence against the Vikings, medieval Scotland, Napoleon and C20 Germany. The Benedictine priory was founded in 1090 on the site of an ancient Anglian monastery.

* Restored magazines of a coastal defence gun battery on view at weekends

Location
In Tynemouth, nr North Pier

Opening
Daily; Apr–Sep 10am–6pm; Oct 10am–4pm; Nov–Mar Thu–Mon 10am–4pm.

Admission
Adult £3, Child £1.50, Concs £2.30

Contact
Tynemouth

t 0191 257 1090
w english-heritage.org.uk

883 Holy Island–Lindisfarne

Lindisfarne Priory

1 hr+   All year

A holy site since being founded by St Aidan in AD 635, Lindisfarne remains a place of pilgrimage today. Lindisfarne Priory was the site of one of the most important early centres of Christianity in Anglo-Saxon England. Check tides before visiting.

* Anglo-Saxon carvings in museum
* Refurbished museum

Location
Holy Island, 6 miles E of A1, across causeway

Opening
Daily; Apr–Sep 10am–6pm, Feb, Mar & Oct 10am–4pm; Nov–Jan Sat & Sun only 10am–4pm
Subject to tides.

Admission
Adult £3.50, Child £1.80, Concs £2.60

Contact
Holy Island,
Berwick-upon-Tweed TD15 2RX

t 01289 389200
w english-heritage.org.uk

884 Morpeth

Belsay Hall, Castle & Gardens

3 hrs   All year

A dramatic, well-preserved medieval towerhouse, to which a Jacobean manor house was added in 1614. Belsay Hall (1807), designed by Sir Charles in Greek Revival style after the Temple of Theseus in Athens, has great architectural importance within Europe.

* Two acres of rhododendrons at best May & June
* Formal terraces and winter garden, original planting

Location
In Belsay, 14 miles NW of Newcastle on A696

Opening
Daily; Apr–Sep 10am–6pm; Oct–Mar Thu–Mon 10am–4pm

Admission
Adult £5, Child £2.50, Concs £3.50

Contact
Belsay NE20 0DX

t 01661 881636
w english-heritage.org.uk

885 Morpeth

Carlisle Park

1–3 hrs   All year

In the heart of medieval Morpeth lies historic Carlisle Park complete with a castle, bridges, formal gardens, walks, wooded slopes, recreation areas, play areas, tennis courts, a boating lake and great vantage points.

*Quality Assured Visitor Attraction
* Paddling pool & boating on the river

Location
From A1 follow signs to Morpeth town centre

Opening
Daily; at all times
Turner Garden dawn–dusk

Admission
Free

Contact
Castle Morpeth Borough Council
Kylins Centre,
Morpeth NE61 2EQ

t 01670 500789
w castlemorpeth.gov.uk
e sam.talbot@castlemorpeth.gov.uk

886 Morpeth

Cragside House

3 hrs+   Mar–Oct

The first house in the world to use hydro electricity to power a revolutionary new lighting and internal telephone system. The brainchild of industrialist William Armstrong, the technology amazed contemporaries. Surrounded by beautiful gardens.

* Used to impress important armament customers
* 3-acre rock garden, fruit house and Italian garden

Location
1 mile N of Rothbury on B6341

Opening
House 22 Mar–26 Sep 1pm–5.30pm Oct 4.30pm
Estate 22 Mar–30 Oct 10.30am–7pm
2 Nov–18 Dec 11am–4pm

Admission
Adult £8.50, Child £4

Contact
Rothbury,
Morpeth NE65 7PX

t 01669 620333
w nationaltrust.org.uk
e cragside@nationaltrust.org.uk

880 Greenhead

Roman Army Museum

2 hrs   Feb–Nov

Located next to the superb walltown crags section of Hadrian's Wall, the museum provides fascinating insights into the life of a Roman soldier. Learn about weapons, uniforms, pay, training and off-duty activities through reconstructions, films and displays.

* On Hadrian's Wall
* Life-size models of Roman soldiers

Location
Off B6318, nr Greenhead, 3 miles from Haltwhistle. Follow heritage signs for Hadrian's Wall & Roman Museum

Opening
Daily; Feb–Mar 10am–5pm; Apr–Sep 10am–6pm; Oct–Nov 10am–5pm

Admission
Adult £3.50, Child £2.20, Concs £3

Contact
Greenhead CA6 7JB

t 01697 47485
w vindolanda.com
e info@vindolanda.com

881 Hexham

Cherryburn

1 hr   Mar–Oct

This C19 farmhouse was the birthplace of Thomas Bewick who pioneered wood-engraving. Bewick was an outstanding artist and naturalist and used this passion to produce beautiful engravings of wildlife. The cottage contains an exhibition of his life and works.

* Occasional demonstration of printing
* Stunning views of valley of the River Tyne from garden

Location
A695 to Mickley Square, follow signs, 11 miles from Hexham

Opening
18 Mar–30 Oct Thu–Tue 11am–5.30pm

Admission
Adult £3.50, Child £1.75

Contact
Station Bank, Mickley, nr Stocksfield NE43 7DD

t 01661 843276
w nationaltrust.org.uk
e cherryburn@nationaltrust.org.uk

882 Holy Island–Lindisfarne

Lindisfarne Castle

½ hr   Feb–Oct

Perched on top of a rocky crag and accessible over a causeway at low tide only. Originally a Tudor fort, it was converted into a private house in 1903 by the young Edwin Lutyens. The small rooms are full of intimate decoration and design.

* Charming walled garden planned by Gertrude Jekyll
* Check crossing times before making long journey

Location
Holy Island, 6 miles E of A1, across causeway

Opening
12 Feb–20 Feb , 12 Mar–30 Oct Tue–Sun Dec 30–Jan 2 & Bank Hols. Times vary depending upon tides, usually 10.30am–3pm or 12noon–4pm

Admission
Adult £5, Child £2.50

Contact
Holy Island, Berwick-upon-Tweed TD15 2SH

t 01289 389244
w nationaltrust.org.uk

877 Bamburgh

Bamburgh Castle

2 hrs Mar–Oct

Probably one of the finest castles in England. Perched on a basalt outcrop on the very edge of the North Sea. Restored in 1750 and again extensively by C19 industrialist, Lord Armstrong. Tour includes magnificent King's Hall, Cross Hall, reception rooms and armoury.

* Still home to the Armstrong family
* Exhibits include fine furniture, tapestries and arms

Location
20 miles S of Berwick–upon–Tweed by B1342

Opening
Daily; 13 Mar–31 Oct 11am–5pm

Admission
Adult £5.50, Child £2.50, Concs £4.50

Contact
Bamburgh NE69 7DF

t 01668 214 515
w bamburghcastle.com
e bamburghcastle@aol.com

878 Carlisle–Newcastle

Hadrian's Wall

1 hr+ All year

One of the most important monuments built by the Romans in Britain. It is the best-known frontier in the entire Roman Empire and is designated a World Heritage site. Various attractions along the wall include Roman forts and several museums.

* Museum brings Roman history to life
* 84 mile coast-to-coast walk along wall now open

      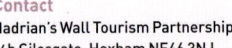

Location
A69 between Newcastle & Carlisle runs parallel to Hadrian's Wall (approximately 2–5 miles S)

Opening
Times vary, please phone for details

Admission
Prices vary, please phone for details

Contact
Hadrian's Wall Tourism Partnership, 14b Gilesgate, Hexham NE46 3NJ

t 01434 322002
w hadrians-wall.org
e info@hadrians-wall.org

879 Chillingham

Chillingham Castle

1 hr+ May–Sep

This remarkable castle with alarming dungeons and torture chamber has been in the family of the Earls Grey and their relations since the C13. See active restoration of complex masonry, metalwork and ornamental plaster in a wide diversity of rooms and styles.

* Beautiful grounds with commanding views
* Formal gardens and woodland walks open to public

Location
Signposted from A1 & A697

Opening
May–Sep Sun–Fri 12 noon–5pm
Oct–Apr by appointment

Admission
Adult £6, Child £3, Concs £5.50
(under 5s £1)

Contact
Chillingham NE66 5NJ

t 01668 215 359
w chillingham-castle.com
e enquiries@chillingham-castle.com

874 Alnwick

Alnwick Castle

1 hr+   Apr–Oct

Foreboding medieval castle known as the Windsor of the North. Stunning state rooms, fine furniture and paintings by Canaletto, Van Dyck and Titian. Filming location for *Harry Potter*. Castle overlooks Capability Brown landscape. Peaceful walks with superb views.

* Home to Percy family for 700 years
* Museum of Royal Northumberland Fusiliers

Location
Outskirts of Alnwick, 35 miles N of Newcastle upon Tyne, 1 mile from A1

Opening
Daily; Apr–Oct 11am–5pm

Admission
Adult £7.50, Child (under 16) free, Concs £6.50

Contact
Alnwick NE66 1NQ

t 01665 510777
w alnwickcastle.com
e enquiries@alnwickcastle.com

876 Ashington

Wansbeck Riverside Park

2–5 hrs   All year

Stretching along the banks of the River Wansbeck, the park provides miles of pleasant walks and trails right down to the sea at Sandy Bay. There are picnic areas for families and play facilities for children. The river can be used for fishing and boating for a small fee.

* Picnic & play areas
* 4-mile riverside walk

Location
Take A1068. The park is located between Ashington & Bedlington

Opening
Daily; 8am–dusk

Admission
Free

Contact
Green Lane,
Ashington NE63 8TX

t 01670 843444

875 Amble

Warkworth Castle

1 hr+   All year

The magnificent eight-towered keep stands high on a hill overlooking the River Coquet. Home to the Percy family who at times wielded more power in the north than the King. Most famous was Harry Hotspur (Sir Henry Percy) immortalised in Shakespeare's *Henry IV*.

* Opening scenes of *Henry IV* were set in Warkworth
* Duke's rooms first opened in 2003

Location
8 miles SE of Alnwick, on A1068

Opening
Daily; Apr–Sep 10am–6pm, Oct 10am–4pm; Nov–Mar Sat, Sun & Mon 10am–4pm

Admission
Adult £3, Child £1.50, Concs £2.30

Contact
Nr Amble,
Morpeth NE65 0UJ

t 01665 711423
w english–heritage.org.uk

©English Heritage Photographic Library

870 Durham

Prince Bishop River Cruiser

1 hr   All year

The 150-seater cruiser sails regularly from Durham city centre. The one-hour trip offers spectacular views of the cathedral and other tourist attractions. There is wheelchair access to the open-air upper deck and saloons.

* Sun deck & on-board BBQ
* 1-hour Santa Cruises in Dec

Location
The cruiser is found below the Prince Bishop shopping centre in Durham

Opening
Sailing times 12.30pm, 2pm, 3pm

Admission
Adult £4.50, Child £2 Senior £4

Contact
The Boathouse, Elvet Bridge, Durham DH1 3AH

t 0191 386 9525

871 Hartlepool

HMS *Trincomalee* – Hartlepool Quay

1 hr   All year

Built for the Admiralty in Bombay in 1817, HMS *Trincomalee* is the oldest ship afloat in the UK. An award-winning restoration provides a unique opportunity to experience the atmosphere of a classic British frigate from the time of Nelson's navy.

* Excellent disabled access to most decks
* One of several attractions around Historic Quay

Location
Follow signs for Hartlepool Historic Quay

Opening
Daily; Apr–Oct 10.30am–5pm
Nov–Mar 10.30am–4pm

Admission
Adult £4.25, Child £3.25, Concs £3.25

Contact
HMS Trincomalee Trust, Jackson Dock, Hartlepool TS24 0SQ

t 01429 223193
w hms-trincomalee.co.uk
e office@trincomalee.co.uk

872 Saint Mary-le-Bow

Durham Heritage Centre

1 hr+   Apr–Oct

This local history museum, located in a historic church, tells Durham's story from C10 to the present day. Displays include Durham people, Durham as a centre of pilgrimage, the world-renowned Harrison organ makers, lost industries, mining life and railways.

* Brass rubbing
* Hands-on exhibits

Location
In the centre of Durham off A690, A177 or A691

Opening
Apr–May & Oct Sat, Sun, Bank Holidays 2pm–4.30pm; Jun daily 2pm–4.30pm; Jul–Sep daily 11am–4.30pm;

Admission
Adult £1.20, Child (5–16) 50p, Concs 80p

Contact
Saint Mary-le-Bow, North Bailey DH1 3ET

t 0191 384 5589/386 8719

873 Upper Weardale

Killhope Lead Mining Museum

4 hrs   Mar–Oct

This fully-restored lead mine explores the lives of Victorian mining families. Guided tours take visitors along the original tunnels (wellingtons, hard-hat and cap lamp provided). Woodland walk gives access to further reminders of lead mining.

* Warm clothes required even during summer
* Winner of family friendly museum 2004

Location
Off A689 between Stanhope & Alston

Opening
Daily; Mar 19–Oct 30 10.30am–5pm

Admission
Adult £6, Child £3 Concs £5.50
No under 4s are allowed in the mine

Contact
The North of England Lead Mining Museum, nr Cowshill, Upper Weardale DL13 1AR

t 01388 537505
w durham.gov.uk/killhope
e killhope@durham.gov.uk

867 Durham

Crook Hall Gardens

1 hr+   May–Sep

On the banks of the River Wear with views of Durham cathedral and castle, Crook Hall is a Grade I medieval manor house with C13 hall. There are a variety of beautiful gardens including ancient and modern planting schemes and an established maze.

* Fruit trees wreathed in rambling roses
* 'A tapestry of colourful blooms', Alan Titchmarsh

Location
Short walk from Durham's Millburngate shopping centre, opposite the Gala theatre

Opening
May & Sep Sun only 1pm–5pm
Jun–Aug Sun–Thu 1pm–5pm
Easter Sat–Mon & all other Bank Hols 1pm–5pm

Admission
Adult £4, Concs £3.50

Contact
Frankland Lane, Sidegate, Durham DH1 5SZ

t 0191 384 8028
w crookhallgardens.co.uk
e info@crookhallgardens.co.uk

868 Durham

Durham Castle

1 hr   Mar–Sep

Dating from 1072, this is one of the largest Norman castles and one of the grandest Romanesque palaces to survive in England. It was the seat of the Prince Bishops until 1832 and now is a residential college for the University of Durham. Entrance by guided tour only.

* World Heritage Site

Location
Durham city centre. Uphill walk or bus service 40 to Palace Green

Opening
Daily; Mid Mar mid Apr, Jul, Aug & Sep, 10am–12.30pm & 2 - 4.30pm. Other times usually Mon, Wed, Sat & Sun afternoons but phone to confirm

Admission
Adult £5, Child £2.50, Concs £2.50

Contact
Durham DH1 3RW

t 0191 334 3800
w durhamcastle.com
e university-college.www@durham.ac.uk

869 Durham

Oriental Museum

1 hr   All year

The only museum of its kind in the UK, entirely devoted to art and archaeology from cultures throughout the Orient. The collections range from prehistoric Egypt and China to the work of living artists. The museum is part of Durham university.

* Used as resource by researchers around the world
* Students of higher education enter for free

Location
S side of Durham, signed from A177

Opening
Daily; Mon–Fri 10am–5pm
Sat & Sun 12 noon–5pm

Admission
Adult £1.50, Concs 75p

Contact
Elvet Hill, off South Road, Durham DH1 3TH

t 0191 334 5694
w dur.ac.uk/oriental.museum
e oriental.museum@durham.ac.uk

865 Darlington

Darlington Railway Centre & Museum

2 hrs   All year

Celebrating nearly 180 years of railway history in the town and the North East of England in general. Of greatest significance is Stephenson's Rocket which hauled the inaugural multi-carriage train on the Stockton and Darlington Railway.

* Including an 1840s Darlington-built locomotive
* The museum is in the 1842 railway station

Location
1 mile from town centre on A167

Opening
Daily; 10am–5pm

Admission
Adult £2.50, Child/Concs £1.50

Contact
North Road Station,
Darlington DL3 6ST
t 01325 460532
w drcm.org.uk
e museum@darlington.gov.uk

866 Darlington

Raby Castle

3 hrs+   May–Sep

Built in the C14, Raby Castle is one of the largest and most impressive of English medieval castles, with towers, turrets, embattled walls, interiors and artworks from the medieval, Regency and Victorian periods. Walled gardens, deer park and children's adventure playground.

* Great kitchen little altered in 600 years
* Paintings by Reynolds and other masters

Location
1 mile N of Staindrop on A688

Opening
Easter Sat–Wed 11am–5.30pm
May & Sep Wed & Sun 11am–5.30pm
Jun–Aug Sun–Fri 11am–5.30pm

Admission
Adult £9, Child £4, Concs £8

Contact
PO Box 50, Staindrop,
Darlington DL2 3AH
t 01833 660 202
w rabycastle.com
e admin@rabycastle.com

861   Barnard Castle

Barnard Castle

1 hr+   All year

This imposing English Heritage property sits high above the River Tees. The C12 stone castle was once one of the largest castles in northern England, the principal residence of the Baliol family, and a major power base in the many conflicts between England and Scotland.

* Beautiful views of River Tees
* Home to Richard III & Henry VII

Location
In Barnard Castle town, off Galgate on A688

Opening
Daily; Apr–Sep 10am–6pm; Oct 10am–4pm; Nov–Mar Thu–Mon 10am–4pm

Admission
Adult £3.00, Child £1.50, Concs £2.30

Contact
Barnard Castle

t 01833 638212
w english-heritage.org.uk

862   Barnard Castle

Bowes Museum

3 hrs   All year

Founded by local businessman, John Bowes, and his French wife, Josephine, this magnificent museum, which opened in 1892, houses one of Britain's finest collections of paintings, ceramics, furniture and textiles. Special outdoor events and family fun days.

* Set in 23 acres of parkland, with parterre garden
* Outstanding temporary art exhibition programme

Location
Just off A66, 20 mins from Scotch Corner (A1)

Opening
Daily; 11am–5pm

Admission
Adult £6, Child free, Concs £5

Contact
Barnard Castle DL12 8NP

t 01833 690606
w bowesmuseum.org.uk
e info@bowesmuseum.org.uk

863   Beamish

Beamish, The North of England Open Air Museum

4 hrs+   All year

Beamish is a unique living, working experience of life as it was in the north of England in both the early C18 and C19. It shows how the region was transformed in that time from its thinly populated rural roots to being the home to heavy industrialisation.

* Costumed guides explain each attraction
* Former European Museum of the Year

Location
Follow signs from junction 63 of A1M

Opening
Apr–Oct Tue–Thu & Sat–Mon 10am–5pm Nov–Apr 10am–4pm

Admission
Adult £12, Child £7, Concs £10

Contact
Beamish DH9 0RG

t 0191 370 4000
w beamish.org.uk
e museum@beamish.org.uk

864   Bishop Auckland

Hamsterley Forest

2–4 hrs   All year

Covering some 2,000 hectares, Hamsterley Forest has something for everyone – play and picnic areas, several walks and cycle routes ranging from a 1½ mile easy-access footpath to a 7-mile black cycle route and downhill descent course for the more adventurous.

* The largest forest in County Durham

Location
From the A68 at Witton-le-Wear follow the brown tourist signs

Opening
Forest: Daily; 7.30am–sunset
Visitor Centre: Apr–Oct Mon–Fri 10am–4pm, Sat & Sun 11am–5pm. Please phone for details in Nov & Dec

Admission
Free. Toll for forest drive & car park charge (£2 per car)

Contact
Redford,
Bishop Auckland DL13 3NL

t 01388 488312
w forestry.gov.uk

High Force Waterfall, Durham

North East

Durham Northumberland Tyne & Wear

858 Liverpool

The Walker

  1 hr All year

The Walker holds one of the finest collections of fine and decorative art in Europe. The gallery has recently undergone a major £4.3m refurbishment programme. These improvements include special exhibition galleries which display important touring shows.

* Refurbishment of the C17 European galleries
* New craft & design gallery of decorative arts

Location
Opposite entrance to Birkenhead tunnel, 5 mins from Tourist Information Centre

Opening
Daily 10am–5pm

Admission
Free

Contact
William Brown Street, Liverpool L3 8EL

t 0151 478 4199
w thewalker.org.uk
e thewalker@liverpoolmuseums.org.uk

© National Trust Photographic Library

859 Prescot

Knowsley Safari Park

  3 hrs+ All year

During the 5-mile-long drive visitors can see a wide range of wild animals, including camels, buffalo, white rhino, emu, wallabies, elephants, giraffes and lions. A separate reptile house is home to snakes, iguanas, lizards, scorpions and stick insects.

Location
Leave the M62 at junction 6, the M57 at junction 2 & follow the signs

Opening
1 Mar–31 Oct open daily 10am–4pm; 1 Nov–28 Feb open daily 10.30am–3pm; closed 25 Dec

Admission
Adult £9, Child/Concs £6

Contact
Prescot
Merseyside L34 4AN

t 0151 430 9009
w www.knowsley.com
e safari.park@knowsley.com

860 Southport

Formby Squirrel Reserve

  2 hrs All year

This nature reserve is home to one of Britain's last thriving colonies of red squirrels. These squirrels can be seen in the pine trees and the shoreline attracts waders such as oystercatchers and sanderlings. As well as the beautiful beach there are miles of walks across the sand dunes.

Location
15 miles N of Liverpool, 2 miles W of Formby, 2 miles off A565 & 6 miles S of Southport

Opening
All year, dawn to dusk

Admission
Free, Car park £3.10

Contact
Blundell Avenue, Formby L37 1PH

t 01704 878 591
w nationaltrust.org.uk
e formby@nationaltrust.org.uk

856   Liverpool

Speke Hall, Garden & Estate

2 hrs   Mar–Dec

Behind the black-and-white half-timbered façade of this hall are interiors which represent many centuries. The Great Hall and priests' holes evoke Tudor times, while the oak parlour and smaller rooms show the Victorian desire for privacy and comfort.

* Fine Jacobean plasterwork & carved furniture
* A fully-equipped Victorian kitchen and servants' hall

Location
8 miles SE of central Liverpool, next to Liverpool airport, signposted

Opening
Mar–Oct Wed–Sun 1pm–5.30pm
Oct–Dec Sat & Sun 1pm–4.30pm

Admission
Adult £6.25, Child £3.50

Contact
The Walk, Speke, Liverpool L24 1XD
t 0151 427 7231
w nationaltrust.org.uk
e spekehall@nationaltrust.org.uk

857   Liverpool

Tate Liverpool

2 hrs   All year

Tate Liverpool houses two main types of exhibits – art selected from the Tate Collection, and special exhibitions of contemporary art. Over 80 different presentations featuring work by more than 300 artists, have taken place since the gallery opened.

* Photography, printmaking, painting & sculpture
* Video, performance & installation

 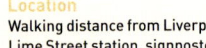

Location
Walking distance from Liverpool Lime Street station, signposted from city centre

Opening
Tue–Sun 10am–5.50pm

Admission
Tate Collection Free
Exhibition Adult £4, Child & Concs £3

Contact
The Colonnades, Albert Dock, Liverpool L3 4BB
t 0151 702 7400
w tate.org.uk/liverpool
e liverpoolinfo@tate.org.uk

853 Liverpool

Mathew Street Gallery

1 hr   All year

The gallery has John Lennon drawings, Beatles' photography, artwork by Klaus Voorman and photography by Astrid Kirchherr.

* Prints are numbered and signed by Yoko Ono
* Robert Whitaker exhibition on display

Location
Situated above the Beatles shop, yards from the Cavern Club

Opening
Mon–Sat 10am–5 pm Sun 11am–4pm

Admission
Free

Contact
31 Mathew Street, Liverpool L2 6RE

t 0151 236 0009
w lennonart.co.uk
e mathewstreetgallery@lennonart.co.uk

855 Liverpool

Sefton Park Palm House

1 hr   All year

Sefton Park Palm House is a Grade II listed Victorian glasshouse, it is an octagonal three-tiered structure, showcasing the Liverpool botanical collection which was brought to the city from all over the world during its maritime history.

* One of the largest municipal collections in the country
* Four sculptures by Leon-Joseph Chavailiaur

Location
M62 onto the A5058 toward Queen's Drive & Alliton Road

Opening
Nov–Mar 10.30am–4pm
Apr–Oct 10.30am–5pm
Restricted opening during events

Admission
Free

Contact
Sefton Park, Liverpool L17 1AP

t 0151 726 2415
w palmhouse.org.uk
e info@palmhouse.org.uk

854 Liverpool

Mendips & 20 Forthlin Road

2 hrs   Mar–Oct

This is a joint tour of Mendips, the childhood home of John Lennon, and Forthlin Road, the home of the McCartney family, where the Beatles met, rehearsed and wrote many of their earliest songs. Displays include contemporary photographs and Beatles' memorabilia.

* Audio tour features Sir Paul McCartney
* Evocative photographs of life at 20 Forthlin Road

Location
Tours leave from Albert Dock in central Liverpool, or Speke Hall

Opening
Tours depart 10.30am & 11.20am from Albert Dock & 2.15pm & 3.55pm from Speke Hall

Admission
Adult £12, Child £1

Contact
20 Forthlin Road, Allerton, Liverpool L24 1YP

t 0151 708 8574/0151 427 7231
w nationaltrust.org.uk
e spekehall@nationaltrust.org.uk

850 Liverpool

Liverpool Cathedral

2 hrs   All year

This is the largest Anglican cathedral in Europe and one of the great buildings of the C20. The massive tower stands over the city and the cathedral boasts the highest gothic arches, the largest organ and the heaviest ring of bells. The cathedral hosts exhibitions, concerts and recitals.

* Designed by Sir Giles Gilbert Scott
* The grand organ has 9765 pipes

Location
Half a mile from city centre

Opening
8am-6pm (subject to services)

Admission
Free, donations welcome

Contact
St James' Mount, Liverpool L1 7AZ
t 0151 709 6271
w liverpoolcathedral.org.uk
e info@liverpoolcathedral.org.uk

851 Liverpool

Liverpool Football Club

1 hr   All year

A tour of Anfield includes a walk down the players' tunnel and the opportunity to touch the famous sign that proclaims 'This is Anfield'. Experience the dressing room where the manager delivers his team talks. The museum is packed with things to do, see and listen to.

* Film takes visitors through the life of the club
* Hillsborough memorial tribute to 96 fans who died in 1989

Location
3 miles from city centre, 4 miles from M62 & 7 miles from end of M57 & M58

Opening
Daily 10am–5pm
(closes 1 hour before kick off)

Admission
Adult £9, Child/Concs £5.50

Contact
Anfield Road, Liverpool L4 0TH
t 0151 260 6677
w liverpoolfc.tv
e events@liverpoolfc.tv

852 Liverpool

Liverpool Museum

2 hrs   All year

This is the largest of the National Museums of Liverpool venues. The fascinating and varied collections cover archaeology, ethnology and the natural and physical sciences. Special attractions include the award-winning natural history centre and the planetarium.

* Exhibition galleries include Egypt & the Near East
* Space & time gallery

Location
Opposite entrance to Birkenhead tunnel,5 mins walk from Tourist information Centre in Queen's Square

Opening
Daily 10am–5pm

Admission
Free

Contact
William Brown Street, Liverpool L3 8EN
t 0151 478 4399
w liverpoolmuseum.org.uk
e themuseum@liverpoolmuseums.org.uk

847 Liverpool

Customs & Excise National Museum

2 hrs   All year

This museum tells the story of smuggling and contraband from the 1700s to the present day. The collection includes a display of tools of the trade, prints, paintings and photographs relating to the work of the Department of Customs and Excise.

* Collection of Department of Customs & Excise
* Discover how far people will go to avoid paying duty

Location
Follow signposts to Albert Dock

Opening
Daily 10am–5pm

Admission
Free

Contact
Albert Dock, Liverpool L3 4AQ

t 0151 478 4499
w customsandexcisemuseum.org.uk
e info@1001daysout.com

849 Liverpool

Fingerprints of Elvis

1 hr   All year

Elvis Presley's enormous influence on the emergence of the Beatles and the whole Merseybeat scene is legendary. The legend of the King lives on through a number of his personal items, including a set of fingerprints, his Harley Davidson and stage costumes.

* Extraordinary jewellery & army insignia
* Audio tour by David Stanley – Elvis' stepbrother

Location
Follow the M62, then the brown signposts to Albert Dock

Opening
Daily 10am–6pm

Admission
Adult £7.95, Child £4.95, Concs £5.45

Contact
19 The Colonnades, Albert Dock, Liverpool L3 4AA

t 0151 709 1790
w fingerprintsofelvis.com

848 Liverpool

Everton Football Club

2 hrs   All year

A tour of Goodison Park will include a behind-the-scenes look at what it's like to play for the Toffees. Walk down the tunnel and imagine the roar of 40,000 fans, explore the dressing room and see where the players relax after a game.

Location
3 miles N of Liverpool city centre

Opening
Daily, except on match days

Admission
Adult £8.50, Child & Concs £5
Pre-booking essential

Contact
Goodison Park, Liverpool L4 4EL

t 0151 330 2277
w evertonfc.com
e boxoffice@evertonfc.com

844 Liverpool

Beatles Story

2 hrs   All year

Imagine experiencing the greatest story the pop world has ever known - in the City where it all began! Take a nostalgic trip through the multi-award winning Beatles story experience, on Liverpool's historic Albert Dock.

* New in 2004 a living history audio tour
* The Cavern Club, the music & the instruments

Location
Follow signposts to Albert Dock

Opening
Daily 10am–6pm, last admission 4.30pm

Admission
Adult £8.45, Child £4.95, Concs £5.75

Contact
Albert Dock, Britannia Vaults, Liverpool L3 4AD
t 0151 709 1963
w beatlesstory.com

---

845 Liverpool

The Cavern Club

4 hrs+   All year

Visit the most famous club in the world and learn all there is to know about the Cavern Club, from its early days as a jazz club in the cellar of a fruit warehouse, to the live music venue of today. This is a carbon copy of the original club where the Beatles found fame.

* Paul McCartney played his last gig of the century here
* Wall of Fame

Location
City Centre

Opening
Mon–Wed 11am–6pm
Thu 11am–2am
Fri–Sat 11am–2.45am
Sun 12pm–12.30am

Admission
Adult £4

Contact
Mathew Street, Liverpool L2 6RE
t 0151 236 1965
w cavern-liverpool.co.uk
e office@thecavernliverpool.com

---

846 Liverpool

Conservation Centre

1 hr   All year

This Conservation Centre is housed in the former Midland Railway goods depot which was built in the 1870s. The centre cares for all of the National Museums' Liverpool collections. There are over a million objects, ranging from tiny natural history specimens to space rockets.

* Conservation science section
* Many world-famous masterpieces are cared for

Location
Nr Queen's Square bus station

Opening
Mon–Sat 10am–5pm
Sun 12 noon–5pm

Admission
Free

Contact
Whitechapel, Liverpool L1 6HZ
t 0151 478 4999
w Liverpoolmuseums.org
e conservation@liverpoolmuseums.org.uk

841 Liverpool

Aintree Racecourse & Visitor Centre

2 hrs   All year

A visit to Aintree Racecourse includes the museum, picture gallery and race of champions. Explore the weighing room, stables, parade ring, Red Rum's grave and statue.

Location
5 miles from Liverpool city centre, well signposted

Opening
Group visits only, phone for details

Admission
Adult £7, Child & Concs £4

Contact
Ormskirk Road, Aintree, Liverpool
L9 5AS

t 0151 522 2921
w aintree.co.uk

842 Liverpool

Albert Dock

4 hrs+   All year

The Albert Dock is an architectural triumph. Opened in 1846, it became a treasure house of precious cargoes from all over the world. Today, redevelopment has transformed it into a busy and cosmopolitan centre as well as a top heritage attraction.

* Converted C19 warehouse buildings
* Visit albertdock.com for a web-cam view of the attraction

Location
Situated on Liverpool's waterfront adjacent to the Pier Head

Opening
Any reasonable time

Admission
Free

Contact
Edward Pavillion, Albert Dock, Liverpool L3 4AE

t 0151 708 7334
w albertdock.com
e enquiries@albertdock.com

843 Liverpool

Cains Brewery

1 hr+   All year

Cains has always been renowned for producing award-winning cask ales. Incorporating the Brewery Tap, now one of Liverpool's drinking landmarks, Robert Cains' original mersey brewery stands today as a fine example of Victorian brewhouse architecture.

* Tours include buffet & 2 pints in the Brewery Tap pub

Location
In West Parliament Street, near Albert Dock

Opening
Mon–Thu, closes at 6.30pm

Admission
Advance booking essential

Contact
Stanhope Street, Liverpool L8 5XJ

t 0151 7098734
w gew@cainsbeer.com
e brewerytour@cainsbeers.com

837 Birkenhead

Historic Warships

3 hrs   All year

This is the largest collection of C20 fighting vessels in the UK. The collection includes the submarine *Onyx* and the anti submarine frigate HMS *Plymouth*. On the quayside explore the Bofors Gun and the LCVP which is ex HMS *Intrepid*, also the minehunter HMS Bronington.

* U534, the last U-boat to leave Germany in the Second World War
* LCT 7074, last surviving LCT of D-Day landings

Location
Leave M53 at junction 1, follow signs to All Docks. Signposted from there

Opening
Apr–Sep 10am–5pm
Oct–Mar 10am–4pm

Admission
Adult £6, Child £4, Concs £5

Contact
East Float, Dock Road, Birkenhead CH41 1DJ

t 0151 650 1573
w warships.freeserve.co.uk

838 Birkenhead

Williamson Art Gallery & Museum

1 hr   All year

This purpose-built gallery houses the majority of Birkenhead's collection of artistic masterpieces. On display are Victorian oil paintings, English watercolours, Liverpool porcelain, Della Robbia pottery. Collections feature local history, ship models and decorative arts.

* Part of the Merseyside embroidery trail
* Varied programme of temporary exhibitions

Location
Slatey Road

Opening
Tue–Sun & Bank Hols 10am–5pm

Admission
Free

Contact
Slatey Road, Birkenhead CH 43 4UE

t 0151 652 4177
w williamsonartgallery@wirrial.gov.uk

839 Knowsley

National Wildflower Centre

2 hrs   Apr–Sep

The National Wildflower Centre is set in a Victorian park within 35 acres of parkland. It has an innovative visitor centre where visitors can learn about wildflowers. It places an emphasis on creative conservation and putting wildflowers back into Britain.

* Seasonal wildflower demonstration areas
* A working garden nursery & shop

Location
Situated in Knowsley's Court Hey Park, off junction 5 of M62

Opening
Apr–Sep daily 10am–5pm

Admission
Adult £3, Child free, Concs £1.50

Contact
Court Hey Park, Knowsley L16 3NA

t 0151 738 1913 / 0151 7228292
w nwc.org.uk
e info@nwc.org.uk

840 Knowsley

Prescot Museum

1 hr   All year

This museum is located in a Georgian townhouse, which was once the site of the local cockerel-fighting pit. Exhibits reflect local history, in particular the clock- and watch-making tradition. On display are local longcase clocks, tools and a reconstruction of a C18 clockmaker's home.

* Displays of pottery manufacture and cable making
* Varied programme of exhibitions

Location
Signposted from the A56

Opening
Tue–Sat 10am–5pm Sun 2pm–5pm
closed bank hols

Admission
Free

Contact
34 Church Street, Prescot, Knowsley L34 3LA

t 0151 430 7787
w knowsley.gov.uk
e knowsley.gov.ukleisure/museum

833 Manchester

Urbis

2 hrs   All year

This museum is set in a shimmering, high-rise, glass building. State-of-the-art interactive displays and exhibits lead visitors through an inspirational journey exploring life in different cities of the world, including Manchester, Los Angeles, São Paulo, Singapore and Paris.

* A visit begins with a sky glide in the glass elevator
* Combination of audio, visual & sensory environments

Location
City centre

Opening
10am–6pm

Admission
Permanent exhibition free, other Adult £5, Child & Concs £3.50

Contact
Cathedral Gardens, Manchester M4 3BG

t 0161 605 8200
w urbis.org.uk
e info@urbis.org.uk

834 Manchester

The Whitworth Art Gallery

1 hr   All year

This gallery houses an impressive range of watercolours, prints, drawings, modern art and sculpture, as well as the largest collection of textiles and wallpapers outside London. The Whitworth uses its collections to create changing exhibitions exploring different themes.

* A programme of innovative touring exhibitions
* Specialist centre for works on paper and textiles

Location
Oxford Road to the S of Manchester city centre and to the S of the University of Manchester campus

Opening
Mon–Sat 10am–5pm, Sun 2pm–5pm
Sat afternoon free eye-opener tour at 2pm

Admission
Free

Contact
The University of Manchester, Oxford Road, Manchester M15 6ER

t 0161 275 7450
w whitworth.man.ac.uk
e whitworth@man.ac.uk

835 Birkenhead

Birkenhead Priory & St Mary's Tower

1 hr   All year

This Benedictine monastery, established in 1150 is the oldest building on Merseyside. Much of the original building remains and other parts have been restored to their former stature. Visit St Mary's Church (1822), climb the tower and experience panoramic views.

* Views of Birkenhead, Oxton Ridge, Bidston and Wirral
* Concerts on Sundays in August

Location
M53 onto the A41, follow signposts to Birkenhead

Opening
Easter–Oct Tue–Sun 1pm–5pm
Nov–Easter Tue–Sun 12 noon–4pm

Admission
Free

Contact
Priory Street, Birkenhead CH41 5JH

t 0151 666 1249
w wirral.gov.uk
e comments@wirral.gov.uk

836 Birkenhead

Birkenhead Tramway & Wirral Transport Museum

1 hr   All year

Birkenhead is the home of the first street tramway in Europe. Take the tramway from Woodside visitor centre to the Old Colonial pub at the Taylor Street terminus. From there visit the heritage centre, which houses a collection of restored and part-restored local buses and trams.

* Open-topped 1901 Birkenhead tram 20
* Day-to-day service operated by two Hong Kong trams

Location
Signposted to Taylor Street from the Woodside ferry terminal

Opening
Apr–Oct Sat–Sun 1pm–5pm
Nov–Mar Sat–Sun 12 noon–4pm

Admission
Adult £1, Child 50p

Contact
1 Taylor street, Birkenhead, CH41 1DG

t 0151 647 6780

829 Manchester

Museum of Science & Industry

4 hrs+   All year

Situated in the oldest-surviving passenger railway buildings in the world, the museum tells the story of the history, science and industry of Manchester – the world's first industrial city. Stimulate the senses in Xperiment, an interactive science gallery.

* Demonstrators operate thunderous cotton machinery
* See the Avro Shackleton plane in the air & space hall

Location
On Liverpool Road in Castlefield, signed from the city centre

Opening
Daily 10am–5pm

Admission
Free, exhibitions may charge

Contact
Liverpool Road, Castlefield, Manchester M3 4FP

t 0161 832 2244
w msim.org.uk
e marketing@msim.org.uk

830 Manchester

Manchester Museum

1 hr   All year

This museum, with its four floors of displays and exhibitions in 15 galleries, houses collections from all over the world. Visit the famous Egyptology galleries, the new science for life gallery and the zoology gallery which contains mammals, birds and live animals.

* Ethnology collections from South America
* Collections of fossils & minerals

Location
In Oxford Road to the S of the city centre

Opening
Daily; Mon–Sat 10am–5pm
Sun & Bank Hols 11am–4pm

Admission
Free, exhibitions may charge

Contact
The University of Manchester, Oxford Road, Manchester M13 9PL

t 0161 275 2634
w museum.man.ac.uk
e michael.rooney@man.ac.uk

831 Manchester

Museum of Transport

2 hrs   All year

Housed in a former bus depot, this wonderfully quirky museum is packed with vintage vehicles, including buses, fire engines and lorries, some 100 years old. The vehicles are lovingly maintained and restored in workshops on the premises.

* The biggest collection of vintage buses in the UK

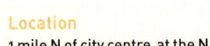   

Location
1 mile N of city centre at the N end of Boyle Street, next to Queen's Road bus garage

Opening
Mar–Oct Wed, Sat, Sun & Bank Hols 10am–5pm;
Nov–Feb, 10am–4pm;
closed Christmas & New Year

Admission
Adult £3, Child £1.75, Concs £1.75

Contact
Boyle Street, Cheetham, Manchester M8 8UW

t 0161 205 2122
w www.gmts.co.uk
e email@gmts.co.uk

832 Manchester

Old Trafford Museum & Tour

2 hrs   All year

Britain's first purpose-built football museum covers the history of Manchester United from 1878 to the present day. There are frequently-updated exhibits and guided tours of the stadium. Picture yourself with the players, using the latest digital imaging technology.

* Play your own commentary on United games
* Multi-award winner

Location
From Chester Road (A56), turn into Sir Matt Busby Way, or use Old Trafford Metrolink station

Opening
Daily; 9.30am–5pm
Museum closes 30 mins before kick-off (please phone for details of times and to book tours)

Admission
Museum only Adult £5.50, Child £3.75, Concs £3.75

Contact
Sir Matt Busby Way, Old Trafford, Manchester M16 0RA

t 0870 442 1994
w www.manutd.com

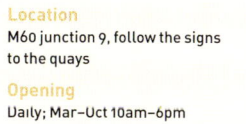

827 Manchester

Imperial War Museum North

1 hr+   All year

The museum, situated on the banks of the Manchester Ship Canal, offers people of all ages thought-provoking displays and direct access to the museum's collections. It offers insights into the enormous impact of war on the C20 and C21.

Location
M60 junction 9, follow the signs to the quays

Opening
Daily; Mar–Oct 10am–6pm
Nov–Feb 10am–5pm

Admission
Free

Contact
Trafford Wharf Road, The Quays, Trafford Park M17 1TZ
t 0161 836 4000
w iwm.org.uk
e info@iwm.org.uk

828 Manchester

Manchester Art Gallery

4 hrs+   All year

This gallery houses one of the world's finest collections of art, displayed in spectacular surroundings. There are fun interactive displays and special exhibitions to enjoy including the gallery of craft and design.

* Collection spans six centuries of fine & decorative art
* Exceptional for C19 British oil & watercolour paintings

Location
City centre

Opening
Tue–Sun 10am–5pm;
closed Mon except Bank Hols

Admission
Free

Contact
Mosley Street, Manchester M2 3JL
t 0161 235 8888
w manchestergalleries.org

823 Manchester

Castlefield Urban Heritage Park & Visitor Centre

1 hr+ All year

See evidence of Manchester's great industrial past, including railway viaducts and canal systems. Visit the remains of the Roman fort of Mamucium, take a pleasant walk or boat trip and enjoy many events in the outdoor arena.

* Britain's first urban heritage park

Location
Manchester city centre, follow signs for the Museum of Science & Industry

Opening
Park Daily
Centre Mon–Fri 10am–4pm
Sat, Sun & Bank Hols 12noon–4pm;
closed Christmas to New Year

Admission
Free

Contact
Castlefield, Manchester
w www.manchester.gov.uk

824 Manchester

Chinese Arts Centre

2 hrs All year

This new building offers changing contemporary art exhibitions, workshops, education programmes and information about Chinese art and culture, with a particular emphasis on supporting Sino-British artistic expression.

* The centre has a state-of-the-art education suite
* Traditional Chinese tea rooms

Location
Market Buildings, Thomas Street

Opening
Mon–Sat 10am–6pm
Sun 11am–5pm

Admission
Free

Contact
Thomas Street, Manchester M4 1 EU

t 0161 832 7271
w chinese-arts-center.org
e info@chinese-arts-center.org

825 Manchester

Gallery of Costume

1 hr All year

Housed in Platt Hall, an C18 textile merchant's house, this is one of the largest collections of clothing and fashion accessories in Britain. The collection contains clothes worn by men, women and children from the C18 to the present day.

* Many of the clothes represent high fashion of the day
* Fashions of Manchester's South Asian communities

Location
In Platt Fields Park, Wilmslow Road in South Manchester

Opening
Last Sat of every month 10am–5pm,
Mon–Fri 10am–5pm by appointment

Admission
Free

Contact
Platt Hall, Rusholme,
Manchester M14 5LL

t 0161 224 5217
w manchestergalleries.org.uk

826 Manchester

Heaton Hall

2 hrs Easter–Sep

Heaton Hall is a magnificent C18 neo-classical country house set in 650 acres of rolling parkland. The hall is Grade I listed and its interiors have been beautifully restored to reflect late C18/C19 life at Heaton.

* 1772 architect James Wyatt re-modelled the house
* One of the finest neo-classical houses in the country

Location
In the middle of Heaton Park off Middleton Road in East Manchester

Opening
Easter–Sep, Wed–Sun & Bank Hols
10am–5.30pm

Admission
Free

Contact
Heaton Park, Prestwich,
Manchester M25 5SW

t 0161 2358888
w manchestergalleries.org

819 Preston

National Football Museum

2 hrs   All year

Travel on a journey through football's history. Learn how the game was invented, how it has developed over the last 150 years, and what the future will hold for players and supporters. Discover the individuals and teams who have helped to shape the game we know today.

* Football Hall of Fame exhibit
* Enjoy our new penalty shoot out game

Location
2 miles from junction 31, 31A or 32 on M6, follow signs

Opening
Tue–Sat 10am–5pm, Sun 11am–5pm

Admission
Free

Contact
Sir Tom Finney Way, Deepdale, Preston PR1 6RU
t 01772 908403/442
w nationalfootballmuseum.com
e enquiries@nationalfootball museum.com

820 Rossendale

Helmshore Textile Museums

2 hrs   Easter–Oct

Experience two original textile mills, a waterwheel and textile machines from the Industrial Revolution. At Whitaker's Mill, a C19 cotton-spinning mill, visitors can see working spinning mules.

* Watch live demonstrations by skilled workers
* Activities programme includes talks & workshops

Location
Holcome Road

Opening
Daily; Mon–Fri 12noon–4pm
Sat & Sun 12noon–5pm

Admission
Adult £3, Child free, Concs £1.50

Contact
Holcombe Road, Helmshore, Rossendale BB4 4NP
t 01706 226459/218838
w museumoflancs.org.uk
e helmshoremuseum@ museumoflancs.org.uk

821 Rivington

Lever Park

3 hrs+   All year

Sited on the West Pennine moors, this park has facilities for fishing and walking as well as an arboretum, a pinetum, refreshments and toilets. Other interesting features include the remains of Lord Leverhulme's gardens and two cruck barns.

* Ruined replica of Liverpool Castle & Rivington Pike
* Reservoir

Location
Rivington Lane, Horwich

Opening
Wed–Sun & Bank Hols
10.30am–4.30pm

Admission
Free

Contact
Great House Information Centre, Rivington Lane, Horwich BL6 7SB
t 01204 691549
w unitedutilities.com

822 Wigan

Haigh Country Park

5 hrs+   All year

This park includes an art and craft gallery with exhibitions of pottery, embroidery and paintings. The model village features a railway, helipad, pub and castle. The walled garden originally supplied the hall with fruit and vegetables and now provides a peaceful retreat.

* Ranger guided walks around the park
* Miniature railway

Location
Nr B5238 and B5239

Opening
Dawn to dusk
Visitor Centre Mon–Sun 9am–5pm

Admission
Free

Contact
Haigh, Wigan WN2 1PE
t 01942 832895
w haighhall.net
e hhgen@wict.org

816 Preston

British Commercial Vehicle Museum

2 hrs   Apr–Oct

This is one of Britain's most important heritage collections. It contains a unique line-up of historic commercial vehicles and buses representing a century of truck and bus building. It is located in the heart of Leyland.

* Sound & light Second World War theme
* Pope mobile

Location
M6 Junction 28, follow the signs

Opening
Apr–Sep Sun, Tue–Thu 10am–5pm
Oct open Sun only

Admission
Adult £4, Child £2

Contact
King Street, Leyland,
Preston PR25 2LE
t 01772 451011
w commercialvehiclemuseum.co.uk

817 Preston

Harris Museum & Art Gallery

2 hrs   All year

Discover the best of Preston's heritage in a beautiful Grade I listed building. The Harris has large collections of paintings, sculpture, textiles, costume, glass and ceramics, as well as the Story of Preston gallery which brings the history of the town to life.

* Exciting programme of exhibitions
* National reputation for contemporary art shows

Location
City centre

Opening
Daily; Mon–Sat 10am–5pm
Sun 11am–4pm

Admission
Free

Contact
Market Square, Preston PR1 2PP
t 01772 258 248
e harris.museum@preston.gov.uk

818 Preston

Museum of Lancashire

2 hrs   All year

Located in the Old Sessions' House, which was built in 1825, this museum traces the history of the county and its people, from the Middle Ages through to recent times. It houses a collection of military objects and memorabilia, from three Lancashire regiments.

* Colourful uniforms & splendid swords are displayed
* Reconstruction of a First World War trench

Location
On the A6, Stanley Street, Preston

Opening
Mon–Wed, Fri & Sat 10.30am–5pm

Admission
Adult £2, Child free, Concs £1

Contact
Stanley Street, Preston PR1 4YP
t 01772 264075
w lancsmuseums.gov.uk
e museums.enquiries@mus.lanc-scc.gov.uk

Eric Morecambe statue

1 hr   All year

Unveiled by the Queen in 1999, the larger-than-life statue depicts Eric Morecambe in a characteristic pose with a pair of binoculars around his neck (he was a keen ornithologist). The statue is set against the backdrop of Morecambe Bay and the Lake District hills.

* People queue to have their photograph taken here

Location
Leave M6 at junction 34 or 35 & follow signs for Morecambe & statue is located on central promenade area

Opening
Any reasonable time

Admission
Free

Contact
Central Promenade, Morecambe or the Tourist Information Centre

t 01524 582808
w visitmorecambe.co.uk

© National Trust Photographic Library

Rufford Old Hall

2 hrs+   Apr–Oct

This is a fine C16 building, famed for its Great Hall which has an intricately carved 'moveable' wooden screen and hammerbeam roof. It is rumoured that Shakespeare performed in this hall for the owner, Sir Thomas Hesketh.

* Fine collections of C16–C17 oak furniture
* Arms, armour and tapestries

     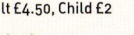

Location
7 miles N of Ormskirk in village of Rufford on E side of A59

Opening
3 Apr–27 Oct Sat–Wed 1pm–5pm
Check opening hours before visit

Admission
Adult £4.50, Child £2

Contact
Rufford, Ormskirk L40 1SG

t 01704 821254
w nationaltrust.org.uk
e ruffordoldhall@ntrust.org.uk

811 Horwich

Horwich Heritage Centre

1 hr   All year

This centre aims to preserve and present the rich history and heritage of Horwich, by featuring specific aspects of Horwich life over the centuries, using videos, displays, artifacts and exhibits. There is a guest speaker on the second Tuesday of every month.

* Exhibition of local historic works
* Full range of publications on Horwich available

Location
Junction 6 M61 and A673

Opening
Wed 2pm–4pm Sat 10am–12noon
2nd Tue every month 7.30pm–9pm

Admission
Free

Contact
Longworth Road, Horwich BL6 7BG
t 01204 847797
w horwichheritage.co.uk

812 Lancaster

Judges' Lodgings

1 hr   Easter–Oct

This is Lancaster's oldest townhouse, home to Thomas Cavell, keeper of the castle during Lancashire's witch trials of 1612. Later used as a residence for judges visiting Lancaster Castle, it is now a museum displaying a wealth of furniture, porcelain, silver and paintings.

* Collection of Gillow furniture in period rooms
* Collection of dolls, toys & games from C18 to today

Location
Nr train station, on the cobbled roads just down from the castle

Opening
Easter–Jun & Oct Mon–Fri 1pm–4pm
Sat & Sun 12noon–4pm
Jul–Sep Mon–Fri 10am–4pm
Sat & Sun 12noon–4pm

Admission
Adult £2, Child free, Concs £1

Contact
Church Street, Lancaster LA1 1YS
t 01524 32808
w lancsmuseums.gov.uk
e judgeslodgings@mus.lancsscc.
   gov.uk

813 Lancaster

Lancaster Maritime Museum

2 hrs   All year

Lancaster Maritime Museum occupies two historic buildings on St George's Quay, the main C18 harbour. The former Customs House of 1764, designed by Richard Gillow, contains displays on the history of the port of Lancaster and the local fishing industry.

* Lancaster Canal & Morecambe Bay ecology displays
* Vessels, *Sir William Priestley* & *Coronation Rose*

 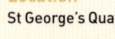   

Location
St George's Quay

Opening
Easter–Oct 11am–5pm
Nov–Easter 12.30pm–4pm

Admission
Adult £2, Child free, Concs £1

Contact
St George's Quay, Lancaster LA1 1RB
t 01524 64637
w lancaster.gov.uk /
   nettingthebay.org.uk
e awhite@lancaster.gov.uk

808 Clitheroe

Clitheroe Castle Museum

½ hr   Feb–Dec

Set on a prominent limestone mound close to the ruined Norman keep of Clitheroe Castle, this museum houses collections of local history and geology. Displays cover the history of the Ribble Valley, the Hacking ferryboat, witchcraft, local birds and roadside geology.

* There is a reconstructed lead mine & a clogger's shop
* Edwardian kitchen

Location
Castle Hill

Opening
Daily; Easter–Oct 11am–4.30pm
Mar–Apr Sat–Wed 11am–4pm
Feb, Nov & Dec Sat & Sun 11am–4pm

Admission
Adult £1.70, Child 25p, Concs 80p

Contact
Castle Hill, Clitheroe BB7 1BA

t 01200 424635/01200 425566
  (Tourist Information)
w ribblevalley.gov.uk
e museum@ribblevalley.gov.uk

809 Colne

British In India Museum

1 hr   Apr–Nov

The museum was opened in 1972 and contains a fascinating collection of material, including model soldiers, dioramas, postage stamps, picture postcards, paintings and military uniforms.

* Shows British & Indian military artifacts

Location
A56–A6068 between Burnley and Keighley

Opening
Apr–Nov Wed & Sat 2pm–5pm

Admission
Adult £3, Child 50p

Contact
Newtown Street, Colne BB8 0JJ

t 01282 613129

810 Fleetwood

Fleetwood Museum

1 hr   Apr–Nov

Built in 1838 and occupying the old Customs House designed by architect Decimus Burton, this fascinating museum brings the story of Fleetwood and the surrounding coast to life. Trace the story of Fleetwood, its cargo trade and famous fishing industry.

* Discover a fisherman's life & the harsh working conditions
* *Harriet* the last surviving northwest fishing smack

Location
M55 signed Fleetwood follow the A585

Opening
Daily; Mon–Sat 10am–4pm
Sun 1pm–4pm

Admission
Adult £2, Child free, Concs £1

Contact
Queen's Terrace, Fleetwood FY7 6BT

t 01253 876621
w nettingthebay.org.uk
e fleetwoodmuseums@mus.
  lancscc.gov.uk

805 Bolton

Turton Tower

2 hrs | Feb–Nov

This distinctive English country house on the edge of the West Pennine Moors was built by the Orrell family. The house was lavishly furnished and extended in the Tudor and early Stuart periods. After falling into decline during the Georgian era, the house was rescued by the Kay family.

* Collection of decorative woodwork & paintings
* Victorian follies, a Victorian tennis court

Location
A66 and A676, follow the signs

Opening
May–Sep Mon–Thu 11am–5pm
Sat & Sun 1pm–5pm;
Mar, Apr & Oct Mon–Wed 1pm–5pm
Sat & Sun 1pm–4pm
Nov & Feb Sat & Sun 1pm–4pm

Admission
Adult £3, Child free, Concs £1.50

Contact
Turton, Bolton BL7 0HG
t 01204 852203
w lancashire.gov.uk
e turtontower.lcc@btinternet.com

806 Carnforth

Leighton Hall

2 hrs | May–Sep

Leighton Hall is the home of the famous furniture-making Gillow dynasty. Explore the past of this ancient, Lancashire family, wander through the grounds and pretty gardens and witness displays from trained birds of prey.

* C19 walled garden, landscaped parkland & woodland
* Entertaining guides reveal the family's history

Location
Junction 35A M6, North Canthorp

Opening
May–Sep Tue–Fri & Sun 2pm–5pm
Aug Tue–Fri & Sun 12.30pm–5pm

Admission
Adult £5.50, Child £4, Concs £5

Contact
Carnforth LA5 9ST
t 01524 734 474
w leightonhall.co.uk
e leightonhall@yahoo.co.uk

807 Chorley

Astley Hall Museum & Art Gallery

1 hr | Easter–Sep

This hall dates back to Elizabethan times but changes have been made over the centuries. The collections range from C18 creamware and glass to the first Rugby League Cup and the contents of a clog-maker's workshop.

* Programme of special exhibitions, events & activities
* Textile collection includes civic robes and militaria

Location
W of Chorley town centre off A581
Chorley-Southport road

Opening
Easter–Sep Sat, Sun & Bank Hols
12pm–5pm

Admission
Adult £2.95, Child £1.95, Concs £1.95

Contact
Astley Park, Chorley PR7 1NP
t 01257 515555
w astleyhall.co.uk
e astleyhall@lineone.net

801 Bolton

Bolton Museum & Art Gallery

2 hrs All year

This building houses an impressive collection of fine and decorative art dating from C18 to C20, including watercolours and drawings, a prominent collection of modern British art prints, and C20 sculpture and contemporary ceramics.

* Varied programme of events & exhibitions
* Ancient Egyptian sculpture The Princess

Location
Town centre

Opening
Mon–Sat 10am–5pm;
closed Bank Hols

Admission
Free

Contact
Le Mans Crescent, Bolton BL1 1SE

t 01204 332211
w boltonmuseums.org.uk
e museums@bolton.gov.uk

802 Bolton

Bolton Wanderers Football Club

2 hrs All year

Look behind the scenes at the Reebok Stadium, home of Bolton Wanderers. Begin at the interactive museum where the history of the club is brought to life. Visit the players' dressing and warm-up rooms, the officials' changing rooms and the manager's dug-out.

Location
Junction 6 off the M61

Opening
Daily; Mon–Fri 9am–5pm
Sat 9am–4pm Sun 11am–4pm

Admission
Adult £2.50, Child £1.50. Concs £1.50

Contact
Burnden Way, Bolton BL6 6JW

t 01204 673670
w bwfc.premiumtv.co.uk
e sparker@bwfc.co.uk

803 Bolton

Hall i' th' Wood Museum

1 hr All year

This half-timbered hall, built in C15, was owned by wealthy yeomen and merchants. After 1697 it was rented out to various tenants. During this period a young Samuel Crompton lived here with his parents. He invented the spinning mule, which revolutionised the cotton industry.

* In 1902, Lord Leverhulme gave the hall to the people of Bolton
* Discover life in Tudor & Stuart times by dressing in period costumes

Location
Town centre

Opening
23 Mar–Oct Wed–Sun 11am–5pm
Nov–Mar Sat & Sun 11am–5pm

Admission
Adult £2, Child £1, Concs £1

Contact
Green Way, Bolton BL1 8UA

t 01204 332370
w boltonmuseums.org.uk
e hallithwood@bolton.gov.uk

804 Bolton

Smithills Hall

1 hr All year

This is one of the earliest examples of a Lancashire manor house, which has recently had additional rooms restored to their full splendour. The house has been developed by generations of owners and mirrors changes in fashion and living conditions from the late C14 to C19.

* Various events including ghost evenings
* Stained glass windows in the chapel

Location
Follow the M62 for Bolton

Opening
Apr–Sep Tue–Sat 11am–5pm
Sun 2pm–5pm;
Oct–Mar Tue & Sat 1pm–5pm,
Sun 2pm–5pm

Admission
Adult £3, Child £1.75, Concs £1.75

Contact
Smithills Dean Road, Bolton BL1 7NP

t 01204 332377
w smithills.org
e office@smithills.org

798 Blackpool

Blackpool Tower

5 hrs+   Easter–Nov

Inside the tower visitors will find a circus and a world-famous ballroom. Explore the Charlie Cairoli exhibition, Under Sea World, the Hornpipe Gallery, Tower Top ride and the Walk of Faith.

* Contact venue for evening entertainment

Location
M55 for Blackpool, follow signs

Opening
Daily; Apr–May 10am–6pm
Mar–Nov 10am–11pm

Admission
Tower & Circus
Adult £12, Child £10, Concs £10

Contact
Leisure Parcs Ltd,
Blackpool FY1 4BJ
t 01253 622242 /01253 292029
w blackpooltower.co.uk
e website@leisure-parcs.co.uk

799 Bolton

Animal World & Butterfly House

1 hr   All year

Animal World provides a living environment for a variety of animals and birds, from farm animals to chipmunks and from wildfowl to tropical birds. Butterfly House features free-flying butterflies and moths in a tropical environment, as well as insects, spiders and reptiles.

* Collection of tropical plants

Location
Bolton A58 to Moss Bank Way

Opening
Daily; Apr–Sep 10am–4.30pm
Oct–Mar Sat–Thu 10am–3.30pm
Fri 10am–2.30pm

Admission
Free

Contact
Moss Bank Park, Moss Bank Way,
Bolton BL1 6NQ
t 01204 334050
w bolton.gov.uk
e animal.world@bolton.gov.uk

800 Bolton

Bolton Aquarium

2 hrs   All year

Fish from all over the world are displayed here. Visitors can view the behaviour of freshwater species at close quarters. A new addition is a species of fish from Australia, the closest relatives of which were last present in the area over 200 million years ago.

* Collection of piranha fish
* Predatory blue-head knifefish from Venezuela

Location
Town centre

Opening
Mon–Sat 10am–5pm;
closed Bank Hols

Admission
Free

Contact
Le Mans Crescent, Bolton BL1 1SE
t 01204 332211
w boltonmuseums.org.uk
e aquarium@bolton.gov.uk

Blackpool Lifeboat Station & Visitor Centre

1 hr   Easter–Nov

This lifeboat station accommodates an Atlantic 75 B-class and 2 D-class lifeboats, launching vehicles and ancillary equipment. The visitor centre incorporates current and historic displays and sea-safety information. There is an accessible public viewing area.

* This station was established by the Institution in 1864
* 1897 Nelson's flagship *Foudroyant* wrecked in gale

Location
Central Promenade

Opening
Easter–Nov 10am–4pm

Admission
Free

Contact
Central Promenade,
Blackpool FY1 5JA

t 01253 620424/290816
w rnli.org.uk
e khorrocks@rnli.org.uk

The Blackpool Piers

4 hrs+   Easter–Nov

The Central Pier offers a traditional seaside experience for the entire family; the North Pier has dare-devil rides, including the reverse bungee jump which reaches 200kmph in 2 seconds; the South Pier is home to classic fairground rides such as the waltzer and dodgems.

* Children's entertainer (all piers)
* Fairground rides (South & Central Pier)

Location
North Pier on the North Promenade;
South Pier on the South Promenade &
Central Pier on Central Promenade

Opening
Daily; Easter–Nov from 10am

Admission
Free, except North Pier (30p toll)
Charges for individual rides

Contact
c/o Leisure Parks Ltd
97 Church Street, Blackpool FY1 1HU

t 01253 629600
w www.blackpoollive.com

794 Blackburn

Whalley Abbey Gatehouse

1 hr   All year

Situated beside the River Calder, this is the outer gatehouse of the nearby Cistercian abbey. There was originally a chapel on the first floor. The adjacent parish church has further remains including three pre-Norman Conquest cross shafts. The nearby abbey has an exhibition centre.

* Vast display of remains

Location
In Whalley, 6 miles NE of Blackburn on minor road off A59

Opening
Any reasonable time

Admission
Free

Contact
Whalley, Clitheroe BB7 9SS

t 01793 414910
w english-heritage.org.uk

795 Blackpool

Blackpool Illuminations

2 hrs   Sep–Nov

Experience Blackpool's annual spectacular event. Six miles of lights electrify this well-loved resort's promenade as the world-famous illuminations shine every night for 66 nights. Enjoy a grandstand seat aboard a cleverly disguised tram.

* View the giant clifftop tableaux
* 1879 electric arc lamps bathe promenade in light

Location
Central Promenade

Opening
2 Sep–6 Nov

Admission
Free

Contact
Blackpool Tourism,
1 Clifton Street FY1 1LY

t 01253 478222
w www.blackpooltourism.com
e tourism@blackpool.gov.uk

790   Accrington

Haworth Art Gallery

2 hrs   All year

This Edwardian house, set in parkland houses the finest public collection of Tiffany art glass outside America. There is also an excellent collection of oil paintings from the C19 .

* Regularly changing exhibitions

Location
Leave M65 at junction 7,
M61 junction 9, M6 junction 29

Opening
Wed–Fri 2pm–5pm
Sat & Sun 12noon–4.30pm

Admission
Free

Contact
Haworth Park, Manchester Road,
Accrington BB5 2JS

t 01254 233782
w hyndburnbc.gov.uk

791   Burnley

Gawthorpe Hall

2 hrs   Easter–Oct

An Elizabethan gem, Gawthorpe resembles the great Hardwick Hall and is probably by the same architect, Robert Smythson. In the mid–C19, Sir Charles Barry was commissioned to restore the house. Charlotte Brontë was a frequent visitor.

* There are many notable paintings & C17–C19 furniture
* Unparalleled collection of British C19–C20 needlework

Location
On E outskirts of Padiham, N of A671

Opening
Easter–Oct Tue–Thu Sat & Sun
1pm–5pm

Admission
Adult £3, Child free, Concs £1.50

Contact
Padiham, Burnley BB12 8UA

t 01282 771004
w Lancsmuseum.gov.uk
e gawthorpehall@ntrust.org.uk

792   Burnley

Queen Street Mill

1 hr   Mar–Nov

A unique survivor of the textile industry, Queen Street Mill represents the last commercial steam-powered textile mill in Europe. The mill closed in 1982 but is preserved as a museum which recreates the days when steam ran the world.

* Smell the oil, hear the hiss & breathe the atmosphere
* 300 Lancashire looms

Location
Brier Cliff Road, Harle Syke

Opening
Mar & Nov Tue–Thu 12noon–4pm
Apr & Oct Tue–Fri 12noon–5pm
May–Sep Tue–Sat 12noon–5pm

Admission
Adult £2.50, Child free, Concs £1.25

Contact
Harle Syke, Burnley BB10 2HX

t 01282 412555
w lancashire.gov.uk
e info@1001daysout.com

793   Blackburn

Blackburn Museum & Art Gallery

2 hrs   All year

The museum is housed in an Arts and Crafts-style building which opened in 1872 as a museum and a library. Highlights include the Hart Collection of over 10,000 rare coins, 500 books and illuminated manuscripts, and a superb collection of Victorian oils and watercolours.

* The Lewis Collection of over 1000 Japanese prints
* The award-winning South Asian gallery

 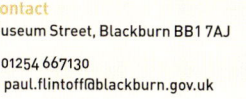

Location
Town centre

Opening
Tue–Sat 10am–4.45pm

Admission
Free

Contact
Museum Street, Blackburn BB1 7AJ

t 01254 667130
e paul.flintoff@blackburn.gov.uk

787 Ulverston

Laurel & Hardy Museum

1 hr   Feb–Dec

Visit the world famous museum devoted to Laurel & Hardy in Ulverston, the town where Stan was born on 16 June 1890. Everything you want to know about them is here. The collection includes letters, photographs, personal items and furniture.

* Small cinema shows films & documentaries all day

Location
Town centre

Opening
Daily; Feb–Dec 10am–4.30pm

Admission
Adult £2.50, Child £1.50, Concs £1.50

Contact
4C Upper Brook Street, Ulverston LA12 7BH
t 01229 582292
w laurel-and-hardy-museum.co.uk

788 Windermere

Lake District National Park

4 hrs   All year

Enjoy some of England's dramatic mountain and lake scenery in the largest of the country's national parks. Get a better understanding of the area at the visitor centre at Brockhole on Lake Windermere.

* Exhibition, displays & gardens down to the lake
* Gardens designed by Mawson

Location
Visitor centre on A591 between Windermere & Ambleside

Opening
Visitor Centre Daily; 19 Mar–30 Oct 10am–5pm
Garden & Grounds All year

Admission
Free, car park £3

Contact
The Lake District Visitor Centre, Brockhole, Windermere LA23 1LJ
t 01539 446601
w lake-district.gov.uk

789 Windermere

Windermere Lake Cruises

3 hrs   All year

Steamers and launches sail daily between Ambleside, Bowness and Lakeside with main season connections for the Lakeside & Haverthwaite Steam Railway, Wray Castle and the Lake District National Park (Brockhole). Daily sailings to the aquarium and the World of Beatrix Potter.

* 24 hour 'Freedom' tickets for unlimited travel
* Other links to lake's attractions – see website

Location
Leave the M6 at junction 36, follow the A590 to the lakeside or the A591 to Bowness (Windermere) & Ambleside

Opening
Daily during daylight hours

Admission
Adult £5, Child £2.50

Contact
Lakeside, Newby Bridge, Ulverston LA12 8AS
t 01539 531188
w windermere-lakecruises.co.uk
e mail@windermere-lakecruises.co.uk

783 Penrith

Dalemain Historic House & Gardens

2 hrs   Mar–Oct

A medieval, Tudor and early Georgian house that has been home to the Hasell family since 1679. The Tudor legacy is a series of winding passageways, unexpected rooms and oak panelling. A good example of the Georgian period is the breathtaking Chinese room.

* C15 medieval hall
* The estate includes many famous valleys and fells

Location
On A592 Penrith to Ullswater road

Opening
20 Mar–Aug
Gardens Sun–Thu 10.30am–5pm
House Sun–Thu 11am–4pm
Sep–Oct
Gardens Sun–Thur 10.30–4pm
House Sun–Thur 11am–3pm

Admission
Adult £5.50, Child £3.50

Contact
Penrith CA11 0HB

t 01768 486450
w dalemain.com
e admin@dalemain.com

784 Ulverston

Conishead Priory & Buddhist Temple

1 hr   All year

A stunning example of early Victorian gothic architecture. It is dominated by two 100 ft (30m) octagonal towers. Special features include decorative ceilings and a vaulted great hall with fine stained glass. The Kadampa Temple was established at the priory in 1997.

* Anyone welcome to visit the temple
* Prayers for world peace every Sunday morning

Location
A5087, 2 miles S of Ulverston

Opening
26 Apr–Oct Sat & Sun & Bank Hols 2pm–5pm, Winter temple only Sat–Sun 10am–4pm

Admission
Free

Contact
Priory Road, Ulverston LA12 9QQ

t 01229 584029
w manjushri.org.uk
e info@manjushri.org.uk

785 Ulverston

Gleaston Water Mill

1 hr   All year

This imposing watermill has been part of the local landscape for over 400 years. Located close to the ruins of Gleaston Castle, the present building dates from 1774. Visitors can see the 18 ft (5½ m) waterwheel and machinery operating most days.

* Last major rebuild in 1700s

Location
Follow signs from A5087 Ulverston to Barrow-in-Furness road

Opening
Tue–Sun & Bank Hols 10.30am–5pm

Admission
Adult £2.50, Child £1.50

Contact
Gleaston, nr Ulverston LA12 0QH

t 01229 869244
w watermill.co.uk

786 Ulverston

Holker Hall, Gardens & Lakeland Motor Museum

3 hrs   Mar–Dec

Only a short distance from the sea, Holker Hall is situated on the magnificent wooded slopes of the Cartmel Peninsula. The house exhibits all the grandeur and prosperity of the late-Victorian era and is set in immaculate gardens.

* Home to Lakeland Motor Museum
* The Campbell Legend Bluebird exhibition

Location
Follow signs from A590 from Barrow or M6 junction 36

Opening
Hall & Gardens 20 Mar–30 Oct Sun–Fri 10am–5.30pm
Museum Daily; Mar–18 Dec 10.30am–4.45pm

Admission
Adult £9.25, Child £5.50

Contact
Cark-in-Cartmel, Cumbria LA11 7PL

t 015395 58328
w holker-hall.co.uk
e publicopening@holker.co.uk

779 Newby Bridge

Aquarium of the Lakes

1 hr   All year

Discover the fascinating wildlife in and alongside the lakes in over 30 displays. A dramatic mountain-top waterfall marks the start of the journey, leading down a moorland stream. Next you will see the otters before moving on to see nocturnal life on the riverbank.

* New for 2005 - Midnight at the water's edge
* Great number of nocturnal creatures

Location
15 mins from junction 36 of M6, take A590 to Newby Bridge, follow signs

Opening
Daily; Apr–Oct 9am–6pm
Nov–Mar 9am–5pm

Admission
Adult £6.25, Child £3.95, Concs £5.95

Contact
Aquarium of the Lakes,
Newby Bridge LA12 8AS

t 01539 530153
w aquariumofthelakes.co.uk
e aquariumofthelakes@reallive.co.uk

780 Newby Bridge

Scott Park Bobbin Mill

1 hr   Apr–Oct

This gem of the industrial revolution has remained largely unchanged since it was built by John Harrison in 1835. Stott Park created the wooden bobbins vital to the spinning and weaving industries of Lancashire.

* Mill worked continuously until 1971
* Steam days Tue, Wed & Thu show engines working

Location
2 miles N of Newby Bridge, off A590

Opening
Daily; Apr–Oct 10am–6pm
Oct ring for details

Admission
Adult £3.80, Child £1.90, Concs £2.90

Contact
Finsthwaite, nr Newby Bridge,
Ulverston LA12 8AX

t 01539 531087
w english-heritage.org.uk
e northwest@english-heritage.org.uk

781 Penrith

Acorn Bank Garden & Watermill

2 hrs   Easter-Oct

Ancient oaks and the high enclosing walls keep out the extremes of the Cumbrian climate, resulting in a spectacular display of shrubs, roses and herbaceous borders. Sheltered orchards contain a variety of traditional fruit trees. The watermill is under restoration.

* Famed herb garden has huge collection of plants
* Watermill remains open to public during restoration

Location
N of Temple Sowerby, 6 miles E of Penrith on A66

Opening
Easter–Oct 30 Wed–Sun 10am–5pm

Admission
Adult £3, Child £1.50

Contact
Temple Sowerby,
nr Penrith CA10 1SP

t 01768 361893
w nationaltrust.org.uk
e acornbank@nationaltrust.org.uk

782 Penrith

Brougham Castle

1 hr   Apr–Oct

Brougham Castle was built in 1092 on the site of a Roman fort, by William Rufus. The original castle was destroyed in 1172 and rebuilt by Henry II. His tower survives but later buildings were destroyed by fire in 1521. A stone-curtain wall was added around 1300.

* Once home to Lady Anne Clifford
* Introductory exhibition includes Roman carved stone

Location
½ mile SE of Penrith off A66

Opening
Daily; Apr–Sep 10am–6pm
Oct Thu–Mon 10am–4pm

Admission
Adult £2.50, Child £1.30, Concs £1.90

Contact
North West Region, Canada House,
3 Chepstow Street, Manchester M1 5FW

t 01768 862488
w english-heritage.org.uk
e northwest@english-heritage.org.uk

776 Grasmere

Dove Cottage & Wordsworth Museum

1 hr   All year

This was the home of William Wordsworth from December 1799 to May 1808, the years of his best work as a poet. The cottage remains very much as it was during this time. The garden was a passion for Wordsworth and he spent many hours developing his 'domestic slip of mountainside'.

* Museum includes original manuscripts & rare books
* Also shows period images of Grasmere

Location
S of Grasmere on A591
Kendal/Keswick

Opening
Daily; 7 Feb–Dec 9.30am–5.30pm

Admission
Adult £5.95, Child £3, Concs £5.30

Contact
Grasmere LA22 9SH

t 01539 435544
w wordsworth.org.uk
e enquiries@wordsworth.org.uk

777 Hawkshead

Beatrix Potter Gallery

½ hr   Mar–Oct

This gallery houses annually-changing exhibitions of original sketches and watercolours painted by Beatrix Potter for her children's stories. This C17 building was once the office of Beatrix's husband, William Heelis.

* The interior remains substantially unaltered
* 2005 exhibition *The Tale of Mrs Tiggy-Winkle*

Location
Town centre

Opening
19 Mar–30 Oct Sat–Wed
10.30am–4.30pm

Admission
Adult £3.50, Child £1.70

Contact
Beatrix Potter Gallery,
Main Street, Hawkshead LA22 0NS

t 01539 436355
w nationaltrust.org.uk
e beatrixpottergallery@
    nationaltrust.org.uk

778 Keswick

Derwent Water Marina

1 hr +   All year

This centre specializes in watersports with RYA sailing courses, windsurfing courses, canoe, kayak and dinghy hire available. Other activities include ghyll scrambling, abseiling, climbing and walking.

Location
From Keswick take the A66 & follow
the signs for Portinscale

Opening
Daily; 9am–5pm; closed 20 Dec–12 Jan

Admission
Activities priced individually

Contact
Portinscale, Keswick,
Cumbria CA12 5RF

t 01768 772912
w www.derwentwatermarina.co.uk
e info@derwentwatermarina.co.uk

773 Kendal

Museum of Lakeland Life

1 hr   Jan–Dec

In 1973 the museum was the first winner of the coveted Museum-of-the-Year award. The permanent collections include displays linked to the Arts and Crafts movement, *Swallows and Amazons* author Arthur Ransome and the Victorian period.

* Temporary displays largely from costume collection
* Large shop selling local crafts & toys

Location
Next to Albert Hall Gallery, junction 36 M6

Opening
Apr–Oct Mon–Sat 10.30am–5pm
20 Jan–Mar, Nov & Dec
Mon–Sat 10.30am–4pm

Admission
Adult £3.50, Child £2.50

Contact
Kendal LA9 5AL

t 01539 722464
w lakelandmuseum.org.uk
e ws@lakelandmuseum.org.uk

---

774 Coniston

Brantwood

3 hrs   All year

As the home of John Ruskin, Brantwood became a great literary and artistic centre. The house is filled with Ruskin's work as well as his original furniture, books and personal items. Brantwood's attraction is increased through its 250 acres of woodland and lakeside meadows.

* The gardens cover 30 acres
* A well-marked nature trail winds through the estate

Location
E shore of Coniston Water
on B5285

Opening
Mid-Mar–mid Nov daily 11am–5.30pm;
winter Wed–Sun 11am–4.30pm

Admission
Adult £5.50, Child £1

Contact
Coniston LA21 8AD

t 01539 441396
w brantwood.org.uk
e enquiries@brantwood.org.uk

---

775 Dalton-in-Furness

South Lakes Wild Animal Park

2 hrs+   All year

The Lake District's only zoological park is recognised as one of Europe's leading conservation zoos. Its 17 acres are home to the rarest animals on Earth which are saved from almost certain extinction in the wild thanks to co-ordinated breeding programmes.

* Many animals are free to roam
* Home of the Sumatran Tiger Trust

Location
Follow signs from junction 36
of M6

Opening
Summer 10am–5pm;
winter 10am–4.30pm

Admission
Adult £9.50, Child £6, Concs £6

Contact
South Lakes Wild Animal Park,
Dalton-in-Furness LA15 8JR

t 01229 466086
w wildanimalpark.co.uk
e office@wildanimalpark.co.uk

769 Cockermouth

Lakeland Sheep & Wool Centre

2 hrs   All year

This centre offers visitors the opportunity to meet Cumbria's most famous residents – 19 different breeds of sheep. Discover interesting facts about each breed, see a shearer at work and see the great skills of the sheepdogs handling a flock.

* Show theatre holds up to 300 people
* Extensive retail outlet for woollen goods

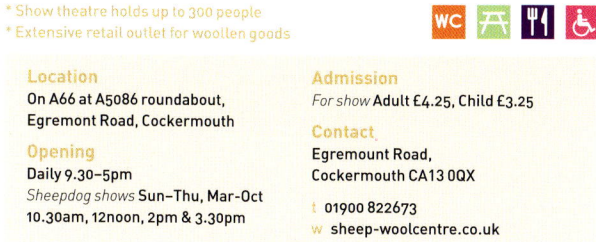

Location
On A66 at A5086 roundabout, Egremont Road, Cockermouth

Opening
Daily 9.30–5pm
Sheepdog shows Sun–Thu, Mar–Oct 10.30am, 12noon, 2pm & 3.30pm

Admission
For show Adult £4.25, Child £3.25

Contact
Egremount Road,
Cockermouth CA13 0QX

t 01900 822673
w sheep-woolcentre.co.uk

---

770 Cockermouth

Wordsworth House

2 hrs   Easter–Oct

William Wordsworth was born here in 1770, moving out after his mother's death in 1778. There are seven rooms furnished in Regency style, with some personal effects of the poet. Explore the walled Georgian garden with terrace overlooking the River Derwent.

* Wordsworth Lake District video in the stables
* Limited disabled access

Location
Main street in Cockermouth

Opening
Easter–Oct Mon–Sat 11am–4.30pm

Admission
Adult £4.50, Child £2.50

Contact
Cockermouth CA13 GRX

t 01900 824805
w nationaltrust.org.uk
e rwordh@smtp.ntrust.org.uk

---

771 Kendal

Kendal Museum

1 hr+   Feb–Dec

Founded in 1796, Kendal Museum houses one of the country's oldest collections of local archaeology, history, geology, an international natural history collection and lakeland flora and fauna from prehistory to the C20.

* A wildlife garden simulates local habitats
* Changing programme of temporary exhibitions

Location
10 mins from junction 36 of M6

Opening
Apr–Oct Mon–Sat 10.30am–5pm
Feb, Mar, Nov & Dec Mon–Sat 10.30am–4pm

Admission
Adult £2.50, Concs £2, Child free

Contact
Station Road,
Kendal LA9 6BT

t 01539 721374
w kendalmuseum.org.uk
e info@kendalmuseum.org.uk

---

772 Kendal

Levens Hall

2 hrs   Apr–Oct

This world-famous C17 topiary garden was designed by Guillaume Beaumont who also laid out the gardens at Hampton Court. The original designs have remained largely unchanged for 300 years. The house has many beautiful Elizabethan rooms with many notable paintings.

* Dining room has embossed leather wall coverings
* Sundays & Bank Holidays ride on traction engines

Location
5 miles S of Kendal on A6

Opening
Mid Apr–mid Oct Sun–Thu
House 12noon–5pm
Garden from 10am

Admission
Adult £7.50, Child £3.70

Contact
Kendal LA8 0PD

t 01539 560321
w levenshall.co.uk
e emaildlevenshall.tsnet.co.uk

766 Carlisle

Carlisle Castle

1 hr   All year

This is a formidable border fortress with a rich and colourful history spanning over 900 years. Once commanding the western end of the Anglo-Scottish border, Carlisle Castle has witnessed countless sieges over the centuries.

* Admission includes entrance to Roman exhibition
* See the legendary 'licking stones'

Location
City centre

Opening
Daily; Apr–Sep 9.30am–6pm
Daily; Oct–Mar 10am–4pm

Admission
Adult £3.80, Child £1.90, Concs £2.90

Contact
Carlisle CA3 8UR

t 01228 591922
w english-heritage.org.uk
e northwest@english-heritage.org.uk

767 Carlisle

Carlisle Cathedral

2 hrs   All year

Founded in 1122 and battered by centuries of warfare, the cathedral retains many items of interest, perhaps most notably the east window with its fine tracery containing C14 stained glass. Other items include the magnificent C16 Brougham triptych and notable medieval painted panels.

* Beautifully painted ceiling in the choir
* Display of cathedral & diocesan silver in the treasury

Location
City centre

Opening
Daily; Mon–Sat 7.30am–6.15pm
Sun 7.30am–5pm

Admission
Free, donations welcome

Contact
7 The Abbey, Castle Street,
Carlisle CA3 8TZ

t 01228 535169
w carlislecathedral.org.uk
e office@carlislecathedral.org.uk

768 Carlisle

Tullie House

2 hrs   All year

Tullie House museum and art gallery offers a multi-faceted visitor experience, combining the features of an historic house with a modern museum. Tullie House has a superb collection of Roman artifacts. The displays include many hands-on exhibits that appeal to all ages.

* Underground space brings to life Carlisle's past
* Displays of key artworks by the Pre-Raphaelites

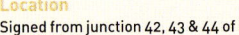

Location
Signed from junction 42, 43 & 44 of M6

Opening
Daily; Jul–Aug Mon–Sat 10am–5pm
Sun 11am–5pm
Nov–Mar Mon–Sat 10am–4pm
Sun 12noon–4pm
Apr–Jun & Sep–Oct Mon–Sat
10am–5pm, Sun 12noon–5pm

Admission
Adult £5.20, Child £2.60, Concs £3.60

Contact
Castle Street, Carlisle CA3 8TP

t 01228 534781
w tulliehouse.co.uk
e enquiries@tullie-house.co.uk

763 Barrow-in-Furness

Dock Museum

3 hrs   All year

A spectacular modern museum built over an original Victorian graving dock. Displays explore the history of Barrow-in-Furness and how it grew from a tiny C19 hamlet to become the biggest iron and steel centre in the world and a major shipbuilding force in just 40 years.

* Attractions include film shows & model ships
* Fine art gallery

Location
Follow signs in Barrow

Opening
Easter–Oct Tue–Fri 10am–5pm
Sat & Sun 11am–5pm
Nov–Easter Weds–Fri 10.30am–4pm
Sat & Sun 11am–4.30pm

Admission
Free

Contact
North Road,
Barrow-in-Furness LA14 2PW

t 01229 894444
w dockmuseum.org.uk
e dockmuseum@barrowbc.gov.uk

---

764 Barrow-in-Furness

Furness Abbey

1 hr   All year

St Mary of Furness was founded in 1123 by Stephen, later King of England. It originally belonged to the small Order of Savigny but passed to the Cistercians in 1147, and became one of the richest monasteries in England, second only to Fountains Abbey in Yorkshire.

* A romantic building, often visited by Wordsworth
* Visitor centre with exhibition about the abbey

Location
½ mile NE of Barrow-in-Furness

Opening
Apr–Sep daily 10am–6pm
Oct–Mar Thu–Mon 10am–4pm

Admission
Adult £3, Child £1.50, Concs £2.30

Contact
North West Region, Canada House,
3 Chepstow Street, Manchester M1 5FW

t 01229 823420
w english-heritage.org.uk
e northwest@english-heritage.org.uk

---

765 Brampton

Lanercost Priory

1 hr   Easter–Oct

Situated near the Scottish border in Cumbria are the impressive remains of this C12 Augustinian priory. It boasts a rich history, from the tranquillity of life as a monastic house to its involvement in the turbulent Anglo-Scottish wars of the C14 and eventual dissolution.

* Hadrian's Wall is close by, audio guide available
* West front is fine example of C12 English architecture

Location
Off minor road S of Lanercost, 2 miles NE of Brampton

Opening
Daily Easter–Oct 10am–6pm

Admission
Adult £2.50, Child £1.30, Concs £1.90

Contact
Lanercost, Brampton CA8 2HQ

t 01697 73030
w english-heritage.org.uk
e northwest@english-heritage.org.uk

759 Tarporley

Hack Green Secret Nuclear Bunker

1 hr+ Jan–Nov

One of the nation's most secret defence sites, Hack Green has played a central role in the defence of Britain for almost 60 years. Through the blast doors visitors are transported into the chilling world of the Cold War to learn what living conditions were like.

* The sounds & smells of a civil defence HQ
* Labyrinth of fully-equipped rooms & corridors

Location
Off A530 Whitchurch road, outside Nantwich, 30 mins from Chester

Opening
Mar–Oct 10.30am–5.30pm
Nov & Jan–Feb 11am–4.30pm

Admission
Adult £5.80, Child £4, Concs £5.50

Contact
PO Box 127, Nantwich CW5 8AQ
t 01270 623353
w hackgreen.co.uk
e coldwar@hackgreen.co.uk

760 Warrington

Warrington Museum & Art Gallery

1 hr+ All year

This museum houses exhibitions on Warrington and the surrounding area, together with exhibitions by renowned artists. Exhibitions have included etchings by Picasso and fashions by Warrington designer, Ozzie Clark. There is also a new geology gallery with a fossil-handling section.

* Temporary exhibition programme
* Education department for schools

Location
Town centre

Opening
Mon–Fri 9am–5.30pm
Sat 9am–4.30pm

Admission
Free

Contact
3 Museum street,
Warrington WA1 1JB
t 01925 442392
w warrington.gov.uk
e museum@warrington.gov.uk

761 Widnes

Catalyst Science Discovery Centre

3 hrs+ All year

This is the only science centre solely devoted to chemistry and how the products of chemistry are used in everyday life – from medicines to Meccano. This centre aims to inform visitors about chemistry and its role in our lives, past, present and future.

* Four interactive galleries with 100+ exhibits
* Panoramic views from the roof-top observatory

Location
Junction 12 of the M56 & junction 7 of the M52

Opening
Tue–Fri & Bank Hols 10am–5pm
Sat & Sun 11am–5pm

Admission
Adult £4.95, Child £3.50, Conc £3.95

Contact
Mersey Road, Widnes WA8 0DF
t 0151 420 1121
w catalyst.org.uk
e paul@catalyst.org.uk

762 Wirral

Port Sunlight Village & Heritage Centre

4 hrs+ All year

Picturesque C19 village founded by William Hesketh Lever for his soap factory workers and named after his famous Sunlight soap. The Heritage Centre explores the history of the village and community. The Lady Lever Art Gallery houses rich and varied collections.

* C18 furniture and Wedgwood china
* Gift shop and garden centre

Location
20 mins from Liverpool, Junction 5 off the M53 take the A41 to Birkenhead, follow signs

Opening
Daily; Apr–Oct Mon–Fri 10am–4pm
Sat–Sun 10am–4pm
Nov–Mar Mon–Fri 10am–4pm
Sat–Sun 11am–4pm

Admission
Adult £1, Child 65p

Contact
95 Greendale Road, Port Sunlight, Wirral CH62 4XE
t 0151 644 6466
w portsunlightvillage.com

©English Heritage Photographic Library

757 Tarporley

Beeston Castle

1 hr+   All year

Standing majestically on sheer, rocky crags, Beeston has stunning views. Its history stretches back more than 4000 years, to when it was a Bronze Age hill fort. The castle was built from 1226 and soon became a royal stronghold, only falling centuries later in the English Civil War.

* Exhibition outlines the history of this strategic site
* Panoramic views of the Cheshire Plain

Location
11 miles SE of Chester on a minor road off A49

Opening
Daily; Apr–Sep 10am–6pm
Oct–Mar 10am–4pm

Admission
Adult £3.50, Child £1.80, Concs £2.60

Contact
Tarporley CW6 9TX

t 01829 260464
w english-heritage.org.uk

758 Tarporley

Oulton Park Race Circuit

All day   Apr–Oct

Set in 320 acres of glorious Cheshire countryside, Oulton Park offers spectacular car and bike racing, including British superbikes, touring cars, Formula 3 and family-fun days. Experience the thrill for yourself with racing, rally and early-drive activities.

* Full racing programme
* 'Drive like a professional' courses

Location
Take junction 18 off the M6 & follow the A54 to Chester for 12 miles. Turn left onto the A49 to Whitchurch & follow the signs

Opening
Apr–Oct open Sat for minor meetings; Sun or Bank holidays open for major meetings

Admission
Please phone for details

Contact
Brands Hatch Circuits Ltd
Little Budworth, Tarporley
Cheshire CW6 9BW

t 01829 760301
w www.motorsportvision.co.uk

©National Trust Photographic Library

755 Stockport

Bramall Hall

2 hrs   All year

This is a grand black and white timber-framed building. The hall was built in the traditional local style with oak framework, joined using mortice and tenon joints and held in place with oak pegs. Wattle and daub or lath and plaster were used to fill the spaces in the timbers.

* Guided tours available on request
* Beautiful landscaped grounds

Location
Junction 1 or 27 of M60

Opening
Daily; Easter–Sep 1pm–5pm
Sun & Bank Hols 11am–5pm
Oct–Jan 1pm–4pm
Sun & Bank Hols 11am–4pm
Feb–Easter 1pm–4pm
Sun 11am–4pm

Admission
Adult £3.95, Child £2.50, Concs £2.50

Contact
Bramall Park,
Stockport SK7 3NX
t 0161 485 3708
w stockport.gov.uk/heritage
attractions
e bramall.hall@stockport.gov.uk

756 Stockport

Lyme Park

2 hrs+   Apr–Oct

Originally a Tudor house, Lyme was transformed by the Venetian architect Leoni into an Italianate palace. Some of the Elizabethan interiors survive and contrast dramatically with later rooms. The state rooms are adorned with Mortlake tapestries.

* Featured in BBC's *Pride & Prejudice*
* Important collection of English clocks

Location
On A6, 6 miles S of the city centre,
follow signs

Opening
Park Daily Apr–Oct 8am–8.30pm
House Apr–Oct Fri–Tue 1pm–5pm
Gardens Apr–Oct Fri–Tue 1pm–5pm

Admission
House Adult £6.20, Child £3.10
Gardens £3.60, £1.50

Contact
Disley, Stockport SK12 2NX
t 01663 762023/766492
w nationaltrust.org.uk
e lymepark@nationaltrust.org.uk

Runcorn

Norton Priory Museum

1 hr   All year

This 38-acre site includes a museum, a magnificent 800-year-old vaulted storage range, a historic priory, remains excavated by archaelogists, and the unique St Christopher statue. The woodland gardens are the setting for a collection of contemporary sculpture.

* Four North-West-in-Bloom awards
* BBC2's *Hidden Gardens* filmed here

Location
From junction 11 off M56. Turn for Warrington and follow signs

Opening
Daily; Nov–Mar 12noon–4pm
Apr–Oct Mon–Fri 12noon–5pm
Sat & Sun 12noon–6pm

Admission
Adult £4.25, Concs £2.95

Contact
Tudor Road, Manor Park,
Runcorn WA7 1SX

t 01928 569895
w nortonpriory.org
e info@nortonpriory.org

Sandbach

Sandbach Crosses

½ hr   All year

Rare Saxon stone crosses, carved with animals and biblical scenes, stand in the cobbled market square of Sandbach. The crosses are believed to date from the C7. Close inspection reveals the ancient carvings.

* One of the most photographed sights in Cheshire
* Restored in 1816 after destruction by iconoclasts

Location
Market Square, Sandbach

Opening
Any reasonable time

Admission
Free

Contact
English Heritage, Canada House,
3 Chepstow St, Manchester M1 5FW

t 0161 242 1400
w english-heritage.org.uk
e northwest@english-heritage.
org.uk

Scholar Green

Rode Hall

2 hrs+   Apr–Sep

The house was constructed in two stages, the earlier two-storey wing and stable block around 1705 and the main building in 1752. The house contains examples of furniture by Gillow of Lancaster, a collection of portraits and an important collection of English porcelain.

* Rode stands in a Repton landscape
* Formal rose garden was designed by Nesfield in 1860

Location
5 miles SW of Congleton between A34 and A50

Opening
Apr–Sep Wed & Bank Hols 2pm–5pm

Admission
House Apr–Sep Wed & Bank Holidays 2pm–5pm

Garden Adult £3, Concs £2

Contact
Scholar Green,
Cheshire ST7 3QP

t 01270 873237
w rodehall.co.uk
e roddehall@scholargreen.fsnet.co.uk

749 Macclesfield

Macclesfield Silk Museum

2 hrs   All year

This building was once the Macclesfield School of Art, built in 1877 to train designers for the silk industry. It now houses exhibitions exploring the properties of silk, design education, Macclesfield's diverse textile industries, workers' lives and historic machinery.

* Displays of costume & textiles
* Try your hand at weaving & designing

Location
Town centre

Opening
Daily; Mon–Sat 11am–5pm
Sun & Bank Hols 1pm–5pm

Admission
Adult £4.20, Concs £3.20

Contact
Roe Street, Macclesfield SK11 6UT

t 01625 613210
w silk-macclesfield.org
e silkmuseum@tiscali.co.uk

750 Neston

Ness Botanic Gardens

1 hr+   All year

When a Liverpool cotton merchant began to create a garden in 1898, he laid the foundations of one of the major botanic gardens in the UK. Now internationally renowned, the collection includes breathtaking rhododendrons and azaleas.

* Adopt a tree scheme
* Water, rose & herb gardens

Location
6 miles from exit M53, 5 miles from
Western End M56, off A540 Chester
Hoylake Road

Opening
Daily; Mar–Oct 9.30am–5pm
Nov–Feb 9.30am–4pm

Admission
Adult £4.70, Child free, Concs £4.30

Contact
Ness, Neston,
South Wirral CH64 4AY

t 0151 3530123
w nessgardens.org.uk
e nessgdns@liv.ac.uk

751 Northwich

Arley Hall & Garden

2 hrs   Apr–Sep

This charming English garden features a double herbaceous border laid out in 1846, a pleached lime avenue, giant cylinders of Quercus Ilex, topiary and collections of roses, rhododendrons and azaleas. The hall reveals fine panelling and plasterwork.

* Voted one of the top 50 gardens in Europe
* Gardens include rose & fallen timber gardens

Location
Junction 19 or 20 of the M6, or junction
9 or 10 of the M56

Opening
Apr–Sep Tue–Sun & Bank Hols
11am–5pm

Admission
Adult £4.50, Child £2, Concs £3.90

Contact
Arley, Northwich CW9 6NA

t 01565 777353
w arleyhalland gardens.com
e enquiries@arleyhalland gardens.
  com

746 Macclesfield

Capesthorne Hall

2–4 hrs   Apr–Oct

A turreted, red brick C18 Jacobean-style hall. Collections include fine art, marble sculptures and tapestries, plus Regency, Jacobean and rococo antiques. Enjoy the treasured collection of Americana and children's toys.

* Guided tours by arrangement
* Grounds include a chapel, gardens & lakes

Location
Off A34 between Manchester & Stoke-on-Trent 3 miles S of Alderly Edge, Junction 6 of the M6

Opening
Apr–Oct Sun, Wed & Bank Hols 12noon–5pm

Admission
Adult £6, Child £3, Concs £5

Contact
Siddington, Macclesfield SK11 9JY

t 01625 861221
w capesthorne.com
e info@capesthorne.com

747 Macclesfield

Gawsworth Hall

1 hr+   Apr–Oct

An ancient manor house which includes the Fitton family chapel, licensed in 1365. The original Norman house was rebuilt in 1480 and remodelled in 1701. A famous duel took place in 1712 between Lord Mohun and the Duke of Hamilton in which both duellists were killed.

* Samuel Johnson, the last professional jester, lived here
* Open-air theatre season Jun–Aug

Location
On A536 between Macclesfield & Congleton

Opening
Apr–Oct Sun–Wed 2pm–5pm
Jun–Aug daily 2pm–5pm

Admission
Adult £5, Child £2.50

Contact
Church Lane, Macclesfield SK11 9RN

t 01260 223456
w gawsworthhall.com
e enquiries@gawsworthhall.com

748 Macclesfield

Jodrell Bank Science Centre & Arboretum

2 hrs+   Mar–Oct

This is the visitor centre for the Lovell radio telescope, there is a small exhibition area, 3D theatre and observational pathway.

* The 35-acre arboretum is a tree-lover's paradise
* Environmental discovery centre

Location
Between Holmes Chapel & Chelford, on A535, 8 miles W of Macclesfield

Opening
Daily; Mar–Oct 10.30am–5.30pm
The centre is under development so please phone for details

Admission
Adult £1, car park charge £3

Contact
Lower Withington, Macclesfield SK11 9DL

t 01477 571339
w jb.man.ac.uk/scicen
e visitorcentre@jb.man.ac.uk

743 Knutsford

Tabley House Collection

1 hr+   Apr–Oct

The house was designed by John Carr of York and completed in 1767. Its nine-bay, south-facing block is flanked by pavilions and quadrant passages and the splendid doric portico is reached by curved stairs. Tabley is the only C18 Palladian country house in the region.

* First collection of English paintings ever made
* Furniture includes pieces by Gillow & Bullock

Location
2 miles W of Knutsford, on Northwich road

Opening
Apr–Oct Thu–Sun & Bank Hols
2pm–5pm

Admission
Adult £4, Child & Concs £1.50

Contact
Knutsford WA16 0HB
t 01565 750151
w tableyhouse.co.uk
e enquiries@tableyhouse.co.uk

745 Macclesfield

Adlington Hall

4 hrs   Jun–Aug

The present structure dates back to 1315 and incorporates Tudor and Elizabethan architecture. Key features are the black and white Tudor manor, the south front and west wing. The great hall is supported by two oak trees from the original hunting lodge.

* Tudor, Elizabethan and Georgian architecture
* Gardens include a rose garden & wilderness area

Location
Just off the A523, follow signs

Opening
Jun–Aug Wed 2pm–5pm

Admission
Adult £3, Child £2

Contact
Adlington, Macclesfield SK10 4LF
t 01625 820875
w adlingtonhall.com
e enquiries@adlingtonhall.com

744 Knutsford

Tatton Park

4 hrs+   Mar–Oct

An impressive estate with over 1000 acres of stunning parkland with herds of red and fallow deer. Its major attractions include a neo-classical mansion, Tudor hall, working farm and award-winning gardens.

* Classic car show, fine food fairs & classical concerts
* Victorian kitchens & servants' quarters

Location
Signed from junction 19 of M6, & junction 57 of M56

Opening
Mar–Oct Tue–Sun 12noon–5pm
Times for individual attractions vary, please phone for details

Admission
Adult £3, Child £2

Contact
Knutsford WA16 6QN
t 01625 534400
w tattonpark.org.uk
e tatton@cheshire.gov.uk

739 Chester

Grosvenor Museum

1 hr+   All year

Hear the story of Chester from the Roman fortress of Deva to the present day. Learn about its Roman people, army and buildings, visit a Roman graveyard with tombstones of the 20th Legion's soldiers and enjoy artists' views of the city's past.

* Explore natural history of Cheshire
* Georgian house with re-created period rooms

Location
Chester city centre

Opening
Daily; Mon–Sat 10.30am–5pm
Sun 1pm–4pm

Admission
Free

Contact
27 Grosvenor Street, Chester CH1 2DD
t 01244 402008
w grosvenormuseum.co.uk
e srogers@chestercc.gov.uk

740 Congleton

Little Moreton Hall

2 hrs   Mar–Dec

This moated house, with its irregular half-timbered façades opening onto a cobbled courtyard, was originally built in the mid C15. The house was extended between 1570 and 1580 when the Long Gallery was added, giving the hall its curious top-heavy look.

* A warren of rooms, some no larger than cupboards
* *Moll Flanders* and *Lady Jane* were filmed here

Location
4 miles S of Congleton on A34, 10 mins from junctions 16 & 17 of M6

Opening
Mar–Oct Wed–Sun 11.30am–5pm
Nov–Dec Sat & Sun 11.30am–4pm

Admission
Adult £5.25, Child £2.50

Contact
Congleton CW12 4SD
t 01260 272018
w nationaltrust.org.uk
e littlemoretonhall@ntrust.org.uk

741 Ellesmere Port

Boat Museum

4 hrs+   All year

Board some of the boats from the world's largest floating collection of traditional canal craft. Discover how people lived in homes no larger than the hallway of a modern house. Tour the Georgian and Victorian buildings full of fascinating exhibitions.

* Visit the Pump House & Power Hall
* Experience domestic life in dock workers' cottages

Location
Junction 9 off the M53, follow signs

Opening
Daily Apr–Oct 10am–5pm
Nov–Mar Sat–Wed 11am–4pm

Admission
Adult £5.50, Child £3.70, Concs £4.30

Contact
South Pier Road,
Ellesmere Port CH65 4FW
t 0151 355 5017
w boatmuseum.org.uk
e paul.taylor@thewaterwaystrust.org

742 Ellesmere Port

Blue Planet Aquarium

2 hrs   All year

The aquarium features one of the world's largest underwater viewing tunnels. Visitors can get up close to huge sharks, graceful rays and hundreds of other fish. Exhibits encompass Scottish Highlands, the mighty Amazon, the depths of Lake Malawi and mangroves.

* A shark-inhabited Caribbean reef
* Touchpools with anemones & rays

Location
Nr junction 10 of M53, adjacent to Cheshire Oaks designer outlet village

Opening
daily; Apr–Nov Mon–Fri 10am–5pm
Sat & Sun 10am–6pm
Nov–Mar Mon–Fri 10am–5pm
Sat & Sun 11am–5pm

Admission
Adult £8.95, Child £6.50, Concs £6.95

Contact
Cheshire Oaks, Ellesmere Port
CH65 9LF
t 0151 357 8800
w blueplanetaquarium.com
e info@blueplanetaquarium.com

736 Altrincham

Dunham Massey

2 hrs | Mar–Nov

This early Georgian house was extensively renovated in the early C20. The result is one of Britain's most sumptuous Edwardian interiors housing collections of C18 walnut furniture, paintings and Huguenot silver. You can also visit the extensive servants' quarters.

* Beautiful gardens with richly planted borders
* Orangery, Victorian bark house and well house

Location
3 miles SW of Altrincham, M6 junction 19, M56 junction 7

Opening
Mar–Oct Sat–Wed 12noon–5pm
Oct–Nov Sat–Wed 12noon–4pm

Admission
Adult £5.80, Child £2.90

Contact
Altrincham WA14 4SJ
t 0161 941 1025
w national-trust.org.uk
e dunhammassey@ntrust.org.uk

---

737 Chester

Chester Cathedral

1 hr | All year

This is the most complete medieval monastic complex standing in the UK. Records show a church has existed on this site since the early C10, and the foundation of a Benedictine monastery in 1092. In 1541, it became the Cathedral Church of Christ and the Blessed Virgin Mary.

* Restoration in latter part of C19 by Sir Gilbert Scott
* Stunning stained glass, fabrics & sculptures

Location
Chester city centre

Opening
Daily; Mon–Sat 8am–6pm
Sun 1pm–6pm

Admission
Adults £4, Child £1.50, Concs £3

Contact
12 Abbey Square, Chester CH1 2HU
t 01244 324756
w chestercathedral.com
e fry@chestercathedral.com

---

738 Chester

Chester Zoo

5 hrs+ | All year

Founded in 1934 and covering an area of over 100 acres, Chester Zoo is one of the largest zoos in the UK and receives over 1 million visitors each year. It is home to over 7000 animals, representing around 500 different species, and a spectacular plant collection.

* Award-winning gardens
* Internationally renowned for innovative enclosures

Location
Easily accessible from the M53 & M56; follow the brown tourist signs

Opening
Daily from 10am; closing times vary; closed 25 Dec

Admission
Adult £13, Child £9.50, Concs £10.50

Contact
Upton-by-Chester, Chester CH2 1LH
t 01244 380280
w www.chesterzoo.org
e reception@chesterzoo.co.uk

Ullswater, Cumbria

North West

Cheshire Cumbria Greater Manchester
Lancashire Merseyside

733 Wakefield

Sandal Castle

1 hr+   All year

Originally a motte and bailey castle dating from C12, the stone castle overlooking the river Calder was demolished on the orders of Parliament after being besieged during the Civil War in 1645. It was restored to its present state in the 1970s and 80s.

* Overlooks site of Battle of Wakefield
* Spectacular views

Location
On the A61, 2 miles from the city centre in the direction of Barnsley

Opening
Castle Daily; dawn–dusk
Visitor centre Daily; Easter–Oct half-term open 11am–5pm otherwise weekends only Please phone for details

Admission
Free

Contact
Manygates Lane, Sandal, Wakefield, WF2 7DG

t 01924 249779

734 Wakefield

National Coalmining Museum

3 hrs+   All year

Tours take visitors 140 metres underground and trace mining techniques and conditions through the ages from the C19 when women and children worked underground, to how pit ponies were used before mechanical systems were implemented.

* Exhibition of modern mining methods
* Each guide is a former local miner

Location
On A642 between Wakefield and Huddersfield

Opening
Daily; 10am–5pm

Admission
Free

Contact
Caphouse Colliery, New Road, Overton, Wakefield WF4 4RH

t 01924 848806
w ncm.org.uk
e info@ncm.org.uk

735 Wakefield

Yorkshire Sculpture Park

2 hrs+   All year

One of Europe's leading open-air galleries showing modern and contemporary work by leading UK and international artists. A changing programme of exhibitions, displays and projects is held throughout 500 acres of C18 landscaped grounds.

* Three indoor galleries
* New underground gallery for spring 2005

Location
1 mile from M1 junction 38 on A637

Opening
Daily; *Summer:* 10am–6pm
Winter: 10am–5pm

Admission
Free, parking £3

Contact
West Bretton, Wakefield WF4 4LG

t 01924 832631
w ysp.co.uk
e info@ysp.co.uk

729 Leeds

Royal Armouries Museum

4 hrs   All year

The Royal Armouries Museum in Leeds was opened in 1996 as the new home for the national collection of arms and armour. Five themed galleries cover war, tournament, self-defence, hunting and the arms and armour of the Orient.

* See Henry VIII's tournament armour
* Live action events and interactive technology

Location
S of Leeds city centre, near junction 4 of M621

Opening
Daily; 10am–5pm

Admission
Free, on-site parking £3

Contact
Armouries Drive, Leeds LS10 1LT
t 08700 344344
w armouries.org.uk
e enquiries@armouries.org.uk

---

730 Leeds

Temple Newsam House & Farm

2 hrs   All year

This magnificent country house contains one of the most important collections of decorative arts in Britain, including splendid Chippendale furniture and silver. The 1,500 acres of parkland, woodland, farmland & gardens include a rare-breed centre with over 400 animals.

* The largest rare-breed centre in the world

Location
Temple Newsam Road, off Selby Road, 4 miles from Leeds city centre, of A63

Opening
Nov–Mar Tue–Sat 10am–4pm; Sun, 12pm–4pm
Apr–Oct Tue–Sat 10am–5pm; Sun, 1pm–5pm

Admission
House Adult £3, Child £2
Farm Adult £3, Child £2

Contact
Temple Newsam Road, Leeds LS15 0AE
t 0113 2647321
w www.leeds.gov.uk/templenewsam
e tnewsamho.leeds@virgin.net

---

731 Leeds

Thackray Museum

3 hrs   All year

Established in a former workhouse building adjacent to St James's Hospital, the museum houses displays, which show how people's lives have changed over the last 150 years as a result of improvements in public health, medicine and healthcare.

* Vast range of surgical instruments from C19 to today
* Unique collection of pharmacy ceramics

  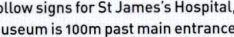

Location
Follow signs for St James's Hospital, museum is 100m past main entrance

Opening
Daily; 10am–5pm, last admission 3pm

Admission
Adult £4.90, Child £3.50, Concs £3.90
Parking £1

Contact
Beckett Street, Leeds, LS9 7LN
t 0113 244 4343
w thackraymuseum.org
e info@thackraymuseum.org

---

732 Leeds

Tropical World

2 hrs   All year

Explore the tropics in the butterfly house, home to 30–40 species, and the coronation house, filled with unusual plants. The Amazon is recreated in the South-American house and is home to whistling ducks and macaws. The nocturnal zone has bush babies and fruit bats.

* Largest collection of tropical plants outside Kew

Location
Off A58 at Oakwood, 3 miles N of Leeds city centre

Opening
Daily; 10am–6pm
Closed 25 Dec

Admission
Adult £3, Child (8–15) £2

Contact
Canal Gardens, Roundhay Park, Leeds LS8 2ER
t 0113 266 1850

726 Halifax

Shibden Hall

1–2 hrs   All Year

Built in 1420, the hall was home to the Lister family for over 300 years. It contains furnishings from several different centuries. The barn houses a collection of horse drawn-vehicles and the folk museum is a reconstruction of an early C19 village.

* See coopers, wheelwrights, pharmacies, a Crispin Inn and an old Ale Brewery

Location
Signed from Halifax and M62

Opening
Daily; Mar–Nov Mon–Sat 10am–5pm
Sun 12 noon–5pm
Dec–Feb Mon–Sat 10am–4pm
Sun 12 noon–4pm

Admission
Adult £3.50, Child & Concs £2.50

Contact
Lister's Road, Halifax HX3 6XG

t 01422 352 246
w calderdale.gov.uk/tourism
e shibden.hall@calderdale.gov.uk

727 Leeds

Harewood House & Bird Gardens

3–4 hrs   Feb–Nov

This is one of the country's premier avian collections. Over 100 species of threatened and exotic birds are housed in sympathetic environments with the aim of promoting conservation and education. The Capability Brown gardens also provide many attractions.

* Boat trips across the lake & adventure playground
* Extensive collections of art & furniture in the house

Location
On A61, 7 miles from Leeds & Harrogate

Opening
Daily; Feb 4–Nov 10am–5pm

Admission
All attractions, Adult £10.50, Child £5.50, Concs £8.25
Grounds, £7.25, £4.50, £6.25

Contact
Harewood Estate, Harewood, Leeds LS17 9LQ

t 0113 218 1010
w harewood.org
e info@harewood.org

728 Leeds

Leeds City Art Gallery

2 hr   All year

There is something for everyone at Leeds City Art Gallery from traditional prints, watercolours, paintings and sculptures to contemporary works. The exhibitions are ever changing, displaying some of the most outstanding works of British art outside of London.

* Designated as a collection of national importance
* Features work by Turner, Rembrandt & Henry Moore

Location
City centre, next to central library

Opening
Daily; Mon–Sat 10am–5pm
Wed 10am–8pm, Sun 1pm–5pm
Closed on Bank Hols

Admission
Free

Contact
The Headrow, Leeds LS1 3AA

t 0113 247 8248
w leeds.gov.uk/gallery

724 Bradford

National Museum of Photography, Film & Television

2 hrs+   All year

This is one of the most visited national museums outside London. Located in Bradford in recognition of the city's historic contribution to the development of cinema and film–making in the UK. The museum's archive includes the first negative and the earliest television footage.

* First moving pictures – 1888 film of Leeds Bridge
* More than 3 million historical items

Location
City centre off Little Horton Lane

Opening
Tue–Sun 10am–6pm & Bank & Public Hols

Admission
Free, except for cinemas

Contact
Bradford BD1 1NQ

t 0870 70 10 200
w nmpft.org.uk
e talk.nmpft@nmsi.ac.uk

---

725 Bradford

Colour Museum

1 hr   All year

Britain's only museum of colour. The Colour Museum is the place to come to find out about the weird and wonderful world of colour. Along with its interactive galleries and special exhibitions, the museum holds workshops on all aspects of colour.

* Situated in a former wool warehouse
* Workshops and educational programme (see website)

Location
City centre, near Metro Interchange

Opening
Tue–Sat 10am–4pm,
Closed between Christmas and New Year

Admission
Adults £2, Child £1.50, Concs £1.50

Contact
PO Box 244, Perkin House,
1 Providence Street, Bradford BD1 2PW

t 01274 390955
w sdc.org.uk/museum
e museum@sdc.org.uk

721 Sheffield

Millennium Galleries

2 hrs+   All year

With four individual galleries under one roof, there is something for everybody to enjoy. Explore treasures from the past, masterpieces from Britain's national collections and discover new creations by contemporary artists and makers.

* Material regularly borrowed from Tate and V&A
* Metalwork Gallery

Location
City centre near the Winter Garden

Opening
Mon–Sat 10am–5pm
Sun 11am–5pm

Admission
Free, exhibitions may charge

Contact
Arundel Gate, Sheffield S1 2PP

t 0114 278 2600
w sheffieldgalleries.org.uk
e info@sheffieldgalleries.org.uk

722 Sheffield

Sheffield Ski Village

3½ hrs   All year

This all-season dry-slope ski resort offers skiing, snowboarding, and toboggan rides for all ages and abilities with lessons available at all levels and equipment for hire. Afterwards relax in the authentic mountain lodge. Ideal for groups and parties.

* Over 1 mile of piste
* Thunder Valley Toboggan Run

Location
5 minutes from Sheffield city centre, off A61 Penistone Road

Opening
Daily; *Summer* Mon–Fri 4pm–10pm, Sat & Sun 10am–8pm, Bank holidays 10am–10pm; *Winter* open Mon–Fri 10am–10pm, Sat, Sun, Bank Holidays & 26 Dec–2 Jan 9am–10pm

Admission
Please phone for details

Contact
Vale Road, Sheffield S3 9SJ

t 0114 276959
w www.sheffieldskivillage.co.uk
e info@sheffieldskivillage.co.uk

723 Batley

Bagshaw Museum

1 hr+   All year

Follow the Bagshaws, the museum's founders, on their world travels. Roam from an ancient Egyptian tomb to a tropical rainforest, see the vibrant colours of the orient and the mythical beasts of four continents. This Victorian mansion is set in the wood and parkland of Wilton Park.

* Butterfly centre open in summer
* Enchanted Forest

Location
The A652, A62 & M62 are all nearby & within easy access

Opening
Daily; Mon–Fri 11am–5pm; Sat & Sun open 12pm–5pm; Closed Good Fri

Admission
Free

Contact
Wilton Park, Batley WF17 0AS

t 01924 326155
w www.kirkleesmc.gov.uk
e bagshaw.museum@kirkleesmc. gov.uk

717 Maltby

Roche Abbey

1 hr   Apr–Sep

Founded in 1147, the fine early–Gothic transepts of this Cistercian monastery still survive to their original height. In the C18, Capability Brown transformed an already beautiful valley incorporating the ruins. Excavation has revealed the complete layout of the abbey.

* See website for full programme of special events

Location
1½ miles S of Maltby off A634

Opening
Daily; Apr–Sep 10am–5pm
Aug 10am– 6pm

Admission
Adult £2.50, Child £1.30, Concs £1.90

Contact
The Abbey Lodge, Maltby,
nr Rotherham

t 01709 812739
w english-heritage.org.uk

718 Rotherham

Magna Science Adventure Centre

3 hrs+   All year

Set within a vast former steelworks, Magna is a new, hands-on visitor attraction that explores the powerful themes of earth, air, fire and water. Operate a real JCB, fire a water cannon or explode a rock face. Visit four pavilions, two shows and the outdoor adventure park.

* Feel the force of a tornado in the air pavilion
* Test your bravery as a virtual fireball races at you

Location
Just off M1, 1 mile along A6178 from
Meadowhall shopping centre

Opening
Daily; 10am–5pm

Admission
Adult £9, Child £7 & Concs £7

Contact
Sheffield Road, Templeborough,
Rotherham S60 1DX

t 01709 720002
w visitmagna.co.uk
e info@magnatrust.co.uk

719 Sheffield

The Graves Art Gallery

1 hr   All year

Displays the city's collections of C19 and C20 British and European Art. The collection encapsulates the story of the development of Modern Art, the main trends traced through works by many well-known artists including Picasso, Pierre Bonnard and Sir Stanley Spencer.

* Exciting programme of temporary exhibitions
* Restored to 1930s splendour in 2001

Location
City centre above Central Library

Opening
Mon–Sat 10am–5pm

Admission
Free

Contact
Surrey Street, Sheffield S1 1XZ

t 0114 278 2600
w sheffieldgalleries.org.uk
e infosheffieldgalleries.org.uk

720 Sheffield

Renishaw Hall Gardens

4 hrs+   Apr–Sep

Home to the Sitwell family for over 350 years, the beautiful Italianate garden, park and lake were the creation of the eccentric Sir George Sitwell. Today visitors can enjoy lakeside walks, various galleries and a sculpture trail.

* Hall open by special arrangement only
* Regular calendar of events

Location
Just 2 miles from junction 30 off the
M1, between Ecrington & Renishaw on
the A6135

Opening
8 Apr–26 Sep Thu–Sun &
Bank Holiday Mon 10.30am–4.30pm
Please phone for details of separate
events

Admission
Adult £6, Child Free, Concs £4

Contact
Renishaw Hall, Sheffield

t 01246 432310
w www.sitwell.co.uk
e info@renishawhall.free-online.co.uk

714 Barnsley

Cannon Hall Farm

3 hrs   All year

This farm is home to lots of animals, including lambs, goats, ponies, alpacas, wallabies, chickens, rabbits, and guinea pigs some of which visitors can hand feed. There's an adventure playground and a farm shop selling local produce.

* White Rose Special Award for Tourism 2002
* Baby animals

Location
Take the A635 from Barnsley just after Cawthorne village. Signed on right

Opening
Daily; Mon–Sat 10.30am–4.30pm, Sun & Bank Holidays 10.30am–5pm

Admission
Adult £2.95 Child/Senior £2.50

Contact
Barnsley S75 4AT

t 01226 790427
w www.cannonhallfarm.co.uk

---

715 Conisbrough

Conisbrough Castle

2 hrs+   All year

The white, circular keep of this C12 castle is a spectacular structure made of magnesian limestone and is the oldest of its kind in England. Recently restored, with two new floors and a roof, it is a fine example of medieval architecture.

* Inspiration for Sir Walter Scott's classic novel Ivanhoe
* Closed for private functions some summer Saturdays

Location
NE of Conisbrough town centre on A630

Opening
Daily; Apr–Sep 10am–5pm
Oct–Mar 10am–4pm

Admission
Adult £3.75, Child £2.00, Concs £2.50

Contact
Castle Hill Conisbrough DN12 3BU

t 01709 863329
w conisbroughcastle.org.uk
e info@conisbroughcastle.org.uk

---

716 Doncaster

Earth Centre

3 hrs+   All year

This amazing collection of attractions is centred around a mission to achieve a better understanding of sustainable development in everyday life. Attractions include indoor and outdoor exhibitions, unique 'eco' buildings, adventure playgrounds, gardens and wetlands.

* Built above two old collieries
* Recycling exhibition has attracted huge media attention

Location
From junction 36 of A1M follow signs along A630 and A6023

Opening
Daily; Easter– 29 Sep 10am–5pm
30 Sep –Easter 10am–3.30pm

Admission
Pricing by attractions used –

see website, £10 for access to all adventure activities, other prices vary

Contact
Denaby Main, Doncaster DN12 4EA

t 01709 513 933
w earthcentre.org.uk
e info@earthcentre.org.uk

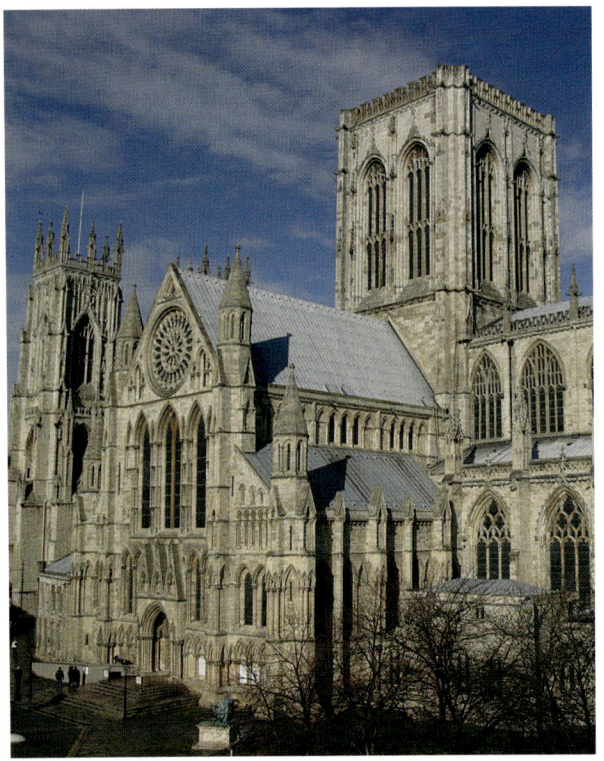

711 York

York Dungeons

1 hr   All year

Deep in the heart of historic York, buried beneath its paving stones, lies the North's most chilling horror attraction. The York Dungeon brings more than 2,000 years of gruesomely authentic history vividly back to life... and death.

* See how torture was part of everyday life until C19

Location
City centre

Opening
Daily; Oct–Mar 10.30am–4.30pm
Apr–Sep 10am–5pm

Admission
Adult £9.95, Child 5–14 years £5.95, U 5's free, Concs £7.95

Contact
The York Dungeon
12 Clifford Street, York YO1 9RD

t 01904 632599
w thedungeons.com
e yorkdungeons@ merlinentertainments.biz

712 York

York Minster

1½ hrs   All year

Built C12–C15, York Minster is the largest Gothic cathedral in England. It is 524 feet long, 249 feet wide and over 90 feet high. The present building was constructed on the site of a Norman cathedral, which was itself built on the foundations of a Roman fort.

* The largest Gothic cathedral in northern Europe
* Visited by 2 million people every year

Location
York city centre

Opening
Summer Mon 9am–5pm,
Sun 12pm–5.30pm
Winter Mon–9.30am–5pm, Sun 12–5pm
(Tower: 30 mins before dusk)

Admission
Free but donations requested

Contact
Deangate, York YO1 2HG

t 01904 557216
w www.yorkminster.org
e info@yorkminster.org

713 York

Yorkshire Museum & Gardens

2 hrs   All year

Walk in the footsteps of Romans and Vikings. See beasts turned to stone from a time when dinosaurs ruled the planet and a host of outstanding archaeological finds. The museum is set in 10 acres of botanical gardens.

* Ruins of St Mary's Abbey in grounds
* Preserved section of York's Roman fortress

Location
5–10 mins walk from railway station

Opening
Daily; 10am–5pm

Admission
Adult £4, Child £2.50, Conc £3

Contact
Museum Gardens, York YO1 7FR

t 01904 687687
w york.trust.museum
e yorkshire.museum@ymt.org.uk

708 York

Yorkshire Air Museum

3 hrs   All year

A fascinating authentically based on a Second World War Bomber Command Station. The unique displays include the original Control Tower, Air Gunners' Collection, Barnes Wallis' prototype 'bouncing bomb' and an Airborne Forces Display.

* See the only restored Halifax bomber
* Historical aircraft from earliest days of flight

Location
Take the B1228 off the A63/A1079 roundabout

Opening
Daily; Summer (Apr–Sep) 10am–5pm
Winter 10am–3.30pm

Admission
Adult £5, Child £3, Concs £4

Contact
Halifax Way, Elvington, York YO41 4AU

t 01904 608595
w yorkshireairmuseum.co.uk
e museum@yorkshireair
    museum.co.uk

709 York

York Art Gallery

1 hr+   All year

See some of Europe's finest art with examples of oil and canvas, watercolours and ceramics. The gallery houses 600 years of British and European art, from the time of the Wars of the Roses right up to the present day.

* Outstanding collection of pioneer studio pottery
* Full programme of temporary exhibitions

Location
Opposite Tourist Information centre, 3 minutes walk from Minster

Opening
Daily; 10am–5pm

Admission
Free

Contact
Exhibition Square, York YO1 7EW

t 01904 697979
w yorkartgallery.org.uk
e art.gallery@ymt.org.uk

710 York

York Castle Museum

1 hr+   All year

Experience life as a Victorian. Walk down cobbled streets and peer through windows of shops long gone. Take a journey through 400 years of life in Britain, from parlours to prisons, marriages to the mill house and see the toys that children used to treasure.

* Stumble into the underworld of the highwayman
* City at War exhibition

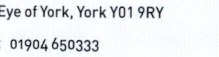

Location
City Centre

Opening
Daily; 9.30am–5pm

Admission
Adult £6, Child £3.50 & Concs £4.50

Contact
Eye of York, York YO1 9RY

t 01904 650333
w york.trust.museum
e castle.museum@ymt.org.uk

705 York

Jorvik

1 hr   All year

Discover what life was like over 1000 years ago, see over 800 Viking items uncovered here, and journey through a reconstruction of actual Viking–Age streets. Witness the skills of Viking craftsmen in a new interactive exhibition – Fearsome Craftsmen!

* Jorvik is the name given to York by Vikings in AD975
* Wheelchair users please ring 01904 543402

Location
A64 to York

Opening
Daily; Apr–Oct 10am–4/5pm
Nov–Apr 10am–4pm

Admission
Adult £7.20, Child £5.10, Concs £6.10

Contact
Jorvik, Coppergate, York Y01 9WT
t 01904 543403 / 643211
w vikingjorvik.com
e jorvik@yorkarchaeology.co.uk

---

707 York

Rievaulx Abbey

4 hrs+   All year

Founded by St Bernard of Clairvaux in C13, this Cistercian abbey was once home to some 150 monks and 500 lay brethren. Although much of what was built by the monks is in ruins, recent digs reveal the monks ate strawberries and ran a flourishing iron industry.

*Towering medieval architecture
* Explore its maze of ancillary buildings

Location
In Rievaulx, 2¼ miles W of Helmsley on a minor road off B1257

Opening
Daily; 1 Apr–30 Sep 10am–6pm; 14–22 Feb & 1–31 Oct 10am–5pm; 1 Nov–13 Feb & 23 Feb–31 Mar 10am–4pm

Admission
Adult £3.80, Child £1.90, Concs £2.90

Contact
Rievaulx,
York,
North Yorkshire YO62 5LB
t 01439 798228
w www.english-heritage.co.uk

---

706 York

National Railway Museum

3 hrs+   All year

The collection includes 103 locomotives and 177 items of rolling stock from the Rocket to the Eurostar. Permanent displays include Palaces on Wheels with pre–Victorian Royal saloons and a Japanese Bullet Train.

* See 'Mallard' the world's fastest steam locomotive
* Literally millions of photographs and artefacts

Location
600 yards from railway station, signed from centre

Opening
Daily; 10am–6pm

Admission
Free except for special events

Contact
Leeman Road, YO26 4XJ
t 01904 621261
w nrm.org.uk
e nrm@nmsi.ac.uk

702 York

The Bar Convent

1 hr+   All year

The oldest working convent in England (established in 1686). The Foundress of the order, Mary Ward, was a pioneer of education for women and its members ran a school for 299 years. The Bar Convent Museum tells the early history of Christianity in the North of England.

* C18 neo-classical chapel still used for weekly service
* School moved to comprehensive system in 1985

Location
2 mins walk from train station

Opening
Museum tours Mon–Fri 10.30am & 2.30pm. 10am–5pm for non tours

Admission
Adult £3, Child £1, Concs £2

Contact
17 Blossom Street,
York YO24 1AQ
t 01904 643 238
w bar-convent.org.uk
e info@bar-convent.org.uk

703 York

Castle Howard

2 hrs+   Mar–Oct

One of Britain's finest stately homes, located in the beautiful Howardian hills. The magnificent house is distinguished by its famous dome and inside there are enormous collections of important art treasures. Spectacular gardens form part of 10,000 acre estate.

* Adventure playground, boat trips and farm shop
* Outdoor guided tours and historical characters

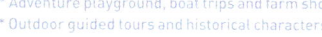

Location
15 miles NE of York

Opening
Daily; Mar–Oct 10am–4pm

Admission
Adult £9.50, Child £6.50, Concs £8.50

Contact
North York YO60 7DA
t 01653 648 333
w castlehoward.co.uk
e house@castlehoward.co.uk

704 York

Clifford's Tower

½ hr   All year

Clifford's Tower is all that remains of York Castle. The original wooden tower was burned down during anti-Jewish riots. The height of the motte was increased and the tower was rebuilt in stone. Today the tower is just a shell, but you can climb to the top for a good view of York.

* Used as prison after English Civil War
* Castle continued to be used for executions until 1896

Location
Eye of York, opposite York Castle museum

Opening
Daily; Apr–Sep 10am–6pm (Oct 5pm)
Nov–Mar 10am–4pm

Admission
Adult £2.50, Child £1.30, Concs £1.90

Contact
Tower Street, York YO1 9SA
t 01904 646940
w english-heritage.org.uk/
cliffordstower.com
e cliffords.tower@
english-heritage.org.uk

700 Skipton

Skipton Castle

1 hr+   All year

Over 900 years old, Skipton Castle is one of England's most complete and best-preserved medieval castles – surviving a three–year siege during the Civil War. Climb from the depths of the dungeons to the very top of the Watch Tower, and visit the fantastic book shop.

* View banqueting hall, kitchen, bedchambers
* Comprehensive tour sheets

Location
Centre of Skipton

Opening
Mar–Sep Mon–Sat 10am–6pm,
Sun 12 noon–6pm
Oct–Feb 10am–4pm

Admission
Adult £5, Child £2.50, Concs £4.40

Contact
Skipton BD23 1AQ

t 01756 792442
w skiptoncastle.co.uk
e info@skiptoncastle.co.uk

701 Skipton

Bolton Abbey

2 hrs+   All year

This Estate covers 30,000 acres of beautiful countryside in the Yorkshire Dales. There are medieval buildings, C12 priory ruins to explore, and 80 miles of moorland, woodland and riverside footpaths. Guide book and walks leaflet available.

* Landscape was inspiration for Wordsworth & Turner
* Grounds include 6-mile stretch of River Wharfe

Location
Between Harrogate & Skipton, off A59
on B6160

Opening
Daily; 9am–dusk

Admission
Vehicle pass £4 (occupants free),
£2.50 for disabled badge holders

Contact
Skipton BD23 6EX

t 01756 718009
w boltonabbey.com
e tourism@boltonabbey.com

696 Ripon

Fountains Abbey
& Studley Royal Estate

2 hrs+   All year

The spectacular ruins of this C12 Cistercian Abbey sit alongside a deer park, a Victorian Church and an elegant C18 landscape garden with water features and follies.

* Best surviving example of a Monastic mill
* Declared a World Heritage site in 1987

Location
4 miles W of Ripon

Opening
Daily; Nov-Feb 10am-4pm
Mar-Oct 10am-5pm
Nov, Dec, Jan Closed Fri

Admission
Adult £5.50, Child £3

Contact
Ripon HG4 3DY

t 01765 608 888
w fountainsabbey.org.uk
e webinfo@fmtp.ntrust.org.uk

697 Ripon

Newby Hall & Gardens

4 hrs   Apr-Sep

One of England's renowned Adam houses, this is an exceptional example of C18 interior decoration, recently restored to its original beauty. Contents include the Gobelins Tapestry Room, a renowned gallery of classical statues and some of Chippendale's finest furniture.

* 25 acres of award-winning gardens
* Miniature railway, woodland walk and special events

Location
Off B6265 between Boroughbridge & Ripon

Opening
Daily; Apr-Sep 11am-5pm

Admission
Adult £7.80, Child £5.30, Concs £6.80

Contact
Ripon HG4 5AE

t 01423 322 583
w newbyhall.com
e info@newbyhall.com

698 Scarborough

Scarborough Castle

1 hr   All year

Dominating the headland, this impressive castle was built in the early C13 and later enhanced by King John and Henry III. It suffered naval bombardment in 1914 and during the second world war was home to a secret listening post. Wonderful views of the Yorkshire coastline.

* Vast C13 fortress

Location
Castle Rd, E of town centre

Opening
Daily, Apr-Sep, 10am-6pm; Oct-Mar, Thu-Mon, 10am-4pm

Admission
Adult £3.20, Child £1.60, Concs £2.40

Contact
Castle Road, Scarborough

t 01723 372 451
w www.english-heritage.org.uk

699 Scarborough

Wykeham Lakes

1 hr+   All year

The ideal place to enjoy a range of watersports, including sailing, windsurfing, boating, scuba-diving, and canoeing. Tuition available. If you prefer fishing, choose from one trout and two coarse fishing lakes and pike fishing in winter.

* Watersports lake
* Sailing & watersports tuition

Location
Situated 6 miles W of Scarborough off the A170 between West Ayton & Wykeham

Opening
Boating & watersports lake Daily; dawn-dusk; *Fishing* available all year; *Nature trails & bird-watching* available all year

Admission
Prices vary according to activity/duration (please phone for details)

Contact
Charm Park, Wykeham, Scarborough, North Yorkshire

t 01723 863148

693 Middleham

Middleham Castle

fine

1 hr

All year

The commanding views from this impressive fortress cover an area that has been inhabited by prehistoric, Roman, Viking and Norman settlers. The formidable stone keep was one of the largest in England. Many modifications have been made over the centuries.

* Childhood home of Richard III
* James Herriott's Yorkshire was filmed in the area

Location
2 miles S of Leyburn on A6108

Opening
Daily; Apr–Sep 10am–6pm
Oct–Mar Thu–Mon 10am–4pm

Admission
Adult £3, Child £1.50, Concs £2.30

Contact
Castle Hill, Middleham,
Leyburn DL8 4QR

t 01969 623899
w english–heritage.org.uk

---

694 Ormesby

Ormesby Hall

2 hrs+

Apr–Nov

Set in 270 acres of parkland, this C18 Palladian mansion, now owned by the National Trust, is notable for its fine plasterwork and carved wood decoration. Visit the Victorian laundry, kitchen, game larder and stable block. There is also an attractive garden and holly walk.

* National Trust property

Location
3 miles SE of Middlesborough. Take A174, A172 & follow the signs

Opening
Apr–Nov, Tue–Thu, Sun,
Bank Holidays & Good Friday
1.30pm–4.30pm

Admission
Adult £3.90, Child £1.80

Contact
Ormesby Hall,
Ormesby TS7 9AS

t 01642 324188
e yorkor@smtp.ntrust.org.uk

---

695 Ripley

Ripley Castle & Gardens

2 hrs+

All year

Home to the Ingilby family for over 700 years, the castle is famous as the place where Jane Ingilby held Oliver Cromwell at gunpoint. Impressive collection of arms and armour from the English Civil War. Extensive hot houses, gardens and grounds.

* Guided tours leave front door every hour
* Home to the National Hyacinth Collection

Location
3 miles N of Harrogate on the A61

Opening
Daily; Jun–Aug 10.30am–3.30pm
Sep–Jun Tue, Thu, Sat, Sun & Bank Hols

Admission
Adult £6, Child £3.50, Concs £5

Contact
The Ripley Castle Estate,
Harrogate HG3 3AY

t 01423 770152
w ripleycastle.co.uk
e enquiries@ripleycastle.co.uk

689 Kirby Misperton

Flamingo Land Theme Park & Zoo

6 hrs + Apr–Dec

The zoo is home to over 1000 animals, including tigers, zebras, camels, monkeys, sea lions, penguins and meerkats, and the largest flock of pink flamingoes in the country. The bird walk has birds of all sizes from finches to ostriches. The park has eight coaster rides.

* Lost Kingdom display
* Children's farm

Location
Off the A64 Scarborough–York road on A169 Malton–Pickering road

Opening
Daily; Apr–Nov 10am–5pm or 6pm; Theme park closed Dec–Mar; Zoo open 6–7, 13–14 & 18–24 Dec 10am–5pm

Admission
Please phone for 2005 prices

Contact
Kirby Misperton, Malton YO17 6UX

t 01653 668287
w www.flamingoland.co.uk

690 Knaresborough

Mother Shipton's Cave

1 hr+ Feb–Nov

Mother Shipton is perhaps England's most famous Prophetess, foretelling the Spanish Armada and the Great Fire of London. She lived 500 years ago during the reign of King Henry VIII and Queen Elizabeth I. Cave, petrifying well, museum and 12 acres of historic woodland park.

* Visitor attraction for 300 years
* Free all-day parking

Location
Signed from A1 on A51

Opening
Daily, Mar–Oct 10am–5.30pm
Nov & Feb Sat & Sun 10am–4.30pm
Closed Dec & Jan

Admission
Adult £4.95, Child £3.75, Concs £4.25

Contact
Prophecy House, Knaresborough HG5 8DD

t 01423 864600
w mothershipton.co.uk
e adrian@mothershipton.co.uk

691 Leyburn

Bolton Castle

1 hr+ All year

This spectacular medieval fortress in the heart of the Yorkshire Dales was completed in 1399. Today visitors can explore five floors of displays depicting castle life in C15 and see where Mary Queen of Scots was imprisoned.

* Film venue for *Ivanhoe*, *Elizabeth* and *Heartbeat*

Location
6 miles W of Leyburn, just off the A648. Signed from Wensley

Opening
Daily; Mar–Nov open 10am–5pm;
Dec–Feb open 10am–4pm
Please phone for details

Admission
Please phone for details

Contact
Leyburn, North Yorkshire DL8 4ET

t 01969 623981
w www.boltoncastle.co.uk

692 Malton

Eden Camp Modern History Museum

4 hrs All year

In this military museum, historical scenes are reconstructed using movement, lighting, sound, smells and smoke machines. Attractions include an original Prisoner of War Camp built in 1942. New exhibition areas being opened.

* Covers complete C20 British military history
* Multiple award–winning attraction

Location
At the junction of A64 with A169

Opening
Daily; 10am–5pm
Closed Dec 24–2nd Mon in Jan

Admission
Adult £4.50, Child/Concs £3.50

Contact
Malton YO17 6RT

t 01653 697777
w edencamp.co.uk
e admin@edencamp.co.uk

685 Bedale

Big Sheep & Little Cow Farm

2 hrs   All year

This small, family-run, family-friendly attraction is home to many farm animals, including lambs, piglets, cows and sheep, which can be bottle-fed, bathed and petted under the supervision of a guide. Afterwards enjoy a homemade ewes-milk ice-cream.

* Sand play area
* Quad bikes and pony rides

Location
11miles S of Scotch Corner & 1 mile from the A1 on the A684 towards Bedale. Follow brown 'Farm Visitor Centre' signs

Opening
Daily; Mar–Sep 10.30am–5pm, Sep–Mar Sat–Wed 10.30am–5pm

Admission
Adult £4, Child £3, Concs £3.50

Contact
nr Bedale, North Yorkshire

t 01677 422125
w www.farmattraction.co.uk
e enquiries@farmattraction.co.uk

686 Harrogate

RHS Garden Harlow Carr

3 hrs   All year

Created from mixed woodland and pasture land in 1950, Harlow Carr's chief aim was to create a trial ground where the suitability of plants for growing in northern climates could be assessed. The garden has year-round interest for the novice and expert alike.

* Built on site of former spa (sulphur water)

Location
Off B6162, 1½ miles from Harrogate town centre

Opening
Daily ,Summer 9.30am–6pm
Winter 9.30am–5pm

Admission
Adult £5, Child £1.50, Concs £4
RHS members free

Contact
Crag Lane, Harrogate HG3 1QB

t 01423 565418
w rhs.org.uk./gardens/harlowcarr
e admin–harlowcarr@rhs.org.uk

687 Helmsley

Duncombe Park

3 hrs   All year

Used as a girls' school for 60 years, Duncombe Park has been restored as a grand family home (200 rooms), housing a fine collection of English and Continental furniture. Its naturally landscaped gardens have fine views over valley and moors.

* 450 acres of parkland is National Nature Reserve
* Way-marked walks through woods and river valley

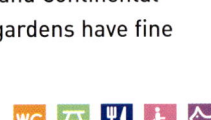

Location
1 mile from Helmsley centre

Opening
Daily; 11am–5.30pm
House by guided tour only
12.30pm–3.30pm every 30 mins

Admission
Adult £6.50, Child £3, Concs £5

Contact
Helmsley YO62 5EB

t 01439 770 213
w duncombepark.com
e info@duncombepark.com

688 Hull

The Deep

2-3 hrs   All year

Experience marine-life and sea-life history in this museum shaped like a ship. Take an underwater lift, walk through sub-aqua tunnels and watch sharks swim overhead. Explore exhibitions about corals, Arctic sea life, and the Big Bang. Lots of hands-on and interactive activities.

* 10m deep tank containing 2.5 million litres of water
* Sharks galore

Location
Within walking distance of the town centre on the banks of the Humber

Opening
Daily, 10am–6pm,
closed 25-26 Dec

Admission
Adult £6.75, Child £4.75, Concs £5.25

Contact
Hull, North Yorkshire HU1 4DP

t 01482 381000
w www.thedeep.co.uk
e info@thedeep.co.uk

683 Kingston upon Hull

Ferens Art Gallery

1 hr+ All year

Opened in 1927, the award-winning Ferens Art Gallery combines internationally-renowned permanent collections with exhibitions and Live Art. The first-class permanent collection of paintings and sculpture spans the medieval period to the present day.

* European Old Masters, particularly Dutch & Flemish
* Masterpieces by Canaletto, Spencer, Hockney

Location
City centre

Opening
Mon–Sat 10am–5pm
Sun 1.30pm–4.30pm

Admission
Free

Contact
Queen Victoria Square,
Kingston upon Hull HU1 3RA

t 01482 613902
w hullcc.gov.uk/museums/ferens
e museums@hull.gov.uk

684 Pocklington

Burnby Hall Gardens

4 hrs Easter–Oct

Burnby Hall Gardens is world famous for its national collection of water lilies, which contains more varieties than anywhere else in Europe. There is also an extensive range of ornamental trees, plants, shrubs and numerous fish and birds.

* Winner of Yorkshire in Bloom 2004
* Two large lakes in 10 acres of beautiful gardens

Location
20 mins E of York off A1079

Opening
Daily, Easter–Oct, 10am–5pm

Admission
Adult £3, Child £1.50, Concs £2.50
Gardens free in winter

Contact
The Ball, Pocklington, YO42 2QF

t 01759 307125
w burnbyhallgardens.co.uk
e burnbyhallgardens@hotmail.com

680 Hornsea

Hornsea Museum

1 hr+   Easter–Sep

This award-winning museum shows how village life has changed in North Holderness from the pre-industrial age of the early C17 through to post world war two. Sited in an C18 farmhouse.

* Local industrial display, photographic exhibition
* Hornsea pottery collection

Location
Hornsea town centre, off B1242

Opening
Easter–Sep, autumn half-term & Bank Hol Mons, Tue–Sat 11am–5pm Sun 2pm–5pm

Admission
Adult £2, Child £1.50, Concs £1.50

Contact
Burns Farm, 11 Newbegin, Hornsea HU18 1AB
t 01964 533443
w hornseamuseum.com
e contact@hornseamuseum.com

---

681 Hull

Hull Maritime Museum

1 hr   All year

Formerly the town docks' offices, this impressive building now houses a fine collection of paintings, artefacts, models, a full-size whale skeleton, and detailed displays on whaling, fishing and the maritime history of Hull and the River Humber.

* 700 years of history
* History of whaling, fishing & merchant shipping

Location
In Queen Victoria Square in the centre of Hull

Opening
Daily Mon–Sat 10am–5pm & Sun 1.30pm–4.30pm; closed 1 Jan, Good Friday & Christmas week

Admission
Free

Contact
Queen Victoria Square, Hull HU1 3RA
t 01482 613902
w museums@hullcc.gov.uk

---

682 Kingston upon Hull

Streetlife Museum of Transport

2 hrs+   All year

Major new developments, opened in 2003, include a new motor car gallery, a major extension of the popular carriage gallery, a larger street–scene with several new shops and a hands-on interactive exhibition area.

* Supported by Heritage Lottery Funding

Location
High Street nr Wilberforce House

Opening
Daily, Mon–Sat 10am –5 pm Sun 1.30pm–4.30

Admission
Free

Contact
High Street, Hull HU1 1PS
t 01482 613902
w hullcc.gov.uk/museums/streetlife
e museums@hull.gov.uk

676 Bridlington

Bempton Cliffs Nature Reserve

  2 hrs All year

One of the best places in England to see seabirds. More than 200,000 birds nest on the cliffs, including gannets, puffins, guillemots, razorbills and kittiwakes. Five safe viewing areas are situated along 3 miles of chalk cliffs. First mile is suitable for wheelchairs.

* Gannets first colonised cliffs in 1920s
* Puffins can be seen in spring & summer

Location
On cliff road from Bempton, on B1229 from Flamborough to Filey

Opening
Visitor centre Daily Mar–Nov
9.30am–4pm
Dec–Feb 9.30am–4pm

Admission
£3 car park fee for non–members

Contact
11 Cliff Lane, Bempton,
Bridlington YO15 1JD

t 01262 851179
w rspb.org.uk

677 Bridlington

Bridlington Leisure World

  4 hrs+ All year

The complex includes three swimming pools, one with waves, slides, storm effects and water features; a 25m training pool and a learner pool. There is also a multi-purpose hall for indoor bowling, family activities and a fitness studio.

* Small theatre and bar
* One of East Ridings premier leisure attractions

Location
Off the A165 (off the M62). Nearest town, Scarborough

Opening
Please phone for details

Admission
Activities individually priced

Contact
The Promenade,
Bridlington,
Yorkshire YO15 2QQ

t 01262 606715
w www.bridlington.net/leisureworld

678 Bridlington

Park Rose Owl & Bird of Prey Centre

  3 hrs Mar–Oct

Set in 3½ acres of natural woodland, the centre has 40 aviaries displaying hundreds of owls and birds of prey. There are daily guided information tours. A honey bee exhibition gives visitors the opportunity to view a working hive.

* Flying displays throughout the summer season
* Adventure playground

Location
On A165/A166, 2 miles S of Bridlington

Opening
Daily; Mar–Oct 10am–5pm;
Closed 25–31 Dec

Admission
Adult £2.50, Child £1.50

Contact
Carnaby Covert Lane,
Bridlington YO15 3QF

t 01262 606800

679 Bridlington

Sewerby Hall & Gardens

  3 hrs Apr–Sep

Set in 50 acres of early C19 parkland in a dramatic cliff–top position, overlooking Bridlington Bay. The Hall contains a magnificent orangery, period rooms and art and photographic galleries. Attractions in the grounds include a beautiful walled garden.

* Display of Amy Johnson's awards & trophies
* Children's zoo includes monkeys & penguins

Location
From Bridlington, follow signs for Flambourgh and then Sewerby

Opening
Daily; Apr–Sep 10am–5.30pm

Admission
Adult £3.10, Child £1.20, Concs £2.40

Contact
Church Lane, Sewerby,
Bridlington YO15 1EA

t 01262 673769
w yorkshire-tour.co.uk
e sewerbyhall@yahoo.com

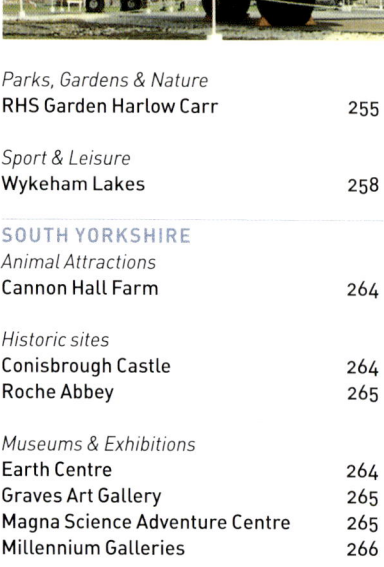

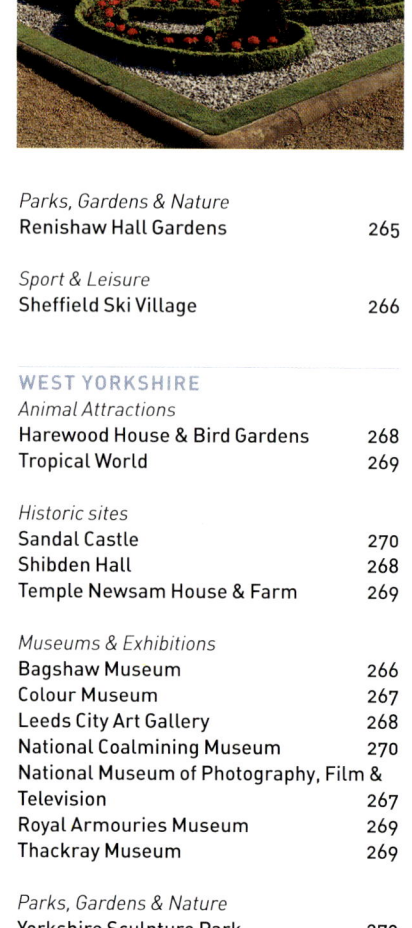

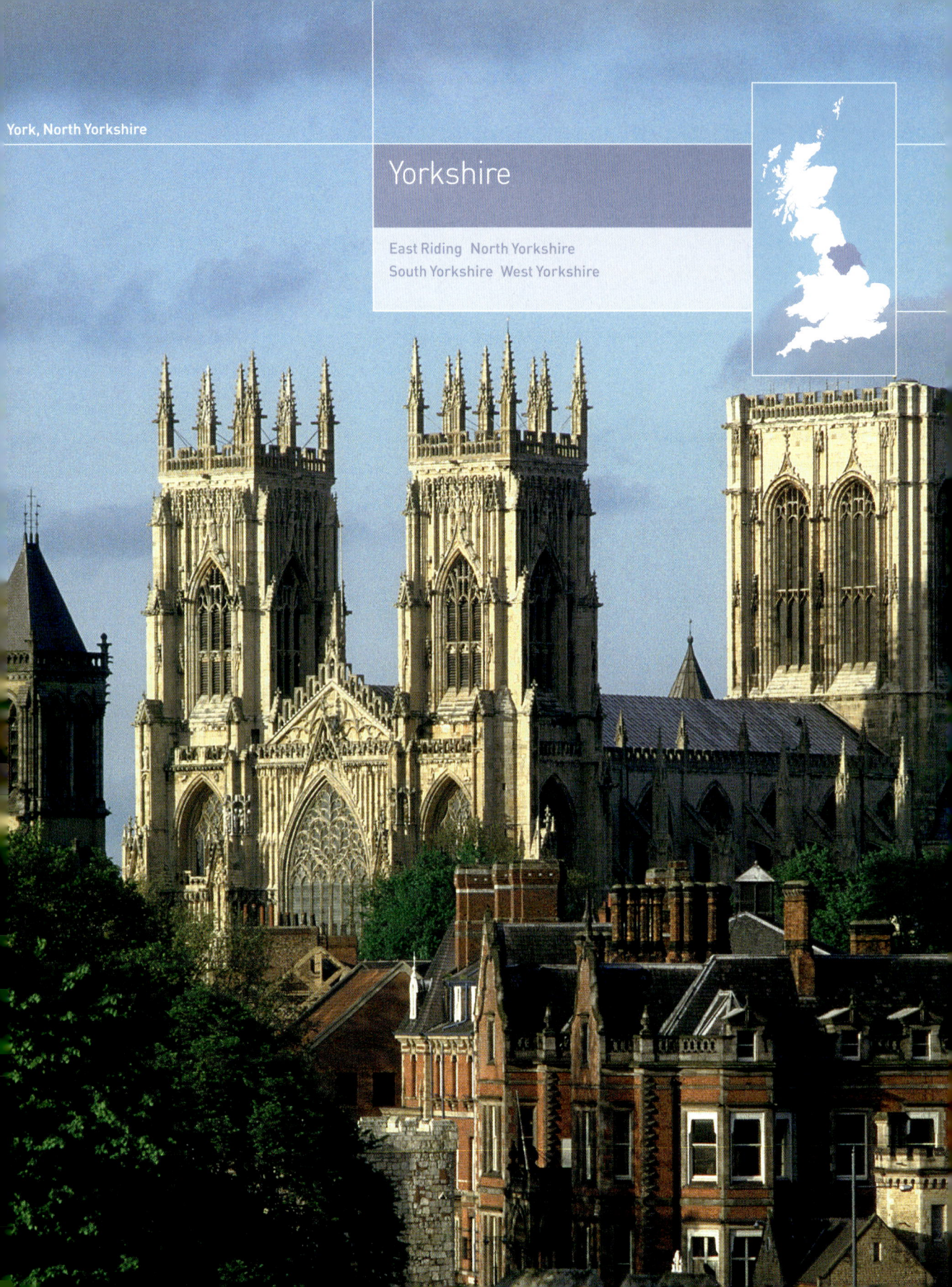

Yorkshire

East Riding North Yorkshire
South Yorkshire West Yorkshire

673   Tenby

Manor House Wild Animal Park

4 hrs   Easter–Sep

Set in landscaped wooded grounds and floral gardens beside a C18 manor house, the zoo has a close-encounters unit where visitors can feed and pet animals, including snakes. There are daily falconry displays and informative talks. Visitors may be allowed to hold certain birds of prey.

Location
3 miles outside Tenby on the B4318

Opening
Daily; Easter–Sep 10am–6pm

Admission
Adult £4.80, Child £3.80, Concs £4.30

Contact
St Florence, Tenby
Pembrokeshire SA70 8RJ

t 01646 651201
w manorhousewildanimalpark.co.uk
e mail@manorhousewildanimal
    parkfreeserve.co.uk

674   Treharris

Llancaiach Fawr Manor

1 hr+   All year

This splendid Tudor, semi-fortified manor house, has been refurbished to its C17 state. Step back in time to the year 1645 where the servants of the household will tell you tales of their lives during the Civil War years.

* Listen to the gossip of the day – 300 years ago
* Stroll in the formal gardens

Location
On the B4254 between Nelson and Gelligaer, 2½ miles from the A470

Opening
Daily; Mon–Fri 10am–5pm
Sat & Sun 10am–6pm;
Nov–Feb closed Mon

Admission
Adult £4.95, Child £3.25, Concs £3.25

Contact
Nelson, Treharris CF46 6ER

t 01443 412248
w caerphilly.gov.uk/visiting

675   Trelewis

Welsh International Climbing & Activity Centre

4 hrs+   All year

In addition to climbing, the centre offers a wealth of indoor and outdoor activities for all abilities, including abseiling, caving, potholing, gorge walking, kayaking, mountain walking and expeditions. It also has a fitness suite and family and bunkhouse accommodation.

* One of the biggest indoor climbing walls in Europe
* High-ropes assault course

Location
From the B4255, follow signs to
Bedlinog, then ½ mile from Trewelis

Opening
Daily; Mon–Fri 9am–10pm
Sat & Sun 9am–6pm

Admission
Prices vary according to activity

Contact
Taff Bargoed Centre, Trelewis,
Merthyr Tydfil CF46 6RD

t 01443 710749
w www.indoorclimbingwalls.co.uk
e enquiries@indoorclimbingwalls.
    co.uk

669 Rhossili

Rhossili Visitor Centre

3 hrs+   All year

This National Trust visitor centre is situated adjacent to the Warren, the Down, Worm's Head, the beach and coastal cliffs, and provides information about one of the most beautiful areas of Wales. It is very popular with walkers, hang-gliders, paragliders and surfers.

* Exhibition of local history

Location
Gower Peninsula, from Swansea via A4118 and then B4247

Opening
Jan–Mar Sat & Sun 11am–4pm
Apr–Oct daily 10.30am–5.30pm
Nov & Dec Wed–Sun 11am–4pm

Admission
Free

Contact
Coastguard Cottages, Rhossili, Swansea SA3 1PR
t 01792 390707
w nationaltrust.org.uk
e rhossili@nationaltrust.org.uk

670 Swansea

Craig-y-nos Country Park

2 hrs   All year

An ideal place for a stroll through trees, alongside water and in grassy meadows. There are no rides, amusements, playgrounds or machines, just 40 acres of historic gardens to enjoy. The centre has a 'go-wild' zone for kids where they can listen to bats and climb inside a rotten tree.

Location
Mid-way between Brecon & Swansea on the A4067

Opening
Please phone for details

Admission
Free. Car park charge

Contact
Brecon Road, Pen-y-cae, Swansea Valley SA9 1GL
t 01639 730395
w breconbeacons.org
e cyncp@breconbeacons.org

671 St David's

St David's Cathedral

1 hr+   All year

This beautiful cathedral is built on the site of St David's C6 monastery. It has been a site of pilgrimage and worship for hundreds of years and continues to serve the local community. It is the only chapter within the UK of which the Queen is a member.

* Exhibition of Celtic carved stone
* 90-minute tours

Location
Near the centre of St David's

Opening
Tours Jul & Aug Mon, Tue, Thu, Fri at 2.30pm. Please book 3 weeks ahead at other times

Admission
Free, but suggested donation of £1–£2
Tours Adult £3, Child £1.20

Contact
RG Tarr, 23 Maes–yr–Hedydd, St David's, Pembrokeshire SA62 6QW
t 01437 720691
w stdavidscathedral.org.uk
e tours@stdavidscathedral.org.uk

672 Tenby

Heatherton Country Sports Park

4 hrs   All year

This leisure park has a wide range of activities including clay-pigeon shooting, coarse fishing, archery, pitch and putt, indoor bowls, baseball, karting, paintball, adventure golf, horse-riding, bumper boats, a driving range and a maze. Suitable for groups and birthday parties.

Location
2 miles outside Tenby on the B4318 Tenby–Pembroke road

Opening
Daily; Jun–Sep 10am–10pm
Oct–May 10am–6pm;
closed 25, 26 Dec & 1 Jan

Admission
Free. Pay-as-you-go activities

Contact
St Florence, Tenby, Pembrokeshire SA69 9EE
t 01646 651025
w heatherton.co.uk

667 Narbeth

Colby Woodland Garden

3 hrs   Apr–Oct

This attractive woodland garden has a fine collection of rhododendrons and azaleas. There are beautiful walks through secluded valleys along open and wooded pathways. The house is not open to the public but there is access to the walled garden.

* Regular guided walks with garden staff

Location
1 mile inland from Amroth, follow signs from A477 (Tenby/Carmarthen)

Opening
Daily; Apr–Oct 10am–5pm

Admission
Adult £3.40, Child £1.70

Contact
Amroth, Narberth SA67 8PP

t 01834 811885
w nationaltrust.org.uk

668 Neath

Aberdulais Falls

½ hr+   Mar–Dec

For over 400 years this famous waterfall provided the energy to drive the wheels of industry, from copper to tinplate. A unique hydro-electricity scheme makes Aberdulais Falls energy self–sufficient, producing power using a giant waterwheel.

* The waterwheel is the largest used in Europe
* Visited by famous artists, such as Turner in 1796

Location
On A4109, 3 miles NE of Neath, 4 miles from junction 43 of M4

Opening
Mar Fri–Sun 11am–4pm
Daily; April–Oct Mon–Fri 10am–5pm
Sat & Sun 11am–6pm
7 Nov–21 Dec Fri–Sun 11am–4pm

Admission
Adults £3.20, Child £1.60

Contact
Aberdulais,
nr Neath SA10 8EU

t 01639 636674
w nationaltrust.org.uk

663 Carmarthen

National Botanic Garden of Wales

2 hrs+   All year

The first national botanic garden in the UK for over 200 years, it is dedicated to conservation, science, education, leisure and the arts. Set in the former C18 park of Middleton Hall, this 568-acre estate enjoys a pollution-free environment, spectacular views and a rich heritage.

* Outdoor art installations
* Regular calendar of special events

Location
On the A48 near Carmarthen, signed from the M4 and A40

Opening
Daily; Easter–Oct 10am–6pm
Oct–Mar 10am–4.30pm

Admission
Adult £6.95, Child £3.50, Concs £5

Contact
Garden of Wales, Llanarthne, Carmarthenshire SA32 8HG
t 01558 668768
w gardenofwales.org.uk
e reception@gardenofwales.org.uk

664 Chepstow

Tintern Abbey

1 hr   All year

This Cistercian abbey is one of the greatest monastic ruins of Wales. Since the early C20 every effort has been made to maintain one of the finest and most complete abbey churches in the country. A favourite of many artists.

* Site exhibition
* Audio tour & Braille plan

Location
Off the A466 4m N of Chepstow

Opening
Daily; 1 Apr–1 Jun 9.30am–5pm
2 Jun–28 Sep 9.30am–6pm
29 Sep–26 Oct 9.30am–5pm
27 Oct–31 Mar Mon–Sat 9.30am–4pm
Sun 11am–4pm

Admission
Adult £3, Child £2.50, Concs £2.50

Contact
Cadw, Welsh Historic Monuments, Cathays Park, Cardiff CF10 3NQ
t 01291 689251
w cadw.wales.gov.uk
e phillip.stallard.cadw@wales.gsi.gov.uk

665 Dan-yr-Ogof

National Showcaves Centre for Wales

2 hrs+   Apr–Oct

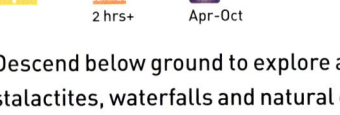

Descend below ground to explore a wonderland of stalactites, waterfalls and natural cave formations extending over 10 kilometres. The tour of the showcaves is self-guided but commentaries play at selected points so you can enjoy a visit at your own speed.

* Wales Top Day Out award winner 2003
* Heritage Education Trust winner 2003

Location
On A4067 between Swansea and Brecon. Signed from junction 45 of the M4

Opening
Daily; Apr–Oct 10am–3pm

Admission
Adult £9, Child £6

Contact
Dan-yr-Ogof, nr Abercraf, Upper Swansea Valley, Powys SA9 1GJ
t 01639 730801
w www.showcaves.co.uk
e james@showcaves.co.uk

666 Monmouth

Caldicot Castle & Country Park

2 hrs+   Mar–Oct

Founded by the Normans, developed in royal hands as a stronghold in the Middle Ages and restored as a Victorian family home, the castle is set in 55 acres of beautiful park-land. Take an audio tour, explore the medieval towers and enjoy breath-taking views from the battlements.

Location
From the M4 take junction 23 & the B4245. From the M48 take junction 2, the A48 & B4245. Signed from the B4245

Opening
Daily; Mar–Oct 11am–5pm

Admission
Please phone for details

Contact
Church Road
Monmouthshire NP26 4HU
t 01291 420241
w caldicotcastle.co.uk

661 Cardiff

Techniquest

2 hrs+   All year

This Science Discovery Centre in Cardiff Bay has over 150 hands–on exhibits that will bring science and technology to life. Among the amazing activities, visitors can fire a rocket, launch a hot–air balloon, play a giant keyboard and much more.

* Explore the universe in the planetarium
* Enjoy a fascinating interactive Science Theatre Show

Location
Exit M4 at junction 33 and follow signs on the A4232

Opening
Daily; Mon–Fri 9.30am–4.30pm
Sat, Sun & Bank Holidays
10.30am–5pm

Admission
Adult £6.90, Child £4.80, Concs £4.80

Contact
Stuart Street, Cardiff CF10 5BW

t 02920 475475
w techniquest.org
e info@techniquest.org

662 Cardigan

Cardigan Heritage Centre

1 hr   Mar–Oct

Set in a converted C18 warehouse on Teifi Wharf, the centre has permanent exhibits tracing the history of Cardigan from the days before the coming of the Normans. There are also static and interactive computer displays and regularly changing exhibitions.

* Special summer interactive exhibitions
* Guided tours by appointment

Location
Take the A487 to Cardigan. The centre is on the bank of the River Teifi, next to Cardigan bridge

Opening
Daily; Mid Mar–Oct from 10am–5pm

Admission
Adult £2, Child £1, Concs £1.50

Contact
Teifi Wharf, Cardigan, Wales

t 01239 614404

659 Cardiff

Millennium Stadium Tours

1 hr   All year

Experience the moments before a match when Wales charge down the players' tunnel cheered on by tens of thousands of rugby and football fans. Feel the pre-match tension and the joy of victory in the changing rooms before celebrating in the Cardiff Arms Suite.

* Sit in the Royal box & lift a trophy

Location
Cardiff city centre

Opening
Daily 10am–5pm

Admission
Adult £5, Child £2.50, Concs £3

Contact
Millennium Stadium Shop,
Gate 3, Westgate St,
Cardiff CF10 1GE

t 02920 822040
w cardiff-stadium.co.uk

660 Cardiff

Museum of Welsh Life

3 hrs+   All year

Standing in the grounds of the magnificent St Fagan's Castle, this museum shows how the people of Wales have lived, worked and spent their leisure time over the last 500 years. Over 30 buildings have been moved from various parts of Wales and reassembled here.

* Exhibitions of costume, daily life & farming tools
* Regular festivals of traditional music & dance

Location
4 miles W of Cardiff city centre
Exit junction 33 from the M4

Opening
Daily 10am–5pm

Admission
Free

Contact
St Fagan's, Cardiff CF5 6XB

t 02920 573500
w nmgw.ac.uk
e post@nmgw.ac.uk

656 Blaenafon

Big Pit National Mining Museum

3 hrs+   Feb–Nov

This is a real colliery. Kitted out in helmet, cap–lamp and battery pack, you descend 300 feet (90 metres) to another world. This is a world of shafts, coal faces and levels, of underground roadways, air doors and stables. Includes new interactive exhibitions.

* Enjoy simulated mining
* Winding engine–house, blacksmith's workshop

Location
Leave M4 at junction 25a/26, follow signs from the A465

Opening
Daily; Feb–Nov 9.30am–5.00pm
Underground tours run from 10.00am–3.30pm

Admission
Free

Contact
Blaenafon, Torfaen NP4 9XP
t 01495 790311
w nmgw.ac.uk
e bigpit@nmgw.ac.uk

657 Caerphilly

Caerphilly Castle

1 hr+   All year

Caerphilly Castle is one of the most impressive examples of medieval castle building in Great Britain. Spread over some 30 acres of land, this is the second largest castle in the UK after Windsor. In the words of the poet Tennyson, 'It isn't a castle – it's a town in ruins'.

* 45-minute audio tours
* Many summer demonstrations & events

Location
Exit the M4 at junction 32 and take the A470 or A469 for Caerphilly

Opening
Daily; 1 Apr–1 June 9.30am–5pm
2 Jun–28 Sep 9.30am–6pm
29 Sep–26 Oct 9.30am–5pm
27 Oct–31 Mar Mon–Sat 9.30am–4.30pm
Sun 11am–4pm

Admission
Adult £3, Child £2.50, Concs £2.50

Contact
Bridge Street, Caerphilly,
Wales CF83 1JD
t 02920 883143
w cadw.wales.gov.uk
e caerphilly.castle@cadw.co.uk

658 Cardiff

Cardiff Castle

2 hrs+   All year

Cardiff Castle is one of Wales' leading tourist attractions. Situated in the very heart of the capital, alongside city-centre shopping and the magnificent Bute Park, the Castle's enchanting fairytale towers conceal an elaborate and splendid interior.

* Guided tours of lavish & opulent interiors
* Set in beautiful grounds

Location
Cardiff city centre

Opening
Daily Mar–Oct 9.30am–6pm
Nov–Feb 9.30am–5pm

Admission
Adult £6, Child £3.70, Concs £3.70

Contact
Castle Street, Cardiff CF10 3RB
t 029 20 878100
w cardiffcastle.com
e cardiffcastle@cardiff.gov.uk

654 Minfford

Portmeirion

4 hrs+   All year

This unique village is set on a private peninsula on the southern shores of Snowdonia. It was created by Welsh architect Clough Williams-Ellis (1883–1978) to demonstrate how a naturally beautiful place could be developed without spoiling it.

* Used as location for cult TV series *The Prisoner*
* Cottages in the village let by Portmeirion Hotel

Location
Signed off the A487 at Minffordd between Penrhyndeudraeth and Porthmadog

Opening
Daily 9.30am–5.30pm

Admission
Adult £6, Child £3, Concs £5

Contact
Gwynedd, LL48 6ET

t 01766 770000
w portmeirion-village.com
e info@portmeirion-village.com

655 Porthmadog

The Ffestiniog Railway

4 hrs+   All year

Take a 13-mile ride on this historical railway. For 140 years, steam-hauled trains have run from the harbour at Porthmadog to the mountains at Blaenau Ffestiniog, passing farmland and forest, mountains and moors, lakes and waterfalls.

* Regular special events
* Refurbished café/bar at Harbour Station

Location
Next to harbour in Porthmadog on A487.

Opening
Daily Mar–Nov, limited winter service please phone for details

Admission
Adult £14, Child £7 (adult price includes 1 child)

Contact
Harbour Station, Porthmadog, Gwynedd LL49 9NF

t 01766 516000
w festrail.co.uk
e info@festrail.co.uk

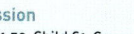

652 Llanberis

Snowdon Mountain Railway

2¹/₂ hrs   Mar–Nov

This tremendously ambitious feat of engineering, is unique in Britain. The rack and pinion railway, which rises to within 66ft of the summit of the highest mountain in England and Wales (3560ft), was built and opened in 1896.

* 30-minute stay at the top, single tickets available
* Breathtaking views from the train & the summit

Location
Llanberis Station on the A4086, 7¹/₂ miles from Caernarfon. 15 mins drive from A55/A5 junction at Bangor. Nearest railway station is Bangor

Opening
Daily mid-March–1 Nov
Please phone for details

Admission
Adult £20, Child £14, Concs £17

Contact
Llanberis,
Gwynedd LL55 4TY

t 0870 4580033
w snowdonrailway.co.uk
e info@snowdonrailway.co.uk

653 Llanrwst

Amgueddfa Sir Henry Jones Museum

1 hr   May–Sep

The childhood home of Sir Henry Jones is now a museum of rural life where visitors can learn more about him. See the tiny kitchen where a family of six once ate, see displays of Victorian life in Wales, or relax in the authentically restored cottage garden.

Location
On the A548 Abergele to Llanrwst road in Llangernyw. Follow the signs from the car park

Opening
May–Sep Tue–Fri & Bank Hols
10.30am–1pm & 2pm–5pm,
Sat & Sun 2pm–5pm

Admission
Adult £1.50, Child £1, Concs £1

Contact
Y Cwm, Llangernyw Abergele,
North Wales LL22 8PR

t 01745860661
w sirhenryjones-museums.org
e info@sirhenryjones-museums.org

648 Conwy

The Royal Cambrian Academy

½ hr+   All year

The most prestigious Art institution in Wales has been in Conwy for over 121 years. Members come from all parts of the UK, but the majority come from Wales. The work shown is a true reflection of contemporary Welsh art.

* Exhibited paintings are for sale
* Exhibitions change regularly

Location
In the centre of Conwy, just off High Street behind Plas Mawr

Opening
Tue–Sat 11am–5pm
Sun 1pm–4.30pm

Admission
Free

Contact
Crown Lane,
Conwy LL32 8AN
t 01492 593413
w rcaconwy.org
e info@rcaconwy.org

649 Ffestiniog

Hydro Centre – Ffestiniog Power Station

1 hr   Jun–Sep

After a talk about generating electricity, visitors are taken on a tour of Britain's first hydro-electricity station. See the machine hall, generators, turbines, interactive models and displays. Drive to the top of the dam for magnificent views.

* Visitors must be able to climb 160 steep steps
* No children under four

Location
A487 N of Ffestiniog

Opening
Jun–Sep Sun–Fri 10am–4.30pm
Easter & half-terms Sun–Fri
10am–4.30pm

Admission
Adult £4, Child £2, Concs £2.50
Visit to Stwlan Dam £3 per car

Contact
Tan-y-Grisiau,
Blaenau Ffestiniog LL41 3TP
t 01766 830465
w fhc.co.uk
e hydrocentre@edisonmission.com

650 Gwynedd

Greenwood Forest Park

4 hrs+   Mar–Oct

Lots of fun for the whole family. Pull yourself on a boat through the jungle, use a traditional longbow, build a den in the wildwood, put your brain cells to the test in the puzzle barn, explore the maze, walk on stilts, see bees at work, feel the heat of the desert and the force of a sandstorm.

* The only forest park in North Wales
* The longest sledge slide in Wales

Location
Take the A4144, leading to the B4366

Opening
Daily; 20 Mar–31 Aug 10am–5.30pm
Sep & Oct 10am–5pm

Admission
Please phone for details

Contact
Y Felinheli, Gwynedd
North Wales LL56 4QN
t 01248 671493
w greenwood-centre.co.uk
e info@greenwood-centre.co.uk

651 Llangollan

Llangollan Wharf

1 hr+   Easter–Oct

Take a horse-drawn boat trip or a motorised aqueduct cruise along the beautiful Llangollen Canal. Longer horse-drawn trips can be arranged for large groups, and lunches and cream teas can be pre-ordered. Self-steer day-hire boat for groups of up to 10 people also available.

Location
Off the A5 Shrewsbury road & near the A483 to Chester

Opening
Daily; Easter–Oct 10am–5pm

Admission
Horse-drawn boats Adult £4, Child £2.50
Aqueduct cruise Adult £7.50, Child £6.50

Contact
Welsh Canal Holiday Craft Ltd
The Wharf,
Llangollen LL20 8TA
t 01978 860702

645 Chirk

Pony & Quad Treks

1-4 hrs   Easter–Oct

Explore the beautiful and spectacular scenery of the Ceiriog Valley and stunning Ceiriog River in North Wales on horseback or quad bike. Horses and ponies for all abilities, off-roading for all tastes.

* Full safety equipment provided
* Full protective clothing available

Location
8 miles from Chirk on B4500

Opening
Daily; Easter–Oct 10.30am–4pm

Admission
Pony trekking day £45, 2 hrs £25, 1 hr £15.
Quad trekking 1 hr £25, 1/2 hr £15

Contact
Pont-y-Meibion, Pandy, Glyn Ceiriog, Chirk, Llangollen, North Wales LL20 7HS

t 01691 718333/718413
w ponytreks.co.uk
e enquiry@ponytreks.co.uk

646 Colwyn Bay

The Welsh Mountain Zoo

4 hrs+   All year

Set within 37 acres of woodland, the zoo has a wide range of animals from lions and tigers to monkeys and pandas. The gardens are home to hardy and tropical plants, some rare and endangered. Facilities include a Tarzan trail adventure playground and a media centre.

* Children's farm & Jungle Adventureland

Location
3 mins from the A55 (Rhos-on-Sea exit), follow the signs

Opening
Daily; summer 9.30am–6pm, winter 9.30am–5pm

Admission
Adult £6.95, Child £4.95, Concs £5.95

Contact
Old Highway, Colwyn Bay, North Wales LL28 5UY

t 01492 532938
w welshmountainzoo.org

647 Conwy

Conwy Castle

1 hr+   All year

This gritty, dark-stoned fortress has the rare ability to evoke an authentic medieval atmosphere. Commanding a rock above the Conwy Estuary, the castle demands as much attention as the dramatic Snowdonia skyline behind it.

* One of the great fortresses of medieval Europe
* Marvellous floodlit night time views

Location
On the B5106 off the A55. Railway station is next to the castle

Opening
Daily; 1 Apr–1 Jun 9.30am–5pm
2 Jun–28 Sep 9.30am–6pm
29 Sep–26 Oct 9.30am–5pm
27 Oct–31 Mar Mon–Sat 9.30am–4pm
Sun 11am–4pm

Admission
Adult £3.75, Child £3.25, Concs£3.25

Contact
Cadw,
Conwy LL32 8LD

t 01492 592358
w cadw.wales.gov.uk

641 Caernarfon

Caernarfon Castle

1 hr+   All year

Designed to replicate the walls of Constantinople, with its unique polygonal towers, intimidating battlements and colour-banded masonry, the castle dominates the town. In 1969, the castle was the setting for the investiture of Prince Charles as Prince of Wales.

* A World Heritage site
* Houses the museum of the Royal Welsh Fusiliers

Location
In Caernarfon town centre on the A55
Nearest railway station, Bangor

Opening
Daily: Apr–May 9.30am–5pm
Jun–Sep 9.30am–6pm
29 Sep–26 Oct 9.30am–5pm
27 Oct–31 Mar Mon–Sat 9.30am–4pm
Sun 11am–4pm

Admission
Adult £4.50, Child £3.50, Concs £3.50

Contact
Castle Ditch, Caernarfon,
Gwynedd LL55 2AY

t 01286 677617
w cadw.wales.gov.uk

642 Caernarfon

Plas Menai National Watersports Centre

2–7 days   All year

Sailing, canoeing, windsurfing, yachting, powersports and mountain activities. This centre has a fantastic range of activity courses scheduled all year round for every level of ability.

* Residential & non-residential courses
* Great low-season savings during the winter

Location
2 miles N of Caernarfon on A487

Opening
Daily

Admission
Prices vary per course. Please phone or check website for details

Contact
Llanfairisgaer, Caernarfon,
Gwynedd LL55 1UE

t 01248 670964
w plasmenai.co.uk
e plas.menai@scw.co.uk

643 Caernarfon

Welsh Highland Railway

3 hrs   All year

Take a 12-mile ride, from the coast to the slopes of Snowdon, on North Wales' newest railway. Enjoy the spectacular scenery of lakes, mountains and forest en route to the heart of Snowdonia itself.

Location
Main station on St Helens Road in Caernarfon, signed from A487

Opening
Daily Mar–Nov, limited winter service, please phone for details

Admission
Adult £14, Child £7, Concs £11.20
(Adult price includes 1 child)

Contact
Harbour Station, Porthmadog,
Gwynedd LL49 9NF

t 01766 516073
w festrail.co.uk
e info@festrail.co.uk

644 Chirk

Chirk Castle

2 hrs   Mar–Oct

A magnificent Marcher fortress, completed in 1310. The austere exterior belies the comfortable and elegant state rooms inside, with elaborate plasterwork, superb Adam-style furniture, tapestries and portraits. Formal garden of clipped yew, roses and climbers.

* Informal area with thatched cottage
* Terrace with stunning views, a classical pavilion

Location
1 mile off A5, 2 miles W of Chirk

Opening
18 Mar–30 Oct Wed–Sun 12noon–5pm

Admission
Adult £6.40, Child £3.20

Contact
Chirk,
Wrexham LL14 5AF

t 01691 777701
w nationaltrust.org.uk
e chirkcastle@nationaltrust.org.uk

638 Anglesea

Anglesey Sea Zoo

2 hrs+   Feb–Oct

This is Wales' largest marine aquarium, nestling on the shores of the Menai Strait. With over 50 displays, the Sea Zoo has recreated the habitats of the fauna and flora found around Anglesey and the North Wales coastline.

* Major seahorse conservation project
* Lobster hatchery & gift shop

Location
On the A55, cross the Britannia Bridge onto Anglesey and follow the brown lobster signs to Brynsiencyn. Nearest train station Bangor then no. 42 bus.

Opening
Daily; Feb–Mar 11am–3pm
Easter–Oct 10am–6pm

Admission
Adult £5.95, Child £4.95, Concs £5.50

Contact
Brynsiencyn,
Isle of Anglesey LL61 6TQ

t 01248 430411
w angleseyseazoo.co.uk
e info@angleseyzoo.co.uk

640 Blaenau Ffestiniog

Llechwedd Slate Caverns

2 hrs   All year

Two underground train rides: The Miner's Tramway takes passengers into the mountain, past early Victorian mining remains and spectacular caverns. The Deep Mine descends on Britain's steepest passenger railway, with a gradient of 1 to 1.8.

* Explore ten chambers on foot
* Experience life in theVictorian Village

Location
On the A470 between Blaenau Ffestiniog & Dolwyddelan

Opening
Daily from 10am

Admission
Adult £8.25, Child £6.25, Concs £7

Contact
Blaenau Ffestiniog LL41 3NB

t 01766 830 306
w llechwedd-slate-caverns.co.uk
e info@llechwedd-slatecaverns.co.uk

639 Anglesey

Plas Newydd

3 hrs   Mar–Nov

This C18 house built by Wyatt is an interesting mixture of classical and Gothic. Restyled in the 1930s, the house is famous for its association with Whistler, whose work is exhibited.There is also a museum for the 1st Marquess of Anglesey who led the cavalry at The Battle of Waterloo.

* A marine walk on the Menai Strait
* Fine spring garden with Australasian arboretum

Location
Junction 7 & 8 off A55

Opening
19 Mar–2 Nov Sat–Wed
Gardens 11am–5pm
House 12pm–5pm

Admission
Adult £5, Child £2.50

Contact
Llanfairpwll,
Anglesey LL61 6DQ

t 01248 715272/714795
w nationaltrust.org.uk
e plasnewydd@nationaltrust.org.uk

637 Welshpool

Powis Castle & Garden

3 hrs   Mar–Oct

This world-famous garden, overhung with enormous clipped yews, shelters rare and tender plants, statues, an orangery and an aviary on the terraces. The medieval castle contains one of the finest collections of paintings and furniture in Wales.

* Collection of Indian treasures at the Clive museum
* Beautiful interiors dating from 1600–1904

Location
1 mile S of Welshpool signed from A483

Opening
31 Mar–31 Oct Thu–Mon
Garden 11am–6pm
Castle 1pm–5pm
Mar & Oct 1pm–4pm

Admission
Adult £8.80, Child £4.40

Contact
Welshpool, SY21 8RF

t 01938 551944
w nationaltrust.org.uk
e powiscastle@nationaltrust.org.uk

© Eithel Powell 2003

633 Machynlleth

Celtica

1 hr+   All year

A unique and stimulating experience of Celtic heritage and culture. Your journey takes you through eight galleries – the foundry, the origins gallery, the village, the roundhouse, the forest, the otherworld, the vortex and Yma o Hyd. A headset provides commentary.

* Award-winning attraction
* Member of Dyfi Valley Attractions

Location
In Machynlleth village

Opening
Daily 10am–6pm; closed Christmas

Admission
Adult £4.95, Child £3.95, Concs £4.30

Contact
Y Plas, Machynlleth,
Powys SY20 8ER

t 01654 702702
w www.celticawales.com
e celtica@celticawales.com

634 Machynlleth

Centre for Alternative Technology

3 hrs+   All year

This is a 40-acre haven of biodiversity. It has examples of wind, water and solar power; energy conservation; environmentally-sound buildings; self-builds; organic agriculture and alternative sewage systems. In summer, entry is via a unique water-balanced cliff railway.

* The largest public display centre of its kind in Europe
* Multi-award winner

Location
3 miles N of Machynlleth on the A487 to Dolgellau. Clearly signed

Opening
Daily; Sep–Oct 10am–5pm
Nov–Mar 10am–4pm
Apr–Jul 10am–5pm
Aug–Sep 9.30am–6pm

Admission
Adult £7.90, Child £4.50, Concs £5.50

Contact
Machynlleth,
Powys, SY20 9AZ

t 01654 705950
w www.cat.org.uk
e information@cat.org.uk

635 Machynlleth

King Arthur's Labyrinth

2 hrs+   Mar–Nov

Take a boat underground through a waterfall and deep into the spectacular caverns under the mountains where tales of King Arthur are told with stunning sound and light effects. Back above ground, join the Bard's Quest to search for legends lost in the Maze of Time.

* Large fully operational craft centre
* Shop sells items on the Arthurian theme

Location
On the A487 between Machynlleth and Dolgellau

Opening
Daily; 19 Mar–6 Nov 10am–5pm

Admission
Adult £5.15, Child £3.60, Concs £4.60

Contact
Corris, Machynlleth,
Powys SY20 9RF

t 01654 761584
w kingarthurslabyrinth.com
e king.arthurs.labyrinth@corriswales.
   co.uk

636 Rhayader

Gigrin Farm

1 hr+   All year

A family-run, upland sheep farm with wonderful views of the Wye and Elan valleys. It has 400 breeding ewes along with ponies, assorted ducks and a number of pea fowl. In 1994 it became the Official Kite Country, Red Kite feeding station.

* Farm & nature trail
* New wetland project

Location
On the A470, ½ mile south of Rhayader

Opening
Daily 1pm–5pm

Admission
Adult £2.50, Child £1, Concs £2

Contact
South Street, Rhayader,
Powys LD6 5BL

t 01597 810243
w redkitecentre.co.uk
e kites@gigrin.co.uk

630 Llangorse

Llangorse Rope and Riding Centre

4 hrs+   All year

The centre offers a range of indoor and outdoor climbing and riding activities, from rock surfaces and rope bridges to trekking and hacking. There's also caving, canoeing and mountain-biking for all ages and abilities, plus qualified instructors and on-site accommodation.

* Largest indoor climbing & riding centre in Wales
*WTB's Best New Business in Wales award

Location
On B4560, off A40 (Brecon to Abergavenny road)

Opening
Climb Daily; Mon–Sat 9am–10pm, Sun 9am–6pm
Ride Daily; 9.30am–4.30pm; closed 25,26 Dec and 1 Jan

Admission
Adult climb: £12, Trek £16

Contact
Gilfach Farm, Llangorse, Brecon Beacons, Powys, LD3 7UH

t 01874 658 272
w www.activityuk.com
e info@1001daysout.com

631 Llannwrda

Dolaucothi Gold Mines

2 hrs   Easter–Oct

These unique gold mines are set amid wooded, hillsides overlooking the beautiful Cothi Valley. The Romans, who exploited the site almost 2000 years ago, left behind a complex of pits, channels, adits and tanks. Mining resumed in the C19 and peaked in 1938.

* Historical tours
* Opportunity to pan for gold

Location
Between Lampeter and Llanwrda on A482

Opening
Daily; Easter–Oct 10am–5pm

Admission
Adult £3, Child £1.50

Contact
Pumsaint,
Llanwrda SA19 8US

t 01558 650177
w nationaltrust.org.uk
e dolaucothi@nationaltrust.org.uk

632 Llanwyddyn

Lake Vyrnwy Nature Reserve

2 hrs+   All year

This man-made lake was completed in 1888. In dry weather, if the water level drops far enough, the ruins of the submerged village of Llanwyddyn reappear. With various hides, vantage points and nature trails, it is a spectacular place for birdwatching.

* Moorland, woodland & water habitats
* Good birdwatching all year round

Location
10 miles W of Llanfyllin

Opening
Apr–Dec 10.30am–5.30pm
Jan–Mar Sat & Sun only

Admission
Free

Contact
Brynawel, Llanwyddyn, Powys SY10 0LZ

t 01691 870278
w rspb.org.uk
e vyrnwy@rspb.org.uk

626 Aberystwyth

Animalarium

3 hrs   All year

Home to a wide collection of exotic and domestic animals, birds and reptiles, including monkeys, marmosets, lemurs, and wallabies. Pony rides twice daily from Easter–September. There is a petting barn, a fruit bat cave and a daily snake-handling demonstration.

* Wales Tourist Board seal of approval

Location
At Borth, between Aberystwyth & Machynlleth

Opening
Daily; summer 10am–6pm
winter 11am–4pm

Admission
Adult £4.90, Child £2.80, Concs £4

Contact
Borth,
Ceredigion SY25 6RA

t 01970 871224

627 Aberystwyth

Vale of Rheidol Railway

1 hr+   Apr–Oct

Take a ride on a steam train for 11 miles from Aberystwyth to Devil's Bridge. During the hour-long journey you'll have spectacular views of the wooded Rheidol Valley. From Devil's Bridge, there are walks to Mynach Falls, Devil's Punchbowl and Jacob's Ladder.

* One of the Great Little Trains of Wales
* The last steam railway owned by British Rail

Location
Trains depart from Aberystwyth centre, beside the main railway station

Opening
Please phone for details

Admission
Return Adult £11.50, Child from £2.50, Concs £10.50

Contact
Park Avenue, Aberystwyth, Cardiganshire SY23 1PG

t 01970 625819
w www.rheidolrailway.co.uk
e vor@rheidolrailway.co.uk

628 Brecon

Brecon Beacons National Park Visitor Centre

1 hr+   All year

The attractions of the Brecon Beacons National Park range from lush, green, open countryside to historical and cultural heritage. There are attractions to suit all the family including museums, theatres and family activity centres, plus beautiful walks and rides.

* Centre of internationally renowned festivals
* Selection of guided walks available

Location
The National Park Mountain Centre is 5½ miles SW of Brecon

Opening
Daily; Mar–Jun & Sep–Oct
9.30am–5pm,
Jul–Aug 9.30am–6pm
Nov–Feb 9.30am–4.30pm

Admission
Free, car park charges vary

Contact
NPVC, Libanus, Brecon,
Powys LD3 8ER

t 01874 623366
w breconbeacons.org
e mountaincentre@breconbeacons.org

629 Cardigan

Felinwynt Rainforest & Butterfly Centre

1 hr+   Easter–Oct

This tropical rainforest in the heart of Wales is home to exotic and unusual plants, birds, insects and butterflies from all over the world. You'll see the American glass-wing butterfly, the Asian scarlet swallowtail and the Indian moon moth.

* Welsh Tourist Board star attraction

Location
Off the A487, 6 miles N of Cardigan. Follow the brown tourist signs

Opening
Daily; Easter–Oct 10.30am–5pm
Limited opening in winter

Admission
Adult £3.75, Child £1.50, Concs £3.50

Contact
Felinwynt, Cardigan
Ceredigion SA43 1RT

t 01239 810882/810250
w butterflycentre.co.uk

The Gribbin Cliffs, Dyfed

Wales

Mid Wales North Wales South Wales

623 Worcester

Witley Court

  2 hrs All year

An early Jacobean manor house, Witley Court was converted in the C19 into a vast Italianate mansion with porticoes by John Nash. The spectacular ruins of this once great house are surrounded by magnificent landscaped gardens.

* Huge stone fountains that once shot 120 feet upwards
* £1m garden renovation in last two years

Location
10 miles NW of Worcester on A443

Opening
Daily; Apr–Oct 10am–6pm (Oct 5pm);
Nov–Mar Wed–Sun 10am–4pm

Admission
Adult £4.60, Child £2.30, Concs £3.50

Contact
Great Witley WR6 6JT

t 01299 896636
w english-heritage.org.uk
e mark.badger@english-heritage.
   org.uk

624 Worcester

Worcester Cathedral

  1 hr All year

Worcester Cathedral has been a place of prayer and worship since 680 AD. The present building was begun in 1084. Its many attractions include: King John's tomb, Prince Arthur's Chantry, the early C12 Chapter House and St Wulstan's crypt.

* Tower open 10am–4.30pm, Sat & summer holidays
* Magnificent Victorian stained glass windows

Location
City centre, off College Street

Opening
Daily; 7.30am–6pm,
services three times daily

Admission
Free, donations welcome

Contact
10A College Green, Worcester,
WR1 2LH

t 01905 28854
w cofe-worcester.org.uk
e info@worcestercathedral.org.uk

625 Upton-upon-Severn

Upton Heritage Centre

  1 hr+ All year

Located in the oldest surviving building in Upton, the Pepperpot, are displays illustrating the growth and development of the town and its involvement in the Civil War of 1651.

* Battle of Upton display
* Sited in old bell tower

Location
On the B4211 from Great Malvern &
the A38 & A4104 from Worcester

Opening
Daily, 1 Apr 30 Sep 1.30pm 4.30pm,
Open some mornings
Please phone for details

Admission
Free

Contact
Church Street, Upton-upon-Severn,
Worcester, WR8 0HT

t 01684 592679

620 Worcester

Royal Worcester Porcelain Works

  3 hrs+   All year

Recently refurbished and doubled in size, the museum displays the world's largest collection of Worcester Porcelain. See Georgian, Victorian and C20 galleries that showcase how styles dramatically changed through time, using room sets, shop fronts and period scenes.

* One of the world's leading ceramics museums
* Huge variety of porcelain, bone china & earthenware

Location
3 miles from junction 7 of M5, follow signs to city centre – near cathedral

Opening
Daily; Mon–Sat 9am–5.30pm Sun 11am–5pm

Admission
Prices vary. See website or phone for details

Contact
Severn Street, Worcester WR1 2NE

t 01905 746 000
w royalworcester.com
e rwgeneral@royal-worcester.co.uk

621 Worcester

Sir Edward Elgar Birthplace Museum

  1 hr   Feb–Dec

The cottage and the Elgar Centre together tell the story of Sir Edward Elgar, the composer of much of England's best known classical music. Visit his study with his gramophone. See family photographs and countless mementos including his books and his golf clubs.

* In the Elgar Centre see manuscripts and music scores
* Watch historic film of his final years

Location
3 miles from Worcester on A44 towards Leominster

Opening
Daily; 11am–5pm
Closed 23 Dec–1 Feb

Admission
Adult £4.50, Child £2, Concs £4

Contact
Crown East Lane, Lower Broadheath WR2 6RH

t 01905 333 224
w elgarmuseum.org
e birthplace@elgarmuseum.org

622 Worcester

Spetchley Park Garden

  2 hrs   Apr–Sep

Virtually hidden from the road and largely unaltered in the last century, this lovely 30-acre Victorian paradise boasts an enviable collection of plant treasures from every corner of the globe. Clipped hedges and tumbling borders to olives and pineapple–scented flowers.

* Year round colour
* Unexpected vistas provide views of the Malvern Hills

Location
2 miles E of Worcester on A44, leave M5 at junction 6

Opening
Apr–Sep Tue–Fri 11am–5pm
Sun 2pm–5pm, Bank Hols 11am–5pm
Deer park closed in Jun

Admission
Adult £4, Child £2

Contact
Spetchley, Worcester WR5 1RS

t 01905 345 213
w spetchleygardens.co.uk

616   Pershore

Croome Park

2 hrs   Mar–Dec

Croome was Capability Brown's first complete landscape, making his reputation and establishing a new style of parkland design which became universally adopted over the next 50 years. The park buildings are mostly by Robert Adam and James Wyatt.

* Ten-year restoration plan including water features
* Restoration of park buildings also in progress

Location
8 miles S of Worcester & E of A38

Opening
Park 5 Mar–31 Oct Wed–Sun 10am–5pm, 3 Nov–19 Dec Wed–Sun 10am–4pm, Open all Bank Hols 10am–4pm

Admission
Adult £3.50, Child £1.70

Contact
NT Estate Office, The Builders' Yard, High Green, Severn Stoke WR8 9JS
t 01905 371006
w nationaltrust.org.uk
e croomepark@nationaltrust.org.uk

617   Stourbridge

Hagley Hall

1 hr   Jan & Feb

Commissioned in 1756 and designed by Sanderson Miller, it was the last of the great Palladian houses to be built. Van Dyck paintings, Chippendale furniture and exquisite rococo plasterwork are displayed throughout the house.

* Surrounded by 350 acres of landscaped deer park
* See where two of the gunpowder conspirators hid

Location
E of Kidderminster, junction 4 of M5, signed from junction of A456 and A491

Opening
Jan–Feb Sun–Fri 2pm–5pm
All Bank Hols and their weekends
Times limited, please phone or check website for details

Admission
Adult £4, Child £1.50, Concs £2.50

Contact
Hagley DY9 9LG
t 01562 882408
w hagleyhallcom
e contact@hagleyhall.info

618   Worcester

The Commandery

1½ hrs   All year

The building was originally founded as a hospital in 1085 by the then Bishop of Worcester, Saint Wulfstan. Over the centuries it has been adapted for different uses while retaining the fabric of its history. It currently houses a variety of historical exhibitions.

* Try on original armour and weapons
* Relive the Battle of Worcester

Location
Just outside city walls at Sidbury Gate

Opening
Daily; Mon–Sat 10am–5pm
Sun 1.30–5pm

Admission
Adult £3.95, Child £2.95, Concs £2.95

Contact
Sidbury, Worcester WR1 2HU
t 01905 361821
w worcestercitymuseums.org.uk
e thecommandery@cityofworcester.gov.uk

619   Worcester

Leigh Court Barn

½ hr+   Apr–Sep

This is a striking example of medieval architecture. At 130 feet long and 36 feet wide (40 x 11m), the barn is the largest cruck structure in the UK. Once part of Leigh Court Manor, the barn has ten bays and two porches.

* Originally built for the monks of Pershore Abbey

Location
5 miles W of Worcester on unclassified road off A4103

Opening
Daily, Apr–Sep 10am–6pm

Admission
Free

Contact
Leigh, Worcester WR6 5LB
t 01902 765105
w english-heritage.org.uk

613 Kidderminster

Harvington Hall

2 hrs   Mar–Oct

A moated medieval and Elizabethan manor house. Many of the rooms still have their original Elizabethan wall–paintings that were discovered under whitewash in 1936. The hall also contains the finest series of priest–holes anywhere in the country.

* Elizabethan malthouse and Georgian chapel in garden
* Moat broadens into a small lake, home to waterfowl

Location
3 miles SE of Kidderminster just off A450 Birmingham to Worcester road

Opening
Mar & Oct Sat & Sun 11.30am–4.30pm
Apr–Sep Wed–Sun 11.30am–4.30pm

Admission
Adult £4.50, Child £3, Concs £3.80

Contact
Harvington, Kidderminster DY10 4LR
t 01562 777 846
w harvingtonhall.com
e thehall@harvington.
    fsbusiness.co.uk

614 Kidderminster

Worcestershire County Museum

2 hr   Feb–Nov

The museum is housed in Hartlebury Castle, home to the Bishops of Worcester for over a thousand years. In the former servants quarters of the north wing a wide range of permanent exhibitions show the past lives of the county's inhabitants, from Roman times to the C20.

* Displays include a Victorian room & transport gallery
* Programme of temporary exhibitions & events

Location
Signed from A449

Opening
Feb–Nov Mon–Thu 10am–5pm
Fri & Sun 2pm–5pm

Admission
Adult £2.50, Child & Concs £1.20

Contact
Hartlebury Castle, Stourport Road,
Hartlebury, Kidderminster DY11 7XZ
t 01299 250 416
w worcestershire.gov.uk
e museum@worcestershire.gov.uk

615 Malvern

Great Malvern Priory

½ hr   All year

Malvern Priory is one of the greater parish churches in the country. It was founded in 1085 and contains the finest collection of stained glass after York Minster, together with carved miserichords from the C15 and C16 and the largest collection of medieval floor and wall tiles.

* Venue for many concerts
* Newly restored organ for 2004

Location
Just off A449 in Malvern

Opening
Daily; Apr–Sep 9am–6.30pm
Oct–Mar 9am–4.30pm

Admission
Free, donations welcome

Contact
Church Street, Malvern WR14 2AY
t 01684 561020
w greatmalvernpriory.org.uk
e gmpriory@hotmail.com

611 Droitwich

Hanbury Hall

2 hrs+   Mar–Oct

Completed in 1701, this homely William & Mary-style house is famed for its beautiful painted ceilings and staircase, and has other fascinating features including an orangery, ice house, pavilions and working mushroom house.

* Tercentenary exhibition opened in 2001
* Garden surrounded by 160 acres of parkland

Location
Near junction 5 of M5, 5 miles
E of Droitwich

Opening
12 Mar–29 Oct Sat–Wed 1pm–5pm

Admission
Adult £5.40, Child £2.70

Contact
School Road, Droitwich WR9 7EA

t 01527 821 214
w nationaltrust.org.uk
e hanburyhall@nationaltrust.org.uk

612 Kidderminster

Bodenham Arboretum

2 hrs+   All year

Bodenham Arboretum is a collection of over 2,700 trees set in 156 acres, with 11 pools, 5 miles of footpaths and a working farm with a herd of pedigree Herefords. In addition there is an award–winning 'Earth Visitor Centre' set in the hillside overlooking the Big Pool.

* Christmas Nativity trail
* Laburnum Tunnel is a highlight in late May/June

Location
Signed from Wolverley

Opening
1 Mar–Dec daily 11am–5pm;
Jan–Mar Sat & Sun 11am–5pm

Admission
Adult £4, Child £1.50

Contact
Wolverley, Kidderminster DY11 5SY

t 01562 852 444
w bodenham-arboretum.co.uk

608   Bewdley

West Midland Safari & Leisure Park

3 hrs+   Apr–Oct

A 4-mile drive-through safari covers an area of over 150 acres and is home to a variety of exotic and unusual animals including rare and beautiful white tigers, elephants, rhinos, giraffes, lions, wallabies, emus, camels, zebras, bison, wolves, and llamas.

Location	**Contact**
On the A456 between	Spring Grove,
Kidderminster & Bewdley	Bewdley DY12 1LF
Opening	t 01299 402114
Apr–Oct	w wmsp.co.uk
Please phone for details	e info@wmsp.co.uk
Admission	
Please phone for details	

609   Broadway

Broadway Tower & Country Park

½ hr+   All year

Built on an ancient beacon site, the tower has a colourful history as – amongst others – home to the renowned printing press of Sir Thomas Phillips and country retreat for Pre-Raphaelite artists, notably the artist, designer, writer, craftsman, and socialist William Morris.

* Today houses exhibition connected with its past
* Said to be one of England's outstanding viewpoints

Location
Off A44 one mile SE of Broadway

Opening
Daily Apr–Oct 10.30–5pm;
Nov–Mar Sat, Sun 11am–3pm

Admission
Adult £3, Child £1.50, Concs £2.50

Contact
Middle Hill, Broadway WR12 7LB
t 01386 852 390
w broadway-cotswolds.co.uk
e broadwaytower1@aol.com

610   Bromsgrove

Avoncroft Museum of Historic Buildings

 ...

3 hrs   Mar–Nov

Avoncroft is a fascinating world of historic buildings covering seven centuries, rescued and rebuilt on a beautiful open–air site. You can see craftsmen working in a C19 workshop, furnished historic houses and a variety of craft demonstrations.

* Visit rural Victorian England at the Toll Cottage
* See a church, gaol and a working windmill

Location
2 miles S of Bromsgrove off A38

Opening
Mar–Oct Tue–Sun 10.30am–4.30;
Nov Sat & Sun 10.30am–4pm

Admission
Adult £6, Child £3, Concs £5

Contact
Stoke Heath,
Bromsgrove B60 4JR
t 01527 831 363
w avoncroft.org.uk
e avoncroft1@compuserve.com

605 Wolverhampton

Bantock House & Park

1 hr+   All year

This Grade II listed family home was built in 1788. The ground floor has recently been restored to its Edwardian splendour, while the upstairs features superb displays of enamels, Japanned ware and steel jewellery, with lots of hands-on activities for all ages.

* Gottle of Gear, a tribute to ventriloquism
* Programme of changing exhibitions

Location
Signed from Wolverhampton ring road

Opening
Nov–Mar Fri–Sun 12 noon–4pm
Apr–Oct Tue–Sun 10am–5pm

Admission
Free

Contact
Finchfield Road, Wolverhampton
WV3 9LQ

t 01902 552195
w wolverhampton.gov.uk

---

606 Wolverhampton

Wightwick Manor

2 hrs   Mar–Dec

This is a fine example of a house built and furnished in the Arts and Crafts movement style. The house features many original William Morris wallpapers and fabrics, Pre-Raphaelite paintings, Kempe glass and tiles by de Morgan.

* Beautiful garden designed by Thomas Mawson
* Talks and tours bring the house to life

Location
Off A454, beside the Mermaid Inn,
3 miles W of Wolverhampton

Opening
Mar–24 Dec Thu & Sat 1.30pm–5pm

Admission
Adult £6, Child £3
Timed ticket and guided tour only

Contact
Wightwick Bank, Wolverhampton
WV6 8EE

t 01902 761400
w nationaltrust.org.uk
e wightwickmanor@
nationaltrust.org.uk

---

607 Wolverhampton

Wolverhampton Art Gallery

1 hr+   All year

The gallery has an innovative programme of temporary exhibitions, alongside a series of workshops and special events. The collection includes British and American pop art as well as traditional C18 and C19 paintings by Gainsborough, Turner and Landseer.

* Contemporary art collection is the finest in the region
* Sensing Sculpture, a tactile sculpture court

Location
Opposite Tourist Information Centre

Opening
Mon–Sat 10am–5pm

Admission
Free

Contact
Lichfield Street, Wolverhampton
WV1 1DU

t 01902 552055
w wolverhamptonart.org.uk
e info@wolverhamptonart.org.uk

602 Kingswinford

Broadfield House Glass Museum

2 hrs   All year

The museum has a collection of British glass, much of which was made locally, from C18 tableware to Victorian cameo vases to modern sculptural pieces. Permanent displays and temporary exhibitions celebrate the art of glassmaking. There is also a glassmaking studio.

* Watch and wonder at the glassblowers' skills
* The Glass Dance windows made by David Prytherch

Location
Off A491, between Stourbridge & Wolverhampton

Opening
Tue–Sun & Bank Hols 10am–4pm

Admission
Free

Contact
Compton Drive, Kingswinford
DY6 9NS

t 01384 812745
w glassmuseum.org.uk
e glass.museum@dudley.gov.uk

603 Walsall

New Art Gallery

2 hrs   All year

This Arts Lottery-funded gallery opened in 2000 and is said to be one of the most exciting art galleries to be built in the UK in the last 20 years. Traditional art is showcased in the Garman Ryan Collection, donated by Lady Kathleen, widow of sculptor Sir Jacob Epstein.

* Building designed by Caruso St John Architects
* Exhibitions dedicated to best of contemporary art

Location
A454 on Wolverhampton Street

Opening
Tue–Sat & Bank Hols 10am–5pm
Sun 12 noon–5pm

Admission
Free

Contact
Gallery Square, Walsall WS2 8LG

t 01922 654400
w artatwalsall.org.uk
e info@artatwalsall.org.uk

604 Walsall

Walsall Leather Museum

2 hrs   All year

Located in the heart of Britain's saddlery and leather goods trade, this fascinating museum tells the story of Walsall's leather workers, past and present. Regular demonstrations of traditional leather crafts take place in historic workshops.

* Collection of contemporary designer leather work
* Regular exhibitions and special events

Location
On A4148

Opening
Mar–Oct Tue–Sat 10am–5pm
Sun 12 noon–5pm
Nov–Apr Tue–Sat 10am–4pm
Sun 12 noon–4pm

Admission
Free

Contact
Littleton Street West, Walsall WS2 8EQ

t 01922 721153
w walsall.gov.uk/leathermuseum
e leathermuseum@walsall.gov.uk

600 Dudley

Dudley Museum & Art Gallery

½ hr+   All year

This museum contains a collection of C17, C18 and C19 British and European paintings, furniture and ceramics, together with oriental ceramics, Japanese netsuke and inro, Bilston enamels, commemorative medals, and Greek, Roman and Egyptian pottery.

* Geological collection of fossils, rock and minerals
* Regular and varied art exhibitions

Location
Off Priory Street, nr bus station

Opening
Mon–Sat 10am–4pm

Admission
Free

Contact
St James' Road, Dudley DY1 1HU

t 01384 815575
w dudley.gov.uk
e dudley.museums@dudley.gov.uk

601 Edgbaston

Birmingham Botanical Gardens & Glasshouses

2 hrs+   All year

The gardens originally opened in 1832 and today tropical, Mediterranean and desert glasshouses stand in 15 acres of beautiful gardens. This fine collection of plants includes over 200 trees and the National Bonsai Collection.

* Designed by J.C. Loudon, a leading garden planner
* Sculpture trail, waterfowl and exotic birds

Location
Signposted from Edgbaston

Opening
Daily; Mon–Sat 9am–5pm
Sun 10am–5pm

Admission
Adult £5.50, Child £3

Contact
Westbourne Road, Edgbaston, Birmingham B15 3TR

t 0121 4541860
w birminghambotanicalgardens. org.uk
e admin@birminghambotanical gardens. org.uk

597 Coventry

Coventry Cathedral

1 hr+   All year

Coventry Cathedral was bombed and destroyed in 1940, during the Second World War. The striking new cathedral, designed by Basil Spence, was consecrated in 1962 and is filled with work from leading artists of the time, including John Hutton's screen Saints and Angels.

* Sutherland's Christ in Glory in the Tetramorph
* Works by Elizabeth Frink, John Piper and Ralph Beyer

Location
Central Coventry

Opening
Daily; 9am–5.30pm (services permitting)

Admission
Free

Contact
1 Hilltop, Coventry CV1 5AB

t 02476 521200
w coventrycathedral.org.uk
e information@coventrycathedral.org.uk

598 Coventry

Herbert Art Gallery & Museum

1 hr   All year

As a focus for Coventry's cultural heritage, the museum offers a fascinating visit. Enjoy the Godiva City exhibition – one thousand years of the city's history, told through historical treasures and artefacts, interactive games and archive film.

* Archaeological finds from Saxon and medieval times
* Objects from Coventry's Asian communities

Location
Central Coventry, nr Cathedral, next to Tourist Information Centre

Opening
Daily; Mon–Sat 10am–5.30pm
Sun 12 noon–5pm

Admission
Free

Contact
Jordan Well, Coventry CV1 5QP

t 0247 6832381
w coverntrymuseum.org.uk
e artsandheritage@coventry.gov.uk

599 Dudley

Black Country Living Museum

3 hrs+   All year

The museum occupies an urban heritage park in the shadow of Dudley Castle. Historic buildings from around the Black Country have been moved and rebuilt to create a tribute to the traditional skills and enterprise of the people that lived in the heart of industrial Britain.

* Tramcars and trolleybuses transport visitors
* Costumed demonstrators and working craftsmen

Location
On A4037, 3 miles from M5 junction 2

Opening
Daily; Mar–Oct 10am–5pm;
Nov–Feb Wed–Sun 10am–4pm

Admission
Adult £9.60, Child £5.50, Concs £8.50

Contact
Tipton Road, Dudley DY1 4SQ

t 0121 5579643
w bclm.co.uk
e info@bclm.co.uk

593 Birmingham

Tolkien's Birmingham

2 hrs   Apr–Sep

J.R.R. Tolkien garnered inspiration from childhood haunts in Birmingham. The imagery he skilfully created can be attributed to various places and buildings in the city. See where Tolkien dreamt up *The Hobbit* and *Lord of the Rings* for yourself or choose a guided tour.

* In-depth knowledge from specialist tour guide for groups only
* Appropriate clothing must be worn, including footwear

Location
Various areas of Birmingham

Opening
Apr–Sep by appointment
Phone for details of guided tours

Admission
£5 per person

Contact
50 Springfield Road,
Kings Heath,
Birmingham B14 7DU
t 0121 4444046
w birminghamheritage.org.uk
e balti1@compuserve.com

594 Bournville

Cadbury World

3 hrs   All year

Chocolate through the centuries – from Aztec rainforests to Victorian England. Learn about the Cadbury family and their early triumphs and struggles to develop the business. Follow the journey of chocolate from its origins as cocoa to liquid chocolate in the factory.

* Learn how chocolate is used to make famous brands
* Chocolate Coronation Street!

Location
Signed from M42

Opening
Times vary, phone for details

Admission
Adult £8.75, Child £6.60, Concs £7
Pre-booking recommended

Contact
Linden Road, Bournville,
Birmingham B30 2LD
t 0121 4514159
w cadburyworld.co.uk
e cadbury.world@csplc.com

595 Bournville

Selly Manor

2 hrs   All year

Dating to at least 1327, Selly Manor is a medieval timber-framed manor house with Tudor extensions. By the late C19, it was due for demolition but was saved by George Cadbury who had it moved piece by piece and rebuilt in the village of Bournville.

* In the unique village of Bournville

Location
3 miles S of Birmingham city centre on Maple Road next to Bournville village green

Opening
Tue–Fri 10am–5pm
Apr–Sep, Sat, Sun & Bank Holidays only, 2pm–5pm

Admission
Adult £2.50, Child 50p, Concs £1.50

Contact
Bournville, Birmingham B30 1UB
t 0121 472 0199
w bvt.org/sellymanor
e sellymanor@bvt.org.uk

596 Castle Bromwich

Castle Bromwich Hall Gardens

2 hrs+   Apr–Oct

This unique example of an English baroque garden is being restored to the period 1680–1740. The 10-acre walled garden contains rare and interesting period plants, vegetables and herbs. Classical patterned parterres can be seen at the end of the Holly Walk.

* C19 holly maze, plant and gift shop
* Restored summer house and green house

Location
Signed from M6 junction 5

Opening
Apr–Oct Wed–Fri 12 noon–4.30pm
Sat, Sun & Bank Hols 1pm–5pm

Admission
Adult £3.50, Child £1.50, Concs £2.50

Contact
Chester Road, Castle Bromwich,
Birmingham B36 9BT
t 0121 7494100
w cbhgt.colebridge.net
e Admin@cbhgt.colebridge.net

590 Birmingham

National Sea Life Centre

  3 hrs All year

A unique insight into the lives of a myriad creatures – from shrimps to sharks. The unique, one-million-litre tropical ocean display has a Hawaiian volcanic theme, and the completely transparent 360 degree submarine tunnel provides a home for two giant green turtles.

* Programme of talks and feeding demonstrations
* Brand new feature for 2004

Location
Between National Indoor Arena & International Convention Centre

Opening
Daily in Summer 10am–5pm;
Winter Mon–Fri 10am–4pm
Sat & Sun 10am–5pm

Admission
Adult £8.95, £Child £6.95, Concs £7.50

Contact
The Waters Edge, Brindleyplace, Birmingham B1 2HL
t 0121 643 6777 / 633 4700
w sealifeeurope.com
e slcbirmingham@merlinentertainments.biz

591 Birmingham

Royal Birmingham Society of Artists Gallery

  2 hrs All year

One of the oldest art societies in the UK, the Royal Birmingham Society of Artists was given royal status in 1868 by Queen Victoria and played an important part in the Pre-Raphaelite movement. The gallery exhibits the work of members and local designers.

* Regularly changing programme of exhibitions
* Craft gallery, including ceramics, jewellery and more

Location
Follow New Hall Street to Brook Street

Opening
Mon–Wed & Fri 10.30am–5.30pm
Thu 10.30am–7pm Sat 10.30am–5pm

Admission
Free

Contact
4 Brook Street, St Paul's Square, Birmingham B3 1SA
t 0121 2364353
w rbsa.org.uk
e secretary@rbsa.org.uk

592 Birmingham

Think Tank

  4 hrs All year

Think Tank is an invigorating science attraction which examines the past, investigates the present and explores what the future may bring. Learn about the canal, road and railway networks that connected Birmingham to the rest of Britain.

* Unravel the mysteries of the body
* Medical tour covers techniques and instruments

Location
Follow blue banners, 15 mins walk from New Street

Opening
Daily; 10am–5pm

Admission
Adult £6.95, Child £4.95, Concs £5.50

Contact
Curzon Street, Birmingham B4 7XG
t 0121 2022222
w thinktank.ac
e findout@thinktank.ac

586   Birmingham

Birmingham Museum & Art Gallery

2 hrs   All year

This magnificent building houses one of the world's finest collections of Pre-Raphaelite art, as well as displays of silver, sculpture, ceramics, archaeology and social history. British watercolours and Arts and Crafts movement work is also on show.

* Permanent collection of the famous Pre-Raphaelites
* Fine and applied art collections

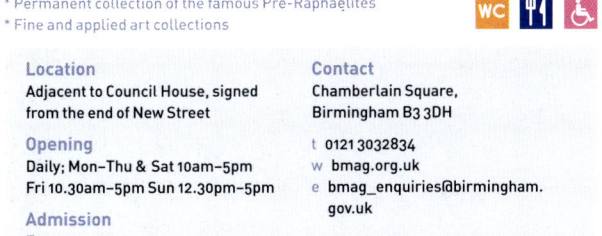

Location
Adjacent to Council House, signed from the end of New Street

Opening
Daily; Mon–Thu & Sat 10am–5pm
Fri 10.30am–5pm Sun 12.30pm–5pm

Admission
Free

Contact
Chamberlain Square,
Birmingham B3 3DH

t   0121 3032834
w bmag.org.uk
e   bmag_enquiries@birmingham.
    gov.uk

587   Birmingham

Cathedral Church of St Philip

½ hr   All year

A dramatic and elegant building at the heart of the city, this is a notable C18 church and a rare example of English baroque style. It contains renowned, massive Pre-Raphaelite stained glass windows by Edward Burne-Jones.

* Italianate domed tower
* Designed and built by Thomas Archer in 1715

Location
City centre

Opening
Daily; 7.30am–7pm

Admission
Suggested donation £1

Contact
Colmore Row, Birmingham B3 2QB

t   0121 2364333
e   enquiries@
    birminghamcathedral.com

588   Birmingham .

Ikon Gallery

1 hr   All year

One of Europe's leading contemporary art galleries, Ikon exhibits the best in international and British art in a changing programme of exhibitions and events. A variety of media are represented, including sound, video, mixed media, photography, painting, sculpture and installation.

* Exhibitions in Ikon's events room and tower room
* Situated in a converted neo-gothic school building

Location
15 mins from city centre, signed from Victoria Square

Opening
Tue–Sun & Bank Hols 11am–6pm

Admission
Free

Contact
1 Oozells Square, Brindleyplace,
Birmingham B1 2HS

t   0121 2480708
w ikon-gallery.co.uk
e   art@ikon-gallery.co.uk

589   Birmingham

Museum of the Jewellery Quarter

1 hr+   Apr–Oct

Visit a real jewellery factory that has changed little since the early part of the last century. The museum tells the story of jewellery making in Birmingham from its origins in the Middle Ages to the present day, and includes an explanation of jewellery-making techniques.

* Free entry includes a guided tour of the factory

Location
Adjacent to Jewellery Quarter Clock & Jewellery Quarter Station

Opening
Apr–Oct Tue–Sun 11.30am–4pm

Admission
Free

Contact
75-79 Vyse Street, Birmingham
B18 6HA

t   0121 5543598
w bmag.org.uk

582 Aston

Aston Hall

1 hr Easter–Oct

A fine Jacobean house, built between 1618 and 1635 by Sir Thomas Holte, featuring elaborate plasterwork ceilings and friezes, a magnificent carved oak staircase and a spectacular 136foot (40m) Long Gallery. Period rooms contain fine furniture, paintings, textiles and metalwork.

* Biennial candlelight event
* Regular programme of events

Location
M6 junction 6, 3 miles N of city centre

Opening
Easter–Oct Tue–Sun & Bank Hols 11.30am–4pm

Admission
Free

Contact
Trinity Road, Aston, Birmingham B6 6JD
t 0121 3270062
w birmingham.gov.uk

583 Baginton

Lunt Roman Fort

2 hrs Apr–Oct

This is a partial reconstruction of the fort established here in AD60. Visitors enter the fort by the reconstructed eastern gateway which is built entirely of timber and based on depictions from Trajan's column. There is also a museum of Roman military life with archaeological finds.

* Events & re-enactments with the XIII Legion
* Museum of army life

Location
In Baginton Village, near Coventry. It can be approached from A45 & A46

Opening
1 Apr–31 Oct open weekends & Bank Holidays 10am–5pm; 31 May–4 Jun daily; 12 Jul–30 Aug open daily except Wed

Pre-booked parties at other times (please phone for details)

Admission
Adult £2 Child £1 Concs £1

Contact
Coventry Road, Baginton CV8 3AJ
t 02476 832565/303567

584 Baginton

Midland Air Museum

2 hrs All year

Exhibits range from the Avro Vulcan bomber through more than 30 other historic aircraft, both civil and military, aero engines and other artefacts, to a wide range of memorabilia. The Heritage Centre houses a collection of material relating to Sir Frank Whittle.

* Giant Armstrong Whitworth Argosy freighter of 1959
* Meteor, Vulcan, Hunter, Starfighter and Phantom

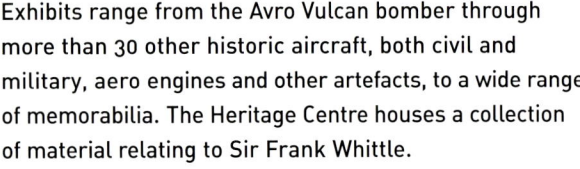 

Location
Off A45, between roundabout & Baginton

Opening
Daily; Apr–Oct Mon–Sat 10am–5pm
Sun 10am–6pm
Nov–Mar 10am–5pm

Admission
Adult £4, Child £2.25, Concs £3.25

Contact
Coventry Airport, Baginton, Coventry CV8 3AZ
t 02476 301033
w midlandairmuseum.org.uk
e midlandairmuseum@aol.com

585 Birmingham

Birmingham Eco Park

2 hrs All year

The Eco Park is a demonstration of the principles of sustainability and provides a stimulating and educational environment. Explore ponds, woodland, flowering meadows and heathland. Frogs, herons, dragonflies, sparrowhawks and foxes are regularly seen here.

* Wildlife and permaculture gardens
* Colourful combination of gardens

Location
From inner ring road take A45 to Heybarnes Circus roundabout, signed from there

Opening
Tue–Thu 12 noon–4pm
Sat 10am–4pm

Admission
Free

Contact
258a Hobmoor Road, Smallheath, Birmingham B10 9HH
t 0121 785 0553
w eco-park.org.uk
e ecopark@bbcwildlife.org.uk

579 Warwick

Warwick Castle

2–3 hrs   All year

Built by William the Conqueror in 1068, this is a fine example of a medieval castle. Today visitors can see the mill and engine house where the power of the river Avon ground grain for 600 years, the conservatory, peacock garden, and exquisite Victorian rose garden.

* Quality Assured Visitor Attraction

Location
2 miles from junction 15 off M40, Warwick Castle is easily accessible by road or rail

Opening
Daily; Apr–Sep 10am–6pm; Oct–Mar 10am–5pm

Admission
Please phone for details

Contact
Warwick CV34 4QU

t 0870 442 2000
w warwick-castle.co.uk

581 Wellesbourne

Wellesbourne Watermill

2 hrs   Easter–Sep

Visitors to this historic watermill can see the mill's machinery being driven by one of the country's largest wooden waterwheels. There are regular demonstrations of how stoneground flour is milled. Coracles are used on the millpond, which is a tranquil haven for wildlife.

Location
On B4086, between Kineton & Stratford-upon-Avon

Opening
Easter–Sep Thu–Sun & Bank Hols 10am–5pm

Admission
Adult £3.50, Child £2.50, Concs £3

Contact
Kineton Road, Wellesbourne CV35 9HG

t 01789 470237
w wellesbournemill.co.uk
e andrew@mill.spacomputers.com

580 Wellesbourne

Charlecote Park

2 hrs+   Mar–Dec

The mellow brickwork and great chimneys of Charlecote sum up the essence of Tudor England. There are associations with both Queen Elizabeth and Shakespeare – he knew the house well and is alleged to have been caught poaching the estate deer.

* Contains objects from Beckford's Fonthill Abbey
* Formal garden and Capability Brown deer park

Location
1 mile W of Wellesbourne, 5 miles E of Stratford, on N side of B4086

Opening
House 6 Mar–2 Nov Fri–Tue noon–5pm
Park & Gardens 6 Mar–2 Nov Fri–Tue 10.30am–6pm 7 Nov–19 Dec Sat & Sun 10.30am–4pm

Admission
Adult £6.40, Child £3.20

Contact
Warwick CV35 9ER

t 01789 470277
w nationaltrust.org.uk
e charlecote.park@nationaltrust.org.uk

© National Trust Photographic Library

575 Stratford-upon-Avon

The Shakespeare Countryside Museum & Mary Arden's House

1 hr+   All year

Mary Arden was the mother of William Shakespeare and this site contains her family home. Comprising two C16 farmhouses – Mary Arden's house itself and Palmer's farm – these houses, outbuildings and the adjoining land demonstrate life on a Tudor working farm.

* Falconry displays
* Rare breeds farm

Location
3 miles outside Stratford

Opening
Daily; Jun–Aug Mon–Sat 9.30am–5pm
Sun 10am–5pm
Apr–May & Sep–Oct Mon–Sat
10am–5pm Sun 10.30am–5pm;
Nov–Mar Mon–Sat 10am–4pm
Sun 10.30am–4pm

Admission
Adult £5.50, Child £2.50, Concs £5

Contact
Station Road, Wilmcote CV37 9UN
t 01789 293455
w shakespeare.org.uk
e info@shakespeare.org.uk

576 Warwick

Lord Leycester Hospital

1 hr   All year

The buildings of the Warwick Guilds were converted into a retreat for old soldiers and this continues to the present day. The 'Brethren', as the inhabitants are known, still wear their blue gowns and flat Tudor hats on ceremonial occasions.

* Museum of Queen's Own Hussars in Chaplain's Hall
* Masters garden

Location
Nr tourist information centre

Opening
Tue–Sun & Bank Hols 10am–5pm

Admission
Adult £3.40, Child £2.40, Concs £2.90

Contact
High Street, Warwick CV34 4BH
t 01926 491422

577 Warwick

St John's House

1 hr+   May–Sep

A charming Jacobean house dating from about 1620, St John's became a branch of the Warwickshire Museum in 1961 and houses the social history collection. The galleries have themes such as costume, domestic life and school life, and are changed frequently.

* Museum of Royal Warwickshire Regiment
* Ever-changing display of costume

Location
Signed from town centre

Opening
May–Sep Tue–Sat & Bank Hols
10am–5pm Sun 2.30pm–5pm

Admission
Free

Contact
Warwick CV34 4NF
t 01926 4120041
w warwickshire.gov.uk/museum
e museum@warwickshire.gov.uk

578 Warwick

Warwickshire Museums

1 hr+   All year

The Warwickshire Museum Service is housed in the C17 market hall. This is one of the few buildings in central Warwick that survived a huge fire in the town in 1694. Displays of geology, biology and archaeology illustrate the natural and historical heritage of the county.

* The famous Sheldon tapestry map of Warwickshire
* 180 million-year-old plesiosaur from the Jurassic Period

Location
In town centre

Opening
May–Sep Tue–Sat 10am–5pm
Sun and Bank Hols 11.30–5pm
Oct–Apr Tue–Sat 10am–5pm

Admission
Free

Contact
Market Place, Warwick CV34 4SA
t 01926 412827
w warwickshire.gov.uk
e museums@warwickshire.gov.uk

©National Trust Photographic Library/Keith Hewitt

573 Stratford-upon-Avon

Packwood House

2 hrs   Mar–Nov

The original C16 house was restored between the world wars by Graham Baron Ash. The interior contains a fine collection of C16 textiles and furniture. The gardens have renowned herbaceous borders and a famous collection of yews.

* A curious feature is the large number of sundials
* Glorious gardens

Location
On A3400, 2 miles E of Hockley Heath

Opening
House 3 Mar–7 Nov Wed–Sun
12 noon–4.30pm
Garden 3 Mar–7 Nov Wed–Sun
11am–4.30pm

Admission
Adult £5.40, Child £2.70

Contact
Lapworth, Solihull B94 6AT

t 01564 783294
w nationaltrust.org.uk
e packwood@nationaltrust.org.uk

572 Stratford-upon-Avon

Nash's House & New Place

1 hr   All year

This building belonged to Thomas Nash, a rich property owner who married Elizabeth Hall, Shakespeare's granddaughter. In addition to the exceptional collection of C17 tapestries and oak furniture, Nash's House also contains exhibits on the history of Stratford-upon-Avon.

* Stratford's first Shakespeare festival
* Elizabethan style knot-garden

Location
Signed from town centre

Opening
Daily; Nov–Mar 11am–4pm, Apr–May
& Sep–Oct 11am–5pm Jun–Aug
Mon–Sat 9.30am–5pm Sun 10am–5pm

Admission
Adult £3.50, Child £1.70, Concs £3

Contact
Chapel Street, Stratford-upon-Avon
CV37 6EP

t 01789 292325
w shakespeare.org.uk
e info@shakespeare.org.uk

574 Stratford-upon-Avon

Shakespeare's Birthplace

1 hr   All year

Experience the Tudor world of William Shakespeare by visiting the house where, in 1564, he was born. Shakespeare's Birthplace provides an insight into his childhood. Family rooms have been recreated with furniture, utensils and wall hangings from the period.

* Exhibitions tell the story of the house
* Exhibits of rare period items including *First Folio* 1623

Location
Signed from town centre

Opening
Nov–Mar Mon–Sat 10am–4pm
Sun 10.30–4pm
Apr–May & Sep–Oct Mon–Sat
10am–5pm Sun 10.30am–5p
Jun–Aug Mon–Sat 9am–5pm
Sun 10.30am–4pm

Admission
Adult £6.50, Child £2.50, Concs £5.50

Contact
Henley Street, Stratford-upon-Avon
CV37 6QW

t 01789 201823
w shakespeare.org.uk
e info@shakespeare.org.uk

569 Stratford-upon-Avon

Hall's Croft

1 hr   All year

One of the finest half-timbered, gabled houses in Stratford-upon-Avon, named after Dr John Hall, who married Shakespeare's daughter, Susanna. Dr Hall was a pioneering medical practitioner and displays in the house reflect his wealth and status in the community.

* Outstanding paintings and furniture
* Exhibition of medical artefacts from C16 and C17

Location
Nr town centre

Opening
Daily; Nov–Mar 11am–4pm
Apr–May & Sep–Oct 11am–5pm
Jun–Aug Mon–Sat 9.30am–5pm
Sun 10am–5pm

Admission
Adult £3.50, Child £1.70, Concs £3

Contact
Old Town, Stratford-upon Avon CV37

t 01789 292107
w shakespeare.org.uk
e info@shakespeare.org.uk

570 Stratford-upon-Avon

Harvard House

1 hr   May–Sep

Harvard House was home to Katherine Rogers, mother of John Harvard, whose bequest founded Harvard University. Built in 1596, the property is a fine example of an Elizabethan townhouse. It boasts the most ornately timber-framed frontage in Stratford.

* Home to the first museum of British pewter
* Many architectural features of interest

Location
In town centre

Opening
May–Sep Fri–Sun & Bank Hols
11am–4pm

Admission
Adult £2, Child free

Contact
High Street, Stratford-upon-Avon

t 01789 204507
w shakespeare.org.uk
e info@shakespeare.org.uk

571 Stratford-upon-Avon

Holy Trinity Church

½ hr+   All year

Visit Shakespeare's grave and the graves of Anne Hathaway, Dr John Hall and his wife Susanna Shakespeare and Thomas Nash in the chancel of Holy Trinity Church. Also in the chancel are 26 fine C15 carved misericords.

* Beautiful church situated on banks of River Avon
* Church is approached along an avenue of lime trees

Location
Signed from Stratford town centre

Opening
Mar–Oct Mon–Sat 8.30am–6pm
Sun 2pm–5pm, Nov–Feb Mon–Sat
9am–4pm Sun 12 noon–5pm

Admission
Shakespeare's Grave Adult £1, Child &
Concs 50p *Church* free

Contact
Old Town, Stratford-upon-Avon
CV37 6BG

t 01789 266316
w stratford-upon-avon.org.uk
e office@stratford-upon-avon.org.uk

567 Sutton Cheney

Bosworth Battlefield Visitor Centre & Country Park

2 hrs+   Mar-Dec

Site of one of the most famous battles in English history, between Richard III and Henry Tudor. The result gave England a new king and marked the beginning of the Tudor dynasty. Walk down a medieval street, discover what it was like to be a soldier and follow the battle trail.

* Site of one of the most famous battles in England
* Annual re-enactment of the battle

Location
2 miles S of Market Bosworth nr the village of Sutton Cheney

Opening
Visitor Centre Mar, Sat-Sun, 11am–5pm; Apr-Oct, daily, 11am-5pm; Nov-Dec, Sun, 11am-4pm
Country Park all year

Admission
Adult £3.25, Concs £2.25

Contact
Sutton Cheney, Nuneaton, Warwickshire CV13 0AD

t 01455 290429
w www.leics.gov.uk
e bosworth@leics.gov.uk

568 Stratford-upon-Avon

Anne Hathaway's Cottage

1 hr   All year

Anne Hathaway's cottage was home to Shakespeare's wife before they married in 1582. Besides being the place where the teenage Shakespeare courted his future bride, the Hathaway home is regarded as the quintessential English country cottage.

* Inhabited by Hathaway family until C19
* Shakespeare tree garden, maze, orchard and brook

Location
1 mile from Stratford town centre

Opening
Daily Nov–Mar 10am–4pm,
Apr–May & Sep–Oct Mon–Sat
9.30am–5pm Sun 10am–5pm
Jun–Aug Mon–Sat 9am–5pm
Sun 9.30am–5pm

Admission
Adult £5, Child £2, Concs £4

Contact
Cottage Lane, Shottery CV37 9HH

t 01789 292100
w shakespeare.org.uk
e info@shakespeare.org.uk

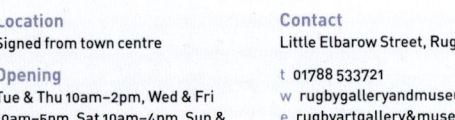

565 Royal Leamington Spa

Royal Pump Rooms

1 hr   All year

The historic Royal Pump Rooms have been redeveloped and now include an art gallery and museum. Visitors can explore life in a Victorian spa town, relax in the magnificent Turkish Room and discover the water treatments used at the Royal Pump Rooms.

* Historic Hammam room
* Temporary exhibition space & interactive gallery

Location
Town centre

Opening
Tue, Wed, Fri–Sat 10.30am–5pm
Thu 1.30–8pm Sun 11am–4pm

Admission
Free

Contact
The Parade, Royal Leamington Spa
CV32 4AA

t 01926 742700
w royal-pump-rooms.co.uk
e prooms@warwickdc.gov.uk

566 Rugby

Rugby Art Gallery

1 hr+   All year

This gallery contains a collection of paintings, prints and drawings by well known British artists such as Sir Stanley Spencer, L.S. Lowry, Percy Wyndham Lewis, Paula Rego, Barbara Hepworth, Bridget Riley and Lucian Freud.

* Rugby's collection of modern art
* Roman artefacts & local social history objects

Location
Signed from town centre

Opening
Tue & Thu 10am–2pm, Wed & Fri
10am–5pm, Sat 10am–4pm, Sun &
Bank Hols 1pm–5pm

Admission
Free

Contact
Little Elbarow Street, Rugby CV21 3BZ

t 01788 533721
w rugbygalleryandmuseum.org.uk
e rugbyartgallery&museum@rugby.
gov.uk

561 Kenilworth

Kenilworth Castle

2 hrs+   All year

The largest castle ruin in England and the scene of many sieges and murders, Kenilworth Castle has been linked with some of the most important names in English history. Explore its impressive Norman keep, Tudor gardens and John of Gaunt's Great Hall.

* Walks to Old Kenilworth & ruined abbey
* Elizabethan festival and Shakespeare performances

Location
In town centre

Opening
Daily Apr–Sep 10am–6pm
Oct 10am–5pm
Nov–Mar 10am–4pm

Admission
Adult £4.50, Child 2.30, Concs £3.40

Contact
Castle Mews, Kenilworth CU8 1NE
t 01926 852078
w english-heritage.org.uk

562 Kineton

Compton Verney Art Gallery

2hrs+   Mar–Oct

An innovative art gallery, in a C18 mansion, designed by Robert Adam and set in 114 acres of Capability Brown landscape. The Peter Moores collections include artefacts from Naples 1450-1800, China 3000 BC–AD 1500 and a collection of British folk art.

* Major temporary exhibitions
* Projects for schools & groups

Location
Off B4086, between Kineton & Stratford-upon-Avon

Opening
Daily; March–Oct 10am–5pm

Admission
Adult £5, Child £2, Concs £4

Contact
Compton Verney CV35 9HZ
t 01926 645500
w comptonverney.org.uk
e info@comptonverney.org.uk

563 Knowle

Baddesley Clinton

3 hrs+   Mar–Nov

This moated manor house dates from C15 and indeed little has changed since 1634. During the Elizabethan era it was a haven for persecuted Catholics and there are three priest-holes. The garden includes stewponds, a lake and a nature walk.

* 70-seater restaurant
* Quiz for children

Location
W of A4141, between Warwick & Birmingham, 7 miles NW of Warwick

Opening
3 Mar–7 Nov Wed–Sun 1.30pm–5pm

Admission
Adult £6.20, Child £3.10

Contact
Rising Lane, Baddesley Clinton, Knowle, Solihull B93 0DQ
t 01564 783294
w nationaltrust.org.uk
e baddesleyclinton@
nationaltrust.org.uk

564 Nuneaton

Arbury Hall

½hr+   Bank Hols

This Elizabethan house was built on the site of a C12 Augustinian priory. Transformed in C18 to become a fine example of Gothic Revival architecture, the house contains collections of antique furniture, pictures, glass and china. Many rooms are open to the public.

* Delightful landscaped gardens, wooded walks & lake
* Chimney piece based on tomb of Aymer de Valence

Location
Signed from Nuneaton

Opening
Sun & Mon of Bank Hols only
2pm–6pm

Admission
House & Gardens Adult £6.50, Child £3
Gardens Adult £4.50, Child £2.50

Contact
Nuneaton CV10 7PT
t 0247 6382804
e brenda.newell@arburyhall.net

557 Coventry

Brandon Marsh Nature Centre

1 hr+   All year

A visit to Brandon Marsh Nature Centre starts at the visitor centre, opened by Sir David Attenborough in 1998. This contains displays, hands-on activities and information about the nature reserve, which covers 220 acres and features many lakes and bird hives.

* Warwickshire Wildlife Trust Centre

Location
Off A45

Opening
Daily; Mon–Sat 9am–4.30pm
Sun 10am–4pm

Admission
Adult £2.50, Child £1, Concs £1.50

Contact
Brandon Lane, Coventry CV3 3GW

t 024 76308999
w wildlifetrust.org.uk
e admin@warkswt.cix.co.uk

558 Gaydon

Heritage Motor Centre

3 hrs   All year

The Heritage Motor Centre is home to the largest collection of classic, vintage and veteran British cars in the world. There are 200 vehicles on display, charting the history of the British car industry from the turn of the century to the present day.

* 1963 Morris Mini Cooper
* Regular programme of events

Location
2 mins from M40 junction 12

Opening
Daily; 10am–5pm

Admission
Adult £8, Child £6, Concs £7

Contact
Banbury Road, Gaydon CV35 0BJ

t 01926 641188
w heritage-motor-centre.co.uk
e enquiries@
heritage-motor-centre.co.uk

559 Henley-in-Arden

Henley-in-Arden Heritage & Visitor Centre

1 hr   Easter–Oct

Henley-in-Arden's history is recorded in the town's oldest house, part of which is C14. Exhibits include a model of the Norman castle which once stood on the mount and information on the ancient Market Cross and the tradition of town criers.

* Chronicle of the origins of the famous ice cream
* Tales of industrial, social & sporting life in the town

Location
In town centre

Opening
Easter–Oct Tue–Fri 10.30am–4.30pm
Sat–Sun 2.30–4.30pm

Admission
Free

Contact
Joseph Hardy House, 150 High Street,
Henley-in-Arden B95 5BS

t 01564 795919
w henley-in-arden-heritage.co.uk
e henleyheritage@lineone.net

560 Henley-in-Arden

The Saxon Sanctuary

½ hr   All year

Warwickshire's oldest church is known as the Saxon Sanctuary. Its tower saw in the last millennium and the drama of English history has swept through it ever since. Every age has left its own story, so a visit to St Peter's Church is a real adventure.

* The tomb of Francis Smith, 1604
* Millennium exhibition in the barn-roofed Lady Chapel

Location
Take A3400 from Stratford-upon-Avon
N for 4½ miles

Opening
Daily; 9am–dusk

Admission
Free

Contact
Stratford Road, Wootton Wawen,
Henley-in-Arden B95 6BD

t 01564 792659
w saxonsanctuary.org.uk
e saxon@btopenworld.com

555 Banbury

Upton House

1 hr+   Apr–Dec

Once owned by Walter Samuel, 2nd Viscount Bearsted and chairman of Shell 1921–46, Upton contains an outstanding collection of English and continental Old Master paintings, including works by Hogarth, Stubbs, Guardi, Canaletto, Brueghel and El Greco.

* Exhibition of Shell paintings & publicity posters
* Tapestries, French porcelain and Chelsea figures

Location
On A422, 7 miles NW of Banbury, 12 miles SE of Stratford-upon-Avon

Opening
House 3 Apr–31 Oct Mon–Wed Sat–Sun 1pm–5pm
Garden 3 Apr–19 Dec Sat–Sun 12 noon–4pm

Admission
Adult £6.50, Child £3.50

Contact
nr Banbury OX15 6HT

t 01295 670266
w nationaltrust.org.uk
e uptonhouse@nationaltrust.org.uk

556 Broadway

Snowshill Manor

2 hrs+   Mar–Oct

A Cotswold manor house containing Charles Paget Wade's extraordinary collection of craftsmanship & design, including clocks, toys & Japanese armour. The garden is run on organic principles & is a lively mix of architectural features, bright colour & delightful scents.

* Cottage and organic garden also on display

Location
Signed from Broadway

Opening
19 Mar–Oct Wed–Sun & Bank Hols
11.30am–5.30pm

Admission
Adult £6.40, Child £3.20

Contact
Snowshill, Broadway WR12 7JU

t 01386 852410
w nationaltrust.org.uk
e snowshillmanor@
nationaltrust.org.uk

552 Alcester

Coughton Court

3 hrs   Mar–Oct

This beautiful Tudor house has been a family home since 1409. There is a fine collection of family portraits, furniture and a fascinating exhibition about the Gunpowder Plot. The gatehouse and courtyard are complemented by an Elizabethan knot garden.

* Stunning displays of roses & herbaceous plants
* There are two churches to visit

Location
On A435, 2 miles N of Alcester

Opening
Mar & Oct Sat–Sun 11.30am–5pm
Apr–Jun & Sep Wed–Sun 11.30am–5pm
Jul–Aug Tue–Sun 11.30am–5pm

Admission
Adult £8.25, Child £4.15

Contact
nr Alcester B49 5JA

t 01789 400777
w coughtoncourt.co.uk
e office@throckmortons.co.uk

553 Alcester

Ragley Hall

5 hrs   Apr–Sep

Ragley Hall is set in 27 acres of beautiful formal gardens. The home contains baroque plasterwork, the stunning C20 mural, The Temptation, and a collection of paintings, china and furniture. In addition to the beautiful house, there are the formal gardens and parkland.

* Ever-changing gardens
* Game fair & other events throughout the year

Location
Off Alcester bypass, signed at A46 junction

Opening
House Apr–Sep Thu–Sun & Bank Hols
12 noon–5.30pm
Park & gardens Apr–Sep Thu–Sun &
Bank Hols 10am–6pm

Admission
Adult £7.50, Child £4.50, Concs £6.50

Contact
Alcester B49 5NJ

t 01789 762090
w ragleyhall.com
e info@ragleyhall.com

554 Banbury

Farnborough Hall

2 hrs+   Apr–Sep

A beautiful, honey-coloured stone house, richly decorated in the mid-C18 and the home of the Holbech family for over 300 years. The interior plasterwork is quite outstanding and the charming grounds contain C18 temples, a terrace walk and an obelisk.

* Terrace walk open by prior appointment only

Location
6 miles N of Banbury, W of A423

Opening
2 Apr–28 Sep Wed & Sat 2pm–5.30pm
May Mon & Sat 2pm–5.30pm

Admission
Adult £4, Child £2

Contact
Banbury OX17 1DU

t 01295 6900002
w nationaltrust.org.uk
e farnboroughhall@
nationaltrust.org.uk

549   Tutbury

Tutbury Castle

2 hr   Easter–Sep

Built in the 1070s for one of William the Conqueror's barons, Tutbury Castle has been involved in some of the most dramatic events in English history. A bloody place of siege and battle, on three occasions it acted as a prison for Mary Queen of Scots.

* Authentic Tudor privy garden & medieval herbery
* Secret staircase recently uncovered to the Great Hall

Location
Exit M1 junction 24a or M6 junction 15, nr A50

Opening
Easter Sun–19 Sep Wed–Sun
11am–5pm

Admission
Adult £3.50, Child £3, Concs £3

Contact
Tutbury, Burton-on-Trent DE13 9JF

t 01283 812129
w tutburycastle.com
e info@tutburycastle.com

550   Winkhill

Blackbrook Zoological Park

2–4 hrs   All year

Set amid the Staffordshire Moorlands, this zoo contains a large and varied collection of some of the most rare and endangered species to be found in the world, from swans and geese to vultures and flamingos and from meerkats ands marmots to piranhas and pythons.

* Largest collection of wildfowl in Britain
* Largest collection of cranes & storks in Britain

Location
From Leek, take the A523 & the 1st right, signposted to the park, then the 1st right again

Opening
Daily; 10.30am–5.30pm (earlier closing in winter);
Café: open in summer only

Admission
Adult £6.25 Child £3.95 Concs £5.25

Contact
Winkhill, ST13 7QR

t 01538 308293
w blackbrookzoologicalpark.co.uk

551   Wolverhampton

Moseley Old Hall

2 hrs+   Mar–Dec

An Elizabethan house, famous for its associations with the fugitive King Charles II who hid there in 1651. Faced with brick in the 1870s, inside it remains as Charles would have known it, with timber framing, oak panelling, period furniture and ingenious hiding places.

* Knot garden recreated in the C17 style
* Exhibition of Charles II's escape after Battle of Worcester

Location
4 miles N of Wolverhampton, S of M54 between A449 and A460

Opening
20 Mar–31Oct Wed Sat Sun 1pm 5pm
1 Nov–19 Dec Sun 1–4pm

Admission
Adult £4.60, Child £2.30

Contact
Moseley Old Hall Lane, Fordhouses, Wolverhampton WV10 7HY

t 01902 782808
w nationaltrust.org.uk
e moseleyoldhall@nationaltrust.org.uk

545 Stoke-on-Trent

Biddulph Grange Garden

1 hr+   Easter–Dec

A rare survival of a high Victorian garden, restored by the National Trust. The garden is divided into a series of themed spaces, including a Chinese temple, Egyptian court, pinetum, dahlia walk, glen, avenues and many other settings.

* Inspiration of the C19 horticulturist James Bateman
* The Egyptian garden contains topiary obelisks of yew

Location
Off A527, N side of Biddulph

Opening
19 Mar–30 Oct Wed–Fri 12pm–5.30pm
Sat, Sun & Bank hols 11am–3pm
5 Nov–18 Dec Sat & Sun 11am–3pm

Admission
Summer Adult £5, Child £2.50
Winter Adult £2, Child £1

Contact
Grange Road, Biddulph,
Stoke-on-Trent ST8 7SD

t 01782 517999
w nationaltrust.org.uk

546 Stoke-on-Trent

Spode Museum & Visitor Centre

1 hr+   All year

Visitors will see a collection of Spode ceramics, including teaware, dessert ware and dinnerware, as well as beautiful ornamental pieces. The display includes items from the late 1700s to 1833, illustrating the genius of Josiah Spode I and II.

* Display includes designs for the royal family
* Fully guided factory tours available

Location
From M6 junction 15 take A500, go left at 2nd roundabout, then follow signs

Opening
Daily; Mon–Sat 9am–5pm Sun
10am–4pm Bank Hols 9am–5pm

Admission
Free

Contact
Church Street, Stoke-on-Trent
ST4 1BX

t 01782 744011
w spode.co.uk
e spodemuseum@spode.co.uk
e visitorcentre@spode.co.uk

547 Tamworth

Middleton Hall

2–3 hrs   Apr–Oct

The hall has an interesting architectural history, with its oldest buildings dating from 1300 and others dating from C16 to early C19. Attractions include the 11-bay Georgian west wing and the impressive C16 Great Hall, the restoration of which was completed in 1994.

* 24 embroideries on history of Sutton Coldfield
* Links to Lady Jane Grey, Elizabeth I and Jane Austen

Location
On A4091, 4 miles S of Tamworth, between Belfry & Drayton Manor Park

Opening
Apr–Oct Sun 2pm–5pm
Bank Hols 11am–5pm

Admission
Adult £2.50, Child free, Concs £1.50

Contact
Middleton, Tamworth B78 2AE

t 01827 283 095
w middletonhalltrust.co.uk
e middletonhall@btconnect.com

548 Tamworth

Tamworth Castle

1 hr   All year

This is a Norman shell-keep castle with intact apartments from C12 to C19. Fifteen period rooms are open to visitors, including the Great Hall, dungeon and haunted bedroom. There is also a permanent exhibition on Norman castles.

* The Tamworth Story is an interactive local history exhibit
* Living images also known as 'talking heads'

Location
Take A51 & A453 through town centre, signed from A51

Opening
Tue–Sun 12 noon–5.15pm
Autumn / winter times differ, please telephone for details

Admission
Adult £4.75, Child £2.75, Concs £2.75

Contact
The Holloway, Ladybank
Tamworth B79 7NA

t 01827 709629 / 709626
w tamworth.gov.uk
e heritage@tamworth.gov.uk

543 Milford

Shugborough

3 hrs+   Mar–Sep

In 1693 the original manor house was demolished and a three-storey house was built. This survives and forms the centre of the house today, but between 1745 and 1748 the architect Thomas Wright transformed the property into a magnificent Georgian mansion.

* Living history museum with costumed servants
* Fully working Georgian farm complete with animals

Location
6 miles from M6 junction 13

Opening
Mar–Sep Tue–Sun 11am–5pm

Admission
Adult £6, Concs £4

Contact
Shugborough, Milford ST17 0XB

t 01889 881388
w staffordshire.gov.uk
e shugborough.promotions
@staffordshire.gov.uk

544 Stafford

Stafford Castle

3 hrs+   All year

Built by William the Conqueror to subdue rebellious local people, Stafford Castle has dominated the landscape throughout 900 years of turbulent history. Visitors today will find a more peaceful setting – follow the castle trail, explore the castle ruins and take in the panoramic view.

* Try on armour & chainmail
* Host of archaeological finds

Location
Off A518, 1 mile SW of Stafford

Opening
Apr–Oct Tue–Sun & Bank Hols
10am–5pm
Nov–Mar Sat–Sun 10am–4pm

Admission
Free

Contact
Castle Bank, Newport Road, Stafford
ST16 1DJ

t 01785 257698
w staffordbc.gov.uk
e castlebc@btconnect.com

541 Longton

Gladstone Working Pottery Museum

2 hrs+   All year

Discover the story of the Potteries at Gladstone, the only factory remaining from the days when coal–burning bottle ovens made the world's finest English bone china. This is a unique working museum that allows visitors to see how C19 potters worked.

* Traditional skills & original workshops
* Cobbled yard & huge bottle kilns

Location
From M6, follow A500, take A50 to Longton

Opening
Daily; 10am–5pm

Admission
Adult £4.95, Child £3.50, Concs £3.95

Contact
Uttoxeter Road, Longton,
Stoke-on-Trent ST3 1PQ

t 01782 319232
w stoke.gov.uk/gladstone
e gladstone@stoke.gov.uk

542 Market Drayton

Dorothy Clive Garden

1 hr+   Apr–Oct

A wide range of unusual plants can be seen in this lovely garden. Features include a quarry garden with a waterfall, a woodland garden and a scree and water garden. The summer borders are spectacular and the autumn crocus and dwarf cyclamen are mindblowing.

* Lovely views of three counties
* Japanese maples add to autumn colours

Location
On the A51, between Nantwich & Stone

Opening
Daily; 12 Mar–30 Oct daily
10.30am–5.30pm

Admission
Adult £4, Child £1, Concs £3.40

Contact
Willoughbridge,
Market Drayton TF9 4EU

t 01630 647237
w dorothyclivegarden.co.uk

537 Halfpenny Green

Halfpenny Green Vineyards

1 hr   All year

Information boards describe many of the French, German and hybrid varieties of vine planted here and visitors to Halfpenny Green can follow the self-guided vineyard trail. After touring the vineyard, inspect the winery and taste the wines.

* Award-winning wines
* Vineyard trail & craft centre

Location
Off B4176, nr Halfpenny Green Airfield

Opening
Daily; 10.30am–5pm

Admission
Free, charges for tours

Contact
Tom Lane, Halfpenny Green DY7 5EP

t 01384 221122
w halfpenny-green-vineyards.co.uk
e sales@halfpenny-green-vine-yards.co.uk

538 Lichfield

Erasmus Darwin's House

1 hr   All year

An elegant C18 house near Lichfield Cathedral, this was home to Charles Darwin's grandfather, Erasmus, a renowned doctor, philosopher, inventor, scientist and poet. Period furnishings, an audio-visual and interactive displays tell the story of this remarkable man.

* Cellar tours by arrangement
* Conference facilities

Location
In town centre, nr cathedral

Opening
Thu–Sat 10am–4.30pm
Sun & Bank Hols 12noon–4.30pm

Admission
Phone for details

Contact
Beacon Street, Lichfield WS13 7AD

t 01543 306 260
w erasmusdarwin.org
e erasmus.d@virgin.net

539 Lichfield

Lichfield Heritage Centre

1 hr+   All year

The centre gives an account of Lichfield's varied history. It is home to the Staffordshire Millennium Embroideries, which are displayed in their own gallery, as well as fine examples of city, diocesan and regimental silver, ancient charters and archives.

* Audio-visual presentations
* Collection of photographs of Lichfield, old & new

Location
In town centre

Opening
Daily; 10am–5pm

Admission
Adult £3.50, Child £1, Concs £2.50

Contact
Market Square, Lichfield WS13 6LG

t 01543 256 611
w lichfieldheritage.org.uk
e info@lichfieldheritage.org.uk

540 Lichfield

Wall Roman Site (Letocetum)

1 hr   Apr–Oct

Wall was an important staging post on the Roman military road to North Wales. It provided overnight accommodation and a change of horse for travelling Roman officials and imperial messengers. The foundations of a hotel and bathhouse can be seen.

* Many excavated finds displayed in the museum
* Audio tour with Gallas the Roman soldier

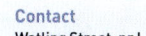

Location
Off A5, nr Lichfield

Opening
Daily; Apr–Sep 10am–6pm
Oct 10am–5pm

Admission
Adult £2.60, Child £1.30, Concs £2

Contact
Watling Street, nr Lichfield WS14 0AW

t 01543 480768
w english-heritage.org.uk

Sudbury Hall & Museum of Childhood

3 hrs   Mar-Oct

This spectacular late C17 house has sumptuous interiors and a fine collection of portraits. The great staircase is one of the most elaborate of its kind in an English house. The C19 service wing is home to the Museum of Childhood with displays about children from C18 onwards.

* Featured in the BBC production of *Pride and Prejudice*
* 'Behind the Scenes' tours

Location
6 miles E of Uttoxeter at junction of A50 Derby–Stoke and A515 Ashbourne

Opening
Hall 6 Mar–30 Oct, Wed–Sun, 1pm–5pm
Grounds 6 Mar–30 Oct, Wed–Sun, 11am–6pm
Museum 6 Mar–30 Oct, Wed–Sun, 1pm–5pm; 4–12 Dec, Sat–Sun, 11am–4pm

Admission
Hall Adult £5, Child £2
Museum Adult £5.50, Child £3.50
Hall & Museum Adult £9 Child £4.50

Contact
Sudbury, Ashbourne DE6 5HT
t 01283 585337
w www.nationaltrust.org.uk
e sudburyhall@nationaltrust.org.uk

Ceramica

1½ hrs+   All year

Ceramica is an interactive experience in the heart of the English Potteries and the centre of the ceramic industry. Learn how clay is transformed into china and the important part ceramics play in everyday life. Discover the past, present and future of ceramics in the displays.

* See a reconstruction of the inside of a bottle oven
* Josiah Wedgewood's kiln, discovered by Channel 4's *Time Team*

Location
In town centre, beside A50

Opening
Daily; Mon–Sat 9.30am–5pm
Sun 10.30am–4.30pm

Admission
Adult £3.50, Child & Concs £2.50

Contact
Market Place, Burslem, Stoke-on-Trent ST6 3DS
t 01782 832001
w ceramicauk.com
e info@ceramicauk.com

The Potteries Museum & Art Gallery

2 hrs   All year

Discover the story of Stoke-on-Trent's people, industry, products and landscapes through displays of pottery, community history, archaeology, geology and wildlife. There is also a large collection of paintings, drawings, prints, costume and glass.

* World's finest collection of Staffordshire ceramics
* A collection of more than 650,000 objects

Location
A500 junction 15 , signed from town centre

Opening
Daily; Mar–Oct Mon–Sat 10am–5pm
Sun 2pm–5pm
Nov–Feb Mon–Sat 10am–4pm
Sun 1pm–4pm

Admission
Free

Contact
Bethesda Street, Hanley ST1 3DW
t 01782 232323
w stoke.gov.uk/museums
e museums@stoke.gov.uk

531   Shrewsbury

Wroxeter Roman City

1 hr   All year

The largest excavated Roman British city to have escaped development, Wroxeter was originally home to 6000 people. The most impressive ruins are the C2 municipal baths and the remains of a huge dividing wall. Local finds are on display in the visitor centre.

* The fourth largest Roman settlement in Britain

Location
On B4380, 5 miles E of Shrewsbury

Opening
Daily; Apr–Sep daily 10am–6pm
Oct daily 10am–5pm
Nov–Mar daily 10am–1pm & 2pm–4pm

Admission
Adult £3.70, Child £1.70, Concs £2.80

Contact
Wroxeter, Shrewsbury SY5 6PH

t 01743 761330
w english-heritage.org.uk

532   Telford

Ironbridge Gorge Museums

1–6 hrs   All year

There are ten award-winning museums spread along what is often called 'the valley that changed the world'. That valley, beside the River Severn, is still spanned by the world's first iron bridge. See the products that set industry on its way and the machines that made them.

* Various workshops, including ceramic and iron working
* Enginuity – hands-on design & tech experiences

Location
5 miles S of Telford, signed from M54 junction 4

Opening
Daily; 10am–5pm – some areas close in winter

Admission
Passport ticket to all ten attractions
Adult £12.95, Child £8.25, Concs £11.25

Contact
Ironbridge, Telford TF8 7DQ

t 01952 884 391
w ironbridge.org.uk
e visits@ironbridge.org.uk

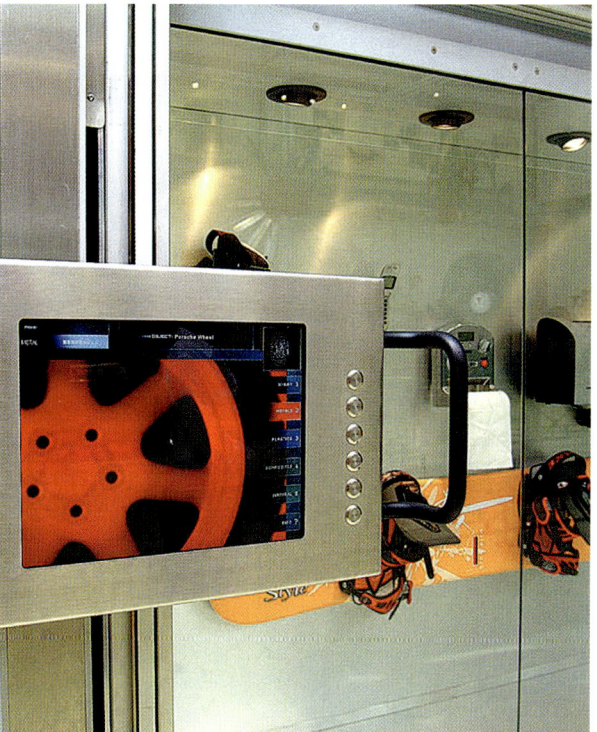

533   Telford

Enginuity

2 hrs   All year

Based in the Ironbridge World Heritage Site, this museum explains the science and design behind the gadgets we see and use every day. Pull a real locomotive, control the flow of water to generate electricity, pitch yourself against a robot, or work as a team to run the crazy boiler.

* World Heritage Site
* Be an apprentice engineer for the day

Location
Follow the brown tourist signs from the M54 (junction 4)

Opening
Daily; 10am–5pm; closed 24–26 Dec

Admission
2004: Adult £5.30 Concs £3.70
Please phone for 2005 prices

Contact
Ironbridge Gorge Museum Trust, Coach Road, Coalbrookdale, Telford TE8 7DQ

t 01952 884391
e tic@ironbridge.org.uk

528 Shrewsbury

Attingham Park

2 hrs+   All year

One of the great houses of the Midlands, this elegant mansion was built in 1785 for the first Lord Berwick, to the design of George Steuart, and has a picture gallery by John Nash. The Regency interiors contain collections of silver, Italian furniture and Grand Tour paintings.

* Park with walk by River Tern landscaped by Repton
* Environmental activity room opened in 2003

Location
On B4380, 4 miles SE of Shrewsbury

Opening
House Mar–Nov Fri–Tue 1pm–4.30pm
Bank Hols 12 noon–5pm
Grounds Mar–Oct daily 9am–8pm
Nov–Feb 9am–5pm

Admission
House & grounds Adult £5.50, Child £2.75
Grounds only £2.90, £1.35

Contact
Shrewsbury SY4 4TP
t 01743 708123
w nationaltrust.org.uk
e attingham@nationaltrust.org.uk

529 Shrewsbury

Hawkstone Park

4 hrs   All year

Created in C18, Hawkstone became one of the greatest historic parklands in Europe. The park is centred around the Red Castle and the awe-inspiring Grotto Hill, and features intricate pathways, ravines, arches and bridges, the towering cliffs and follies.

* Woodland full of ancient oaks
* The attraction has won numerous awards

Location
Off A49, between Shrewsbury
& Whitchurch

Opening
Times vary, phone for details

Admission
Adult £5.50, Child £3.50, Concs £4.50

Contact
Weston-under-Redcastle,
Shrewsbury SY4 5UY

t 01939 200611
w hawkstone.co.uk
e info@hawkstone.co.uk

530 Shrewsbury

Shrewsbury Museum & Art Gallery

1 hrs+   All year

The museum occupies two of Shrewsbury's finest buildings – a C16 timber-framed former merchant's warehouse and a stone and brick building of about 1616. Displays include social history, geology, costume, ceramics and fine art.

* Excavated material from Viroconium
* See pre-Roman & medieval Shrewsbury

Location
City centre

Opening
Jan–Mar & Oct–Dec Tue–Sat
10am–4pm
Apr & May Tue–Sat & Bank Hols
10am–4pm
Daily; Jun–Sep Tue–Sat 10am–5pm
Sun–Mon 10am–4pm

Admission
Free

Contact
Barker Street, Shrewsbury SY1 1QH
t 01743 361196
w shrewsburymuseums.com
e museums@
shrewsbury-atcham.gov.uk

525 Market Drayton

Wollerton Old Hall Garden

2 hrs   Easter–Sep

Wollerton Old Hall Garden is a three-acre plantsman's garden developed around a C16 house (not open) in rural Shropshire. The strong formal design has created many separate gardens, each with its own character, and there are many rare and unusual plants.

* Present garden developed from 1984
* Difficult-to-obtain perennials available in nursery

Location
Off A53, between Market Drayton & Shrewsbury

Opening
Good Friday–Aug Fri, Sun & Bank Hols
12 noon–5pm
Sep Fri 12 noon–5pm

Admission
Adult £4, Child £1

Contact
Wollerton, Market Drayton TF9 3NA

t 01630 685760
w wollertonoldhallgarden.com
e info@wollertonoldhallgarden.com

527 Shifnal

Weston Park

2 hrs+   May–Sep

The house was first mentioned in the *Domesday Book* in the C11, but Weston owes its unique character to the developments of the C17, directed by Lady Wilbraham. The beautiful landscaped gardens are the work of Capability Brown, although they were restored in 1991.

* Mary, daughter of George V, honeymooned here
* One of Disraeli's favourite locations

Location
On A5, 3 miles off M54 junction 3

Opening
Daily;May–Jun Holidays & Sat–Sun
11am–7pm
Jul–Sep 11am–7pm

Admission
Adult £3, Child £2, Concs £2.50

Contact
Weston-under-Lizard,
Shifnal TF11 8LE

t 01952 852 100
w weston-park.com
e enquiries@weston-park.com

526 Shifnal

The RAF Museum – Cosford

3 hrs+   All year

Tells the story of man's flight – the successes and failures – through one of the largest aviation collections in the UK. Over 70 historic aircraft are displayed in three wartime hangars on an active airfield. The collection spans nearly 80 years of aviation history.

* Visitor Attraction of the Year 2003
* State-of-the-art flight simulator

Location
On A41, less than 1 mile from M54 junction 3

Opening
Daily; 10am–6pm (last entry 4pm)
Closed 24–26 Dec & 1 Jan

Admission
Free, charges for special events
Under 16s must be accompanied by an adult

Contact
Cosford, Shifnal TF11 8UP

t 01902 376 200
w rafmuseum.org
e cosford@rafmuseum.com

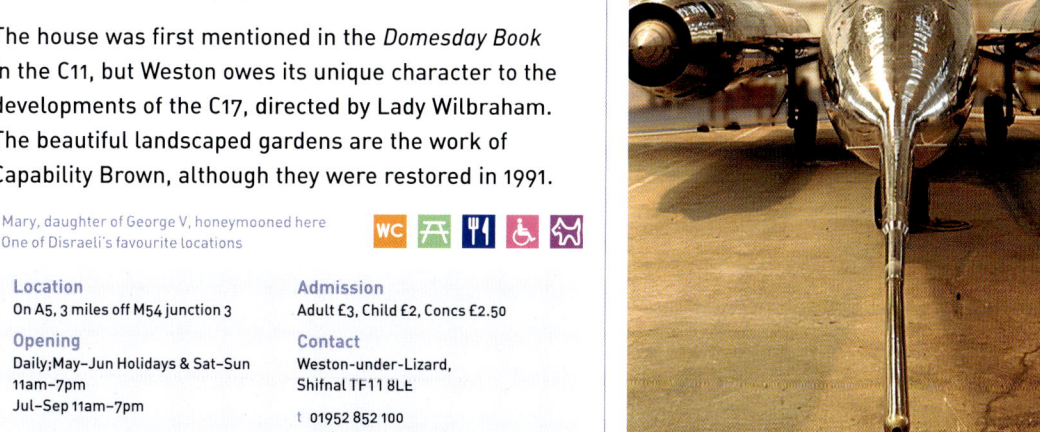

522 Ludlow

Ludlow Castle

  1 hr All year

A dramatic ruined medieval castle, set in glorious Shropshire countryside. Walk through the castle grounds, see the ancient houses of kings, queens, princes, judges and the nobility and get a glimpse of the lifestyle of medieval society.

* Host to the popular Ludlow festival
* Many events throughout the year

Location
On A49, in town centre

Opening
Jan Sat–Sun 10am–4pm
Daily; Feb–Mar & Oct–Dec 10am–4pm
Apr–Jul & Sep 10am–5pm
Aug daily 10am–7pm

Admission
Adult £3.50, Child £1.50, Concs £3

Contact
Castle Square, Ludlow SY8 1AY

t 01584 873355
w ludlowcastle.com
e ludlowcastle@
paperclaydesigns.com

523 Ludlow

Stokesay Castle

  1 hr All year

Strength and elegance are united in this fortified medieval manor house, built by renowned wool merchant Lawrence of Ludlow. In 1291 a 'licence to crenellate' was obtained from Edward I at Hereford for the three-storey south tower.

* Magnificent Great Hall largely untouched
* Timber-framed Jacobean gatehouse

Location
Off A49, 7 miles NW of Ludlow

Opening
Daily; Apr–Sep 10am–6pm
Oct 10am–5pm;
Nov–Mar Wed–Sun 10am–4pm

Admission
Adult £4.50, Child £2.30, Concs £3.40

Contact
Craven Arms SY7 9AH

t 01588 672544
w english-heritage.org.uk

524 Market Drayton

Hodnet Hall Gardens

  2 hrs Apr–Oct

Hodnet Hall features over 60 acres of flowers, forest trees, a chain of ornamental pools and a cultivated garden valley providing a natural habitat for waterfowl and other wildlife. The gardens also include a kitchen garden where the produce can be purchased.

* Woodland walks along chain of pools and lakes
* Planted to give colour from early spring to late autumn

Location
On A53, between Shrewsbury & Market Drayton

Opening
Apr–Sep Tue–Sun & Bank Hols
12 noon–5pm; Oct Sun 12noon–5pm

Admission
Adult £3.75, Child £1.75, Concs £3.25

Contact
Hodnet, Market Drayton TF9 3NN

t 01630 685 786
w hodnethallgardens.co.uk
e marlene@
heber-percy.freeserve.co.uk

519 Broseley

Benthall Hall

1 hr+   Apr–Sep

Situated on a plateau above the gorge of the Severn, this C16 stone house has mullioned and transomed windows and a stunning interior with carved oak staircase, decorated plaster ceilings and oak panelling. There is also an interesting Restoration church.

* Carefully restored plantsman's garden
* Old kitchen garden

Location
On B4375, 1 mile NW of Broseley,
1 mile SW of Ironbridge

Opening
Apr–Jun Tue–Wed, Bank Hols & Sun of Bank Hols
Jul–Sep Tue, Wed, Sun & Bank Hols
House 2pm–5.30pm
Gardens 1.30pm–5.30pm

Admission
Adult £4, Child £2

Contact
Broseley TF12 5RX

t 01952 882159
w nationaltrust.org.uk

520 Church Stretton

Acton Scott

3 hrs   Apr–Oct

Experience daily life on an upland farm at the turn of the century. The waggoner and his team of heavy horses work the land with vintage farm machines. Every day you can see milking by hand and butter making in the dairy. You will also see the farrier and the blacksmith.

* Lambing, shearing, cider making etc in season
* Children's holiday activities

Location
Off A49, 17 miles S of Shrewsbury,
14 miles N of Ludlow

Opening
30 Mar–31 Oct Tue–Sun & Bank Hols
10am–5pm

Admission
Adult £4.25, Child £2, Concs £3.75

Contact
nr Church Stretton SY6 6QN

t 01694 781306
w actonscottmuseum.co.uk
e acton.scott.museum@
shropshire–cc.gov.uk

521 Craven Arms

Secret Hills – Shropshire Hills Discovery Centre

2 hrs+   All year

A stylish and imaginative new building with a grass roof set within 25 acres of the Onny Meadows. Designed to improve understanding of the landscape, culture and heritage of the area, the centre provides a base for year-round entertainment and hands-on activities.

* Craft gallery & activities area
* Find out about earthquakes

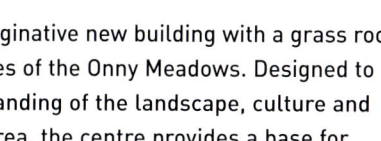

Location
Off A49, 7 miles N of Ludlow

Opening
Daily; Apr–Oct 10am–4.30pm
Nov Mar 10am 3.30pm

Admission
Adult £4.25, Child £2.75

Contact
School Road, Craven Arms SY7 9RS

t 01588 676000 / 676040
w shropshire-cc.gov.uk/discover.nsf
e secrethills@shropshire-cc.gov.uk

516 Bishop's Wood

Boscobel House & The Royal Oak

2 hrs+   Mar–Nov

A refuge for Charles II before he fled to France, this timber-framed farmhouse was later converted into a hunting lodge. It was called Boscobel after the Italian 'bosco bello', meaning 'in the midst of fair woods' and reflecting the woodland that once surrounded it.

* Its true use is thought to have been to hide Catholics
* Escape from Worcester and farm exhibition

Location
8 miles NW of Wolverhampton, on minor road between A41 & A5

Opening
Daily; Mar–Sep 11am–6pm, Oct 11am–5pm, Nov Wed–Sun 11am–4pm

Admission
Adult £4.40, Child £2.20, Concs £3.30

Contact
Brewood, Bishop's Wood ST19 9AR

t 01902 850244
w english-heritage.org.uk
e bascobelhouse@ english-heritage.org.uk

517 Bridgnorth

Dudmaston

2 hrs+   Mar–Sep

A late C17 house with intimate family rooms containing fine furniture and Dutch flower paintings, as well as important contemporary paintings and sculpture. The gardens are a mass of colour in spring and include a wooded valley or dingle.

* C20 art includes Nicholson, Moore & Hepworth
* Oak-panelled study opened to view in 2003

Location
4 miles SE of Bridgnorth, on A442

Opening
House 30 Mar–28 Sep Tue–Wed & Sun 2pm–5.30pm
Garden Mon–Wed & Sun 12 noon–6pm

Admission
House & Garden Adult £4.75, Child £2.40 *Garden only* £3.50, £1.50

Contact
Quatt, nr Bridgnorth WV15 6QN

t 01746 780866
w nationaltrust.org.uk
e dudmaston@nationaltrust.org.uk

518 Bridgnorth

Severn Valley Railway

3 hrs+   All year

A full-size standard-gauge line running regular steam-hauled passenger trains between Kidderminster and Bridgnorth, a distance of 16 miles. For most of the way, the route follows the meandering course of the River Severn closely.

* Crosses impressive Victoria Bridge
* Passengers may break the journey at any station

Location
Stations in Kidderminster, Bridgnorth & Bewdley

Opening
Daily; May–Sep; Oct–Apr Sat–Sun
Full timetable available on website

Admission
See website for full details

Contact
The Railway Station, Bewdley DY12 1BG

t 01299 403 816
w svr.co.uk

513 Ludlow

Wigmore Castle

2 hrs   All year

One of the most remarkable ruins in England, Wigmore Castle was abandoned pre-C17 and left to deteriorate naturally. Today, it has been buried up to first floor level by fallen upper floors, but its towers and curtain walls survive to their full height.

* WARNING: The castle has steep steps to the summit which are hazardous in icy conditions

Location
8 miles W of Ludlow on A4110

Opening
Dawn to dusk

Admission
Free

Contact
English Heritage West Midlands,
112 Colmore Row,
Birmingham B3 3AG

t 0121 6256820
w english-heritage.org.uk
e customers@english-heritage.org.uk

---

515 Symonds Yat

Amazing Hedge Puzzle

1 hr   Mar–Oct

Planted over 20 years ago by brothers Lindsay and Edward Heyes, the fun of the Amazing Hedge Puzzle has made it one of Herefordshire's most popular private tourist attractions. Learn about mazes through history and the myths surrounding them in the maze museum.

* Hands-on displays allow you to build your own maze
* Set in the beautiful countryside of the Wye Valley

Location
Follow signs on B4164, off A40
between Ross-on-Wye & Monmouth

Opening
Daily; Good Friday–Sep
and half terms 11am–5pm
Mar & Oct Sat–Sun 11am–4pm

Admission
Adult £3.50, Child £2, Concs £2.50

Contact
Jubilee Park, Symonds Yat West,
Ross-on-Wye HR9 6DA

t 01600 890360
w mazes.co.uk

---

514 Ross-on-Wye

Goodrich Castle

1 hr   All year

This fortified baronial palace stands majestically on a red sandstone crag, commanding the passage of the River Wye into the picturesque wooded valley of Symonds Yat. Much of the stone used was quarried from the rock around the base of the castle, creating a deep moat.

* Cannon that destroyed the castle in 1645 is now on display
* Views over River Wye & Symonds Yat

WC

Location
5 miles S of Ross-on-Wye off A40

Opening
Daily; Apr–Sep 10am–6pm
Oct 10am–5pm;
Nov–Mar Wed–Sun
10am–1pm & 2–4pm

Admission
Adult £3.70, Child £1.90, Concs £2.80

Contact
Ross-on-Wye HR9 6HY

t 01600 890538
w english-heritage.org.uk

©English Heritage Photographic Library/Jonathan Bailey

509   Kington

Hergest Croft Gardens

2 hrs+   Apr–Oct

In the heart of the Welsh Marches, with stunning views towards the Black Mountains, Hergest Croft was created over 100 years by three generations of the Banks family. There are hidden valleys, woodland glades, open parkland and flower borders for year-round beauty.

* National Collection of birch & maples
* Rhododendrons and azaleas

Location
Signed on A44 from Kington

Opening
3 Apr–31 Oct 12.30–5.30pm

Admission
Adult £4.50, Child free

Contact
Kington HR5 3EG
t 01544 230160
w hergest.co.uk
e gardens@hergest.co.uk

510   Leominster

Berrington Hall

2 hrs   Mar–Oct

With sweeping views to the Brecon Beacons, this elegant Henry Holland house was built in the late C18 and is set in parkland designed by Capability Brown. A rather austere external appearance belies a surprisingly delicate interior.

* Beautiful ceilings & a spectacular staircase hall
* Good collection of furniture & paintings

Location
3 miles N of Leominster

Opening
Times vary, please phone for details

Admission
Adult £5, Child £2.50

Contact
Leominster HR6 0DW
t 01568 615721
w nationaltrust.org.uk
e berrington@nationaltrust.org.uk

511   Leominster

Croft Castle

2 hrs   Mar–Oct

Re-opened in 2003 after a major refurbishment programme, with additional showrooms to complement the fine Georgian interior and period furnishings. The gardens and park offer pleasant walks and magnificent views.

* Joint tickets with Berrington Hall available
* Beautiful period walled garden

Location
5 miles NW of Leominster

Opening
6 Mar–28 Mar Sat–Sun 1pm–5pm
1 Apr–30 Sep Wed–Sun 1pm–5pm
1 Oct–31 Oct Sat–Sun 1pm–5pm

Admission
House & Garden Adult £4.40, Child £2.20
Garden Adult £3.10, Child £1.55

Contact
nr Leominster HR6 9PW
t 01568 780246
w nationaltrust.org.uk
e croftcastle@nationaltrust.org.uk

512   Leominster

Hampton Court Gardens

3 hrs   All year

With the stunning backdrop of a late medieval castle and surrounded by acres of parkland, Hampton Court has much to offer. Water features highly and there are canals, island pavilions, a waterfall and a sunken garden, plus two very different walled gardens.

* A maze of a thousand yews
* Organically managed site

Location
A417 nr junction with A49

Opening
Times vary, phone for details

Admission
Adult £5, Child £3, Concs £4.75

Contact
Hope under Dinmore,
Leominster HR6 0PN
t 01568 797 777
w hamptoncourt.org.uk
e office@hamptoncourt.org.uk

505 Hereford

The Cider Museum

1 hr   All year

Explore the story of traditional cider making: how apples were harvested, milled and pressed, and how the resulting juice was fermented to produce cider. You can also walk through a reconstructed farm ciderhouse and see the 300-year-old travelling cider maker's 'tack'.

* Visit the original champagne cider cellars
* See the distillation process being used for cider brandy

Location
In W Hereford, off A438

Opening
Daily; Apr–Oct 10am–5pm
Nov–Dec 11am–3pm
Jan–Mar Tue–Sun 11am–3pm

Admission
Adult £2.70, Child & Concs £2.20

Contact
21 Ryelands Street, Hereford HR4 0LW

t 01432 354 207
w cidermuseum.co.uk
e info@cidermuseum.co.uk

506 Hereford

Hereford Cathedral, Mappa Mundi & Chained Library

2 hrs   All year

Housed within the cathedral's C15 south west cloister and the new library building is an exhibition that uses models and original artefacts to reveal the secrets of Mappa Mundi, the largest and most elaborate complete pre-C15 world map in existence.

* The world's largest chained library – 1500 rare books
* Working stonemasons yard & cathedral shop

Location
Hereford town centre

Opening
Daily; Summer Mon–Sat
10am–4.15pm
Sun 11am–3.15pm;
Winter Mon–Sat 11am–3.15pm

Admission
Adult £4.50, Child & Concs £3.50

Contact
5 College Cloisters, Cathedral Close,
Hereford HR1 2NG

t 01432 374200
w herefordcathedral.co.uk
e visits@herefordcathedral.co.uk

507 Hereford

The Old House

½ hr   Apr–Sep

Originally completed in 1621, by the end of C19 the building had been taken over by a local bank that later became part of Lloyds Bank. Lloyds moved out in 1928 and donated the house to the city. The Old House is now a museum recreating C17 life.

* One of the finest examples of Jacobean architecture
* Virtual tours for those that can't climb stairs

Location
Centre of High Town, signposted

Opening
Apr–Sep Tue–Sat 10am–5pm
Sun & Bank Hols 10am–4pm

Admission
Free

Contact
High Town, Hereford HR1 2AA

t 01432 260694

508 Hereford

The Weir

1 hr+   Jan–Oct

A delightful riverside garden, particularly spectacular in early spring and with fine views over the River Wye and the Black Mountains. The late C18 house (not open to the public) sits on top of steep slopes that fall away to the river.

* Walks through beech woodland high above the river
* Created by the Parr family in the 1920s

Location
5 miles W of Hereford, signed from
A438

Opening
17 Jan–10 Jan Sat–Sun 11am–4pm
Feb Wed–Sun 11am–6pm
Mar daily 11am–6pm
Apr–Oct Wed–Sun & Bank Hols
11am–6pm

Admission
Adult £3.50, Child £1.75

Contact
Swainshill, nr Hereford HR4 7QF

t 01981 590509
w nationaltrust.org.uk
e theweir@ntrust.org.uk

501 Abbeydore

Dore Abbey

1 hr   All year

Founded by French monks in 1147, Dore Abbey is remarkable for the wealth of features dating back to C12. Today only the chancel area and transepts remain but the foundations of the nave, cloisters, chapter house and domestic buildings are all still in evidence.

* The only Cistercian monastery in Britain founded from Morimond, France

Location
In Abbeydore village on B4347

Opening
Daily

Admission
Free

Contact
Abbeydore, Hereford,
Herefordshire,
HR2 0AD

w www.doreabbey.org.uk

502 Bromyard

Brockhampton Estate

1 hr   All year

This 1,700–acre estate still maintains farms and has extensive areas of woodland, including ancient oak and beech. Visitors can enjoy a variety of walks through both park and woodland. At the heart of the estate lies Lower Brockhampton House, a late C14 moated manor house.

* Timber-framed gatehouse and ruined chapel
* Woodland is home to interesting range of wildlife

Location
2 miles E of Bromyard on A44

Opening
House Mar Sat & Sun 12noon–4pm
Apr–Sep Wed–Sun 12noon–5pm
Oct Wed–Sun 12noon–4pm
Estate all year dawn to dusk

Admission
Adult £3.60, Child £1.80

Contact
Greenfields, Bringsty WR6 5TB

t 01885 488099 / 482077
w nationaltrust.org.uk
e brockhampton@nationaltrust.org.uk

503 Bromyard

Bromyard Heritage Centre

½ hr   Apr–Oct

Based in an C18 stable block, Bromyard Heritage Centre displays aspects of Bromyard's past, together with an extensive exhibition of hops and hop growing. This traces the growing and picking cycle and changing methods of cultivation since C15.

* Host to highly successful Year of the Hop exhibition
* Exhibition of rural & urban developments in the town

Location
Signposted from A44

Opening
Apr–Oct Mon–Sat 10am–4pm

Admission
Free

Contact
Rowberry Street, Bromyard HR7 4DU

t 01885 482341
w visitorlinks.com

504 Bromyard

Shortwood Family Farm

4 hrs+   Easter–Oct

Ideal for all the family, this organic farm offers visitors the opportunity to collect eggs, feed animals, milk a cow by hand, see at first hand the benefits of organic farming, buy fresh produce, visit mini-farm world and pets' corner, follow the farm trail, and take a trailer ride.

Location
Signed from the A417 between Burley Gate, Bodenham & from Pencombe village

Opening
Daily; Easter–Oct from 10am

Admission
Adult £4.50, Child £2.90

Contact
Pencombe,
Bromyard HR7 4RP

t 01885 400205
w shortwoodfarm.co.uk

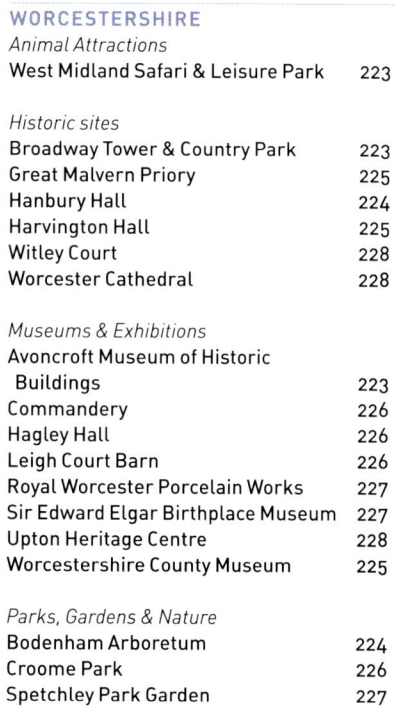

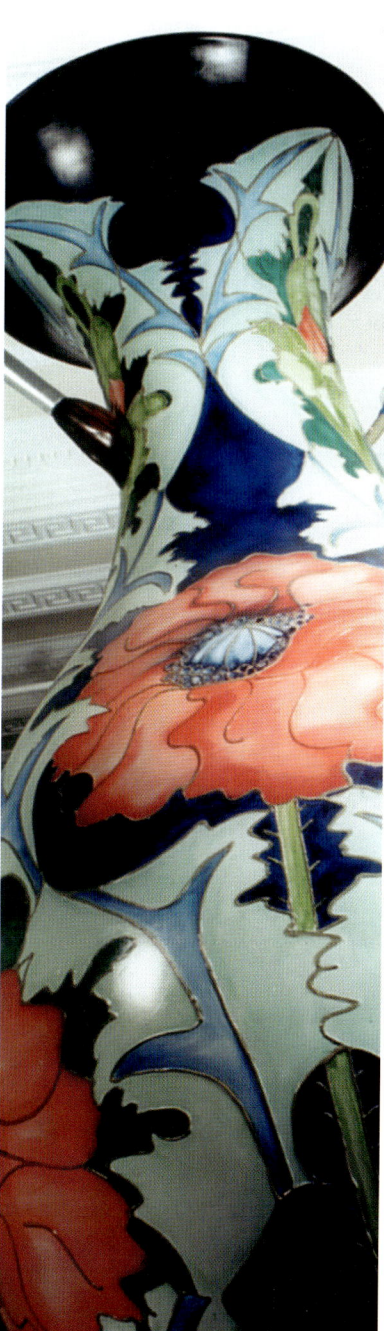

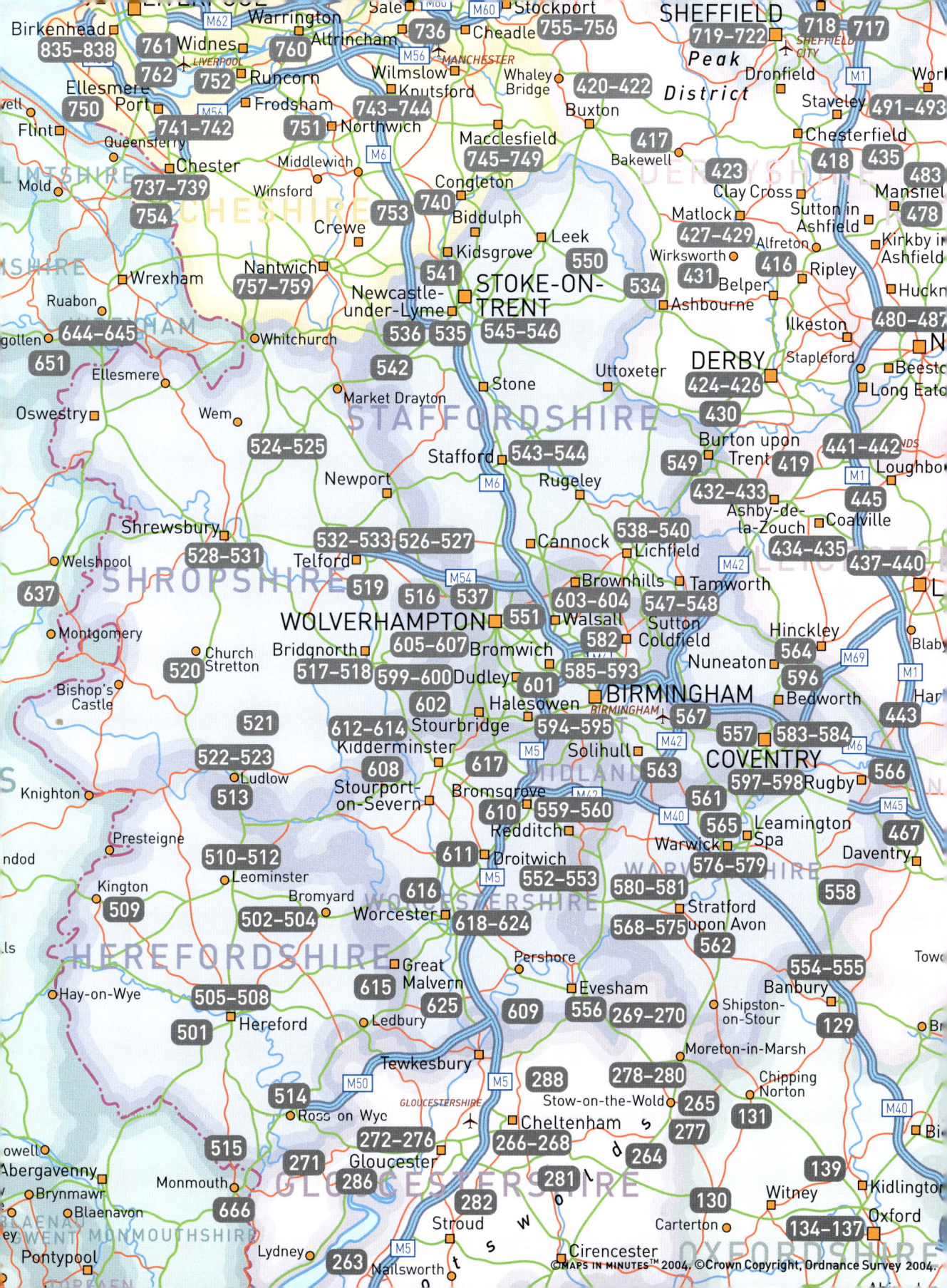

Alstonefield, Staffordhire

West Midlands

Herefordshire Shropshire Staffordshire
Warwickshire West Midlands Worcestershire

498 Oakham

Oakham Castle

½ hr   All year

The Great Hall, built in about 1180-90, is a fine example of late C12 domestic architecture. The remains of other parts of the house lie beneath the grass of the inner bailey. The hall posseses a range of C12 figure sculpture.

* Stonework by masons from Canterbury Cathedral
* Over 200 horseshoes hang on the walls of the castle

Location
In Oakham town centre, just off the market place

Opening
Mon–Sat 10.30am–5pm
Closed 1pm–1.30pm week days
Sun 2pm–4pm

Admission
Free

Contact
c/o Rutland County Museum, Catmose Street, Oakham LE15 6HW

t 01572 758440
e museum@rutland.gov.uk

499 Oakham

Rutland County Museum

1 hr+   All Year

Rutland Museum is a perfect introduction to England's smallest county. The new Welcome to Rutland gallery is a guide to the house of Rutland and leads into displays of local archaeology and history, and an extensive rural life collection.

* A rare Saunderson tractor
* Tools and equipment of village tradesmen

Location
Off A603, near Oakham town centre

Opening
Daily; Mon–Sat 10.30am–5pm
Sun 2pm–4pm

Admission
Free

Contact
Catmose Street, Oakham LE15 6HW

t 01572 758440
e museum@rutland.gov.uk

500 Oakham

Rutland Water

2 hrs+   All year

The largest man-made lake in western Europe, this attractive 3,100-acre reservoir has an international reputation for balancing leisure activities with wildlife conservation. Visitors may windsurf, rock-climb or canoe, hire a dinghy, bike or fishing boat, or just relax.

* Cruise on the *Rutland Belle* from Whitwell Harbour
* Range of craft available for hire or launch your own

Location
Just off A606, signed from A1

Opening
Daily; Jun–Sep 10am–5pm
Oct–May 10am–4pm

Admission
Free, charges for car park

Contact
Tourist Information Centre, Sykes Lane, Empington, Rutland LE 15 8PX

t 01572 653026
w rutlandwater.net
e tic@rutland-water.freeserve.co.uk

494 Barnsdale

Drought Garden & Arboretum

½ hr   All year

Designed by the late Geoff Hamilton with refurbishment by Nick Hamilton, this garden – on a south-facing clay slope at Barnsdale – has survived dry summers and penetrating frost. The arboretum shows the species of trees planted around the reservoir.

* Accolade Winner 2002
* The Best of its Kind 2003

Location
Accessed from A606
Oakham–Stamford road. Turn into Barnsdale car park at Rutland Water

Opening
Daily; All reasonable times

Admission
Free

Contact
Barnsdale, Rutland Water

t 01572 653026
w ruttlandwater.net

495 Clipsham

Clipsham Yew Tree Avenue

1½ hrs   All year

The Yew Tree Avenue is a unique collection of 150 clipped yew trees, most over 200 years old, which was once the drive to Clipsham Hall. The topiary was begun in 1870 by Amos Alexander, the estate's head forester, who lived in the gate lodge at the foot of the avenue.

* Clipping each autumn by Forestry Commission
* Muntjac may be seen crossing the avenue

Location
Less than 1 mile E of Clipsham on Castle Bytham road

Opening
Daily; All reasonable times

Admission
Free

Contact
Forest Enterprise, North Hants
Top Lodge, Fineshade NN17 3BB

t 01780 444394
w forestry.gov.uk
e northants@forestry.gsi.gov.uk

496 Lyddington

Lyddington Bede House

1 hr   Apr–Sept

Lyddington Bede House was originally a wing of a medieval rural palace belonging to the bishops of Lincoln. In 1600, the building was converted into an almshouse and remained a home for pensioners until the 1930s.

* Great Chamber features a beautiful ceiling cornice
* Bedesmen's rooms with tiny windows and fireplaces

Location
In Lyddington, 6 miles N of Corby, 1 mile E of A6003, next to the church

Opening
Please ring for deatails

Admission
Adult £3.20, Child £1.60, Concs £2.40
Prices for events vary

Contact
Bluecoat Lane, Lyddington LE15 9LZ

t 01572 822438
w english-heritage.org.uk

497 Normanton Village

Normanton Church

½ hr   April–Oct

The church, with its semi-circular portico and tower, was built in 1826-29. Its original site would have placed it below the proposed water line of Rutland Water, but it was raised and now stands proudly beside Rutland Water on a pier of stones.

* Museum and exhibition
* History of the building of the reservoir

Location
South of Rutland, off A606

Opening
Daily; Apr–Sep 11am–4pm
Oct Sat & Sun 11am–4pm

Admission
Adult £1, Child 50p

Contact
Tourist Information Centre,
Sykes Lane, Empington LE15 8PX

t 01572 653026
w rutnet.co.uk

491   Worksop

Clumber Park

2–3 hrs   All year

Part of Nottinghamshire's famed 'Dukeries', at Clumber Park there are over 3,800 acres of parkland, peaceful woods, open heath and rolling farmland with a superb serpentine lake at their heart. Although the house was demolished in 1938, many features of the estate remain.

* Outstanding Gothic Revival chapel
* Walled kitchen garden

Location
4 miles SE of Worksop

Opening
Park Daily; Apr–Sep 9am–7pm
Oct–Mar daily 9am–5pm
Garden Daily; Mar–Oct 10am–5pm

Admission
Free, £3.80 per car

Contact
The Estate Office, Clumber Park,
Worksop S80 3AZ

t 01909 476592
w nationaltrust.org.uk/clumberpark
e clumberpark@nationaltrust.org.uk

©National Trust Photographic Library

492   Worksop

Harley Gallery

1 hr   All year

The Harley Foundation, set up as a charitable trust in 1977 by the late Ivy, Duchess of Portland, is based in the Ducal Estate of Welbeck. As well as offering studio space to artists and craftspeople, it also funds an art gallery and programme of exhibitions.

* Historical gallery exhibiting decorative and fine art
* Full programme of events

Location
5 miles S of Worksop on the A60

Opening
15 Jan –Dec Tue–Sun & Bank Hols
10am–5pm

Admission
Free

Contact
Welbeck, Mansfield Road, Worksop
S80 3LW

t 01909 501700
w harleygallery.co.uk
e info@harley-wellbeck.co.uk

493   Worksop

Mr Straw's House

1 hr+   Apr–Nov

This modest, semi-detached, Edwardian house provides a fascinating insight into early C20 everyday life. The interior has remained unaltered since the 1930s and features contemporary wallpaper, Victorian furniture and household objects.

* Displays of family costumes
* A typical suburban garden

Location
Follow signs to Bassetlaw General
Hospital, signed from Blyth Road

Opening
Apr–Nov Tue–Sat 11am–4.30pm

Admission
Pre-booked timed ticket only
Adult £4.60, Child £2.30

Contact
5 Blyth Grove, Worksop S81 0JG

t 01909 482380
w nationaltrust.org.uk
e mrstrawshouse@
nationaltrust.org.uk

488 Ollerton

Rufford Abbey

  4 hrs All year

This ruined, former Cistercian monastery was founded in C12, but following its dissolution in 1536, its lands were granted to George Talbot, 4th Earl of Shrewsbury. The Talbot family then went on to transform the buildings into a country house.

* Stable block houses a contemporary craft exhibition
* The gardens were re-established in the late 1970s

Location
2 miles S of Ollerton, off A614

Opening
Daily; Apr–Oct 10am–5pm
Nov–Mar 10am–4pm

Admission
Free, Sat–Sun & Bank Hols £1.50
for car park

Contact
Ollerton, nr Newark NG22 9DF

t 01623 822944
w notinghamshiretourism.co.uk

---

489 Southwell

Southwell Minster

  2 hrs All year

Southwell Minster, with its majestic Norman nave and glorious C13 chapter house, is one of the least-known jewels in the crown of Nottinghamshire. Nearby is the Minster Centre with an audio-visual theatre showing a film on the life of the Minster, a library, gallery and bookshop.

* Dedicated education officer who organises tours
  and talks for children

Location
Southwell town centre

Opening
Minster daily
Minster Centre Mon–Fri, 9am–5pm;
Sat, 10.30am–3.30pm, Sun 2.30–
4.30pm

Admission
Free but donation welcome

Contact
Southwell, Nottinghamshire

t 01636 812649
w www.southwellminster.org.uk
e nikki-di@southwellminster.org.uk

---

490 Southwell

Southwell Workhouse

  1 hr+ Mar–Nov

The lives of the poor and destitute in the C19 and C20 are revealed at Southwell workhouse. Explore the building and its history, including the segregated staircases and rooms, and unlock the stories of the people who lived and worked there.

* Play the Master's Punishment game
* Meet some of the 'characters' who lived here

Location
13 miles from Nottingham on A612,
8 miles from Newark on A617 & A612

Opening
Mar–Jul & Sep–Nov Thu–Mon 12
noon–5pm
Aug 11am–5pm

Admission
Adult £4.40, Child £2.20

Contact
Upton Road, Southwell NG25 0PT

t 01636 817250
w nationaltrust.org.uk
e theworkhouse@
nationaltrust.org.uk

Tales of Robin Hood

1–2 hrs   All year

The swashbuckling adventures of Robin Hood have inspired storytellers for more than 700 years. Explore the world of this infamous and endearing outlaw and experience medieval life, legend and adventure by fleeing through the forest to escape the evil Sheriff.

* Regular Robin Hood events
* Medieval banquets are held on Fridays and Saturdays

Location
In the city centre, next to the castle, signed from M1

Opening
Daily; 10am–5.30pm

Admission
Adult £6.95, Child £4.95, Concs £5.95

Contact
30-38 Maid Marian Way,
Nottingham NG1 6GF

t 0115 9483284
w robinhood.uk.com
e robinhoodcentre@mail.com

Wollaton Hall Museum

3 hrs+   All year

Set in over 500 acres of historic deer park, Wollaton Hall is a spectacular Tudor building, designed by Robert Smythson and completed in 1588. It is now home to the city's natural history museum, industrial museum, a steam-engine house, a visitor centre, and a gallery.

* Why Change Things? exhibition
* Explore underground caves

Location
3 miles from Nottingham centre

Opening
Natural History Museum Daily; Oct–Mar 11am–4pm; Apr–Sep 11am–5pm
Industrial Museum Daily; Apr–Sep 11am–5pm

Admission
Each museum Adult £1.50, Child £1 (Sat–Sun) Free (Mon–Fri), Concs 80p

Contact
Wollaton Park,
Nottingham NG8 2AE

t 0115 915 3900
w www.nottinghamcity.gov.uk

Holocaust Centre, Beth Shalom

2–3 hrs   All year

Beth Shalom is set in two acres of beautiful gardens and provides a range of facilities for visitors to explore the history and implications of the Holocaust. The main features are its red brick memorial building, permanent exhibition on the Nazi period and memorial gardens.

* Art and photography exhibitions about the Holocaust
* Survivors regularly speak at the centre

Location
Large buildings on right between Laxton and Ollerton

Opening
Daily; Apr–Sep 10am–5pm
Oct–Mar Mon–Fri 10am–5pm

Admission
Adult £6, Child & Concs £4

Contact
Laxton, nr Ollerton NG22 0PA

t 01623 836627
w holocaustcentre.net
e office@bethshalom.com

482 Nottingham

Galleries of Justice

2–3 hrs   All year

A tour through three centuries of crime, punishment and law. Located in the Shire Hall, it includes Victorian courtrooms, an C18 prison, exercise yard, cave cells, a women's prison with bath house and laundry, medieval cave system and an Edwardian police station.

* Costumed interpreters bring the experience to life
* Series of temporary exhibitions

Location
Central Nottingham, nr Broadmarsh Shopping Centre

Opening
Tue–Sun & Bank Hols 10am–5pm

Admission
Adult £6.95, Child £5.25, Concs £5.95

Contact
Shire Hall, High Pavement, Lace Market, Nottingham NG1 1HN
t 0115 9520555
w galleriesofjustice.org.uk

---

483 Nottingham

The Lace Centre

½ hr   All year

Nottingham is famous for its lacemaking heritage and Nottingham lace is a rich, varied fabric, knitted, twisted or embroidered in the UK by a member of the British Lace Federation. The Lace Centre is housed in a C14 medieval house in the heart of the city.

* Weekly bobbin lace demonstrations
* Hands-on experiences on Thursday afternoons

Location
Opposite Nottingham Castle

Opening
Jan–Mar daily 10am–4pm
Apr–Dec Mon–Sat 10am–5pm
Sun 11am–4pm

Admission
Free

Contact
Severns Building, Castle Road, Nottingham NG1 6AA
t 0115 9413539
e nottinghamlace@btopenworld.com

---

484 Nottingham

Nottingham Castle

1–2 hrs   All year

Situated high above the city, Nottingham Castle was originally constructed by William the Conqueror, demolished after the Civil War and then rebuilt in the C17. As well as displays about its turbulent history, the castle has paintings, sculptures, china and silverware.

* Network of caves and passageways beneath the castle
* Robin Hood statue

Location
Central Nottingham

Opening
Daily; 10am–4.30pm

Admission
Weekdays free
Sat–Sun & Bank Hols Adult £2,
Child & Concs £1

Contact
Lenton Road, Nottingham NG1 6EL
t 0115 9153700
w nottinghamcity.gov.uk

479 Newark

Newark Air Museum

2 hrs   All year

The museum's impressive collection currently stands at over 65 aircraft and cockpit sections, including transport, training and reconnaissance aircraft and helicopters and a diverse selection of jet fighters and bombers.

* Post-war air-to-air missile display
* History of RAF Winthorpe, wartime bomber training

Location
Easily accessible from A1, A46, A17, A1133 and Newark bypass

Opening
Daily; Mar–Oct 10am–5pm
Nov–Feb 10am–4pm

Admission
Adult £5.25, Child £3.50, Concs £4.50

Contact
Winthorpe Showground, Newark
NG24 2NY

t 01636 707170
w newarkairmuseum.co.uk
e newarkair@lineone.net

480 Nottingham

Angel Row Gallery

1–2 hrs   All year

This is a one of the region's leading contemporary art galleries, with a programme of exhibitions that covers a whole range of art, including painting, photography, video and installations. The gallery also runs workshops and hosts talks by leading artists.

Location
Central Nottingham

Opening
Mon, Tue, Thu–Sat 10am–5pm
Wed 10am–7pm

Admission
Free

Contact
Central Library Building, 3 Angel Row,
Nottingham NG1 6HP

t 0115 9152869
w angelrowgallery.com
e angelrow.marketing@
nottinghamcity.gov.uk

481 Nottingham

City of Caves

1 hr+   All year

Descend under the city to man-made, Anglo-Saxon tunnels to discover an enchanted well, a medieval tannery which includes a pillar cave (1250 AD), original Victorian slums, and the Anderson shelter, used during the Blitz. Learn more about ongoing archaeological digs.

* Have a go at real archaeology
* Special events throughout the year

Location
Nottingham city centre. Inside the Broadmarsh shopping centre on the upper level

Opening
Daily; 10.30am–4.30pm

Admission
Adult £4.25, Child/Concs £3.50

Contact
Drury Walk,
Broadmarsh Centre,
Nottingham NG1 7LS

t 0115 988 1955
w www.cityofcaves.com

477 Edwinstowe

Sherwood Forest Country Park & Visitor Centre

2 hrs   All year

A good place to begin any exploration of Sherwood Forest is the visitor centre. Find out what life would have been like for outlaws, kings and commoners in Sherwood Forest during the Middle Ages. Enjoy the trails and discover the forest yourself.

* See the Major Oak, Robin Hood's hiding place
* National Nature Reserve

Location
In Edwinstowe village, off B6034

Opening
Visitor Centre Daily; summer 10am–5pm , winter 10am–4.30pm
Park dawn to dusk

Admission
Free, charges for car park

Contact
Edwinstowe, nr Mansfield NG21 9HN

t 01623 823202
w sherwoodforest.org.uk
e sherwood.forest@nott-cc.gov.uk

478 Mansfield

Mansfield Museum & Art Gallery

1 hr   All year

Explore the history of Mansfield and the surrounding area. Permanent displays illustrate the social, industrial and natural history of the area. New 2005 Xplorative hands-on environmental exhibition.

* Pottery pieces from Derby, Pinxton and Mansfield
* Varied programme of temporary exhibitions

Location
5 mins walk from market place

Opening
Mon–Sat 10am–5pm

Admission
Free

Contact
Leeming Street, Mansfield NG18 1NG

t 01623 463088
w mansfield.gov.uk
e lweston@mansfield.gov.uk

474 Towcester

Canal Museum

2–4 hrs   All Year

Housed in an old corn mill on the Grand Union Canal are exhibits from two centuries of canal history, including a reconstructed narrowboat, with all its traditional furniture and equipment. Trips can be taken through the mile-long Blisworth Tunnel.

* Cruise along the Grand Union Canal

Location
S of Northampton, 10 mins from M1 junction 15 and A5, on Grand Union Canal S of Blisworth Tunnel

Opening
Oct–Mar Tue–Sun 10am–4pm
Apr–Sep Mon–Sun 10am–5pm

Admission
Adult £3, Child £2.50, Concs £2.50

Contact
Stoke Bruerne, Towcester NN12 7SE

t 01604 862 229
w waterwaystrust.co.uk
e canal.museum@waterwaystrust.co.uk

475 Wansford

Prebendal Manor House

2 hrs+   May–Sep

This C13 Grade 1 listed manor house is the oldest surviving dwelling in Northamptonshire and is steeped in history. The recreated medieval gardens are unique to the area and are the largest in Europe. Visit the C16 dovecote and the large C18 tithe barn museum.

* Rare breeds of sheep and pigs and medieval farming
* Explore the history of the Prebends

Location
A few miles from A1 and A605, signed from nearby villages

Opening
Please phone for details

Admission
Adult £5.50, Child £2.50, Concs £5

Contact
Nassington, Peterborough PE8 6QG

t 01780 782575
w prebendal-manor.demon.co.uk
e info@prebendal-manor.demon.co.uk

476 Wellingborough

Irchester Country Park

4–6 hrs   All year

Explore a network of trails running across 83 hectares of mixed woodland and observe the wealth of wildlife, including woodpeckers and sparrowhawks. A Forestry Centre of Excellence, the park balances conservation with timber production and recreation.

* Ironstone railway museum
* Accessible trails and orienteering trail

Location
2 miles S of Wellingborough, on B570, in the Nene Valley

Opening
Park Daily; 24 hrs
Car park 9am–5pm

Admission
Free, £1.50 for car park

Contact
Gypsy Lane, Little Irchester, Wellingborough NN29 7DL

t 01933 276866
w northamptonshire.gov.uk
e irchester@northamptonshire.gov.uk

470 Northampton

Holdenby House, Gardens & Falconry Centre

  2 hrs Apr–Sep

Across the fields from Althorp lies Holdenby, a house whose royal connections go back over 400 years. Its history is complemented by a regal collection of birds of prey, including the only naturally reared male black eagle on display anywhere.

* Based on the remaining kitchen wing of the old palace
* Built in 1583 by Sir Christopher Hatton

Location
6 miles NW of Northampton, off A5199 or A428

Opening
Easter–Sep 30 Sun & Bank Hols 1pm–5pm
Sep Sun 1pm–5pm

Admission
Gardens & Falconry Centre
Adult £4.50, Child £3, Concs £4

Contact
Holdenby, Northampton NN6 8DJ
t 01604 770074
w holdenby.com
e enquiries@holdenby.com

471 Northampton

Northampton Museum & Art Gallery

  1 hr All year

Reflecting the town's proud standing as Britain's boot and shoe capital, the Northampton Museum & Art Gallery features the world's largest collection of footwear. Other displays include British and Oriental pottery and porcelain and a display of fine glassware.

* Programme of temporary exhibitions and events
* The town's history from the Stone Age to the present day

Location
Northampton town centre

Opening
Daily; Mon–Sat 10am–5pm, Sun 2–5pm

Admission
Free

Contact
4–6 Guildhall Road,
Northampton NN1 1DP
t 01604 838111
w northampton.gov.uk/museums
e museums@northampton.gov.uk

472 South Northampton

Abington Museum

  3 hrs+ All year

Housed in a C15 manor house which was once the home of Shakespeare's granddaughter, Elizabeth Bernard, the museum is now home to displays of Victorian curiosities, Northamptonshire military history, a costume gallery, local history, and a leathercraft gallery.

* C17 oak panelled room
* C19 fashion gallery

Location
Approximately 1½ miles E of the town centre

Opening
Please phone for details

Admission
Free

Contact
Abington Park,
Park Avenue,
South Northampton NN1 5LW
t 01604 838110
w www.northampton.gov.uk/museums

473 Oundle

Lyveden New Bield

  1 hr+ All year

This incomplete Elizabethan garden lodge remains unaltered since building work stopped 400 years ago. Designed in the shape of a cross, with fascinating architectural stonework, the lodge is set in beautiful countryside adjoining the remains of a moated garden.

* Designed by Sir Thomas Tresham
* Elizabethan water gardens

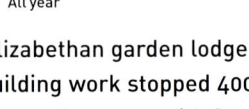

Location
4 miles SW of Oundle on A427, 3 miles E of Brigstock, leading off A6116

Opening
Please phone for details

Admission
Adult £2.50, Child £1.20

Contact
nr Oundle, Peterborough PE8 5AT
t 01832 205358
w nationaltrust.org.uk/lyveden
e lyvedennewbield@nationaltrust.org.uk

467 Daventry

Canons Ashby House

1 hr+   Apr–Oct

Constructed in the mid-C16, this charming house has survived substantially unaltered since 1710. The interior contains wall paintings and Jacobean plasterwork, with rich panelling in the Winter Parlour. Edward Dryden's formal gardens have been restored.

* Remains of an Augustinian priory
* Orchard containing varieties of typical C16 apple trees

Location
Between Northampton and Banbury

Opening
Apr–Sep Sat–Wed 1pm–5pm
Oct Sat–Wed 12 noon–4pm

Admission
Adult £5.60, Child £2.90

Contact
Daventry NN11 3SD

t 01327 860044
w nationaltrust.org.uk
e canonsashby@nationaltrust.org.uk

468 Kettering

Rushton Triangular Lodge

1 hr   Apr–Oct

This triangular building was designed and built by Sir Thomas Tresham in 1593 as a testament to his Catholicism, for which he had been imprisoned. Consequently, the lodge is emblazoned with references to the number three and the Holy Trinity.

* Colourful house adorned with dates and emblems
* Three windows, three floors, three roof gables

Location
1 mile W of Rushton, on A6, on unclassified road 3 miles from Desborough

Opening
Daily; Apr–Sep 10am–6pm
Oct 10am–5pm

Admission
Adult £2, Child £1, Concs £1.50

Contact
Rushton, Kettering NN14 1RP

t 01536 710761
w english-heritage.org.uk

469 Market Harborough

Kelmarsh Hall & Gardens

2 hrs+   Easter–Sep

This early C18 Palladian style house was designed by James Gibbs. It includes a Chinese room with hand-painted wallpaper, interesting gardens, a lake and woodland walks. A herd of British white cattle roam the parkland.

* Managed by the Kelmarsh Trust
* Regular events throughout the season

Location
On A508 at Kelmarsh village

Opening
House Easter–Sep 4 Sun & Bank Hols 2.30pm–5pm
Gardens Apr–Sep Sun & Thu 2pm–5pm

Admission
Adult £4, Child £2, Concs £3.50

Contact
Kelmarsh, Northampton NN6 9LU

t 01604 686543
w kelmarsh.com
e enquiries@kelmarsh.com

464   Corby

Deene Park

2 hrs   Jun–Aug

Deene park is a largely C16 house incorporating a medieval manor. It's built around a courtyard and had important rooms added during the reign of George III. It was the seat of the 7th Earl of Cardigan who led the charge of the Light Brigade at Balaklava in 1854.

* Crimean War exhibition of uniforms and memorabilia
* Beautiful gardens and parkland

Location
6 miles NE of Corby, off A43

Opening
Jun–Aug Sun & Bank Hols 2pm–5pm

Admission
Adult £6, Child £2.50, Concs £5.50

Contact
Corby NN17 3EW

t 01780 450278
w deenepark.com
e admin@deenepark.com

465   Corby

Kirby Hall

1–2 hrs   All year

Featuring decorative carving and ornate gardens fit for a queen, Kirby Hall is one of the great Elizabethan houses, built in the hope of a royal visit. The great hall and state rooms have recently been refitted and redecorated to authentic C17 and C18 designs.

* Elizabethan festivals
* Theatre productions

Location
On an unclassified road off A43, 4 miles NE of Corby

Opening
Daily; 1 Apr–31 Oct 10am–6pm (5pm in Oct); 1 Nov–28 Mar Sat & Sun 10am–4pm

Admission
Adult £3.50, Child £1.80, Concs £2.60

Contact
Kirby Hall Deene, nr Corby NN17 5EN

t 01536 203230
w www.english-heritage.org.uk

466   Cottesbrooke

Cottesbrooke Hall & Gardens

2 hrs+   May–Sep

Architecturally magnificent Queen Anne house with a renowned picture collection, featuring sporting and equestrian subjects. Other collections include fine furniture and porcelain. Cottesbrooke is reputed to be the model for Jane Austen's Mansfield Park.

* HHA / Christie's Garden of the Year 2000
* Guided tours of the house are available

Location
At A14 junction 1 head S on A5199, signposted for Cottesbrooke

Opening
May & Jun, Wed–Thu & Bank Hols, 2pm–5.30pm
Jul, Aug & Sep, Thu & Bank Hols 2pm–5.30pm

Admission
Hall & Gardens Adult £6, Child £3
Gardens Adult £4, Child £2

Contact
Cottesbrooke, Northampton NN6 8PF

t 01604 505808
w cottesbrookehall.co.uk
e hall@cottesbrooke.co.uk

461 Spalding

The Butterfly & Wildlife Park

4hrs   Mar–Oct

Set in the heart of the Fens, the park has a tropical house, a reptile area with crocodiles and snakes, a creepy-crawlie house, and an ant room. Outdoor attractions include a birds-of-prey centre which runs twice-daily flying displays, an animal centre, and an adventure playground.

* Quality Assured Visitor Attraction
* Lincolnshire Family Attraction of the Year 2003

Location
Signposted off the A17 at Long Sutton

Opening
Daily; End Mar–end Oct from 10am
Please phone for details

Admission
Adult £5.50, Child (3–16) £3.80, Senior £4.80

Contact
Long Sutton, Spalding
PE12 9LE

t 01406 363833
w butterflyandwildlifepark.co.uk
e butterflypark@hotmail.com

462 Spilsby

Lincoln Aviation Centre

4 hrs   All year

This aircraft museum is based on a 1940s bomber airfield and has a number of exhibits, ranging from the original control tower and war-time blast shelter to Barnes Wallis' bouncing bomb and squadron and airfield photographs.

* Avro Lancaster bomber NX611 'Just Jane'
* RAF Escaping Society

Location
On A155, between Revesey & East Kirkby

Opening
Easter–Oct Mon–Sat 9.30am–5pm
Nov–Easter Mon–Sat 10am–4pm

Admission
Adult £5, Child £1.50, Concs £4.50

Contact
East Kirkby Airfield, nr Spilsby
PE23 4DE

t 01790 763207
w lincsaviation.co.uk
e enquiries@lincsaviation.co.uk

463 Tattershall

Tattershall Castle

1 hr   Mar–Dec

A large medieval fortified and moated red brick tower, built for Ralph Cromwell, Lord Treasurer of England. The building was restored by Lord Curzon in 1911–14 and contains four great chambers with enormous Gothic fireplaces, tapestries and brick vaulting.

* Spectacular views from the battlements

Location
On S side of A153, 15 miles NE of Sleaford, 10 miles SW of Horncastle

Opening
Apr–Sep Mon–Wed Sat–Sun 11am–5pm
Mar, Nov–Dec, Sat–Sun 12 noon–4pm

Admission
Adult £3.70, Child £1.90

Contact
Tattershall, Lincoln LN4 4LR

t 01526 342543
w nationaltrust.org.uk
e tattershallcastle@nationaltrust.org.uk

459   Spalding

Baytree Garden Centre (Owl Centre)

2 hrs+   All year

Set in 16 acres, this garden centre and nursery has something for all gardeners, including bulbs, plants, pets and aquatics. The centre is also home to over 100 owls and birds of prey, including very rare Mexican striped owls. Regular flying displays.

Location
On the main A151 at Weston between Spalding & Holbeach

Opening
Daily; 10am–5pm

Admission
Adult £2, Child £1, Senior £1

Contact
High Road Weston, Spalding, Lincolnshire PE12 6JU
t 01406 372840
w www.baytree-gardencentre.com

460   Stamford

Burghley House

3 hrs   Mar–Oct

Built between 1555 and 1587 by William Cecil, Lord Treasurer to Queen Elizabeth I, Burghley was based on designs of other great houses of the period, but has European influences. Externally, it is largely as it was when completed by Cecil's masons.

* Paintings include work by John Frederick Herring
* Sculpture park

Location
1½ miles from Stamford, well signed

Opening
House Daily; Mar–Oct 11am–5pm
Sculpture Park Daily; 10am–5pm

Admission
Adult £7.80, Child £3.50, Concs £6.90

Contact
Stamford PE9 3JY
t 01780 752451
w burghley.co.uk
e burghley@burghley.co.uk

Usher Gallery

1 hr+   All year

Set in the beautiful grounds of the Temple Gardens, the gallery houses a collection of fine and decorative arts. The original Usher bequest of clocks and watches, porcelain, silver, enamels, miniatures and coins remains the core of the gallery's permanent collection.

* Neo-classical sculpture to contemporary portraiture
* C17-C20 glass, including English drinking glasses

Location
Lincoln city centre

Opening
Tue–Sat & Bank Hols 10am–5pm
Sun 1pm–5pm

Admission
Free, charges for special exhibitions

Contact
Lindum Road, Lincoln LN2 1NN

t 01522 527980
w lincolnshire.gov.uk
e usher.gallery@lincolnshire.gov.uk

Skegness Natureland Seal Sanctuary

2 hrs   All year

The sanctuary houses seals, penguins and tropical birds. There are reptiles in a tropical house and a display of free-flying tropical butterflies. Natureland is well known for rescuing abandoned seal pups and visitors can view the hospital unit and large seascape pool.

* Family Attraction of the Year 2004

Location
Signposted from town centre

Opening
Daily; Jun–Sep 10am–5pm
Oct–May 10am–4pm

Admission
Adult £4.95, Child £3.25, Concs £3.95

Contact
North Parade, Skegness PE25 1DB

t 01754 764 345
w skegnessnatureland.co.uk
e natureland@fsbdial.co.uk

Gibraltar Point National Nature Reserve & Visitor Centre

2 hrs+   All year

This area of unspoilt coastline comprises sand-dunes, saltmarshes and freshwater habitats for rare plants and animals, including seals, water voles and pygmy shrews. There are four birdwatching hides, a nature trail, an interpretation centre, and various activities and events.

* Area of international scientific interest
* Home to many rare plants, insects and animals

Location
1½ miles S of Skegness, signed from town centre

Opening
Reserve: All year
Visitor Centre: Daily; May-Oct, Nov-Apr, Sat-Sun and Bank Holidays

Admission
Free

Contact
Gilbraltar Rd, Skegness PE24 4SU

t 01507 526667
w www.lincstrust.org.uk
e info@lincstrust.co.uk

453 Grantham

Grantham Museum

½ hr   All year

The museum interprets the archaeology and social history of Grantham and includes exhibits on famous residents such as Sir Isaac Newton and Margaret Thatcher, who has given many personal items to the museum. There is also a section on the Dambusters.

* Dambusters mission planned here
* 1851 Great Exhibition gold medal winning doll

Location
Central Grantham

Opening
Mon–Sat 10am–5pm

Admission
Free

Contact
St Peter's Hill, Grantham NG31 6PY

t 01476 568783
w lincolnshire.gov.uk/
   granthammuseum
e grantham.museum@
   lincolnshire.gov.uk

454 Grimsby

National Fishing Heritage Centre

2 hrs   Mar–Oct

The centre tells the story of the area's fishermen, their boats and the waters they fished in. The dangers and hardships of life at sea are explained and there is a reconstruction of a 1950s sea voyage, complete with authentic aromas and a moving deck.

* Collection of historic vessels in adjacent dock
* Reconstruction of streets and alleys of 1950s Grimsby

Location
Next to Alexandra Dock, 2 minutes walk from town centre

Opening
Daily; Mar–Oct Mon–Fri 10am–5pm
Sat–Sun & Bank Hols
10.30am–5.30pm

Admission
Adult £4.95, Child £3.85

Contact
Alexandra Dock, Grimsby DN31 1UZ

t 01472 323345
w nelincs.gov.uk
e ann.hackett@nelincs.gov.uk

455 Lincoln

Lincoln Medieval Bishop's Palace

1 hr   All year

Standing in the shadow of Lincoln Cathedral, the palace acted as the administrative centre of the largest diocese in medieval England and now forms an impressive bishop's house. Don't miss the East Hall, with its stunning vaulted undercroft, or the chapel.

* Heritage garden
* Panorama of the Roman, medieval and modern city

Location
S side of Lincoln Cathedral

Opening
Apr–Jun, Sep–Oct 10am–5pm
Nov–Mar Thu–Sun 10am–4pm

Admission
Adult £3.50, Child £1.80, Concs £2.60

Contact
Minster Yard, Lincoln LN2 1PU

t 01522 527468
w english-heritage.org.uk

Woolsthorpe Manor

2 hrs   Mar–Oct

This C17 manor house was the birthplace and home of the scientist, Sir Isaac Newton. Visitors can see his childhood scribblings on the walls. A gnarled old apple tree in the garden may be a descendant of the famous specimen which helped Newton with his work.

* An interactive science discovery centre
* Replica of principle of differential calculus

Location
From A1, take B676 at Colsterworth roundabout, turn right at second crossroads and follow signposts

Opening
Jul & Aug Wed–Sun 1pm–6pm
Apr, May & Sep Wed–Sun 1pm–5pm
Mar & Oct Sat & Sun 1pm–5pm

Admission
Adult £4.20, Child £2.10

Contact
23 Newton Way, Woolsthorpe-by-Colsterworth, nr Grantham NG33 5NR
t 01476 860338
w nationaltrust.org.uk

Gainsborough Old Hall

2 hrs   All year

This is a large C15 timber-framed medieval house, with a magnificent Great Hall and brick tower built on the site of an earlier C13 manor house. In 1483 King Richard III stayed at the Old Hall and in 1451 King Henry VIII was a guest.

* Special events throughout the year
* Lectures on first Tuesday of each month

Location
Town centre, off Parnell Street

Opening
Daily; Easter–Oct Mon–Sat 10am–5pm
Sun 1pm–4.30pm
Nov–Easter Mon–Sat 10am–5pm

Admission
Adult £3.20, Child /Concs £2.40

Contact
Parnell Street, Gainsborough DN21 2NB
t 01427 612669
w lincolnshire.gov.uk/gainsborougholdhall
e gainsborougholdhall@lincolnshire.gov.uk

Belton House

6 hrs   Mar–Nov

A stunning example of Restoration country house architecture, Belton was built in 1685-88 and later altered by James Wyatt. The interiors contain fine plasterwork and wood-carving, as well as collections of paintings, furniture, tapestries and silverware.

* Formal gardens, orangery and landscape park
* Edward VIII often came to stay before his abdication

Location
On A607 3miles NE of Grantham, signed from A1

Opening
House Mar–Nov Wed–Sun
12.30pm–5pm
Garden Mar–Nov Wed–Sun
11am–5.30pm
Nov–Dec Sat & Sun 12 noon–4pm

Admission
Adult £6.80, Child £3.40

Contact
Grantham NG32 2LS
t 01476 566116
w nationaltrust.org.uk
e belton@nationaltrust.org.uk

447 Alford

Claythorpe Watermill & Wildfowl Gardens

1 hr+   Easter–Oct

Situated at the tip of the Lincolnshire wolds, Claythorpe is home to over 500 birds and visitors are able to experience their environment and habitat first hand. Visit the Old Bakery, which depicts the history of the site's milling and baking industry.

* Enchanted woods in which fairy tales come to life
* Otters, red squirrels and wallabies

Location
Signposted off A16

Opening
Daily; Easter–Oct 10am–5pm

Admission
Adult £4.25, Child £3.25, Concs £3

Contact
Aby, nr Alford LN13 0DU

t 01507 450687
w claythorpewatermill.
    fsbusiness.co.uk
e info@claythorpewatermill.co.uk

448 Boston

Sibsey Trader Windmill

1 hr   Apr–Oct

Built in 1877 in typical Lincolnshire style, to replace a small post mill, this is one of the few six-sailed mills remaining in England. It's not exceptionally tall, but the slender tower and surrounding flat landscape create the impression that it's bigger than it really is.

* Grade 1 listed working windmill
* Fresh, organic, stoneground flour available

Location
Off A16, 5 miles N of Boston, 1/2 mile W of Sibsey

Opening
Apr–Oct Tue 10am–6pm &
Sat–Sun 11am–6pm
Bank Hols 10am–6pm

Admission
Adult £2, Child £1, Concs £1.50

Contact
Frith Ville Road, Sibsey PE22 0SY

t 01205 750036 / 460647
w sibsey.fsnet.co.uk
e traderwindmill@sibsey.fsnet.co.uk

449 Cleethorpes

Cleethorpes Humber Estuary Discovery Centre

1 hr   All year

Visit this exhibition and observatory to learn more about Cleethorpes and the Humber Estuary through an exciting hands-on exhibition. Discover the ancient, submerged forest that is buried along Cleethorpes beach.

* The centre is on the edge of an important habitat

Location
From A180 & A16 follow signs for the lakeside

Opening
Daily; Jan–Jun , Sep & Oct 10am–5pm
Jul & Aug 10am–6pm,
Nov–Dec 10am–4pm

Admission
Adult £1.95, Child £1.30

Contact
Lakeside, Kings Road, Cleethorpes DN35 0AG

t 01472 323232
w cleethorpesdiscoverycentre.co.uk
e lynne.emery@nelincs.gov.uk

Rockingham Castle

3 hrs All year

Built by William the Conqueror over 900 years ago, the castle is set in beautiful grounds and has magnificent views across the Welland Valley. Apart from its role as a stronghold, it was also an important seat of government. Now home to the Saunders Watson family and open to the public.

* Winner of numerous education awards
* Regular events including kite and Viking days

Location
Off the A6003, 1 mile N of Corby

Opening
Please Phone for details

Admission
Adult £7.50, Child £4.50, Concs £6.50

Contact
Rockingham, Market Harborough, Leicestershire LE16 8TH

t 01536 770240
w www.rockinghamcastle.com
e estateoffice@rockinghamcastle.com

Bradgate Country Park

3 hrs+ All year

With 850 acres of heathland, small woods, herds of deer and the River Lin, this is Leicestershire's largest country park. It also includes the ruins of Bradgate House, the birthplace of Lady Jane Grey, who was famously Queen of England for nine days.

* Old John Tower folly

Location
3 miles from M1 junction 22, signposted on A50

Opening
Dawn to dusk

Admission
Free, charges for car park and visitor centre

Contact
Deerbarn Buildings, Newtown Linford LE6 0HE

t 0116 2362713

Wigston Framework Knitters Museum

1 hr All year

The museum is unique, because when the last master hosier, Edgar Carter, died in 1952, the workshop was locked and left. Inside were eight hand frames for making gloves and fancy ribbed tops, with all the needle moulds and tools.

* Original frames, needle moulds and tools

Location
4 miles S of Leicester on B582, off A5199

Opening
Sun, first Sat of every month & Bank Hols 2pm–5pm

Admission
Adult £1, Child 50p

Contact
42-44 Bushloe End, Wigston LE18 2BA

t 0116 288 3396

440 Leicester

New Walk Museum

1 hr+   All year

The museum's permanent collections include the Ancient Egypt Gallery and the Natural History Room, with dinosaur skeletons and interesting fossils. It is also a major art gallery with a collection of German Expressionist and European art dating from the C15.

* Decorative arts gallery
* Wild space exhibition

Location
Short walk from city centre

Opening
Daily; Apr–Sep Mon–Sat 10am–5pm Sun 1pm–5pm
Oct–Mar Mon–Sat 10am–4pm Sun 1pm–4pm

Admission
Free

Contact
53 New Walk, Leicester LE1 7EA
t 0116 2254900
w leicester.gov.uk/museums
e museums@leicester.gov.uk

441 Loughborough

Great Central Railway

2 hrs+   All year

Main line steam trains run every weekend throughout the year. Re-create the experience of the famous expresses of the steam age. See freight and parcel train demonstrations or relax in the comfort of classic corridor trains, which are steam-heated in winter.

* Steam through the glorious Leicester countryside
* Driver's view of bridges, trains and hidden sidings

Location
SE of Loughborough town centre

Opening
Trains run at weekends all year and midweek Jun–Aug, Please phone for details

Admission
Adult £11, Child & Concs £7.50

Contact
Great Central Road, Loughborough LE11 1RW
t 01509 230 726
w gcrailway.co.uk
e booking_office@gcrailway.co.uk

442 Loughborough

Whatton Gardens

1 hr   Apr–Sep

The gardens and park are early C19. The house was built in 1876 and the garden is laid to lawn punctuated with Irish yews. Other highlights include the Chinese garden with oriental statuary, the kitchen garden, an ice house now used as a grotto and the Bogey Hole.

* Ornate stone loggia with Quattrocento carving
* Arboretum and small lake

Location
Off A6, between Hathern and Kegworth

Opening
Apr–Sep, Mon–Fri 11am–4pm

Admission
Adult £4, Child free

Contact
Whatton House, Loughborough LE12 5BG
t 01509 842268 / 842302
e whatto@compuserve.com

443 Lutterworth

Stanford Hall

1 hr   Easter–Sep

Stanford, on the river Avon, has been the home of the Cave family since 1430. In the 1690s, Sir Roger Cave commissioned Smiths of Warwick to pull down the old manor house and build the present hall, which is a superb example of their work.

* A collection of royal Stuart portraits

Location
Just off M1 / M6 interchange, nr A14

Opening
Easter–Sep Sun & Bank Holidays only.
House 1.30pm–5.30pm
Grounds 12noon–5.30pm

Admission
House & Grounds Adult £5, Child £2
Grounds Adult £3, Child £1
Motorcycle Museum Adult £1, Child 35p

Contact
Lutterworth LE17 6DH
t 01788 860250
w stanfordhall.co.uk

Jewry Wall

1 hr   All year

One of Leicester's most famous landmarks, this rare example of Roman walling has survived for nearly 2,000 years. Originally part of the Roman public baths, it separated the exercise hall, which stood on the site of St Nicholas Church, from the rest of the baths.

* Archaeologists discovered remains of Roman baths
* Museum tells the story of Leicester from the Iron Age

Location
In St Nicholas Street, W of St Nicholas Church

Opening
Apr–Sep Mon–Sat 10am–5pm
Oct–Mar Mon–Sat 10am–4pm

Admission
Free

Contact
St Nicholas Circle, Leicester LE1 4LB

t 0116 2254971
w english-heritage.org.uk

National Space Centre

4–6 hrs   All year

This centre is dedicated to space science and astronomy. From its futuristic Rocket Tower discover the stories, personalities and technology of the past and present, and explore our current understanding of space and how it affects our future.

* Five themed galleries with hands-on activities
* Space theatre show

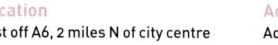

Location
Just off A6, 2 miles N of city centre

Opening
Term time Tue–Sat 10am–3.30
Sat–Sun 10am–4.30pm
School Hols Mon 12 noon–4.30pm
Tue–Sun 10am–4pm

Admission
Adult £8.95, Child £6.95

Contact
Exploration Drive, Leicester LE4 5NS

t 0870 6077223
w spacecentre.co.uk
e info@spacecentre.co.uk

The National Gas Museum, Leicester

1 hr   All year

Established in 1977 to preserve the knowledge and skills of the gas industry during a period of rapid technological and economic change, the museum contains many artefacts collected during the conversion to natural gas and tells the story of gas from 1667 to the present day.

Location
Off the A426, S of Leicester city centre

Opening
All year Tue–Thu
12noon–4.30pm;
closed Bank Holidays
Opening at other times by
special arrangement

Admission
Free

Contact
195 Aylestone Road,
Leicester LE2 7QH

t 0116 2503190
w www.gasmuseum.co.uk
e information@gasmuseum.co.uk

433   Ashby de La Zouch

Conkers

4 hrs+   All year

Located at the heart of the national forest, Conkers offers a great mix of hands-on activities, from 4 indoor discovery zones for all ages to 23 outdoor activities, including lakeside walks, sculpture & nature trails, an assault course, train rides, playgrounds & water play.

* Visitor Attraction of the Year Finalist
* Adventure playground & assault course

Location
3 miles from Ashby de la Zouch on the B5003

Opening
All year open daily; in summer 10am–6pm in winter 10am–dusk

Admission
Adult £5.95, Child £3.95, Concs £4.95

Contact
Rawden Road, Moira
Nr Ashby de la Zouch
Leicestershire DE12 6GA

t 01283 216633
w www.visitconkers.com
e info@visitconkers.com

---

434   Coalville

Manor House at Donington

1 hr+   All year

Donington-le-Heath Manor House was built in the late C13 and renovated early in C17. Visitors can see restored rooms and displays on medieval life. The house is set in recently recreated C17-style gardens with herbaceous borders, herb gardens an orchard and a maze.

* Re-enactments, hands-on and demonstrations
* Temporary exhibitions on a wide range of subjects

Location
1 mile S of Coleville, signed from M1 junction 22, on A50

Opening
Daily; Apr–Sep 11.30am–5pm
Oct–Nov & Mar 11.30am–3pm
Dec–Feb Sat–Sun 11.30am–3pm

Admission
Free

Contact
Donington-le-Heath,
Coalville LE67 2FW

t 01530 831259
w leics.gov.uk/museums

---

435   Coalville

Snibston Discovery Park

6 hrs   Feb-Dec

A popular museum, Snibston is situated on the site of a former colliery. The museum displays a rich collection of historic objects telling the story of transport, mining and quarrying, engineering and the fashion industry. A visit includes a tour of the historic colliery buildings.

* Train ride along the newly restored colliery railway
* A Sculpture trail

Location
On A511, on the edge of Coalville town centre

Opening
Daily; 10am–5pm
Closed in early Jan, ring for details

Admission
Adult £5.70, Child £3.60, Concs £3.90

Contact
Ashby Road, Coalville LE67 3LN

t 01530 278444
w leics.gov.uk/museums
e snibston@leics.gov.uk

---

436   Desford

Tropical Birdland

2 hrs+   Easter–Oct

Created in 1982, this exotic bird lover's dream is set in beautiful surroundings and features over 85 species of our feathered friends. You can walk through aviaries, visit the chick room, see spectacular free-flying birds, take a woodland stroll and visit the koi ponds.

* Take tea with free-to-fly birds in the cafe

Location
Just off M1 at junction 22

Opening
Daily; Easter–Oct 10am–5pm

Admission
Adult £4, Child £3, Concs £3.50

Contact
Lindridge Lane, Desford,
Leicester LE9 9N

t 01455 824603
w www.tropicalbirdland.co.uk
e info@tropicalbirdland.co.uk

Derbyshire

430   Swadlincote

Beehive Farm Woodland Lakes

4–6 hrs   All year

Using specially laid out trails, visitors can explore the beauty of this woodland landscape on foot or horseback. Alternatively, they can simply enjoy the atmosphere of the three tranquil fishing lakes – Horseshoe, Botany Bay and Jubilee.

* Woodland, meadow and wetland habitats
* Caravan & camping park

Location
In Rosliston, nr Burton on Trent

Opening
Daily; 9.30am–5pm, Sun 9.30–4pm

Admission
Adult £1, Child 50p

Contact
Lullington Road, Rosliston, Swadlincote DE12 8HZ
t 01283 763981
w beehivefarm-woodlandlakes.co.uk
e info@beehivefarm-woodlandlakes.co.uk

431   Middleton by Wirksworth

National Stone Centre

2 hrs+   All year

Deep in the heart of the Derbyshire Dales, this dramatic site is steeped in industrial history, but the centre tells the full story of stone. Through artefacts such as 330 million-year-old fossils and tropical reefs, it covers its history, the science and technology and its use in art.

* Gem panning
* Fossil rubbing

Location
On B5035, S of Matlock, between Cromford & Carsington

Opening
Daily; Summer 10am–5pm
Winter 10am–4pm

Admission
Adult £1.80, Child 90p, Concs £1.20

Contact
Porter Lane, Middleton by Wirksworth DE4 4LS
t 01629 824833
w nationalstonecentre.org.uk
e nsc@nationalstonecentre.org.uk

432   Ashby de la Zouch

Ashby de la Zouch Castle

1 hr+   All year

In the C15, Edward IV gave this property to Lord Hastings, who converted what was then a fortified manor house into a grand castle, adding a chapel and the Hastings Tower. Now partly ruined, the tower remains, soaring to the great height of 80ft.

* Wonderful views across Leicestershire
* The setting for jousting scenes in the film *Ivanhoe*

Location
In Ashby de la Zouch, 12 miles S of Derby, on A511

Opening
Please phone for details

Admission
Adult £3.20, Child £1.60, Concs £2.40

Contact
South Street, Ashby de la Zouch LE65 1BR
t 01530 413343
w english-heritage.org.uk
e customers@english-heritage.org.uk

©Chatsworth House Trust

Chatsworth House

4–6 hrs   Mar–Dec

The 'Palace of the Peak' contains one of Europe's finest collections of treasures, displayed in more than 30 rooms, from the grandeur of the 1st Duke's hall and state apartments with their rich decoration and painted ceilings, to the C19 library and dining room.

* Works by Rembrandt, Gainsborough and Freud
* Maze, rose, cottage and kitchen gardens

Location
8 miles N of Matlock, off B6012

Opening
Open Mar–Dec
House 11am–5.30pm
Garden 11am–6pm

Admission
House Adult £9, Child £3.50, Concs £7,
Garden Adult £5.50, Child £2.50,
Concs £4

Contact
Bakewell DE45 1PP

t 01246 565300
w chatsworth.org

Masson Mills Working Textile Museum

1 hr+   All year

Sir Richard Arkwright built these mills as his showpiece on the banks of the River Derwent in 1783. Beautifully restored, Masson Mills house a working textile museum containing a unique and comprehensive collection of authentic historic working textile machinery.

* Internationally famous Grade II listed buildings
* Experience over 200 years of industrial history

Location
On A6, ½ mile S of Matlock Bath

Opening
Daily; Mon–Fri 10am–4pm, Sat 11am–5pm,
Sun 11am–4pm

Admission
Adult £2.50, Child £1.50, Concs £2

Contact
41 Derby Road, Matlock Bath DE4 3PY

t 01629 581001.
w massonmills.co.uk

Matlock Bath Aquarium & Hologram Gallery

1 hr   Easter–Oct

Housed in the original Victorian thermal baths, the collection includes a large thermal pool containing various species of carp, indoor aquaria, a hologram gallery, a petrifying well, gemstone and fossil collections, and a local history exhibition.

* Life in a Lens exhibition

Location
Off A6 in Matlock Bath

Opening
Daily; Easter–end Oct
10am–5.30pm (times extended during high season)

Admission
Adult/Child £1.80 Under-5s Free

Contact
110–114 North Parade,
Matlock Bath,
Matlock DE4 3NS

t 01629 583624

Derby Museum of Industry and History

1 hr   All year

Built on the site of one of the world's oldest factories, dating from 1702 and 1717, the museum tells the story of the industrial heritage and achievement of Derby and its people. There is a special emphasis on the development of Rolls-Royce aero engines and the railway industry.

* On site of City's first silk mill
* History of Midland Railway

Location
Off the A6, near Derby Cathedral

Opening
Daily; Mon 11am–5pm,
Tue–Sat 10am–5pm,
Sun & Bank Holidays 2pm–5pm
Please phone to confirm
holiday opening

Admission
Free

Contact
Silk Mill Lane, off Full Street,
Derby DE1 3AF

t   01332 255308
w www.derby.gov.uk/museums

Melbourne Hall & Gardens

2 hrs   Apr–Sep

An historic house and garden that was once the home of Prime Minister William Lamb, who as Lord Melbourne gave his name to the Australian city. It has interesting and extensive gardens which contain a wrought iron arbour made around 1710 by Robert Bakewell of Derby.

* Formal garden with yew tunnel
* Best surviving example of work by London and Wise

Location
7 miles S of Derby

Opening
House Aug Daily; 2pm–4.15pm
Gardens Apr–Sep Wed, Sat–Sun &
Bank Hols 1.30pm –5.30pm,

Admission
House Adult £3.50, Child £ 2, Concs £3
Gardens Adult £3, Child £2, Concs £3

Contact
Church Square, Melbourne DE73 1EN

t   01332 862502
w melbournehall.com
e   melbhall@globalnet.co.uk

Royal Crown Derby Visitor Centre

2 hrs   All year

Tour the working factory and watch the production of tableware and giftware, from clay through to the finished hand-decorated product. The museum is full of treasures going back to 1750 and there are demonstrations of skills such as flower-making, painting and gilding.

* Working factory tour available on weekdays
* Museum, demonstration studio and factory shop

Location
On A415, nr Derby city centre

Opening
Daily; Mon–Sat 9.30am–4pm,
Sun 10.30am–4pm

Admission
Adult £2.95, Child & Concs £2.75
Tour Adult £4.95, Child & Concs £4.75

Contact
194 Osmaston Road, Derby DE23 8JZ

t   01332 712800
w royal-crown-derby.co.uk
e   enquiries@royal-crown-derby.
     co.uk

422 Castleton

Peveril Castle

1 hr   All year

Built shortly after the Norman Conquest of 1066 by one of King William's most trusted Knights, the elegant tower of this stronghold still stands to its original height. The castle, perched high above the pretty village of Castleton, offers breathtaking views of the Peak District.

* Some of the earliest herringbone masonry
* Sir Walter Scott based a book on the castle

Location
On S side of Castleton, on A6187, 15 miles W of Sheffield

Opening
Please phone for details

Admission
Adult £2.70, Child £1.30, Concs £2

Contact
Market Place, Castleton S33 8WQ

t 01433 620613
w english-heritage.org.uk

423 Crich

The National Tramway Museum

3 hrs+   Mar–Dec

Visit the museum to see a variety of trams, including open, closed, double-deck, single-deck, horse drawn, steam and vintage electric from all the corners of the globe. Electric trams also run through Period Street, and on to open countryside, giving panoramic views.

* Exhibition hall houses impressive displays
* Dramatic 'tram at night' experience

Location
8 miles from M1 junction 28 , via A38, A6, A61 and A52

Opening
Daily; Mar–Nov 10am–5.30pm
Nov & Dec Sat–Sun 10.30am–4pm

Admission
Adult £8, Child £3.50, Concs £6.50

Contact
Crich Tramway Village, Matlock DE4 5DP

t 01773 854321
w tramway.co.uk
e enquiry@tramway.co.uk

Donington Grand Prix Collection

2–4 hrs   All year

Take a spin around the largest collection of Grand Prix cars and journey through motor sport history. Exhibits include a 1999 Ralf Schumacher Williams, a 1997 David Coulthard McLaren and the car in which Ayrton Senna won the 1993 European Grand Prix at Donington Park.

* The world's only complete collection of Vanwalls
* Henry Seagrave's 1922 3-litre GP Sunbeam

Location
M1 junction 23a / 24, access from NW via A50

Opening
Daily; 10am–4pm

Admission
Adult £7, Child £2.50, Concs £5

Contact
Donington Park, Castle Donington
DE74 2RP

t 01332 811027
w doningtoncollection.com
e enquiries@doningtoncollection.co.uk

Blue John Cavern

1 hr   All year

An historic cavern containing the first known mined deposits of the Blue John mineral for which the area is famous. It was worked by the Romans more than 2,000 years ago. Tours take visitors through many colourful caves, including the crystallised and waterfall caverns.

* Exhibition of C19 miners' working implements

Location
2 miles W of Castleton

Opening
Daily; Summer 9.30am–5.30pm
Winter 9.30am–dusk

Admission
Adult £6.50, Child £3.50, Concs £4.50

Contact
Castleton S33 8WP

t 01433 620638 / 620642
w bluejohn-cavern.co.uk
e lesleyldbluejohn.gemsoft.co.uk

Peak Cavern

1 hr   All year

Explore the mystery of the Great Cave and step into the unique world of Peak Cavern, with its unusual rock formations, eerie sounds of running water and echoes of a bygone age. The cavern's imposing entrance chamber is the largest natural cave entrance in the British Isles.

* Riverside walk past historic miners' cottages
* Guided tours and rope-making demonstrations

Location
On the A6187, between Hathersage and Whaley Bridge

Opening
Daily; Apr–Oct 10am–5pm
Nov–Mar Sat–Sun 10am–5pm

Admission
Adult £5.50, Child £3.50, Concs £4.50

Contact
Peak Cavern Road, Castleton, Hope Valley S33 8WS

t 01433 620285
w www.peakcavern.co.uk
e info@peakcavern.co.uk

416 Alfreton

Wingfield Manor

1 hr+   All year

Mary Queen of Scots was imprisoned three times in this C15 manor house. Now an imposing ruin, the building was begun by Ralph, Lord Cromwell, Chancellor of England, around 1441. Over the entrance are carved twin money bags, symbolising Cromwell's status.

* Impressive undercroft of the hall, with a vaulted roof
* *Peak Practice* and Zeffirelli's *Jane Eyre* were filmed here

Location
On B5035, 5 miles S of South Wingfield

Opening
Apr–Sep Thu–Mon 10am–5pm
Oct Wed–Sun 10am–4.30pm
Nov–Mar Sat–Sun 10am–4pm

Admission
Adult £3.20, Child £1.60, Concs £2.40

Contact
Garner Lane, South Wingfield
D55 7NH

t 01773 832060
w english-heritage.org.uk

417 Bakewell

Haddon Hall

2 hrs+   Apr–Oct

Once home to William the Conqueror's illegitimate son, Peverel, little now remains of the original building (1087) but major restoration work undertaken from 1370 onwards means visitors can now experience what this perfect Tudor hall and beautiful gardens were like in their heyday.

* Annual children's weekend
* Film location for *Jane Eyre* and *Elizabeth*

Location
2 miles S of Bakewell on the A6

Opening
Apr–Sep, Daily; 10.30am–4.30pm
Oct, Thu–Sun, 10.30am–4.30pm

Admission
Adult £7.25, Child £3.75, Concs £6.25

Contact
Bakewell, Derbyshire, DE45 1LA

t 01629 812855
w www.haddonhall.co.uk
e iinfo@haddonhall.co.uk

418 Bolsover

Bolsover Castle

1 hr+   All year

Bolsover Castle is a C17 house, built on the site of a Norman fortress, and is a wonderful place to meander and muse. Sir Charles Cavendish, son of Bess of Hardwick, started the construction of the little castle in 1612.

* Symbolic and erotic wall-paintings restored in 1970s
* The Venus fountain garden has been restored

Location
In Bolsover, on A632, 6 miles E of Chesterfield

Opening
Apr, Sep &Oct Thu–Mon 10am–5pm
May–Aug daily 10am–6pm
Nov–Mar Thu–Mon 10am–4pm

Admission
Adult £6.50, Child £3.30, Concs £4.90

Contact
Castle Street, Bolsover S44 6PR

t 01246 822844
w english-heritage.org.uk
e bolsover.castle@english-heritage.org.uk

© English Heritage Photographic Library

©English Heritage Photographic Library

Edale, Derbyshire

East Midlands

Derbyshire Leicestershire Lincolnshire
Northamptonshire Nottinghamshire Rutland

413 Southwold

Coastal Voyager

Varies   All year

Hop aboard this 9-metre rigid inflatable for a short, high-speed, fun trip around Sole Bay or for a longer full-day trip, perhaps as far as Scroby Sands to see the seals. Suitable for individuals or groups. Fully equipped with wrap-round seats, seat belts and lifejackets.

Location
Trips depart from Southwold Harbour

Opening
Please phone for details

Admission
½-hr high-speed blast:
Adult £16 Under-13s £9

Contact
6 Strickland Place,
Southwold IP18 6HN

t 07887 525082
w blythweb.co.uk/sail-southwold
e thrills@southwold.ws

414 Woodbridge

Sutton Hoo

2–3 hrs   All year

Excavations here in 1939 revealed the burial chamber of a 90ft ship, filled with treasures including a warrior's helmet, weapons, armour, ornaments, tableware, and a purse with 37 gold coins from *c.* AD 620. The exhibition hall houses a full-size reconstruction of the chamber.

* The most important archaeological find in the country
* Largest Anglo-Saxon ship ever discovered

Location
Off B1083 Woodbridge–Bawdsey
road, signed from A12

Opening
Daily; Mar–Sep 11am–5pm
Oct Wed–Sun 11am–5pm
Nov–Dec Fri–Sun 11am–4pm

Admission
Adult £5, Child £2.50

Contact
Woodbridge IP12 3DJ

t 01394 389714
w www.nationaltrust.org.uk
e suttonhoo@nationaltrust.org.uk

415 Woodbridge

Orford Castle

1 hr+   All year

Originally a keep and bailey castle with a walled enclosure and a great tower. Henry II constructed the building we see today as a coastal defence during the C12. The unique polygon keep survives almost intact with three immense towers.

* The building records are the earliest in the kingdom
* Audio tours of 50mins

Location
In Orford on B1084, 20 miles NE
of Ipswich

Opening
Daily; Apr–Sep 10am–6pm
Oct 10am–5pm
Nov–Mar 10am–5pm
(closed Tue & Wed)

Admission
Adult £4, Child £2, Concs £3

Contact
Orford, Woodbridge IP12 2ND

t 01394 450472
w english-heritage.org.uk

411 Newmarket

National Horseracing Museum

1 hr+   Apr–Oct

The story of the people and horses involved in racing from Royal origins to Lester Piggott, Frankie Dettori and other modern-day heroes. Highlights include the head of Persimmon, a great Royal Derby winner in 1896 and the colourful jackets of 'Prince Monolulu'.

* Exciting programme of temporary exhibits
* Minibus tours – behind-the-scenes at Newmarket

Location
Centre of Newmarket, well signed

Opening
Apr–Oct Tue–Sun 11am–5pm
Jul–Aug daily 11am–5pm

Admission
Adult £4.50, Child £2.50, Concs £3.50

Contact
99 High Street, Newmarket CB8 8JL

t 01638 667333
w nhrm.co.uk
e museum@nhrm.freeserve.co.uk

412 Sudbury

Gainsborough's House

1 hr   All year

This is the birthplace of Thomas Gainsborough RA (1727–88). The Georgian fronted townhouse with attractive walled garden, displays more of the artist's work than any other gallery. The collection is shown together with C18 furniture and memorabilia.

* Varied exhibitions of contemporary art
* Includes works by Hubert Gravelot and Francis Hayman

 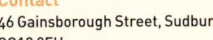

Location
In centre of Sudbury

Opening
Mon–Sat 10am–5pm
Bank Hols & Sun before Bank Hols
2pm–5pm

Admission
Adult £3.50, Child & Concs £1.50

Contact
46 Gainsborough Street, Sudbury
CO10 2EU

t 01787 372 958
w gainsborough.org
e mail@gainsborough.org

409 Long Melford

Long Melford Hall

1 hr
Apr–Oct

One of East Anglia's most celebrated Elizabethan houses, little changed externally since 1578 and with a beautiful panelled banqueting hall. There is a Regency library, as well as Victorian bedrooms and good collections of furniture and porcelain.

* Small collection of Beatrix Potter memorabilia
* Garden contains a charming banqueting house

WC

Location
In Long Melford off A134, 14 miles S of Bury St Edmunds, 3 miles N of Sudbury

Opening
Apr Sat & Sun 2pm–5.30pm
May–Sep Wed-Sun 2pm–5.30pm
Oct Sat & Sun 2pm–5.30pm

Admission
Adult £4.50, Child £2.25

Contact
Long Melford, Sudbury CO10 9AA

t 01787 880286
w nationaltrust.org.uk
e e.melford@nationaltrust.org.uk

410 Lowestoft

Lowestoft Maritime Museum

1 hr+
Easter–Oct

The museum specialises in the history of the Lowestoft fishing fleet and early commercial activities, from early days of sail, to steam through to modern diesel vessels. Methods of fishing are also recorded including the art of herring driftnet fishing.

* Fine exhibition of the evolution of lifeboats
* Collection of shipwright's & cooper's tools

WC

Location
Under the Lighthouse on Whaplode Road in Sparrow's Nest Park

Opening
Daily; May–10 Oct, 23-31 Oct & Easter hols 10am–5pm

Admission
Adult 75p, Child 25p, Concs 50p

Contact
Whapload Road, Lowestoft NR32 1XG

t 01502 561963

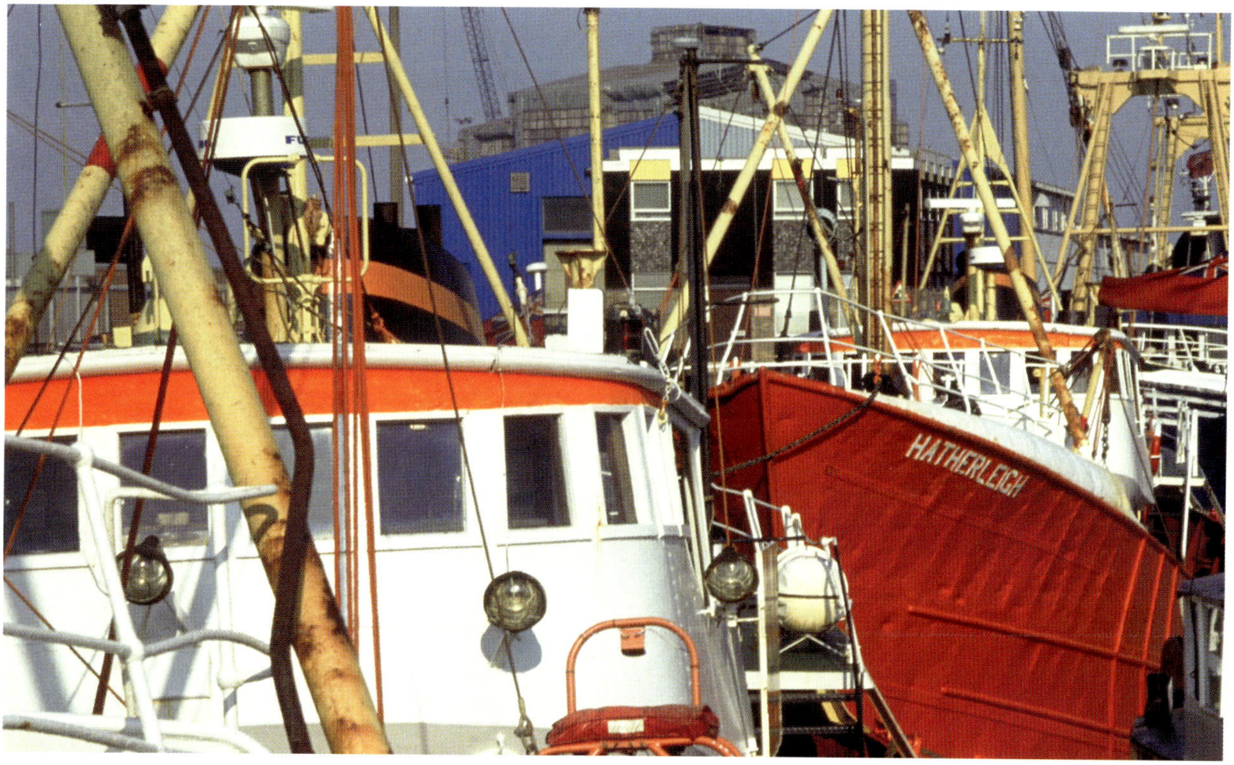

405 Bury St Edmunds

Manor House Museum

1 hr+   All year

The museum, a Georgian townhouse in Bury St Edmunds' Great Churchyard, houses a superb series of collections. The displays feature some of the finest clocks and watches to be found anywhere in the world, costumes and textiles from C17 to the present day.

* Hear the polyphon longcase clock
* 1920s costume collection

Location
Signed within Bury St Edmunds

Opening
Wed–Sun 11am–4pm

Admission
Adult £2.50, Child £2

Contact
5 Honey Hill, Bury St Edmunds
IP33 1RT
t 01284 757076 / 757074
w stedmundsbury.gov.uk/manorhse
e manor.house@stedsbc.gov.uk

406 Framlingham

Framlingham Castle

1 hr+   All year

This is a fine example of a late C12 castle. It has 13 hollow towers connected by a large curtain wall, 42 feet high and 8 feet thick (13 x 2.5m), similar to those at Dover and Windsor castles. The castle has fulfilled a number of roles including fortress, prison, poorhouse and school.

* Walk along the impressive wall walk
* Explore the outer courts, moat and mere

Location
In Framlingham on B1116

Opening
Daily; Apr–Sep 10am–6pm
Oct 10am–5pm
Nov–Mar 10am–4pm

Admission
Adult £4.20, Concs £3.20, Child £2.10

Contact
Framlingham, Woodbridge IP13 9BP
t 01728 724189
w english-heritage.org.uk

407 Ipswich

Ipswich Transport Museum

1 hr   Mar–Nov

The museum has the largest collection of transport items in Britain devoted to just one town. Everything was either made or used in and around Ipswich. The collection, started in 1965, consists of around 100 major exhibits, and numerous smaller transport related items.

* Timetables, photographs, maps, tickets and uniforms
* Varied programme of events as advertised

Location
SE of Ipswich near junction 57 of A14

Opening
Mar–Nov Sun and Bank Hols 11am–4pm, school hols Mon–Fri 1pm–4pm

Admission
Adult £3, Child £2, Concs £2.50

Contact
Old Trolleybus Depot, Cobham Road, Ipswich IP3 9JD
t 01473 715666
w ipswichtransportmuseum.co.uk
e enquiries@ipswichtransportmuseum.co.uk

408 Leiston

Long Shop Steam Museum

 1 hr+   Apr–Oct

The Long Shop was built in 1852 as Britain's first production lines for steam engines. Traction engines, steamrollers, electric trolleybuses and even ammunition were also produced here. Learn how the Victorians worked and explore our industrial heritage.

* Discover the amazing range of Garrett products
* A collection of unique and fascinating exhibits

Location
In Leiston town centre, off A12 at Saxmundham

Opening
Daily; Apr–Oct, Mon–Sat 10am–5pm
Sun 11am–5pm

Admission
Adult £3.50, Child £1, Concs £3

Contact
Main Street, Leiston IP16 4ES
t 01728 832189
w longshop.care4free.net
e longshop@care4free.net

402 Brandon

High Lodge Forest Centre

8 hrs+   All year

This centre in the heart of Thetford Forest offers walks, cycle trails, cycle hire, an adventure playground, a ropes course, one of the largest mazes in Europe, and a giant sculpture trail. Special events include bird walks, deer safari and family-fun walks.

* Largest maze in Europe
* Bird walks & family fun walks

Location
Just off A11 on B1107 midway between Thetford & Brandon

Opening
Daily; 9am–dusk
Phone for details

Admission
£3.50 per car

Contact
Thetford Forest Park,
Santon Downham,
Brandon IP27 0TJ

t 01842 815434 (High Lodge Centre)
   01842 810271 (Forestry Commission)
w forestry.gov.uk

403 Bungay

Norfolk & Suffolk Aviation Museum

2 hrs+   All year

The museum constitutes an impressive collection of aircraft and equipment. It also houses the Royal Observer Corps Museum, the 446th (H) Bomb Group Museum, the RAF Bomber Command Museum and the Air Sea Rescue and Coastal Command Museum.

* 40 aircraft within seven hangers
* Aircraft from pre First World War to present day

Location
On B1062, off A143, 1 mile W of Bungay

Opening
Apr–Oct Sun–Thu 10am–5pm
Nov–Mar Tue Wed & Sun 10am–4pm
15 Dec–15 Jan closed

Admission
Free

Contact
The Street, Flixton NR35 1NZ

t 01986 896644
w aviationmuseum.net
e lcurtis@aviationmuseum.net

404 Bury St Edmunds

Ickworth House

2 hrs+   Mar–Nov

Ickworth is an elegant Italianate house set within spectacular English parkland. The central rotunda and curving wings were intended to house treasures collected from all over Europe. Today, the state rooms display works by Titian, Velasquez and Gainsborough.

* Noted for its Georgian silver and Regency furniture
* Enchanting gardens and woodland walks

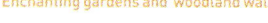

Location
On A143, 2 miles S of Bury St Edmunds signed from A14

Opening
House Mar–Sep 1pm–5pm, Oct–Nov
1pm–4.30pm closed Wed & Thu
Garden Daily; Jan–Feb 10am–4pm
Mar–Oct 10am–5pm
Nov–Dec 10am–4pm Mon–Fri

Admission
House & Gardens; Adult £6.70, Child
£3.00 *Park & Gardens;* £3.10, 90p

Contact
Bury St Edmunds IP29 5QE

t 01284 735 270
w nationaltrust.org.uk
e julia.vinson@nationaltrust.org.uk

399 Norwich

Norwich Cathedral

1 hr+   All year

This is a magnificent Norman building. The nave roof bosses, illustrating The Bible from Creation to the Day of Judgment, and the Saxon Bishop's throne are unique features. The cloisters are the largest monastic cloisters in the country, and spire the second highest.

* Nurse Edith Cavell is buried here
* Famous collection of medieval carvings

Location
Signed from Norwich city centre

Opening
Daily; Mid Sep–mid May 7.30am–6pm
Mid May–mid Sep 7.30am–7pm

Admission
Free, although donations welcome

Contact
62 The Close, Norwich NR1 4EH

t 01603 218 321 / 218300
e vis-proffice@cathedral.org.uk
w cathedral.org.uk

400 Sheringham

The Muckleburgh Collection

2 hrs   Apr–Nov

This is a collection of military vehicles, many of which are in full working order. Further displays feature the Royal Flying Corps and the modern armed forces. Several aero engines and missiles are on show. Frequent live tank demonstrations take place.

* The Meteor is on loan from the Imperial War Museum.
* Gama Goat Rides – in a USA Personnel Carrier

   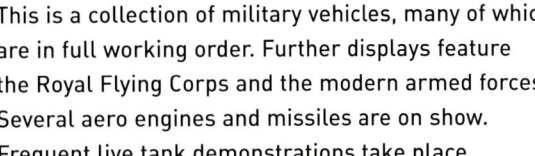

Location
Signed from A149 W of Cromer,
3 miles W of Sheringham

Opening
Please phone for details

Admission
Adult £5.50, Child £3, Concs £4.50

Contact
Weybourne Military Camp,
Holt NR25 7EG

t 01263 588 210
w muckleburgh.co.uk
e info@muckleburgh.co.uk

401 Swaffham

Castle Acre Priory

1 hr   All year

The priory's ruins span seven centuries and include a C12 church with an elaborately decorated great west front which still rises to its full height, a C15 gatehouse and a porch and prior's lodging. Visit the recreated herb garden, growing both culinary and medicinal herbs.

* Regular events held throughout the year
* One of the first Cluniac priories in England

Location
¼ mile W of village of Castle Acre,
5 miles N of Swaffham

Opening
Daily; Apr–Sep 10am–6pm
Oct–Mar Wed–Sun 10am–4pm

Admission
Adult £4.20, Child £2.10, Concs £3.20

Contact
Stocks Green PE32 2XD

t 01760 755394
w english-heritage.org.uk
e castleacre-priory@english-heritage.org.uk

395 King Lynn

Sandringham

3 hrs   Apr–Oct

The country retreat of Her Majesty The Queen and His Royal Highness The Duke of Edinburgh. Sandringham is a friendly and informal place and visits include ground floor rooms within the house, a museum within the stable blocks and beautiful grounds.

* Nature trails and woodland walks in the Country Park
* Collection of vintage Royal motor vehicles

Location
Signed from Kings Lynn

Opening
Daily; Apr–Sep
House 11am–4.45pm Oct 11am–3pm
Museum 11am–5pm Oct 11am–4pm
Gardens 10.30am–5pm Oct 11am–4pm

Admission
House, Garden & Museum Adult £7,
Child £4.50, Concs £5.50
Garden and Museum £5, £3, £4

Contact
Estate Office, Sandringham PE35 6EN
t 01553 612 908
w sandringhamestate.co.uk
e visits@sandringhamestate.co.uk

396 Little Walsingham

Walsingham Shirehall Museum & Abbey Grounds

1 hr+   All year

Walsingham is one of the main centres for Christian pilgrimage in England, it has been an important site since 1061 and in 1153 an Augustinian Priory was founded in the village. It was destroyed in 1538, but the remains and site of the original shrine can still be seen.

* Picturesque and tranquil grounds
* Shirehall Museum – unaltered 'hands-on' courtroom

Location
4 miles NE of Fakenham off A149

Opening
Daily; 10am–4.30pm

Admission
Adut £3, Child £1.50, Concs £1.50

Contact
Common Place, Little Walsingham
NR22 6BP

t 01328 820510 / 820259
e walsingham.museum@farmline.com

397 Norwich

Felbrigg Hall, Garden & Park

2 hrs+   Mar–Oct

This handsome house owes much of its splendour to William Windham II. The interior was remodelled in the 1750s to provide a sumptuous setting for his art treasures. The state rooms contain superb C18 furniture and paintings, and there is an outstanding library.

* The orangery has a fine display of camellias in spring
* Walled garden, extensive parkland, lake and woods

Location
In Felbrigg, 2 miles SW of Cromer, off
B1346. Signed from A140 & A148

Opening
Mar 19–Oct 30 Sat–Wed
Hall 1pm–5pm
Garden 11am–5.00pm

Admission
Hall, Garden & Park Adult £6.60, Child £3
Garden only £2.70, £1

Contact
Felbrigg, Norwich NR11 8PR

t 01263 837444
w nationaltrust.org.uk
e felbrigg@ntrust.org.uk

398 Norwich

Sainsbury Centre for Visual Arts

1 hr   All year

In an internationally renowned building designed by Norman Foster, discover the delights of the Sainsbury art collection. There are over 1,200 items in the collection which spans thousands of years and many cultures. Alongside African masks are works by Picasso and Bacon.

* Degas' Little Dancer
* Giacometti's Standing Woman

Location
On University campus – signed

Opening
Tue–Sun 11am–5pm
Wed 11am–8pm

Admission
Free admission

Contact
University of East Anglia
Earlham Road, Norwich NR4 7TJ

t 01603 593 199
w uea.ac.uk/scva
e scva@uea.ac.uk

392 Great Yarmouth

Tolhouse Museum

1 hr+ Apr–Oct

This C13 museum is one of the oldest civic buildings in the country. Once Great Yarmouth's courtroom and gaol, it illustrates aspects of local history, including the dungeons in which Victorian figures can be seen lurking in their cells. Brass rubbings can be made.

* Audio guide brings to life the stories and characters
* Museum of local history

Location
Great Yarmouth, near 'Historic South Quay'

Opening
Daily; Apr–Oct Mon–Fri 10am–5pm
Sat & Sun 1.15pm–5pm

Admission
Adult £2.70, Child £1.50, Concs £2.30

Contact
Tolhouse Street, Great Yarmouth
NR30 2SH

t 01493 858900
w norfolkmuseumservice.org.uk
e yarmouth.museums@norfolk.gov.uk

394 Hunstanton

Hunstanton Sea Life Centre

1 hr+ All year

At this sanctuary you will see otters, penguins and more than 30 permanent displays all showcasing the diversity of life under the waves. The centre also provides a safe haven for sick, injured or orphaned seal pups which are cared for at the sanctuary.

* Penguin sanctuary, home to rare Humboldt penguins
* Seal adoption programme

Location
Take A140 from Kings Lynn to Hunstanton and follow the signs

Opening
Daily; 10am–4pm.
Times may vary during winter, phone for details

Admission
Adult £7.75, Child £4.95, Concs £5.50

Contact
Southern Promenade,
Hunstanton PE36 5BH

t 01485 533 576
w sealsanctuary.co.uk

393 Holt

Baconsthorpe Castle

1–2 hrs All Year

Reached via a maze of tiny lanes are the remains of this C15 castle, built by Sir John Heydon as a manor house and wool-processing factory during the Wars of the Roses. In the 1560s, Sir John's grandson added the outer gatehouse, which was inhabited until the 1920s.

* English Heritage Property

Location
Off the A148 & B1149, ¾ mile N of the village of Baconsthorpe, off an unclassified road. 3 miles E of Holt

Opening
Daily; at any reasonable time

Admission
Free

Contact
Baconsthorpe, Holt

t 01604 730325
w english-heritage.org.uk

388 Dereham

Roots of Norfolk

4 hrs+   Mar–Nov

Set in 50 acres of beautiful countryside, this collection of rural Norfolk life is housed in a Georgian workhouse dating from 1777. There is a traditional farm, worked by heavy horses. Explore village life, agriculture and the workhouse through hands–on displays.

* Recent £3.5 million refurbishment
* Family friendly displays & adventure playground

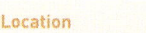

Location
3 miles NW of Dereham, follow signs

Opening
Daily; Mar–Nov 10am–5pm

Admission
Adult £5.70, Child £4.40, Concs £5.00

Contact
Gressenhall, Dereham NR20 4DR

t 01362 860563
w norfolk.gov.uk/tourism/museums
e gressenhall.museum@norfolk.gov.uk

389 Downham Market

Denver Windmill

1–3 hrs   All year

Visit a working windmill set on the edge of the Fens. Recently restored, this unique set of buildings allows visitors to explore the story of windmilling in England and of the people who lived and worked at the windmill since it was built in 1835.

* Tours to the very top of the windmill tower
* See the mill working – wind and the miller permitting

Location
Signed from A10

Opening
Daily; Apr–Oct Mon–Sat 10am–5pm
Sun 12 noon–5pm
Nov–Mar Mon–Sat 10am–4pm
Sun 12 noon–4pm

Admission
Adult £3.50, Child £2, Concs £3

Contact
Denver, Downham Market PE38 0EG

t 01366 384009
w denvermill.co.uk
e enquires@denvermill.co.uk

390 Fakenham

Thursford Collection

2 hrs   Easter–Sep

An Aladdin's cave of old road engines and mechanical organs of magical variety all gleaming with colour. Live musical shows featuring nine mechanical pipe organs and starring Robert Wolfe in the Wurlitzer Show. Old farm buildings, transformed into a small village.

Location
A148 between Fakenham & Holt

Opening
Easter–Sep Sun–Fri 12 noon–5pm

Admission
Adult £5.50, Child £3.30, Concs £5

Contact
Thursford, Fakenham NR21 0AS

t 01328 878 477
e admin@thursfordcollection.co.uk

391 Great Yarmouth

Elizabethan House Museum

1 hr   Apr–Oct

A C16 building with rooms reflecting the lives of families who have lived there. Of particular interest are a Tudor bedroom and dining–room, Victorian kitchen, scullery and parlour, and the Conspiracy Room, where the trial and execution of King Charles I were allegedly plotted.

* Special children's room with replica toys
* Hands–on activities

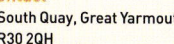

Location
In Great Yarmouth on 'Historic South Quay'

Opening
Daily; Apr–Oct Mon–Fri 10am–5pm
Sat & Sun 1.15pm–5pm

Admission
Adult £2.70, Child £1.50, Concs £2.30

Contact
4 South Quay, Great Yarmouth NR30 2QH

t 01493 855746
w nationaltrust.org.uk

386 Aylsham

Blickling Hall, Garden & Park

3 hrs+   Mar–Nov

One of England's great Jacobean houses, it is famed for its spectacular long gallery, superb library and fine collections of furniture, pictures and tapestries. The gardens are full of colour all year, and the extensive parkland features a lake and a series of beautiful walks.

* Superb Jacobean plaster ceiling in the long gallery
* Formal woodland and wilderness garden

Location
N of B1354, 1½ miles NW of Aylsham on A140

Opening
19 Mar–Nov Wed–Sun
Hall 1pm–4.30pm
Garden & Park 10.15am–5.15pm

Admission
Adult £7.30, Child £3.65
Garden only £4.20, £2.10

Contact
Blickling, Norwich NR11 6NF

t 01263 738030
w nationaltrust.org.uk
e blickling@nationaltrust.org.uk

387 Blakeney

Blakeney Point

3 hrs   All year

One of Britain's foremost bird sanctuaries, the point is a 3½-mile long sand and shingle spit, noted for its colonies of breeding terns and for the rare migrants that pass through in spring and autumn. Both common and grey seals can also be seen.

* Information centre at Morston Quay provides further details
* Restricted access during main bird breeding season

Location
Morston Quay, Blakeney and Cley are all off A149 Cromer to Hunstanton road

Opening
Daily; all times

Admission
Free

Contact
The Warden, 35 The Cornfield, Langham, Holt NR25 7DQ

t 01263 740480 (Apr–Sep)
   01263 740241 (Oct–Mar)
w nationaltrust.org.uk
e blakeneypoint@nationaltrust.org.uk

383 St Albans

The Verulamium Museum

1 hr+   All year

Discover the life and times of a major Roman city at St Albans. This is the museum of everyday life in Roman Britain. Displays and activities include recreated Roman rooms, hands-on discovery areas and some of the best mosaics and wall plasters outside the Mediterranean.

* Excavation video and accessible collections
* Roman soldiers 2nd weekend of every month

Location
Signed from St Albans

Opening
Daily; Mon–Sat 10am–5.30pm
Sun 2pm–5.30pm

Admission
Please ring for details

Contact
St Michaels, St Albans AL3 4SW

t 01727 751 810
w stalbansmuseums.org.uk
e a.coles@stalbans.gov.uk

384 Tring

Walter Rothschild Zoological Museum

1 hr+   All year

This collection, started in 1890 by Walter Rothschild, contains thousands of birds, mammals, reptiles, fish, insects and even dressed fleas. The Victorian setting gives it a unique atmosphere and it's a fascinating insight into the life of a classic English eccentric.

* Come face to face with a giant anaconda
* Part of the Natural History Museum since 1937

Location
Tring is on A41, 12 miles W of Hemel Hempstead and 33 miles N of London. Museum is off Tring High Street

Opening
Daily; Mon–Sat 10am–5pm, Sun 2pm–5pm

Admission
Free

Contact
Akeman Street,
Tring HP23 6AP

t 020 7942 6171
w nhm.ac.uk/museum/tring
e tring-enquiries@nhm.ac.uk

385 Welwyn

Shaw's Corner

1 hr+   Mar–Oct

This Edwardian villa was the home of George Bernard Shaw from 1906 till his death in 1950. The rooms remain much as he left them, with many literary and personal effects and many touches evoking the individuality and genius of this great dramatist.

* An Edwardian Arts & Crafts-influenced house
* Kitchen and outbuildings evocative of early C20 life.

Location
Junction 4 of A1(M) signed from B653 & B656

Opening
20 Mar–31 Oct Wed–Sun & Bank Hols
House 1pm–5pm
Garden 12 noon–5.30pm

Admission
Adult £3.80, Child £1.90

Contact
Ayot St Lawrence,
Welwyn AL6 9BX

t 01438 820307
w nationaltrust.org.uk/shawscorner
e shawscorner@nationaltrust.org.uk

380 Knebworth

Knebworth House

3 hrs+   Mar–Sep

The Lytton family have lived at Knebworth for 500 years. Queen Elizabeth I stayed here, Charles Dickens acted in private theatricals in the house and Winston Churchill's painting of the banqueting hall hangs in the room where he painted it.

* Constance Lytton fought for votes for women in 1900s
* The stately home of rock music

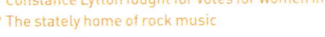

Location
29 miles N of London off junction A1(M) at Stevenage

Opening
27 Mar–26 Sep Sat Sun & Bank Hols 12 noon–5pm
Daily; 3–18 Apr, May 29–Jun 6, Jul 3–Aug 31

Admission
Adult £8.50, Child & Concs £8

Contact
Knebworth SG3 6PY
t 01438 812 661
w knebworthhouse.com
e info@knebworthhouse.com

---

381 Letchworth

Letchworth Museum & Art Gallery

1 hr+   All year

The museum opened in 1914 to house the collections of the Letchworth Naturalists' Society. Today it shows examples of local wildlife in realistic settings, including the famous Letchworth black squirrel, and the two art galleries house changing exhibitions.

* Iron Age chieftain's burial display
* Many examples of Roman pottery and jewellery

Location
In Letchworth town centre, opposite cinema

Opening
Mon, Tue, Thu, Fri & Sat 10am–5pm

Admission
Free

Contact
Broadway, Letchworth SG6 3PF
t 01462 685 647
w north-herts.gov.uk
e letchworth.museum@north-herts.gov.uk

---

382 Stevenage

Fairlands Valley Park

4 hrs+   All year

This beautiful 120-acre park is home to an 11-acre lake used for a range of watersport courses; its waters are kept well stocked for anglers. There is a kids' area with paddling pool and play equipment. The park is also home to a wide selection of wildlife and wildfowl.

* Children's play area
* Paddling pools open

Location
Situated on Six Hills Way, 1 mile E of Stevenage

Opening
Daily; 8am–dusk

Admission
Free

Contact
Six Hills Way, Stevenage SG2 0BL
t 01438 353241
w stevenage-leisure.co.uk/fairlands
e fairland@clara.net

377 Broxbourne

Paradise Wildlife Park

2 hrs+ All year

The park is a special place, with a relaxed and friendly atmosphere. It has a range of animals from monkeys to lions, zebras to tigers and cheetahs to camels. What makes it unique is the fact that you can get really close, meeting and feeding many of the animals.

* Brazilian tapirs and reptilemania
* Parrot olympic training

Location
Junction 25 of M25 onto A10, signed from Broxbourne

Opening
Daily; Mar–Oct 9.30am–6pm
Nov–Feb 10am–5pm

Admission
Adult £10, Child £7, Concs £7

Contact
White Stubbs Lane,
Broxbourne EN10 7QA

t 01992 470 490
w pwpark.com
e info@pwpark.com

378 Hatfield

Mill Green Museum & Mill

1 hr+ All year

This museum is housed in what was for centuries the home of the millers who worked in the adjoining watermill. The watermill is fully restored and operational. It probably stands on the site of one of four Hatfield mills listed in the *Domesday Book*.

* Waterwheel in action every day
* Watch milling of organic flour on Tue, Wed & Sun

Location
Located in Mill Green, between Hatfield and Welwyn Garden City

Opening
Tue–Fri 10am–5pm
Sat, Sun & Bank Hols 2pm–5pm

Admission
Free

Contact
Mill Green, Hatfield AL9 5PD

t 01707 271362
w hertsmuseums.org.uk/millgreen
e museum@welhat.gov.uk

379 Hatfield

Hatfield House

2 hrs+ Easter–Sep

This Jacobean house stands in its own great park and is the home of the Marquess of Salisbury. The state rooms are rich in paintings, furniture, fine tapestries and historic armour. Superb examples of Jacobean craftsmanship can be seen throughout the house.

* Beautifully carved wooden grand staircase
* Rare stained-glass window in the private chapel

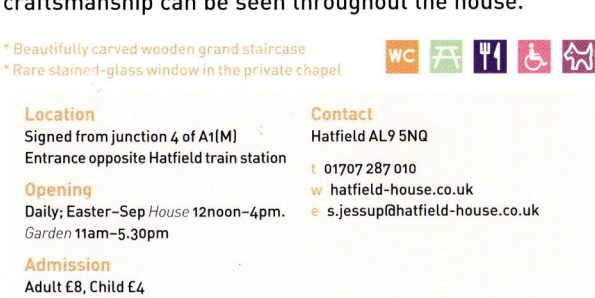

Location
Signed from junction 4 of A1(M)
Entrance opposite Hatfield train station

Opening
Daily; Easter–Sep *House* 12noon–4pm.
Garden 11am–5.30pm

Admission
Adult £8, Child £4

Contact
Hatfield AL9 5NQ

t 01707 287 010
w hatfield-house.co.uk
e s.jessup@hatfield-house.co.uk

374 Barnet

Museum of Domestic Design & Architecture

1 hr · All year

The museum (MoDA) houses one of the most important and comprehensive collections of late C19 and C20 decorative design for the home. MoDA offers a wide ranging programme alongside its permanent exhibition, 'Exploring Interiors: Decoration of the Home 1900–1960'.

* Wallpapers and textiles from 1870s–1960s
* Crown Wallpaper archive

Location
Underground Oakwood, from where there is a university shuttle bus. Or M25 junction 24 onto A111 for 3 miles

Opening
Tue–Sat 10am–5pm, Sun 2pm–5pm

Admission
Free

Contact
Middlesex University, Cat Hill, Barnet EN4 8HT
t 020 8411 5244
w moda.mdx.ac.uk
e moda@mdx.ac.uk

376 Berkhamsted

Berkhamsted Castle

2 hrs+ · All year

Berkhamsted Castle is a good example of a motte and bailey castle where the original wooden defences were later rebuilt in stone. It consists of a large bailey and a motte to one side, on which there are traces of a stone tower. The only double-moated Norman castle in the UK.

* Built in late C11 by Robert of Mortain
* Further improvements were made by King John

Location
Adjacent to Berkhamsted station

Opening
Daily; Apr–Oct 10am–6pm
Nov–Mar 10am–4pm

Admission
Free

Contact
Berkhamsted HP4 1LJ
t 01442 871737
w english-heritage.org.uk
e customers@english-heritage.org.uk

375 Berkhamsted

Ashridge Estate

1 hr+ · All year

This estate, situated along the main ridge of the Chiltern Hills, offers a variety of picturesque walks, supporting a variety of wildlife in the commons, woodlands and chalk downland. The focal point is the Duke of Bridgewater Monument, erected in 1832.

* Splendid views from Ivinghoe Beacon
* Visitor Centre with exhibition room

Location
Between Northchurch & Ringshall just off B4506

Opening
All year

Admission
Estate free
Monument Adult £1.20, Child 60p

Contact
Ringshall, Berkhamsted HP4 1LT
t 01442 851 227
w nationaltrust.org.uk
e ashridge@nationaltrust.org.uk

117 Tower Bridge

Design Museum

2 hrs+   All year

The Design Museum is the world's leading museum of industrial design, fashion and architecture. A programme of critically-acclaimed exhibitions captures the excitement of design's evolution, ingenuity and inspiration through the C20 and C21.

* Permanent collection plus temporary exhibitions
* Full range of talks, courses & kids' activities

Location
Underground Tower Hill, 10 min walk over Tower Bridge
Docklands Light Railway Tower Gateway

Opening
Daily; 10am–5.45pm

Admission
Adult £6, Child £4, Concs £4

Contact
Shad Thames, London SE1 2YD

t 0870 8339955
w designmuseum.org
e info@designmuseum.org

118 Tower Bridge

HMS *Belfast*

1 hr+   All year

HMS *Belfast* was launched in 1938 and served throughout the WWII, playing a leading part in the destruction of the German battle cruiser *Scharnhorst* and in the Normandy landings. In 1971 she was saved as a unique reminder of Britain's naval heritage.

* Experience what life was like for the crew
* Complete tours of this huge & complex warship

Location
Underground London Bridge

Opening
Daily; Mar–Oct 10am–6pm;
Nov–Feb 10am–5 pm;
(last admissions 45 mins before close)

Admission
Adult £7, Child free, Concs £5

Contact
Morgan's Lane, Tooley Street, London SE1 2JH

t 0207 940 6300
w iwm.org.uk/belfast
e hmsbelfast@iwm.org.uk

119 Tower Hill

Tower of London

3 hrs   All year

Founded by William the Conqueror and modified by successive sovereigns, the Tower of London is one of the world's most famous and spectacular fortresses. Discover its 900-year history as a palace, fortress, prison, mint, arsenal, menagerie and jewel house.

* Ceremony of the keys (please apply in writing)
* Constant calendar of special events

Location
Underground Tower Hill

Opening
Mar–Oct Tues–Sat 9am–5pm
Sun & Mon 10am–5pm
Nov–Feb Tue–Sat 9am–4pm
Sun & Mon 10am–4pm

Admission
Adult £13.50, Child £9 , Concs £10.50

Contact
Tower Hill, London EC3N 4AB

t 0870 756 6060
w tower-of-london.org.uk

120 Tower Bridge

Tower Bridge Exhibition

1 hr   All year

This is one of the world's most famous bridges. Visitors can go inside the Gothic towers to discover its history and see the original Victorian engine rooms. From the high-level walkways you can look out across the modern city skyline and down the river to Canary Wharf.

* New interactive computer displays
* Special ticket rate for Tower Bridge & Monument

Location
Underground Tower Hill and London Bridge
Boat from Tower Pier

Opening
Daily; 9.30am–6pm

Admission
Adult £5.50, Child £3, Concs £4.25

Contact
Tower Bridge, London SE1 2UP
t 020 7403 3761
w towerbridge.org.uk
e enquiries@towerbridge.org.uk

121 Trafalgar Square

National Portrait Gallery

2 hrs   All year

Founded in 1856 to collect the likenesses of famous British men and women, the gallery aimed to be about history not art, and this remains its criterion today. The collection is the most comprehensive of its kind in the world.

* Daytime & evening lectures & events
* Roof-top restaurant which boasts stunning views

Location
Underground Charing Cross, Leicester Square

Opening
Daily; 10am–6pm; Thu & Fri 10am–9pm

Admission
Free, exhibitions may charge

Contact
St Martin's Place, London WC2H 0HE
t 020 7306 0055 / 020 7312 2463
w npg.org.uk

122 Trafalgar Square

National Gallery

1 hr+   All year

This gallery houses one of the greatest collections of European painting in the world. The permanent collection spans the period from 1250 to 1900 and includes paintings by artists Leonardo da Vinci, Michelangelo, JMW Turner and Vincent van Gogh.

* Selection of courses & lectures available
* Weekend & school holiday family events

Location
Trafalgar Square
Underground Leicester Square, Charing Cross

Opening
Daily; 10am–6pm; Wed 10am–9pm

Admission
Free, donations welcome, exhibitions may charge

Contact
Trafalgar Square, London WC2N 5DN
t 020 7747 2885
w nationalgallery.org.uk
e information@ng-london.org.uk

123 Twickenham

Museum of Rugby

2 hrs   All year

More than just a collection of interesting artefacts, this museum is an inspirational journey through the history of the ultimate team game. Innovative, interactive exhibits bring to life some of the great moments of the international game.

* Finest collection of rugby memorabilia
* Action-packed films show footage of matches

Location
Mainline Twickenham (from Waterloo)

Opening
Tue–Sat 10am–5pm; Sun 11am–5pm

Admission
Adult £9, Child £6, Concs £6

Contact
Rugby Road, Twickenham, London TW1 1DZ

t 020 8892 8877
w rfu.com
e museum@rfu.com

124 West End

Wallace Collection

3 hrs   All year

This is both a national museum and the finest private collection of art ever assembled by one family. It is displayed against the opulent backdrop of Hertford House. The collection is best known for its magnificent C18 French paintings, furniture and porcelain.

* Paintings by Titian, Rembrandt & Frans Hals
* Superb new restaurant

Location
Underground Bond Street

Opening
Daily; 10am–5pm

Admission
Free

Contact
Hertford House, Manchester Square, London W1U 3BN

t 020 7563 9500
w wallacecollection.org

125 Westminster

Houses of Parliament

2 hrs   July–Oct

The House of Commons and House of Lords meet in the Palace of Westminster, next to the River Thames in London. Parliament has met in the Palace of Westminster since around 1550. UK residents and overseas visitors must book tours in advance.

* See & hear debates
* Tours of the clock tower available on request

Location
Underground Westminster

Opening
Tours available during summer recess end Jul–early Oct
Please phone for details

Admission
Please phone for details

Contact
House of Commons Information Office, Westminster, London SW1A 0AA

t 0870 906 3773
w parliament.uk
e hcinfo@parliament.uk

126 Westminster

Cabinet War Rooms & Churchill Museum

1 hr   All year

In 1940, as the bombs rained down on London, Winston Churchill, his Cabinet, his War Cabinet and his staff met below ground in a fortified basement in Whitehall known as the Cabinet War Rooms. Today, visitors can see them just as they looked during the war years.

* Newly restored Churchill Suite now open
* New Winston Churchill museum opened Apr 2003

Location
Underground Westminster or St James's Park
Mainline Charing Cross or Victoria

Opening
Daily 9.30am–6pm

Admission
Adult £7, Child free, Concs £5.50

Contact
King Charles Street, London SW1A 2AQ

t 020 7766 0120
w iwm.org.uk
e cwr@iwm.org.uk

127 Westminster

Westminster Abbey

1 hr+   All year

An architectural masterpiece of the C13 to C16, Westminster Abbey presents a unique pageant of British history. It has been the setting for most coronations since 1066 and for numerous royal occasions. Today it is still a church dedicated to regular worship and events.

* The tombs of kings & queens
* Tomb of the Unknown Warrior

Location
Next to Parliament Square, opposite the Houses of Parliament.
Underground St James's Park and Westminster

Opening
Mon–Fri 9.30am–3.45pm; Wed 9.30am–7pm; Sat 9.30am–1.45pm Sundays worship only

Admission
Adult £7.50, Child £5, Concs £5

Contact
20 Deans Yard, London SW1 P3PA

t 020 7654 4900
w wesminster–abbey.org
e press@westminster–abbey.org

128 Wimbledon

Wimbledon Lawn Tennis Museum

1 hr+   All year

This museum, on the site of the world's most famous lawn tennis tournament, offers a glimpse of both the centre court and the original trophies. Discover how the original medieval real tennis has become a multi-million pound professional sport.

* Audio/visual presentation of great players in action
* Additional behind-the-scenes tours are also available

Location
Underground Southfields

Opening
Daily; 10.30am–5pm

Admission
Adult £6, Child £3.75, Concs £5

Contact
The All England Lawn Tennis Club, Church Road, Wimbledon, London SW19 5AE.

t 020 8946 6131
w wimbledon.org/museum
e museum@aeltc.com

129 Banbury

Broughton Castle

1 hr+   May–Sep

Historic C14 moated castle enlarged in C16. Home of the family of Lord Saye and Sele for 600 years. Civil war connections, fine walled gardens, old roses and herbaceous borders. There is also a large area of open parkland.

* Location for *Shakespeare in Love*
* Medieval manor house enlarged in 1600

Location
2 miles W of Banbury Cross on the B4035 Shipston-on-Stour road

Opening
1 May–15 Sep Wed & Sun 2pm–5pm; Jul & Aug Thurs 2pm–5pm; Bank Hol & Sun

Admission
Adult £5.50, Child £2.50, Concs £4.50

Contact
Broughton, Banbury OX15 5EB
t 01295 722 547/276070
w broughtoncastle.demon.co.uk
e admin@broughtoncastle.demon.co.uk

130 Burford

Cotswold Wildlife Park & Gardens

3 hrs+   All year

The park, which is set in 160 acres of parkland and gardens around a listed Victorian manor house, has been open to the public since 1970. It's home to a collection of mammals, birds, reptiles and invertebrates, from ants to white rhinos and bats to big cats.

* Insect & reptile houses
* Birds of prey flying demos at weekends in summer

Location
On A361, 2 miles S of Burford

Opening
Daily Mar–Sep 10am–4.30pm
Oct–Feb 10am–3.30pm

Admission
Adult £8, Child £5.50, Concs £5.50

Contact
Burford OX18 4JW
t 01993 823006
w cotswoldwildlifepark.co.uk

131 Chipping Norton

The Rollright Stones

1 hr   All year

The Rollright Stones is an ancient site which consists of three main elements. The King's Men stone circle, the King Stone, and the Whispering Knights. The name is believed to derive from 'Hrolla–landriht', the land of Hrolla.

* Discover the folklore of Kings, witches & faeries
* 5000-year-old burial chamber of a Neolithic barrow

Location
N of Chipping Norton

Opening
Sunrise to sunset

Admission
Adult 50p, Child 25p

Contact
The Friends of the Rollright Stones
PO Box 444,
Bicester OX25 4AT

w rollrightstones.co.uk

132 Henley-on-Thames

Greys Court

1 hr+   Apr–Sep

This intriguing Tudor house, is set beside the ruins of C14 fortifications and one surviving tower dating from 1347. The house has an interesting history involving Jacobean court intrigue. The outbuildings include a wheelhouse, a donkey wheel and an ice house.

* Wisteria walk & ornamental vegetable garden
* Intimate rooms contain beautiful C18 plasterwork

Location
From Henley take A4130 to Oxford.
At Nettlebed roundabout take B481

Opening
Apr–Sep *House* Wed–Fri 2pm–5pm
Garden Tue–Sat 2pm–5pm

Admission
House Adult £5, Child £2.50
Garden £3.50, £1.70

Contact
Rotherfield Greys,
Henley–on–Thames RG9 4PG

t 01491 628529
w nationaltrust.org.uk
e greyscourt@ntrust.org.uk

133 Henley-on-Thames

River and Rowing Museum

2 hrs   All year

The museum has three main galleries devoted to the River Thames, the international sport of rowing and the town of Henley. There are also three special exhibition galleries housed in an astonishing building, raised on columns above water meadows beside the Thames.

* Exhibits from 400 BC to Sydney 2000 Olympic Games
* Architect David Chipperfield designed the building

Location
Signed from the centre of Henley

Opening
Daily; summer 10am–5.30pm
winter 10am–5pm
closed 24, 25, 31 Dec & 1 Jan

Admission
Please phone for details

Contact
Mill Meadows,
Henley–on–Thames RG9 1BF

t 01491 415600
w rrm.co.uk
e museum@rrm.co.uk

134 Oxford

The Ashmolean Museum of Art & Archaeology

2 hrs+   All year

This is a museum of the University of Oxford. Founded in 1683, it is one of the oldest public museums in the world. The collections are divided between five curatorial departments: antiquities, cast gallery, eastern art, heberden coin room and western art.

* Unique collection of early Chinese ceramics
* Sculpture includes an Ideal Head by Antonio Canova

Location
On Beaumont Street, opposite the Randolph Hotel, Oxford .

Opening
Tue–Sat 10am–5pm
Sun 2pm–5pm

Admission
Free

Contact
Beaumont Street, Oxford OX1 2PH UK
t 01865 278000
w ashmol.ox.ac.uk

135 Oxford

The Oxford University Museum of Natural History

1 hr+   All year

This museum houses Oxford University's extensive, natural history collection in a high-Victorian Gothic building. Exhibits include the remains of the dodo, immortalised in *Alice in Wonderland* and extinct since 1680, fossil dinosaur materials and many other exhibits.

* The Oxford dinosaurs & other Mesozoic reptiles
* Historic material donated by scientists like Darwin

Location
In Parks Road facing Keble College, signed

Opening
Daily; 12 noon–5pm
Closed 24–26 Dec & 1 Jan

Admission
Free, donations appreciated

Contact
Parks Road, Oxford OX1 3PW
t 01865 272950
w oum.ox.ac.uk
e info@oum.ox.ac.uk

136 Oxford

Modern Art Oxford

1 hr   All year

The gallery has established an international reputation for its pioneering programme of exhibitions and community events. Artists exhibited at the gallery include Joseph Beuys, Yoko Ono, Ed Ruscha, Louise Bourgeois, Carl Andre, Mike Nelson and Tracey Emin.

* A regular and changing programme of events
* Talks & tours, chidren's events and music evenings

Location
Town centre, 10 mins from train station

Opening
Tue–Sat 10–5pm, Sun 12noon–5pm
Please phone for details

Admission
Free

Contact
30 Pembroke Street,
Oxford OX1 1BP
t 01865 722733
w modernartoxford.org.uk
e foh@modernartoxford.org.uk

©Stephen White

137 Oxford

University Of Oxford Botanic Garden

1 hr+   All year

This garden holds a National Collection and has over 8000 different types of plant – the most compact yet diverse collection in the world. There is even more biological diversity here than in tropical rain forests.

* Water garden, rock garden & Grade I walled garden
* Innovative black border & autumn borders

Location
Opposite Magdalen College in the centre of Oxford

Opening
Daily; Mar–Sep 9am–5pm
Oct–Feb 9am–4.30pm

Admission
Adult £2.50, Child free, Concs £2

Contact
Rose Lane, Oxford OX1 4AZ

t 01865 286 690
w botanic–garden.ox.ac.uk
e postmaster@botanic–garden. ox.ac.uk

138 Wantage

The Vale & Downland Museum

2 hr+   All year

This museum is housed in a converted C17 cloth-merchant's house – a fine example of local vernacular architecture. The collections held at the museum contain geological, archeological and contemporary objects. An important record of both natural and social history.

* The story of Victorian Rural Life in the Vale
* 3D, graphic design and audio-visual presentations

    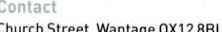

Location
Well signed from Wantage town centre

Opening
Mon–Sat 10am–4.30pm;
Sun 2.30pm–5pm

Admission
Adult £2.50, Child £1

Contact
Church Street, Wantage OX12 8BL

t 01235 771447
w wantage.com/museum
e museum@wantage.com

139 Woodstock

Blenheim Palace

4 hrs   Feb–Dec

This beautiful palace was built for John Churchill, 1st Duke of Marlborough, in 1705. Designed by Sir John Vanbrugh, it is one of the largest private houses in the country and contains a superb collection of tapestries, paintings, sculptures and furniture.

* Special exhibitions devoted to Sir Winston Churchill
* Paintings include works by Reynolds & Van Dyck

Location
Approaching Oxford on M40, exit at junction 9 and follow signs to Blenheim Palace

Opening
Palace Daily; mid Feb–mid Dec 10.30am– 4.45pm;
Nov–Dec closed Mon–Tue
Park Daily; 9am–4.45pm

Admission
Adult £12.50, Child £7, Concs £10, Please phone for details

Contact
Woodstock OX20 1PX

t 08700 602080
w www.blenheimpalace.com
e administrator@blenheimpalace.com

140 Cheam

Whitehall

1 hr+   All year

Whitehall has undergone a major refurbishment to reflect how the house would have looked at stages of its 500-year history. Originally C16, it now shows styles in several periods, all displayed in fully furnished rooms with original architecture.

* Timber framed construction
* Audio tour available & touch-screen information system

Location
Off Broadway, centre of Cheam

Opening
Wed–Fri 2pm–5pm
Sat 10am–5pm Sun & Bank Hols
2pm–5pm
closed 21 Dec–1 Jan

Admission
Adult £1.20, Child 60p

Contact
1 Malden Road, Cheam SM3 8QD

t 020 8643 1236
w sutton.gov.uk
e curators@whitehallcheam.fsnet.co.uk

141 Chertsey

Chertsey Museum

1 hr+   All year

Reopened in 2003 after a major redevelopment. Chertsey is famous as the site of a medieval abbey and has some of the best-preserved Georgian architecture in the county. The museum explores the history of the area and includes many items of national interest.

* Hands-on exhibits in Grade II Regency town house
* Nationally famous Olive Matthews costume collection

Location
Chertsey town centre

Opening
Tue–Fri 12.30–4.30pm Sat 11am–4pm
Closed 24 Dec–1 Jan

Admission
Free

Contact
The Cedars, 33 Windsor Street,
Chertsey KT16 8AT

t 01932 565764
w chertseymuseum.org.uk
e enquiries@chertseymuseum.org.uk

142 Cobham

Painshill Park

2 hrs+   All year

The Hon. Charles Hamilton created one of the great C18 landscape parks before running out of money in 1773. After years of neglect, the garden won a 'Europa Nostra Award for Exemplary Restoration' with its impressive plant collection having been painstakingly reassembled.

* Historic vineyard now replanted for production
* 14-acre lake fed by a spectacular waterwheel

Location
Off A3 and A245 at Cobham

Opening
Mar–Oct 10.30am–6pm, closed Mon
Nov–Feb 11am–4pm or dusk,
closed Mon & Tue

Admission
Adults £6, Child £3.50, Concs £5.25

Contact
Portsmouth Road, Cobham KT11 1JE

t 01932 868 113
w painshill.co.uk
e info@painshill.co.uk

143 Churt

Pride of the Valley Sculpture Park

2 hrs+   All year

Adjoining Frensham Country Park at the foot of Devil's Jumps with the finest views of the county. Some 100 renowned sculptors exhibit works of art in a woodland setting. Ten acres of hills, valleys, arboretum and wild fowl-inhabited water gardens.

* Frensham Country Park provides extensive walks

Location
Jumps Road is off A287 S of Farnham

Opening
Tue–Sun 10am–5pm. closed Mon except Bank Hols

Admission
Adult £4.50, Child £3, Concs £3

Contact
Jumps Road, Churt, nr Farnham GU10 2LE

t 01428 605453
w thesculpturepark.com
e eddiepowell@thesculpturepark.co.uk

144 East Molesey

Hampton Court Palace

3 hrs+   All year

With 500 years of royal history, Hampton Court is one of England's finest attractions. It is a magnificent house with diverse rooms such as a Tudor kitchen and the sumptuous State Apartments. The house is complemented by 60 acres of riverside gardens.

* Horse–drawn carriages through gardens in summer
* World–famous maze in which to get lost

Location
From M25, junction 10 to A307 or junction 12 to A308

Opening
Mar–Oct Tue–Sat 9.30am–6pm; Mon 10.15–6pm Nov–Feb shuts at 4.30pm; closed 24–26 Dec

Admission
Adult £11.80, Child £7.70, Concs £8.70

Contact
East Molesey KT8 9AU

t 0870 752 7777
w hrp.org

145 Esher

Claremont Landscape Garden

1hr+   All year

Claremont's creation and development involved some of the great names in garden history. Begun c.1715, it became famous throughout Europe. Restoration began in 1975 after years of neglect. The many features include a lake, grotto and great views.

* Design by Capability Brown & Sir John Vanbrugh
* Turf amphitheatre & island with pavilion

Location
1 mile outside Esher on the Cobham road, A307

Opening
Tue–Sun 10am–5pm or dusk
Apr–Oct Mon–Fri 10am–6pm
Sat, Sun & Bank Hols 10am–7pm

Admission
Adult £4.40, Child £2.20

Contact
Portsmouth Road, Esher KT10 9JG

t 01372 467806
w nationaltrust.org.uk/claremount
e claremount@nationaltrust.org.uk

Farnham Castle Keep

1 hr   Apr–Sep

From the C12 until 1920, Farnham Castle was the seat of the Bishop of Winchester. Kings and Queens were entertained here and hunted in the nearby park. Damage was caused during the English Civil War, though the medieval shell was maintained.

* Inclusive audio tour available
* Motte & bailey castle design

Location
½ mile N of Farnham on A287

Opening
Apr–Sep weekends 10am–6pm

Admission
Please phone for details

Contact
Castle Street, Farnham GU9 0AG

t 01252 713393
w english–heritage.co.uk

Rural Life Centre

2 hrs+   All year

The Rural Life Centre is a museum of past village life covering the years from 1750 to 1960. It is set in over 10 acres of garden and woodland and housed in purpose-built and reconstructed buildings including a chapel, village hall and cricket pavilion.

* Displays show village crafts & trades
* Arboretum with over 100 species of trees

Location
Off A287, 3 miles S of Farnham

Opening
21 Mar–5 Oct Wed–Sun & Bank Hol Mons 10am–5pm;
Nov–Feb Wed & Sun 11am–4pm

Admission
Adult £5, Child £3, Concs £4

Contact
Old Kiln Museum, Reeds Road
Tilford, Farnham GU10 2DL

t 01252 795 571
w rural–life.org.uk
e rural.life@lineone.net

Winkworth Arboretum

2 hrs   All year

A hillside woodland, created in the C20 and now containing over 1300 different rare shrubs and trees. Impressive displays of magnolias, bluebells and azeleas in spring and stunning colours in autumn. There is a lake and wetland area with wildlife in abundance.

* Trees include Japanese maples & tupelos from US
* Cool, peaceful walks through woodland

Location
2 miles SE of Godalming, off E side of the B2130.

Opening
Daily, dawn–dusk Wed–Sun

Admission
Adult £4, Child £2

Contact
Hascombe Road,
Godalming GU8 4AD

t 01483 208477
w nationaltrust.org.uk
e winkwortharboretum@national-trust.org.uk

149 Guildford

Clandon Park

2 hrs+   Mar–Oct

Built in 1730, this grand Palladian mansion is notable for its magnificent two-storeyed marble hall. The house has a superb collection of C18 furniture and porcelain. The attractive gardens contain a parterre, grotto and a Maori meeting house with a fascinating history.

* Home of Queen's Royal Surrey Regiment museum
* Designed by Venetian architect Giacomo Leoni

Location
Off A247 NE of Guildford

Opening
13 Mar–31Oct Tue–Thu & Sun
11am–5pm
Museum 12noon–5pm

Admission
Adult £6, Child £3

Contact
West Clandon, Guildford GU4 7RQ

t 01483 222 482
w nationaltrust.org.uk/clandonpark
e clandonpark@nationaltrust.org.uk

150 Guildford

Guildford House Gallery

1 hr+   All year

Guildford House is a fascinating C17 townhouse that now contains the council's art gallery showing selections from the borough's collection and varied temporary exhibitions. The house has magnificent plaster ceilings, original panelling and period furniture.

* Original craftwork & jewellery in giftshop
* Spectacular carved oak staircase

Location
Guildford High Street

Opening
Tue–Sat 10am–4.45pm;
closed 25–27, 31 Dec & Good Friday

Admission
Free

Contact
155 Upper High Street,
Guildford GU1 3AJ

t 01483 444740
w guildfordhouse.co.uk
e guildfordhouse@remote.guildford.
   gov.uk

151 Guildford

Hatchlands

2 hrs+   Apr–Oct

Set in the 430-acre Repton Park, Hatchlands is noted for its nautically themed interiors designed by Robert Adam. It is also home to the Cobbe Collection, the world's largest group of keyboard instruments, many associated with famous composers.

* Paintings by Van Dyck & Gainsborough
* Park offers variety of woodland walks

Location
N of A246 Guildford–Leatherhead road

Opening
House: Apr–Jun & Sep–Oct Tue–Thu &
Sun 2pm–5.30pm. Aug Tue–Fri & Sun
Open Bank Hol
Park: Daily 11am–6pm

Admission
Adult £6, Child £3

Contact
East Clandon, Guildford GU4 7RT

t 01483 222 482
w nationaltrust.org.uk
e hatchlands@nationaltrust.org.uk

152 Guildford

Loseley Park

3 hrs+   May–Sep

Built in 1562, Loseley House is a fine example of Elizabethan architecture, set in acres of peaceful gardens and parklands. Highlights of its celebrated garden include an award-winning rose garden, a vine walk and an area of native wild flowers. Relax in the serene fountain garden.

* Herb garden has six areas devoted to specific purposes

Location
A3 SW from Guildford on B3000

Opening
House May–Aug, Tues–Thurs & Sun 1pm–5pm; Bank Hol 11am–5pm
Garden May–Sep Tues–Sun 11am–5pm

Admission
House Adult £6, Child £3, Concs £5
Garden £3, £1.50, £2.50

Contact
Guildford GU3 1HS
t 01483 304440
w loseley-park.com
e enquiries@loseley-park.com

153 Guildford

River Wey & Godalming Navigations & Dapdune Wharf

2 hrs+   Mar–Oct

The Wey was one of the first British rivers to be made navigable (1653). This 15-mile waterway linked Guildford to Weybridge on the Thames. The visitor centre at Dapdune Wharf in Guildford tells the story of the people who lived and worked on the waterway.

* Boat trips available
* The entire 19-mile towpath is open to walkers

Location
Wharf Road is behind Surrey County Cricket Ground, off Woodbridge Road

Opening
End Mar–end Oct, Mon & Thu–Sun 11am–5pm

Admission
Adult £3, Child £1.50

Contact
Wharf Road, Guildford GU1 4RR
t 01483 561389
w nationaltrust.org.uk
e riverwey@nationaltrust.org.uk

154 Morden

Morden Hall Park

2 hrs+   All year

This oasis in the heart of suburbia covers over 125 acres of parkland with the River Wandle meandering through. The historic mill is now used as an environmental centre. The park has a hay meadow and there is an impressive rose garden with over 2000 roses.

* Planned walks & monthly programme of events
* Variety of bridges across the river

Location
Off Morden Hall Road

Opening
Daily; 8am–6pm
closed 25, 26 Dec & Jan 1

Admission
Free

Contact
Morden Hall Road, Morden SM4 5JD
t 020 8545 6850
w nationaltrust.org.uk/places/ mordenhallpark
e mordenhallpark@nationaltrust. org.uk

155 Ockley

The Hannah Peschar Sculpture Garden

2 hrs+   All year

A stunning woodland water-garden is the setting for this specialist exhibition of contemporary sculpture. Hannah Peschar and Anthony Paul are in the vanguard of a C21 revolution in garden design that uses predominantly sculpture and water.

Location
A29 to Ockley, near Oakwood Church

Opening
Mar–Oct, Fri–Sat 11am–6pm;
Sun & Bank Hol 2pm–5pm
Nov–Apr Tues & Thu by appointment

Admission
Adult £8, Child £5, Concs £6

Contact
Black and White Cottage,
Standon Lane, Ockley RH5 5QR

t 01306 627269
w hannahpescharsculpture.com
e hpeschar@easynet.co.uk

156 Richmond

Ham House & Gardens

2 hrs+   Mar–Oct

This outstanding Stuart house, built in 1610, is famous for its lavish interiors and spectacular collections of fine furniture, textiles and paintings. Restoration of the C17 formal gardens over the last 30 years has influenced similar projects in the great gardens of Europe.

* C18 dairy
* Reinstated C17 statuary in wilderness garden

Location
Off A307 W of Richmond

Opening
House Mar–Oct Mon–Wed, Sat & Sun,
1pm–5pm
Gardens Mon–Wed, Sat & Sun,
11am–6pm or dusk. Closed 25, 26 Dec
& 1 Jan

Admission
House Adult £7.50, Child £3.75
Gardens Adult £3.50, Child £1.75

Contact
Ham Street, Richmond TW10 7RS

t 020 8940 1950
w nationaltrust.org.uk/hamhouse
e hamouse@nationaltrust.org.uk

157 Richmond

Royal Botanic Gardens Kew

3 hrs+   All year

Established in 1759, Kew has developed into 300 acres of garden containing a collection of over 40,000 varieties of plant. Also see seven spectacular glasshouses and two art galleries, Japanese and rock gardens and regular exhibitions in the restored museum.

* One of England's top 100 attractions
* Inscribed as a World Heritage site in 2003

Location
Off A307 at Kew

Opening
Daily; from 09.30am–sunset,
closed 25 Dec & 1 Jan

Admission
Adult £8.50, Child free, Concs £6

Contact
Kew, Richmond TW9 3AB

t 020 8332 5655
w kew.org
e info@kew.org

158 Weybridge

Brooklands Museum

3 hrs+   All year

Constructed in 1907, Brooklands was the first purpose-built motor racing circuit in the world. Not only the birthplace of British motorsport but also of British aviation. The track and original buildings have been restored, and a motor museum has been added.

* Concorde in pieces ready to assemble for display
* Large display of cars, bikes & aircraft

Location
Off B374, A3 to A245, follow signs

Opening
Tue–Sun & Bank Hols;
summer 10am–5pm;
winter 10am–4pm;
closed 24–31 Dec & Good Friday

Admission
Adults £7, Child £5, Concs £6

Contact
Brooklands Rd, Weybridge KT13 0QN

t 01932 857381
w brooklandsmuseum.com
e info@brooklandsmuseum.com

159 Windsor

Runnymede

2 hrs+   All year

These historic meads on the banks of the Thames are where the Magna Carta was sealed by King John in June 1215. A network of footpaths links the Magna Carta memorial with two others: one to John F Kennedy and one to the 20,000 Royal Air Force airmen killed in WWII.

* Fairhaven Lodges, designed by Lutyens
* Boat trips along the Thames available

Location
6 miles E of Windsor on S side of A308
M25 junction 13

Opening
Daily; summer 9am–7pm
winter 9am–5pm

Admission
Charges for parking, fishing & mooring

Contact
North Lodge, Windsor Road,
Old Windsor SL4 2JL

t 01784 432891
w nationaltrust.org.uk/runnymede
e runnymede@nationaltrust.org.uk

160 Woking

RHS Garden Wisley

3 hrs+   All year

Wisley is Britain's best-loved garden with 240-acres offering a fascinating blend of beautiful and practical plants plus innovative design and cultivation techniques. It features richly planted borders, luscious rose gardens and the exotica of the glasshouses.

* New plant varieties continuously developed
* Extensive events & educational programmes

Location
Just S of junction 10 of the M25

Opening
Mar–Oct Mon–Fri 10am–6pm
Sat & Sun 9am–6pm
Nov–Feb Mon–Fri 10am–4.30pm
Sat & Sun 9am–4.30pm; closed Dec 25

Admission
Adult £7, Child £2, Concs £5.50

Contact
Woking GU23 6QB

t 01483 224234
w rhs.org.uk

161 Arundel

Amberley Working Museum

3 hrs+   Mar–Nov

Amberley is a 36-acre open air museum set in the South Downs. With its historic buildings, working exhibits and demonstrations the museum aims to show how science, technology and industry have affected people's lives.

* Variety of crafts demonstrated daily
* Trips on vintage bus & narrow gauge railway

Location
Off B2139 between Arundel & Storrington

Opening
Mar–Nov Wed–Sun 10am–5.30pm

Admission
Adult £7.50, Child £4.30, Concs £6.50

Contact
Amberley, Arundel, BN18 9LT

t 01798 831370
w amberleymuseum.co.uk
e office@amberleymuseum.co.uk

162 Arundel

Denmans Garden

2 hrs+   All year

An interesting late C20 garden cultivated to create a 'tamed wilderness'. Great use is made of contrasts in form and foliage, and gravel is widely used as a growing medium to create a very relaxed effect. The herb garden, roses and climbers give inspiration to visiting gardeners.

* Large greenhouse provides shelter to tender plants
* Natural-looking lake is home to moorhens

Location
Off the A27 W between Chichester and Arundel, adjacent to Fontwell Racecourse.

Opening
Daily; 9am–5pm

Admission
Adult £3.50, Child £1.95, Concs £3

Contact
Fontwell, Arundel BN18 0SU

t 01243 542808
w denmans-garden.co.uk
e denmans@denmans-garden.co.uk

163 Arundel

WWT Arundel

2 hrs+   All year

Surrounded by ancient woodland and overlooked by the town's historic castle, the wetlands at Arundel are home to many rare species of wetland wildlife. Many of the thousands of birds you will see are tame enough to eat from your hand.

* Many rare birds regularly sighted
* Eye of the Wind wildlife art gallery

Location
Close to A27 & A29 follow brown duck signs on approaching Arundel

Opening
Daily; 9.30am–5.30pm; 4.30pm in winter closed 25 Dec

Admission
Adult £5.75, Child £3.50, Concs £4.75

Contact
Mill Road, Arundel BN18 9PB

t 01903 883355
w wwt.org.uk/visit/arundel
e enquiries@wwt.org.uk

164 Arundel

Arundel Castle

1 hr+   Apr–Oct

Originally built in the C11 by the Earl of Arundel, this centre has 1000 years of fascinating history. There are fabulous displays of furniture, artefacts and paintings by Gainsborough, Reynolds and Van Dyck. The original motte, constructed in 1068, is over 100 feet (30m) high.

* Situated in magnificent grounds overlooking River Arun
* Seat of the Dukes of Norfolk for over 850 years

Location
At Arundel on A27

Opening
Apr–Oct Sun–Fri 12 noon–5pm; closed Sat & Good Friday

Admission
Adult £9.50, Child £7.50, Concs £6

Contact
Arundel BN18 9AB

t 01903 883136
w arundelcastle.org
e info@arundelcastle.org

165 Ashington

Holly Gate Cactus Garden

1 hr+   All year

This fascinating garden houses a world-renowned collection of over 30,000 exotic plants. Rare plants from the more arid areas of the world such as USA, Mexico, South America and Africa are represented, as well as cacti from the Central and South American jungles.

* 10,000 ft² of glasshouses
* Many plants in flower throughout the year

Location
Off A24 between Horsham & Worthing

Opening
Daily; 9am–5pm (4pm Nov–Jan)

Admission
Adults £2, Concs £1.50, Child £1.50

Contact
Billingshurst Road, Ashington RH20 3BB

t 01903 892930
w hollygatecactus.co.uk
e info@hollygatecactus.co.uk

166 Chichester

Chichester Cathedral

1 hr   All year

For 900 years Chichester Cathedral has been a landmark from land and sea. Famous for its modern art, it boasts a stunning Chagall window. Its more ancient treasures include the 'Arundel Tomb' which inspired Philip Larkin's poem.

* C12 sculpture depicting Lazarus
* Newly commissioned icon of St Richard

Location
City centre

Opening
Daily, subject to services

Admission
Free, donations requested

Contact
The Royal Chantry, Cathedral Cloisters, Chichester PO19 1PX

t 01243 782595
w chichestercathedral.org.uk
e reception@chichestercathedral.org.uk

167 Chichester

Goodwood House

2 hrs   Mar–Oct

Goodwood House is home to one of the most significant private art collections in the country. The state apartments have been richly refurbished to their original Regency elegance and there is an Egyptian state dining room and magnificent ballroom.

* Curator of the collection is author Rosemary Baird
* Fine art collection includes Reynolds, Stubbs and Canaletto

Location
3 miles NE of Chichester of A27

Opening
Mar–Oct Sun & Mon 1pm–5pm
3–30 Aug Sun–Thu 1pm–5pm

Admission
Adult £7, Child £3, Concs £6

Contact
Goodwood, Chichester PO18 0PX

t 01243 755 048
w goodwood.co.uk
e housevisiting@goodwood.co.uk

168 Chichester

Fishbourne Roman Palace & Gardens

2 hrs+   All year

This late C1 palace, discovered in 1960, is the largest Roman residence found to date in Britain. Its treasures include the country's finest collection of Roman mosaic floors and hypocausts. Finds are displayed, while an audio-visual presentation brings the site to life.

* The remains of over 20 mosaics are on display
* Roman garden has been replanted to its original plan

Location
N of A259 off A27 1½ mile W of Chichester

Opening
1 Feb–15 Dec, daily from 10am
16 Dec–31 Jan Sat & Sun only
10am–4pm

Admission
Adult £5.40, Child £2.80, Concs £4.60

Contact
Salthill Road, Fishbourne,
Chichester PO19 3QR

t 01243 785859
w sussexpast.co.uk
e adminfish@sussexpast.co.uk

169 Chichester

Military Aviation Museum

4 hrs+   Feb–Nov

Established in 1982, the museum tells the story of military flying from the earliest days, with emphasis on the RAF at Tangmere, and the air war over southern England from 1939–1945. Displays include the world speed record-breaking Meteor and Hunter.

* Opportunity to 'fly' fighter simulator
* Direct bus service from Chichester to museum, no.55

Location
3 miles E of Chichester off A27

Opening
Daily; Feb & Nov 10am–4.30pm
Mar–Oct 10am–5.30pm

Admission
Adult £5, Child £1.50, Concs £4

Contact
Military Aviation Museum,
Tangmere, Chichester PO20 6ES

t 01243 775 223
w tangmere–museum.org.uk
e admin@tangmere–museum.org.uk

170 Chichester

Royal Military Police Museum

1 hr   All year

The museum catalogues the worldwide activities of military police from Tudor times to the present day, documenting a unique history in a vibrant display. See artefacts from 1800's Britain, plus learn about activities in the Gulf and Balkan conflicts.

* Armoured reconnaissance vehicle
* Display of weapons used

Location
Off A286 Chichester–Midhurst Road

Opening
Tues–Fri 10am–4.30pm
Sat & Sun 2pm–4.30pm
Not open during weekends in winter

Admission
Free, donations appreciated

Contact
Broyl Road, Roussillon Barracks
Chichester PO19 6BL

t 01243 534225

171 Chichester

Weald & Downland Open Air Museum

2 hrs+   All year

This museum set in 50 acres of beautiful Sussex country-side offers a chance to wander through a fascinating collection of historic buildings dating from the C13 to the C19. Many with period gardens and farm animals. There are also woodland walks and a picturesque lake.

* The leading museum of historic buildings in England
* See food prepared in the working Tudor kitchen

Location
Situated 7 miles N of Chichester on the A286

Opening
Mar–Oct 10.30am to 6pm;
Nov–Feb Sat & Sun 10.30am–4pm

Admission
Adult £7, Child £4, Concs £6.50,

Contact
Singleton, Chichester PO18 0EU

t 01243 811363 / 811348
w wealddown.co.uk
e office@wealddown.co.uk

172 Chichester

West Dean Gardens

3 hrs+   Mar–Oct

These Edwardian gardens include 35 acres of ornamental grounds, a 100-yard pergola and herbaceous borders. A two-mile park walk, walled kitchen and fruit gardens, 16 restored greenhouses and a 45-acre arboretum are additional features.

* Christie's Garden of the Year 2002
* English Tourism Council 'Quality Assured Attraction'

Location
6 miles N of Chichester on A286

Opening
Mar–Oct 11am–5pm (last entry 4.30pm), May–Sep 10.30am–5pm

Admission
Adults £5.50, Child £2.50, Concs £5

Contact
West Dean, Chichester PO18 0QZ

t 01243 818210
w westdean.org.uk
e gardens@westdean.org.uk

173 East Grinstead

Standen

2 hrs+   Mar–Dec

Standen shows off pure Victorian style under the influence of the Arts and Crafts movement. It's extensively decorated with William Morris carpets, fabrics and wallpaper, and externally finished in sand stone, weatherboards and brick.

* 12-acre garden with fine views over the countryside
* Custom-made furniture from Heals & Morris

Location
2 miles S of East Grinstead off B2110

Opening
House 18 Mar–30Oct 11am–5pm
Garden 18 Mar–30 Oct 11am–6pm, 5 Nov–18 Dec Fri, Sat & Sun 11am–3pm

Admission
Gardens & House: **Adult £6.50, Child**
£3.25

Contact
West Hoathly Road,
East Grinstead RH19 4NE

t 01342 323029
w nationaltrust.org.uk/standen
e standen@nationaltrust.org.uk

174 Haywards Heath

Borde Hill Gardens

2 hrs+   All year

Borde Hill is set in 200 acres of traditional country estate. The garden was established from 1900 plants gathered from the Himalayas, China, Burma and Tasmania. Today Borde Hill has one of the most comprehensive collections of trees and shrubs in England.

* Magnificent rhododendrons, azaleas and camellias
* Britain's largest private collection of 'champion' trees

Location
1½ miles N of Haywards Heath

Opening
Daily; 10am–6pm

Admission
Summer Adult £6, Child £3.50, Concs £5; Winter £4, £2.50, £4

Contact
Balcombe Road,
Haywards Heath RH16 1XP

t 01444 450326
w bordehill.co.uk
e info@bordehill.co.uk

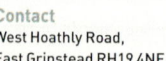

175 Haywards Heath

Nymans Gardens

2 hrs   All year

Nymans is one of the great gardens of the Sussex Weald and is internationally famous for its collection of rare plants. Created by three generations of the Messel family over a period of over a hundred years, Nymans was one of the first gardens to come to the National Trust (1953).

* Huge replanting programme followed 1987 storm
* Garden has individually characterised sections

Location
On B2114 at Handcross, 4½ miles S of Crawley, just off M23/A23

Opening
Garden 18 Feb–31 Oct Wed–Sun 11am–6pm; 6 Nov–20 Feb Sat & Sun 11am–4pm;
House 24 Mar–31 Oct 11am–5pm;

Admission
Adults £6.20, Child £3.10

Contact
Nymans Gardens, Handcross, nr Haywards Heath RH17 6EB

t 01444 400321
w nationaltrust.org.uk/nymans
e nymans@nationaltrust.org.uk

176 Horsham

Leonardslee Lakes & Gardens

3 hrs+   Apr–Oct

A woodland garden set in a 240-acre valley with seven lakes. Leonardslee has many features including a rock garden and Alpine House, as well as deer and wallabies roaming in the parkland. It also houses a collection of Victorian motor cars (1889–1900).

* Gold medal-winning bonsai & 400 species of alpines
* 'Behind the doll's house' exhibition

Location
On the junction on A281 & B2110 in Lower Beeding

Opening
Daily; 1 Apr–31 Oct 9.30am–6pm

Admission
Adult £6–£8, Child £4

Contact
Lower Beeding, Horsham RH13 6PP

t 01403 891212
w leonardslee.com
e gardens@leonardslee.com

177 Petersfield

Uppark

3 hrs   Mar–Sep

A late C17 house set high on the South Downs with magnificent sweeping views to the sea. It was rescued from a fire in 1989 and the restored Georgian interior houses a famous Grand Tour collection that includes paintings, furniture and ceramics.

* HG Wells' mother was a housekeeper
* A C18 doll's house is a star of the collection

Location
5 miles SE of Petersfield off B2146

Opening
House 20 Mar–2 Oct Sun–Thur
1pm–5pm
3–27 Oct Sun–Thurs 1–4pm
Grounds 20 Mar–2 Oct Sun–Thur
11.30am–5.30pm
3–27 Oct Sun–Thurs 11.30am–4.30pm

Admission
Adult £6, Child £3

Contact
South Harting, Petersfield GU31 5QR

t 01730 825415
w nationaltrust.org.uk/uppark
e uppark@nationaltrust.org.uk

178 Petworth

Petworth House & Park

3 hrs+   All year

A magnificent late C17 mansion set in a park landscaped by Capability Brown and immortalised in Turner's paintings. The house contains the National Trust's finest and largest collection of pictures, with numerous works by Turner, Van Dyck, Reynolds and Blake.

* Ancient & neo-classical sculpture
* Fine furniture & carvings by Grinling Gibbons

Location
5½ miles E of Midhurst on A272

Opening
19 Mar–31 Oct Mon–Wed; Sat & Sun
11am–5.30pm. Park open all year

Admission
Adult £7, Child £4

Contact
Petworth GU28 0AE

t 01798 342 207
w nationaltrust.org.uk/petworth
e petworth@nationaltrust.org.uk

179 Pulborough

Parham House & Gardens

2 hrs+   Easter–Sept

In the Middle Ages Parham House was owned by Westminster Abbey. In 1601 it was sold to Thomas Bysshop and it remained in the family until bought in 1922 by Clive Pearson. He purchased many of the paintings, and added his own objets d'art and English furniture.

* Award-winning four-acre walled garden
* Idyllically sited in the heart of an ancient deer park

Location
Off A283 Pulborough–Storrington road

Opening
Gardens: Easter Sun–Sep,
12noon–6pm; Wed, Thu, Sun & Bank
Hol Mons (also Tue & Fri in Aug).
House 2–5pm

Admission
House & Gardens Adult £6.50,
Child £2.50, Concs £5.50
Gardens only £5, £1, £4.50

Contact
Parham Park,
nr Pulborough RH20 4HS

t 01903 742021
w parhaminsussex.co.uk
e enquiries@parhaminsussex.co.uk

180 Pulborough

Bignor Roman Villa

1 hr+   Mar–Oct

Discovered in 1811, the site, which probably dates from C2, comprises 65 rooms in the main complex and nine outbuildings. They include a bathhouse, with one of the best-preserved Roman mosaics in England, and a summer and a winter dining room.

* Spectacular mosaics depicting Venus & Medusa
* One of the largest Roman villas in Britain

Location
6 miles N of Arundel, signed from the
A29 (Bignor-Billinghurst) and the
A285 (Chichester-Petworth)

Opening
Mar–Apr, Tues- Sun and Bank hols
10am–5pm;
Daily; May & Oct 10am–5pm
June–Sep 10am–6pm

Admission
Adult £4, Child £1.70, Concs £2.85

Contact
Bignor Lane,
Pulborough RH20 1PH

t 01798 869259
w pyrrha.demon.co.uk
e bignorromanvilla@care4free.net

Hell's Mouth, Cornwall

South West

Bristol Cornwall Devon Dorset
Gloucestershire Somerset Wiltshire

Strumble
Head

629 Cardigan

631 Lampe

Newcastle
Emlyn

Fishguard

St David's

PEMBROKESHIRE   CARMARTHENS

Carmarthen

671

663   Lla

Narberth

Haverfordwest   667   St Clears

Milford   Neyland   Kidwelly
Haven

Llanelli   M4

672–673   Burry
Pembroke   Port
Dock   Tenby   Swanse

Pembroke   Caldey
Island   SWANSEA   67
SWANSEA

St Govan's   Port
Head   Einon   Mumbles
Head

669

Ilfracombe

Hartland
Point   Barnst

216   Bideford

Great
Torrington   DEV

Bude   228–229

Holsworthy

Okehampton   230

196   Launceston

Tintagel   203   Dartr

214

195   Bodmin
208   Moor   Tavistock

Trevose Head   Wadebridge

Padstow   CORNWALL   Buckfas

Bodmin   PLYMOUTH
PLYMOUTH

NEWQUAY   192–194   Liskeard   PLYMOUTH

Newquay   Saltash   Plympto

St Austell   Looe   232–233
212   Fowey   Torpoint

215   Truro   Salc

St Ives   Camborne   Dodman
213   Redruth   Point

209   197–198

St Just   Penzance   St Mawes

206–207   204   205   Falmouth

Sennen   Helston

Land's End   200–201

210–211   199

202 Isles of Scilly   Lizard

Lizard
Point

181 Brislington

Bristol Blue Glass

1 hr   All year

Glass-blowing in Bristol was fully established by the mid-C17 when the city was fêted as a centre of excellence for glass-making and porcelain. See freeblown, handmade glass and watch glass-blowing demonstrations from the public viewing gallery.

* Glass available to puchase in giftshop
* Join in with exciting hands-on activites

Location
From M32 junction 3 and follow signs to A4

Opening
Daily; Mon–Sat 9am–5pm, Sun 11am–4pm

Admission
Adults £3, Child £1, Concs £2

Contact
Unit 7, Whitby Road, Brislington, Bristol BS4 3QF

t 0117 972 0818
w bristol-glass.co.uk
e info@bristol-glass.co.uk

183 City Centre

Bristol Cathedral

1 hr   All year

This fascinating building is a centre for Bristol's history, civic life and culture. Founded as an abbey in 1140, it became a cathedral in 1542 and developed architecturally through the ages. It is one of the finest examples of a 'hall church' anywhere in the world.

* Fine examples of Saxon stone carvings
* Expressionist window designed by Keith New in 1965

Location
Central Bristol on College Green

Opening
Daily 8am–6pm

Admission
Donation appreciated, £2 per person

Contact
College Green, Bristol BS1 5TJ

t 0117 926 4879
w bristol-cathedral.co.uk
e reception@bristol-cathedral.co.uk

182 City Centre

@Bristol

3 hrs+   All year

This is a unique destination bringing science, nature and art to life. It is a place of discovery and home to three attractions: Wildwalk, a living rainforest in the heart of the city; Explore, a C21 science centre; and a giant IMAX® theatre with digital surround sound.

* Tropical forest with free flying birds & butterflies
* Imaginarium – Bristol's very own planetarium

Location
Off Anchor Road in central Bristol

Opening
Daily 10am–6pm, closed 25 Dec

Admission
Explore
Adult £7.50, Child £4.95, Concs £5.95
Wildwalk & IMAX® £6.50,£4.50,£5.50

Contact
Harbourside, Bristol BS1 5DB

t 0845 345 1235
w at-bristol.org.uk
e information@at-bristol.org.uk

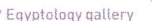

184 City Centre

Bristol Ferry Boat Company

2–4 hrs   All year

Enjoy the exciting world of Bristol's historic harbour – for a round trip tour or just by visiting one of the many attractions. The journey takes in the Pump House, Millennium Square and the SS *Great Britain*.

* River trips & pub ferry can be arranged
* Unique view of Bristol past & present

Location
Bristol Harbour

Opening
Daily, please phone for details

Admission
Multistop Day Ticket:
Adult £5, Child £3, Concs £3

Contact
MV *Tempora*, Welsh Back,
Bristol BS1 4SP

t 0117 9273 416
w bristolferryboat.co.uk
e enquiries@bristolferryboat.co.uk

185 City Centre

City Museum & Art Gallery

2 hrs+   All year

Bristol's major museum and art gallery houses an outstanding and diverse range of objects, from sea dinosaurs to magnificent eastern art. It is one of the few museums to have been awarded Designated status by the government – the mark of an outstanding museum.

* World Wildlife Gallery
* Egyptology gallery

Location
In Clifton, follow brown signs from
town centre

Opening
Daily 10am–5pm, closed 25,26 Dec

Admission
Free

Contact
Queen's Road, Bristol BS8 1RL

t 0117 922 3571
w bristol–city.gov.uk/museums
e general_museum@
   bristol–city.gov.uk

186 City Centre

The British Empire & Commonwealth Museum

2 hrs+   All year

This award–winning national museum presents the dramatic 500-year history of the rise and fall of Britain's overseas empire. Located in Isambard Kingdom Brunel's historic old Bristol station at Temple Meads.

* 16 permanent & interactive galleries
* Special half-term & holiday activities for families

Location
Located right next to Temple Meads, Bristol's main railway station

Opening
Daily 10am–5pm, closed 25,26 Dec. Please phone for details

Admission
Adult £6.50, Child £3.95, Concs £5.50

Contact
Station Approach, Temple Meads, Bristol BS1 6QH

t 0117 925 4980
w empiremuseum.co.uk
e admin@empiremuseum.co.uk

187 City Centre

CREATE Centre

1 hr   All year

The CREATE centre is a showcase of environmental excellence. Bristol's ecological centre is a font of information on environmental initiatives. Visit the Ecohome, a green home of the future, and learn about the challenge of waste in the recycling exhibition.

* A hands-on journey through waste & recycling
* Themed events throughout the year

Location
Cumberland Basin lies at the far end of the docks. CREATE is in a red brick warehouse

Opening
Mon–Fri 9am–5pm, closed 25 Dec

Admission
Free

Contact
Smeaton Road, Bristol BS1 6XN

t 0117 925 0505
w createcentre.co.uk
e create@bristol–city.gov.uk

188 City Centre

The Georgian House

1 hr   All year

This lovely house is an example of Bristol's C18 heritage, illustrating how the city profited from being one of England's premier trading ports. Originally home to John Pinney, a West India merchant, the house is displayed as it might have looked in its heyday.

* Home to the slave Pero
* Illustrating life above & below stairs

Location
Just off Park Street, near the Cabot Tower

Opening
Sat–Wed 10am–5pm

Admission
Free

Contact
7 Great George Street, Bristol BS1 5RR

t 0117 921 1362
w bristol-city.gov.uk
e general_museum@bristol-city.gov.uk

189 City Centre

University Botanic Garden

1½ hrs   All year

This garden cultivates some 4500 plant species from over 200 plant families within its five acre site. This diversity of plants is unique and not found elsewhere in Bristol. Special collections include rare native and threatened plants of the south west.

* Chinese medicinal herb garden
* South African & New Zealand collections

Location
Turning off A369 Bristol to Portishead road, 50 yards from Clifton Suspension Bridge

Opening
Mon–Fri 9am–5pm, closed Bank Hols

Admission
Free

Contact
Bracken Hill, North Road, Leigh Woods, Bristol, BS8 3PF

t 0117 973 3682
w bris.ac.uk/depts/botanicgardens
e nicholas.wray@bristol.ac.uk

190 City Centre

SS *Great Britain*

2 hrs   All year

The world's first great ocean liner, the SS *Great Britain*, is a unique surviving engineering masterpiece from Victorian times. Docked in the original Great Western Dock, this grand passenger liner has been the forerunner of all modern cruise ships.

* Designed by Isambard Kingdom Brunel
* The largest ship of her day

     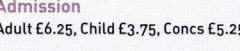

Location
Follow anchor signs in Bristol Historic Dockyard

Opening
Daily; Apr–Oct 10am–5.30pm
Nov–Mar 10am–4.30pm
closed 24,25 Dec

Admission
Adult £6.25, Child £3.75, Concs £5.25

Contact
Great Western Dockyard, Gas Ferry Road, Bristol BS1 6TY

t 0117 926 0680
w ss-great-britain.com
e enquiries@ss-great-britain.com

191 Whitchurch

Horseworld

3 hrs+   All year

This is a registered equine welfare charity. Located in beautiful Mendip stone farm buildings, dating back to the early C19, meet over 40 of the 300 rescued horses, ponies and donkeys. From Shetland ponies to shire-horses, each has a different story to tell.

* Twice daily presentations
* Museum of the Horse & giftshop

Location
Take A37 from Bristol. Through Whitchurch – Horseworld is on left

Opening
Daily; Mar–Sep 10am–5pm (4pm in winter); Sep–Mar closed Mon

Admission
Please phone for details

Contact
Staunton Manor Farm, Staunton Lane, Whitchurch, Bristol BS14 0QJ

t 01275 540173
w horseworld.org.uk
e visitorcentre@horseworld.org.uk

192 Bodmin

Lanhydrock House

3 hrs+   Apr–Oct

Largely rebuilt in 1881 after a fire, this fascinating C19 home captures the atmosphere and trappings of a high Victorian country house. 'Below stairs' has a huge kitchen, larder, dairy and bakehouse. The garden is set in 900 acres on the River Fowey.

* Magnificent gallery with moulded plaster ceiling

Location
2 miles E of Bodmin, follow signs off either A30 or A38

Opening
Apr–Oct Tue–Sun & Bank Hol Mons 11am–5.30pm (5pm in Oct)

Admission
House Adult £7.50, Child £3.75
Garden £4.20, £2.10

Contact
Lanhydrock, Bodmin PL30 5AD
t 01208 265950
w nationaltrust.org.uk
e lanhydrock@nationaltrust.org.uk

193 Bodmin

Military Museum Bodmin

1 hr+   All year

Over 200 years of regimental history is on display at the Duke of Cornwall Light Infantry Museum. The former barracks now houses the regimental museum with uniforms, pictures and medals including one of the country's finest small arms collections.

* General George Washington's bible captured 1777
* Events from the capture of Gibraltar in 1704 to WWII

Location
Outskirts of Bodmin

Opening
Mon–Fri 9am–5pm (Sun in Jul–Aug)

Admission
Adult £2.50, Child £1.50

Contact
The Keep, Bodmin PL31 1EG
t 01208 72810
e dclimus@talk21.com

194 Bodmin

Pencarrow

3 hrs+   Apr–Oct

Pencarrow houses a superb collection of pictures, furniture, porcelain and antique dolls. The house sits in 50 acres of gardens and woodland with a lake, an ice house and a Victorian rockery. There are marked walks through the woodland and gardens.

* Sir Arthur Sullivan composed the music to *Iolanthe*
* Grade II listed garden & Dogs Trust national award

Location
Follow signs off A389, 4 miles NW of Bodmin

Opening
House, Restaurant, Shop Apr–Oct Sun–Thu 11am–5pm
Gardens Daily 9am–6pm

Admission
House & Gardens Adult £7.50, Child £3.75 *Gardens* £3.75, free

Contact
Bodmin PL30 3AG
t 01208 841369
w pencarrow.co.uk
e pencarrow@aol.com

195 Bolventor

Colliford Lake Park

3 hrs+   Easter–Oct

Acres of indoor and outdoor adventure and fun with a 'Beast of Bodmin Moor' theme. Colliford Lake Park is a farm–based attraction with eight acres of woodland and 30 acres of farm stock with sheep, goats, red deer and other animals.

* Extensive indoor and outdoor play areas
* Nature trails around Colliford Lake

Location
500 yards off A30 between Launceston & Bodmin

Opening
Daily; Easter–Oct 11am–6pm

Admission
Adult £5.50, Child £4.50, Concs £4

Contact
Bolventor, Bodmin Moor PL14 6PZ

t 01208 821469
w collifordlakepark.com
e info@collifordlakepark.com

196 Camelford

British Cycling Museum

1 hr+   All year

Excellent display of cycling history from 1818 to the present day. Over 400 machines on display and large exhibition of cycling memorabilia including the first cycle oil lamps as well as candle lamps. Large display of cycling medals, fobs and badges.

* Extensive library of cycling books
* Gallery of cycling pictures

   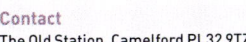

Location
1 mile N of Camelford on B3266

Opening
Sun–Thu 10am–5pm

Admission
Adult £2.90, Child £1.70

Contact
The Old Station, Camelford PL32 9TZ

t 01840 212811
w chycor.co.uk/britishcycling-museum

197 Falmouth

Pendennis Castle

2 hrs   All year

A Cornish fortress, ready for military action since C16. Pendennis and its sister, St Mawes Castle, face each other across the mouth of the River Fal. Constructed c. 1540, they are the Cornish end of a chain of castles built by Henry VIII along the south coast.

Location
Pendennis Head, 1 mile S of Falmouth

Opening
Please phone for details

Admission
Adult £4.50, Child £2.30, Concs £3.40

Contact
Pendennis Head, Falmouth TR11 4LP

t 01326 316594
w english-heritage.org.uk
e jane.kessell@english-heritage.org.uk

198 Falmouth

National Maritime Museum Cornwall

2 hrs   All year

This multi-award winning new generation of Museum, is a hands-on attraction inspired by the sea, and located on the water. With famous boats, access to the water and the opportunity to go under the sea, this Museum has everything for everyone.

* Cimb to the top of the tower for views over harbour
* Display of Cornish maritime heritage

Location
SE end of harbourside. Or follow signs from A39 for Park & Float

Opening
Daily 10am–5pm

Admission
Adult £6.50, Child £4.30, Concs £4.30

Contact
Discovery Quay, Falmouth TR11 3QY

t 01326 313388
w nmmc.co.uk
e enquiries@nmmc.co.uk

200 Helston

Godolphin House & Garden

2 hrs   Apr–Sep

This historic landscape includes Godolphin Hill with its wonderful views over west Cornwall. The house has fine C16 and C17 English oak furniture and equine paintings including Wotton's painting of Godolphin Arabian – one of three ancestors to all British bloodstock.

* The estate has over 400 archaeological features
* House dates from C15

Location
B3303 turn left to Godolphin Cross. Through Godolphin Cross village & house is on the left with brown signs

Opening
Please phone for details

Admission
Adult £6–7, Child £2

Contact
Godolphin Cross, Helston TR13 9RE

t 01736 763194
w godolphinhouse.com
e godo@euphony.zone

199 Goonhilly

Goonhilly Satellite Earth Station

2 hrs+   All year

One of the most striking attractions in Cornwall, on the Lizard Peninsula. Visit Goonhilly, the largest satellite station on Earth, to learn about space and modern communications through the multimedia visitor centre, interactive exhibits and film shows with tour guides.

* 3D virtual head creation & touch-screen internet terminals
* See yourself in space & move a satellite

Location
Follow B3293 Helston to St Keverne road

Opening
Daily from 10am Closing times vary from 4pm–6pm. Phone for details. Closed Mon in Feb, Mar, Nov & Dec

Admission
Adult £5, Child £3.50 Concs £4

Contact
Goonhilly TR12 6LQ

t 0800 679593
w goonhilly.bt.com
e goonhilly.visitorscentre@bt.com

201 Helston

Poldark Mine & Heritage Complex

  3 hrs All year

This Cornish tin mine has several underground routes with tunnels and stairs. Believed to be Europe's most complete mine workings open to the public. Also some machines and waterpumping engines are on display around the garden.

* Entry to the site itself is free
* Family attractions in addition to mine

Location
2 miles from Helston on B3297

Opening
Please phone for details

Admission
Underground tour Adult £5.95, Child £3.75

Contact
Wendron, Helston TR13 0ES

t 01326 573173
w poldark-mine.co.uk
e info@poldark-mine.co.uk

202 Isles of Scilly

Isles of Scilly Museum

  1½ hrs All year

Established following severe gales in the winter of 1962 which yielded up some remarkable Romano-British finds. The museum now houses an extremely diverse collection including material from wrecks, as well as the original Romano-British artefacts.

Location
10 mins' walk from Hugh Town harbour

Opening
Daily; Easter–Sep 10am–4.30pm
Oct–Easter 10am–12 noon

Admission
Adults £2.50, Child 50p, Concs £1.50

Contact
Church Street, St Mary's, Isles of Scilly TR21 0JT

t 01720 422337
w iosmuseum.org
e info@iosmuseum.org

203 Launceston

Launceston Castle

  1 hr Apr–Oct

Set on the high motte of a stronghold built soon after the Norman Conquest, this strategically important building controlled the road and river crossing in and out of Cornwall. As the venue for the county assizes and jail, the castle witnessed many trials and hangings.

* Built first as earthwork after Norman Conquest
* Administrative centre for the Earls of Cornwall

Location
Centre of Launceston

Opening
Daily, Apr–June 10am–5pm
July–Aug 10am–6pm
Sep 10am–5pm
Oct 10am–4pm

Admission
Adult £2.30, Child £1.20, Concs £1.70

Contact
Launceston PL15 7DR

t 01566 772365
w english-heritage.org.uk
e launceston.castle@english-heritage.org.uk

204 Marazion

St Michael's Mount

  2 hrs All year

This former Benedictine priory and castle is one of Britain's most visited properties. Linked to the mainland when the tide is out by a 500-yard causeway. Beautiful gardens contain many rare plants that are not often found growing out of doors in Britain.

* Once an important harbour & home to 300 people
* Castle is full of history including garrison & armoury

Location
Off coast of Marazion on A394

Opening
Please phone for details

Admission
Adult £5.20, Child £2.60

Contact
Marazion TR17 0HT

t 01736 710507
w stmichaelsmount.co.uk
e godolphin@manor-office.co.uk

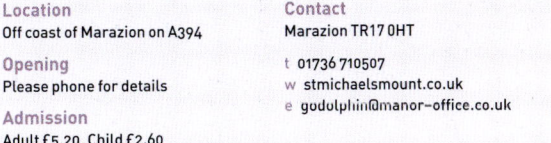

205 Mawnan Smith

Trebah Gardens

3 hrs   All year

This lovely sub–tropical ravine paradise winds through huge plantations of 100-year-old giant tree ferns, rhododendrons, magnolias, camellias, palms and two acres of massed hydrangeas to a private beach on the Helford River.

* Part of the Eden Trail
* Unique collection of rare plants & trees

Location
Follow signs from junction off A39 & A394

Opening
Daily 10.30am–5pm

Admission
Mar–Oct Adult £5.50, Child £3, Concs £5
Nov–Feb £2.60, £1.40, £2.40

Contact
Mawnan Smith,
Falmouth TR11 5JZ

t 01326 250448
w trebah-garden.co.uk
e mail@trebah-garden.co.uk

206 Penzance

Newlyn Art Gallery

½ hr   All year

Initially established to exhibit the work of the Newlyn School, the gallery has developed into one of the south west's leading contemporary art organisations. It enjoys a national and international reputation for its innovative exhibitions.

* The gallery has an active educational programme
* Newlyn Society of Artists still exhibits three times a year

Location
1 mile out of Penzance

Opening
Mon–Sat 10am–5pm

Admission
Free

Contact
New Road, Newlyn,
Penzance TR18 5PZ

t 01736 363715
w newlynartgallery.co.uk
e mail@newlynartgallery.co.uk

207 Penzance

Geevor Tin Mine

2 hrs   All year

The last working mine in West Penwith and now a mining museum and the largest preserved mining site in the UK, extending a mile inland. Some areas of the mine are 200 years old. A museum provides insight into the history of this traditional Cornish industry.

* Expert guides conduct underground tours
* Display of original mining machinery

Location
On B3306, St Ives to Land's End road

Opening
Daily; Apr–Oct 10am–5pm;
Nov–Mar 10am–4pm, closed Sat

Admission
Adult £6.50, Child £4, Concs £6

Contact
Pendeen, Penzance TR19 7EW

t 01736 788662
w geevor.com
e pch@geevor.com

208 Padstow

Prideaux Place

2 hrs   May–Oct

Explore 40 acres of landscaped grounds with terraced walks, formal garden, temple, Roman antiquities and the C9 Cornish Cross. An ancient deer park overlooks the estuary of the River Camel. Also see the Elizabethan plastered ceiling in the Great Chamber.

* Treasures include the Prideaux porcelain collection
* Guided tours of house available

Location
Off B3276, Padstow to Newquay road

Opening
27–31 Mar,
May–Oct Sun–Thurs 1.30pm–4pm

Admission
Adult £6.50, Child £2
Grounds: £2, £1

Contact
Padstow PL28 8RP

t 01841 532411
e office@prideauxplace.fsnet.co.uk

209 Penzance

Land's End Visitor Centre

2 hrs+   All year

Set on the most westerly point of mainland Britain, this privately-owned centre offers a range of facilities, including five pay-as-you-go exhibitions, restaurants, shops and a three-star hotel overlooking the sea. On a clear day you can see the Isles of Scilly, 23 miles away.

Location
At the end of the A30, 12 miles from Penzance

Opening
Daily; summer 10am–4pm
winter 10am–3pm
closed 25,26 Dec

Admission
Adult £10, Child, £6, Concs £5

Contact
Land's End, Sennen
Penzance TR19 7AA

t 01736 871501
w landsend-landmark.co.uk

---

211 Porthcurno

Porthcurno Telegraph Museum

2 hrs   All year

This award-winning industrial heritage museum explains the development of international telegraphy at the site of the first underground cables that linked Britain to the rest of the world (1870). It is housed in an underground station built for protection during the Second World War.

* Staff on hand to show how instruments work
* Adjacent to stunning Minack Theatre

Location
3 miles from Land's End off A30

Opening
Easter–Oct daily 10am–5pm
Nov–Easter Sun & Mon 10am–5pm

Admission
Adult £4, Child £2.50, Concs £3.50

Contact
Porthcurno, Penzance TR19 6JX

t 01736 810966
w porthcurno.org.uk
e mary.godwin@cw.com

---

210 Porthcurno

Minack Theatre

2 hrs+   All year

This has to be one of world's most spectacular theatres – an open-air auditorium carved into the cliffs high above Porthcurno's sandy cove. Founded and largely built by Rowena Cade in the 1930s, its remarkable story is now told in the visitor centre.

* Full programme of performances through summer
* Fantastic views from visitor centre

Location
3 miles from Lands End off A30

Opening
Daily; Apr–Sep 9.30am–5.30pm
Oct–Mar 10am–4pm

Admission
Adult £2.50, Child £1, Concs £1.80

Contact
Porthcurno, Penzance TR19 6JU

t 01736 810181
w minack.com
e info@minack.com

212   St Austell

The Eden Project

3 hrs+   All year

The Eden Project is dominated by two huge biomes – which are effectively the largest greenhouses in the world. The Humid Tropics Biome recreates the conditions and plant life of a lush rainforest while the Warm Temperate biome has a Mediterranean climate.

* Project has two million visitors a year
* See coffee plants, palm trees and pineapples

Location
Follow signs from A390 at St Austell & A30 Bodmin bypass

Opening
Daily; summer 9.30am–6pm
winter 10am–4.30pm

Admission
Adult £12, Child £5, Concs £9

Contact
Bodelva, St Austell PL24 2SG

t 01726 811900
w edenproject.com
e info@edenproject.com

213   St Ives

Tate St Ives

2 hrs   All year

St Ives has been famous as an artist's colony since the early C20 and the opening of Tate St Ives in 1993 provides the opportunity to view modern art in the surroundings and atmospere which inspired them. The gallery also manages the Hepworth Museum and Sculpture Garden.

* Spectacular coastal setting
* Visit Barbara Hepworth's home

Location
Near Porthmeor beach

Opening
Mar–Oct daily 10am–5.30pm
Nov–Feb Tue–Sun 10am–4.30pm

Admission
Adult £5.50, Child free, Concs £2.50

Contact
Porthmeor Beach,
St Ives TR26 1TG

t 01736 796226
w tate.org.uk/stives
e tatestivesinfo@tate.org.uk

214 Tintagel

Tintagel Castle

1 hr+   All year

This is the legendary home of King Arthur and Merlin, and its spectacular setting with the crashing waves on three sides adds fuel to the story. The ruins that stand today are the remnants of a castle built by Earl Richard of Cornwall, brother of Henry III.

* Some of the best sea views in Cornwall
* Put your foot in 'Arthur's Footprint'

Location
½ mile track from village, no vehicles beyond village

Opening
Daily; Apr–Sep 10am–6pm
Oct 10am–5pm
Nov–Mar 10am–4pm

Admission
Adult £3.70, Child £1.90, Concs £2.80

Contact
Tintagel PL34 0HE

t 01840 770328
w english–heritage.org.uk/membership
e tintagel.castle@english–heritage.org.uk

215 Truro

Royal Cornwall Museum

2 hrs   All year

A permanent display on the history of Cornwall from the Stone Age to the present day. Also contains a renowned collection of minerals, and ceramics, collections of ancient Egyptian, Greek, and Roman antiquities and a changing display of fine and decorative art.

* Diverse range of temporary exhibitions
* Restaurant relaunching end of Aug called Stingi Lulu's

Location
Truro town centre

Opening
Mon–Sat 10am–5pm,
closed Sun & Bank Hols

Admission
Free

Contact
River Street, Truro TR1 2SJ

t 01872 272205
w royalcornwallmuseum.org.uk
e enquiries@royalcornwallmuseum.org.uk

216 Barnstaple

Arlington Court

3 hrs+   Easter–Oct

Arlington Court houses the treasures amassed during the travels of Miss Rosalie Chichester. These include model ships, tapestries, pewter and shells. The stable block contains a magnificent collection of horse-drawn vehicles which offer carriage rides around the grounds.

* 'Batcam' films bat colony from May to September
* Spectacular gardens & extensive parkland

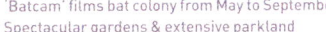

Location
Follow signs off A39, 8 miles N of Barnstaple

Opening
House Easter–Oct 10.30am–5.30pm closed Sat
Garden Jul–Aug daily

Admission
Adult £6.50, Child £3.25

Contact
Arlington, Barnstaple EX31 4LP

t 01271 850296
w nationaltrust.org.uk
e arlingtoncourt@nationaltrust.org.uk

217 Beer

Pecorama Millennium Garden

3 hrs+   Easter–Oct

This unusual garden is one of a number of activities on this hillside site overlooking Beer. Stunning designs include a roof garden enclosed by a ruined tower, a moat garden, rainbow garden, sun and moon garden – all with appropriately coloured plants and foliage.

* Miniature railway with steam & diesel locomotives
* Peco model railway exhibition

Location
Follow signs from Beer turning on A3052

Opening
5 Apr–30 Oct Mon–Fri 10am–5.30pm
Sat 10–1pm
30 May–5 Sep 10am–5.30pm;
open Easter Sunday

Admission
Please phone for details

Contact
Beer,
Nr Seaton EX12 3NA

t 01297 20580
w peco-uk.com
e pecorama@amserve.com

218 Bovey Tracey

Devon Guild of Craftsmen

2 hrs   All year

This is the south west's leading gallery and craft showrooms with work selected from around 240 makers, many with national and international reputations. Riverside Mill, the Guild's showcase, features frequently changing exhibitions.

* Newly refurbished gallery, extended craft shop
* Riverside Mill dates from 1850

Location
Follow signs for Bovey Tracey,
2 miles from A38

Opening
Daily 10am–5.30pm
closed Christmas

Admission
Free

Contact
Riverside Mill, Bovey Tracey TQ13 9AF

t 01626 832223
w crafts.org.uk
e devonguild@crafts.org.uk

219 Budleigh Salterton

Bicton Park Botanical Gardens

3 hrs+   All year

Bicton has sweeping lawns, water features, English borders and a formal Italian garden that survived the Capability Brown period. Its palm house is one of the world's most beautiful garden buildings. The museum contains an enormous collection of rural memorabilia.

* Exhibition of traction engines & vintage machinery
* Children's play area and narrow gauge railway

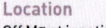 

Location
Off M5 at junction 30, follow signs via Newton Poppleford

Opening
Daily; summer 10am–6pm
winter 10am–5pm, closed 25,26 Dec

Admission
Adult £4.95, Child £3.95, Concs £3.95

Contact
East Budleigh,
Budleigh Salterton EX9 7BJ

t 01395 568465
w bictongardens.co.uk
e info@bictongardens.co.uk

---

220 Buckfastleigh

Buckfast Butterfly Farm & Dartmoor Otter Sanctuary

2 hrs   Easter–Oct

This unusual attraction offers an educational experience for animal lovers. See free-flying moths and butterflies from around the world in the indoor tropical garden. Otters swim in large glass enclosures to ensure spectacular underwater views.

* Butterfly habitat constructed to maximise viewing
* British, Asian & North American otters on show

Location
Follow signs from A38 at A384 to Buckfastleigh

Opening
Easter–Oct 10am–5.30pm

Admission
Adult £5.95, Child £4.50, Concs £5.50

Contact
Buckfastleigh TQ11 0DZ

t 01364 642916
w ottersandbutterflies.co.uk
e info@ottersandbutterflies.co.uk

---

221 Buckfastleigh

Buckfast Abbey

3 hrs+   All year

Buckfast Abbey is the only English medieval monastery to have been restored after the Dissolution and used again for its original purpose. This active Benedictine community provides an insight into monastic life and remarkable church architecture in a peaceful setting.

* Impressive marble flooring
* Original building dates from 1018

Location
Off A38, follow signs on A384

Opening
Daily; summer 9am–5.30pm
winter 9am–5pm

Admission
Free

Contact
Buckfastleigh TQ11 0EE

t 01364 645590
w buckfast.org.uk
e enquiries@buckfast.org.uk

222 Cullompton

Coldharbour Mill
& Working Wool Museum

4 hrs+   Mar–Oct

This 200-year-old waterside mill houses working spinning and weaving machines, and steam engines restored to their former glory. Regular exhibitions throughout the season.

* Guided tours available
* Steam engines can be seen running at special events

Location
2 miles off junction 27 of M5. Follow signs to Willand and the museum

Opening
Daily; Mar–Oct 10.30am–5pm

Admission
Adult £5.75, Child £2.75 Concs £5.25

Contact
Uffculme,
Cullompton EX15 3EE

t 01884 840960
w coldharbourmill.org.uk
e info@coldharbourmill.org.uk

---

224 Dartmouth

Blackpool Sands

1 hr+   Apr–Oct

This award-winning beach offers superb swimming conditions in clean clear water with a lifeguard on duty during the summer. Facilities include restaurants; a shop selling beach clothes and games; surfski, kayak, boogie boards, wet suit and snorkel hire.

* European blue-flag beach
* Secret seaside garden

Location
On the A379, 3 miles from Dartmouth

Opening
Daily; Apr–Oct 9am–7pm;

Admission
Free
Car park charges apply Apr–Oct

Contact
Blackpool,
Dartmouth TQ6 0RG

t 01803 770606
w blackpoolsands.co.uk
e info@blackpoolsands.co.uk

---

223 Dartmouth

Dartmouth Castle

1 hr   All year

Built by C14 merchants (led by mayor John Hawley) to protect themselves from invasion, this brilliantly positioned castle juts out into the narrow entrance to the Dart Estuary. It is said that Hawley was the inspiration for Chaucer's Shipman in *The Canterbury Tales*.

* Hands-on exhibition brings 600 years of history to life
* Complete Victorian gun battery

Location
1 mile SE of Dartmouth on B3025

Opening
Daily; Apr–Jun 10am–5pm
Jul–Aug 10am–6pm
Oct 10am–4pm;
Nov–Mar Sat & Sun 10am–4pm

Admission
Adult £3.50, Concs £2.60, Child £1.80

Contact
Castle Road, Dartmouth TQ6 0JN

t 01803 833588
w english-heritage.org.uk
e Dartmouth@english-heritage.org.uk

225 Exeter

Exeter Cathedral

½ hr   All year

This magnificent Gothic cathedral was largely rebuilt in the C13 though the imposing towers remain from the earlier Norman structure. The cathedral has played an important historical role through the ages, particularly in the C17.

* Elaborately carved choir stalls of particular note
* Visited by William the Conqueror

Location
Just off the High Street in the city centre

Opening
Daily; guided tours Apr–Oct

Admission
Free, donations encouraged

Contact
The Cloisters, Exeter EX1 1HS

t 01392 285983/285970
w exeter-cathedral.org.uk
e admin@exeter-cathedral.org.uk

226 Exeter

Killerton House

2 hrs+   Mar–Oct

An elegant C18 house in a hillside garden. The house has many treasures including the famous Killerton costume collection. The garden features a Victorian rock garden and an interesting ice house. There are fine views across the Devon countryside from the lawns.

* Costume collection extends to over 9000 items
* Costume display changes every year

Location
6 miles from Exeter off B3181

Opening
16 Mar–31 Oct 11am–5pm closed Tue;
Open daily in Aug;
closed Mon & Tues in Oct

Admission
House & Garden
Adult £6.50, Child £3

Contact
Broadclyst, Exeter EX5 3LE

t 01392 881345
w nationaltrust.org.uk
e killerton@smtp.ntrust.org.uk

227 Exeter

Powderham Castle

3 hrs+   Easter–Oct

Visit a succession of magnificent halls and state rooms filled with lavish furnishings, tapestries and historic portraits of the Courtenay family, whose home this has been for over 600 years. Powderham Castle is situated in beautiful parkland beside the Exe estuary.

* Fantastic grand staircase once part of Medieval Hall
* Miniature railway & children's secret garden

Location
8 miles from Exeter on A379 to Dawlish

Opening
Easter–Oct Sun–Fri 10am–5.30pm

Admission
Adult £7.20, Child £4.10

Contact
Kenton, Exeter EX6 8JQ

t 01626 890243
w powderham.co.uk
e caslte@powderham.co.uk

228 Great Torrington

RHS Garden Rosemoor

3 hrs+   All year

RHS Garden Rosemoor is a garden of great importance. To the huge range of plants collected by its former owner, the RHS has added features such as the formal garden, herbaceous borders, herb, fruit, vegetable and cottage gardens. Also Mediterranean and winter gardens.

* Extensive rose garden is most popular feature
* Extensive stream & lakeside planting

Location
Junction 27 of M5, A361 to South Molton. Follow signs.

Opening
Daily; Apr–Sep 10am–6pm
Oct–Mar 10am–5pm, closed 25 Dec

Admission
Adult £5.50, Child £1.50

Contact
Great Torrington EX38 8PH

t 01805 624067
w rhs.org.uk
e rosemooradmin@rhs.org.uk

229 Great Torrington

Dartington Crystal

3 hrs+   All year

Internationally known for handmade contemporary glassware. Discover the history of glass and of the Dartington company in the visitor centre, and watch the craftsmen at work in the factory. The factory shop is thought to be the biggest glass shop in the world.

* See Dartington's innovative glass designs
* Have your hand or foot cast

Location
In centre of Torrington off A386

Opening
Daily; Mon–Fri 9am–5pm, Sat 10am–5pm, Sun 10am–4pm (last tour at 3.15pm), no factory tour at weekends.

Admission
Please phone for details

Contact
Great Torrington EX38 7AN
t 01805 626242
w dartington.co.uk
e sfrench@dartington.co.uk

230 Okehampton

Okehampton Castle

3 hrs+   All year

The impressive ruins of the largest castle in Devon stand on the banks of a river in the foothills of Dartmoor. The central keep is still impressive atop its motte, and there are excellent walks through the woodlands surrounding the castle.

* Free audio tape tour available
* Beautiful picnic grounds

Location
1 mile SW of town centre

Opening
Daily; Apr–Sep 10am–6pm
Oct–Mar 10am–5pm

Admission
Adult £2.50, Child £1.50, Concs £1.90

Contact
Castle Lodge,
Okehampton EX20 1JB
t 01837 52844
w english-heritage.org.uk
e okehampton@english-heritage.org.uk

231 Newton Abbott

Tuckers Maltings

2 hrs+   Easter–Oct

Britain's only working malthouse open to the public, making malt from barley for beer. With its working Victorian machinery, Tuckers Maltings is an education for all ages with video and audio. See and taste real ale from the in-house brewery.

* Guided tours last one hour
* Speciality beer shop open all year

Location
3 mins' walk from Newton Abbot railway station

Opening
Easter–Oct, closed Sun, except Jul & Aug

Admission
Adult £5.25, Child £3.25, Concs £4.75

Contact
Teign Road,
Newton Abbott TQ12 4AA
t 01626 334734
w tuckersmaltings.com
e info@www.tuckersmaltings.com

232 Plymouth

Plymouth Dome

2 hrs　　All year

Over 400 years of Plymouth's great history is brought to life in this high-tech visitor centre. Walk through an Elizabethan street, find out about Drake, Cook and the *Mayflower*, link up a satellite and study weather patterns.

* Walk the gun deck of a galleon
* See the devastation of the Blitz

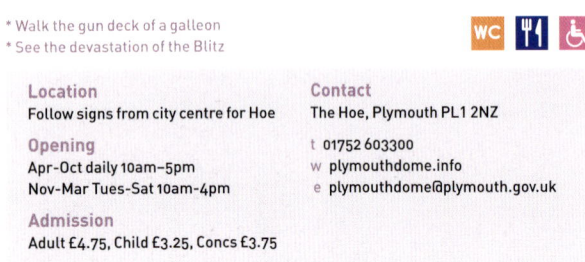

Location
Follow signs from city centre for Hoe

Opening
Apr–Oct daily 10am–5pm
Nov–Mar Tues–Sat 10am–4pm

Admission
Adult £4.75, Child £3.25, Concs £3.75

Contact
The Hoe, Plymouth PL1 2NZ

t 01752 603300
w plymouthdome.info
e plymouthdome@plymouth.gov.uk

233 Plymouth

Royal Albert Memorial Museum

2 hrs　　All year

This outstanding collection of local and national importance ranges from local archaeological finds to natural history displays from around the world as well as works of art. The impact of geology on Devon and its people is explored in the Geology at Work Gallery.

* Fascinating building to commemorate Prince Albert
* Display of clocks, watches & timekeeping

Location
Queen Street is just off High Street in city centre

Opening
10am–5pm, closed Sun
& Bank Hols

Admission
Free

Contact
Queen Street,
Exeter EX4 3RX

t 01392 665858
w exeter.gov.uk
e ramm@exeter.gov.uk

234 South Molton

Quince Honey Farm

2 hrs+　　Easter–Oct

In this world renowned honey farm you can stand and watch bees in complete safety. The unique design of the indoor apiary allows close-up viewing. The glass booths expose the working colonies without interfering with the bees' natural lifestyle.

* One of the largest honey farms in the country
* See the complete story of the production of honey

Location
From centre of South Molton on Barnstable Road

Opening
Daily; Easter–Sep 9am–6pm
Oct 9am–5pm

Admission
Adults £3.50, Child £2, Concs £2.80

Contact
South Molton EX36 3AZ

t 01769 572401
w quincehoney.co.uk
e info@quincehoney.co.uk

235 Tiverton

Tiverton Castle

1 hr　　Easter–Oct

Originally built in 1106 as the home of the Earl of Devon, the building now exhibits aspects of architecture from medieval to modern. Visitors can climb to the roof for views of the town and surrounding hillside, try on some English Civil War armour, and stroll round the gardens.

* Superb holiday accommodation, ring for details

Location
A361 to Tiverton and follow signs

Opening
Easter–Oct Sun, Thu & Bank Hols
2.30–5.30pm.

Admission
Adults £4, Child £2

Contact
Park Hill,
Tiverton EX16 6RP

t 01884 253 200
w tivertoncastle.com
e tiverton.castle@ukf.net

236 Torquay

Torquay Museum

1 hr   All year

Devon's oldest museum (1845) holds an impressive collection of natural history – both local and from across the world. There are also displays of Torquay pottery, pictorial archives, the story of Agatha Christie's life and a model of an old Devon farmhouse.

* Regular temporary exhibitions & events programme
* Over 300,000 natural history specimens in store

Location
Near Torquay harbour, a short walk from the clocktower

Opening
Mon–Sat 10am–5pm
Easter–Oct Sun 1.30pm–5pm

Admission
Adult £3, Child £1.50, Concs £2

Contact
529 Babbacombe Road,
Torquay TQ1 1HG

t 01803 293975
w torquaymuseum.org
e info@torquaymuseum.org

237 Torquay

'Bygones'

2 hrs+   All year

This life-size Victorian street with shops and period rooms also features a giant model railway and railwayana collection, an interactive and illuminated children's fantasy land, a multi-sensory First World War trench with militaria collection and a real Anderson shelter.

* Housed in a former cinema
* Christmas is a winter wonderland in a Victorian street

Location
Town centre, direction St Mary Church

Opening
Jul–Aug Mon–Thu 10am–9.30pm
Fri–Sun 10am–6pm;
Apr–May & Sep–Oct 10am–6pm,
Nov–Feb 10am–4pm

Admission
Adults £4.50, Concs £3.95, Child £3

Contact
Fore Street, St Marychurch
Torquay TQ1 4PR

t 01803 326108
w bygones.co.uk
e info@bygones.co.uk

238 Totnes

Totnes Castle

1 hr   Apr–Oct

Totnes Castle sits high on a hill above the town, commanding the approaches from three valleys. One of the best surviving examples of a Norman motte and bailey castle. The C11 wood structure was replaced by a stone keep in the C13 and C14.

* The keep has survived in excellent condition
* Keep surrounded by a curtain wall – now crumbling

 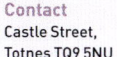

Location
On a hill overlooking Totnes

Opening
Daily; Apr–Jun & Oct 10am–5pm
Jul–Sep 10am–6pm

Admission
Adult £2, Child £1, Concs £1.50

Contact
Castle Street,
Totnes TQ9 5NU

t 01803 864406
w english-heritage.org.uk

239 Totnes

Berry Pomeroy Castle

1 hr   Apr–Oct

The Pomeroy family came from France with William the Conqueror and set up home on land bordering the Dart in 1267. The castle followed from that time. A mansion was added in the Elizabethan period but was damaged in the Civil War. The castle has been largely abandoned since.

* Stands on steep wooded hillside
* Rumoured to be the most haunted castle in Britain

Location
2 miles E of Totnes off A385

Opening
Daily; Apr–Jun & Sep 10am 5pm
Jul–Aug 10am–6pm, Oct 10am–4pm

Admission
Adult £3, Child £1.50, Concs £2.30

Contact
Totnes TQ9 6NJ

t 01803 866618
w english-heritage.org.uk

240 Beaminster

Mapperton Gardens

1 hr+   Easter–Oct

These terraced valley gardens surround a delightful Tudor/Jacobean manor house, stable blocks, dovecote and All Saints Church. Used as location in Jane Austen's *Emma*, *Restoration* and *Tom Jones*. There is also a shop with plants, pots and gift items, and a delightful cafe.

* Spring plant sale

Location
15 mins from Crewkerne via A303 to Beaminster on the B3163

Opening
Garden Daily; Mar–Oct 2pm–6pm
House Weekdays, 2 Jun–11 Jul
26, 25 May 2pm-4.30pm

Admission
Please phone for details

Contact
Mapperton,
Beaminster DT8 3NR
t 01308 862645
w mapperton.com
e office @mapperton.com

241 Bournemouth

Dorset Belle Cruises

1 hr+   All year

Take a glorious coastal and harbour cruise on a number of routes linking Bournemouth, Swanage and Poole Quay as well as Brownsea Island and the Isle of Wight. Specialist cruises are also available along this stunning coastline.

* ½-hour cruise around bay
* Fireworks & magnificent sunset cruises

Location
Boats depart from Bournemouth pier, Swanage or Poole

Opening
Phone or check website for details

Admission
Please phone for details

Contact
Pier Approach,
Bournemouth BH2 5AA
t 01202 558550
w dorsetbelles.co.uk
e info@dorsetbelles.co.uk

242   Bournemouth

Oceanarium Bournemouth

2 hrs   All year

A visit to the aquarium provides an encounter with marine life from across the globe. This is a fully interactive experience with feeding demos and talks, a walk-through underwater tunnel and exhibits to help you discover more about this fascinating underwater world.

* Gift shop & cafe open to the public

Location
Follow signs to Bournemouth beaches & piers

Opening
Daily; 10am–5pm, closed 25 Dec

Admission
Adult £6.95, Child £3.95, Concs £4.95

Contact
Pier Approach,
Bournemouth BH2 5AA

t 01202 311993
w oceanarium.co.uk
e info@oceanarium.co.uk

243   Blandford

Hall & Woodhouse Brewery

1 hr   All year

The brewery visitor centre tells the story of Hall and Woodhouse through the ages. Devise your own beer recipes, enjoy a virtual tour of the brewery, read the guide to beer tasting and view a personal collection of brewery artefacts and old advertising materials

* Fascinating insight into this 225-year-old brewery
* Beer can be bought at the brewery shop

Location
Follow signs from centre of Blandford

Opening
Visitor Centre Mon–Sat
10:30am–5:30pm.
Brewery tours please phone for details

Admission
Free to visitor centre, charge for tour

Contact
Blandford,
St Mary DT11 9LS

t 01258 452 141
w hall-woodhouse.co.uk
e enquiries@hall-woodhouse.co.uk

244   Bovington

Tank Museum

3 hrs+   All year

There are few places in the world where you can touch a Second World War tank. There are even fewer that have tanks that are in fully restored, running condition. Here are examples of tanks from both World Wars to the modern day, along with a good deal of post-war equipment.

* Indoor collection of 150 vehicles from 26 countries
* Vehicle rides & live demonstrations

Location
Off the A352, between Dorchester & Wareham, near Wool. Follow signs from Bere Regis

Opening
Daily; 10am–5pm, closed 25,26 Dec

Admission
Please phone for details

Contact
Bovington BH20 6HG

t 01929 405096
w tankmuseum.co.uk
e info@tankmuseum.co.uk

245 Dorchester

Kingston Maurward Gardens

2 hrs+   All year

Kingston Maurward Gardens are set deep in Hardy's Dorset and are listed on the English Heritage register of gardens. The 35 acres of classical C18 parkland and lawns sweep majestically down to the lake from the Georgian House.

* National Collections of penstemons and salvias
* Edwardian formal & walled demonstration gardens

    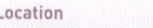

Location
1 mile E of Dorchester off the A35

Opening
Daily; 5 Jan–19 Dec 10am–5.30pm or dusk if earlier, closed Christmas

Admission
Adult £4, Child £2.50

Contact
Dorchester DT2 8PY
t 01305 215003
w www.kmc.ac.uk
e administration@kmc.ac.uk

247 Dorchester

The Keep Military Museum of Devon & Dorset

1 hr+   All year

Learn stories of courage, tradition and sacrifice of those who served in the regiments of Devon and Dorset for over 300 years. Experience spectacular views from the battlements of Dorchester and surrounding countryside, brought to life by the novels of Thomas Hardy.

* Modern interactive & creative displays

Location
On A35 Bridport road on western edge of Dorchester

Opening
Apr–Sep Mon–Sat 9.30am–5pm
July & Aug Sun 10am–4pm.
Oct–Mar Tues–Sat 9am–5pm

Admission
Adult £3, Child £2, Concs £2

Contact
Bridport Road, Dorchester DT1 1RN
t 01305 264066
w keepmilitarymuseum.org
e keep.museum@talk21.com

246 Dorchester

Dorset County Museum

1 hr+   All year

Visit Dorset's main general museum with 16 display rooms exploring aspects of local history, literature, geology, archaeology, fine art and natural science. Winner of the Best Museum of Social History category in the 1998 Museum of the Year awards.

* Interactive audio guide
* Exhibition of Trafalgar

Location
Town centre, follow museum signs

Opening
Oct–Jun Mon–Sat 10am–5pm
Jul–Sep daily 10am–5pm

Admission
Adults £4.20, Child free, Conc £3.20

Contact
High West Street,
Dorchester DT1 1XA
t 01305 262735
w dorsetcountymuseum.org
e nicky@dor-mus.demon.co.uk

248 Dorchester

The Dinosaur Museum

1 hr+   All year

Dedicated to dinosaurs, this award-winning museum is a treat. Audio-visual displays portray the Earth millions of years ago. One fascinating exhibit explores the question of what life would be like today if the dinosaurs had not become extinct.

* Winner of the Dorset Family Attraction award
* Top 10 Hands-on Museum in Britain

Location
Centre of Dorchester

Opening
Daily; Easter–Oct 9.30am–5.30pm
Nov–Mar 10am–4.30pm

Admission
Adults £5.50, Child £3.95

Contact
Icen Way,
Dorchester DT1 1EW

t 01305 269880
w thedinosaurmuseum.com
e info@thedinosaurmuseum.com

249 Dorchester

The Tutankhamun Exhibition

1 hr   All year

This exhibition recreates the original Tutankhamun artefacts found when the pharoah's tomb was reopened. The artefacts are displayed in a model of the tomb chamber as it looked in 1922 when local archaeologist Howard Carter unearthed it.

* A permanent exhibition of the World Heritage Organisation

Location
3 mins walk from Dorchester centre

Opening
Easter–Oct 9.30am–5.30pm
Nov–Easter daily 9.30am–5p;
weekends open 10am,
Sun close 4.30pm

Admission
Adult £5.50, Child £3.95, Concs £4.75

Contact
High West Street,
Dorchester DT1 1UW

t 01305 269571
w tutankhamun-exhibition.co.uk
e info@tutankhamun-exhibition.co.uk

250 Poole

Brownsea Island National Trust

3 hrs+   Mar–Oct

Just a short boat trip from Poole or Bournemouth, the charm of the landscape, the variety of wildlife and an intriguing heritage make Brownsea a fascinating place to visit. It offers magnificent views of the Purbeck Hills and Studland Bay, with a study centre.

* Exhibition of island information & photographs
* Dorset Wildlife Trust Nature Reserve

Location
By boat from Poole, Bournemouth,
Swanage or Sandbanks

Opening
27 Mar–31 Oct from 10am
closing time varies

Admission
Adult £3.70, Child £1.60

Contact
Poole Harbour BH13 7EE

t 01202 707744
w nationaltrust.org.uk/brownsea
e office@brownseaisland.fsnet.co.uk

251 Poole

Waterfront Museum

1 hr   All year

Discover a wealth of intriguing items in the Waterfront Museum. Here, 2000 years of history about trading in the Poole area is on view, housed in a fine C18 warehouse adjoining the medieval town cellars with a historic street scene.

* Artefacts from Studland Bay wreck
* Scaplens Court Museum open opposite in August

Location
End of High Street in town centre

Opening
Nov–Mar Mon–Sat 10am–3pm
Sun 12noon–3pm
Apr–Oct Mon–Sat 10am–5pm
Sun 12noon–5pm

Admission
Free

Contact
4 High Street,
Poole BH15 1BW

t 01202 262600
e museums@poole.gov.uk

252 Portland

Portland Castle

1 hr+   Apr–Oct

Portland Castle was built by Henry VIII as part of his ambitious scheme of coastal defences against the French and Spanish. It has survived largely unaltered since the C16, making it one of the best preserved examples of Henry's castles.

* Audio guides around the castle
* Contemporary heritage gardens

Location
Royal Naval Dockyard at Portland

Opening
Apr–Jun & Sep, daily 10am–5pm
Jul–Aug, daily 10am–6pm
Oct, daily 10am–4pm

Admission
Adult £3.50, Child £1.80, Concs £2.70

Contact
Castletown, Portland Harbour,
Weymouth DT5 1AZ

t 01305 820539
w english-heritage.org.uk

253 Sherborne

Sherborne Castle

2 hrs+   Apr–Oct

Built by Sir Walter Raleigh in 1594 and set in 20 acres of beautiful landscaped gardens around a 50-acre lake, Sherborne Castle has been home to the Digby family since 1617 and contains a fine collection of pictures, porcelain, furniture and decorative arts.

* Capability Brown lake

     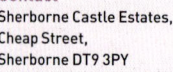

Location
1 mile E of Sherborne, follow signs from A30

Opening
Apr–Oct 11am–4.30pm closed Mon & Fri; Sat 2:30pm–4.30pm

Admission
Adult £6, Child free, Concs £5.50

Contact
Sherborne Castle Estates,
Cheap Street,
Sherborne DT9 3PY

t 01935 813182
w sherbornecastle.com
e enquiries@sherbornecastle.com

254 St Leonards

Avon Heath Country Park

4 hrs+   All year

Dorset's largest country park has nearly 600 acres of heathland with stands of pine trees and birch woodland. Special events include pond dipping, Easter egg trails, bug hunts, den building, orienteering, kite making, animal tracks and signs, and dawn-chorus walks.

* Barbecue hire available
* Nature activity trails

Location
On the A31, 2 miles W of Ringwood

Opening
Park: Daily; Apr–Sep 8am–7.30pm;
Oct–Mar 8.30am–5.30pm
Visitor centre: Daily 11am–4pm

Admission
Free
Car park charge

Contact
Brocks Pine, St Leonards
Ringwood BH24 2DA

t 01425 478470

255 Swanage

Swanage Railway

2 hrs+   All year

This award-winning railway currently operates on the six mile track between Swanage and Norden, through the beautiful Isle of Purbeck, passing the magnificent ruins of Corfe Castle. At present, there is extension work taking place to the north of Norden.

Location
Station in centre of Swanage, a few mins walk from the beach

Opening
Trains daily Apr–Oct. Weekends only rest of year. Daily Dec 26–31

Admission
Adult £7, Child £5, Concs £5

Contact
Station House, Swanage BH19 1HB

t 01929 425800
w swanagerailway.co.uk
e general@swanrail.freeserve.co.uk

256 Studland

Studland Beach & Nature Reserve

3 hrs+   Easter–Oct

Fine sandy beaches stretch for 3 miles from South Haven Point to the chalk cliffs of Handfast Point and Old Harry Rocks. Along the way are Shell Bay and a designated naturist area. The heathland behind the beach is a National Nature Reserve.

Location
Across B'mth & Swanage motor road ferry or via Corfe Castle on the B3351

Opening
Daily

Admission
Parking charges vary through seasons, please telephone for details

Contact
Countryside Office, Studland, Swanage BH19 3AX

t 01929 450259
w nationaltrust.org.uk
e studlandbeach@nationaltrust.org.uk

35027

381

257 Wareham

Corfe Castle

1 hr+   All year

One of Britain's more majestic ruins, this castle once controlled the gateway through the Purbeck Hills and in its time served as a fortress, prison and home. Many fine Norman and early English features remain.

* Special events including historical re-enactments
* Guided tours available

Location
On the A352 Wareham to Swanage road

Opening
Daily; closed 25,26 Dec

Admission
Adult £4.70, Child £2.30

Contact
The National Trust, The Square, Corfe Castle, Wareham BH20 5EZ

t 01929 481294
w nationaltrust.org.uk
e corfecastle@nationaltrust.org.uk

258 Wareham

Monkey World

2 hrs+   All year

Monkey World is a sanctuary for over 160 rescued primates from all over the world. Living at the park is the largest group of chimpanzees outside Africa. Orangutans, gibbons and many more primates inhabit spacious enclosures in a natural woodland setting.

* Adoption scheme
* The south's largest adventure playground

Location
Located between Bere Regis and Wool, 1 mile from Wool station

Opening
Daily 10am–5pm (6pm Jul & Aug)

Admission
Adult £8, Child £6, Concs £6

Contact
Longthorns, Wareham BH20 6HH

t 01929 462537
w www.monkeyworld.org
e apes@monkeyworld.org

259 Wareham

Lulworth Castle

3 hrs+   All year

Lulworth Castle was built between 1608 and 1610 but caught fire in 1929 and was all but ruined. In the 1970s restoration work began and the exterior is now as it was before the fire. This is a unique building with a rich history.

* Lulworth Country Fair & international horse trials
* August jousting shows

Location
3 miles SW of Wareham, follow signs

Opening
Summer 10.30am–6pm
Winter 10.30am–4pm
Closed Sat & 24 Dec to early Jan

Admission
Adults £7, Child £4, Concs £5

Contact
East Lulworth, Wareham BH20 5QS
t 01929 400 352
w www.lulworth.com
e estate.office@lulworth.com

260 Weymouth

Brewers Quay

3 hrs+   All year

Redeveloped Victorian brewery at the heart of Weymouth's Old Harbour, offering speciality shopping, entertainment and eating out. Step back in time at the 'Timewalk and Brewery Days' attraction.

Location
On harbour, 5 mins from town centre

Opening
Daily 10am–5.30pm

Admission
Free entry to complex.
Timewalk attraction Adult £4.50,
Child £3.25, Concs £4.00

Contact
Hope Square, Weymouth DT4 8TR
t 01305 777 622
w brewers-quay.co.uk
e brewersquay@yahoo.co.uk

261 Weymouth

Deep Sea Adventure

3 hrs   All year

Experience the world of underwater exploration from C17 to the present day. Discover the history of Weymouth's Old Harbour, alongside compelling tales of shipwreck and survival. Fascinating exhibitions including 'Scuba diving through the years' and 'The *Titanic*'.

* Sharkey's Play and Party Warehouse for children up to 11 yrs
* Creative workshops, paint your own pottery

Location
A35 into Weymouth, follow signs

Opening
Summer 9.30am–8pm; winter
9.30am–7pm; closed 25,26 Dec &
1 Jan (last entry 1½ hrs before close)

Admission
Adult £3.75, Child £2.75

Contact
9 Custom House Quay, Old Harbour,
Weymouth DT4 8BG
t 0871 222 5760
w deepsea-adventure.co.uk
e enquires@deepsea-adventure.co.uk

262 Wimborne

Kingston Lacy House

3 hrs+   Mar–Nov

Kingston Lacy was home to the Bankes family for over 300 years. All four floors are open to visitors and contain lavish interiors. The Edwardian laundry gives a fascinating insight into life below stairs 100 years ago. Formal gardens and parkland surround the house.

* Special snowdrop days in January
* Events throughout the year

Location
1½ miles from Wimborne on B3082

Opening
House Mar–Nov Wed–Sun & Bank Hols
11am–5pm
Garden Daily; Mar–Nov 10.30am–6pm,
5 Nov–19 Dec, Fri, Sat & Sun
10.30am–4pm

Admission
Please phone for details

Contact
Wimborne BH214EA
t 01202 883402
w www.nationaltrust.org.uk
e kingstonlacy@nationaltrust.org.uk

263 Berkeley

Edward Jenner Museum

1 hr+   Mar–Nov

This was the beautiful Georgian home of Edward Jenner (1749–1823), who discovered the smallpox vaccine and who also studied birds, fossils and balloons. There is an exhibition of modern immunology with the aim of promoting wider public understanding.

* Explore the science of Jenner's work
* See how smallpox has been eradicated

Location
1½ miles W of A38 midway between Bristol & Gloucester

Opening
Mar–Nov Tue–Sat & Bank Hol Mons 12.30pm–5.30pm, Sun 1pm–5.30pm; Oct Sun only 1pm–5.30pm; closed Nov–Mar

Admission
Adult £3.50, Child £2, Concs £2.80

Contact
Church Lane, Berkeley GL13 9BN

t 01453 810 631
w jennermuseum.com
e manager@jennermuseum.com

264 Bourton-on-the-Water

Cotswold Motor Museum & Toy Collection

½ hr   Feb–Nov

A veritable treasure of yesteryear. Though the main focus is on motoring with a fine collection of classic cars, motorcycles and caravans, the museum has its very own toy collection including teddy bears and aeroplanes plus a rare collection of pedal cars.

* Largest collection of historic motoring signs
* Home to TV character 'Brum'

Location
Bourton town centre at junction with Sherborne Street

Opening
Daily; Feb–Nov 10am–6pm

Admission
Adult £2.95, Child £1.95

Contact
The Old Mill, Sherbourne Street, Bourton-on-the-Water, Cheltenham GL54 2BY

t 01451 821255
w cotswold-motor-museum.com
e motormuseum@csma-netlink.co.uk

265 Bourton-on-the-Hill

Bourton House Gardens

1 hr   May–Oct

Bourton House is an C18 Cotswold manor house and C16 tithe barn. Its 3-acre garden, which has been created over the last 20 years, features extravagant borders, exotic plants and fantastic topiary. Much variety including raised alpine troughs and a shade house.

* Fountains & ponds fed by original spring
* Tithe barn has exhibition of local art

Location
On A44, 2 miles W of Moreton-in-Marsh

Opening
May–Aug Wed–Fri 10am–5pm
Sep–Oct Thu–Fri only

Admission
Adult £4.50, Child free

Contact
Bourton-on-the-Hill, nr Moreton-in-Marsh GL56 9AE

t 01386 700754
w bourtonhouse.com
e cd@bourtonhouse.com

266 Cheltenham

Chedworth Roman Villa

2 hrs   Mar–Nov

The site comprises over a mile of walls, several fine mosaics, two bathhouses, hypocausts, a water-shrine and latrine. Set in a wooded Cotswold combe, the site was excavated in 1864 and still has a Victorian atmosphere. The museum houses objects found on site.

* National Trust Property
* One of the largest Roman villas in the country

Location
3 miles NW of Fossebridge on the Cirencester–Northleach road (the A429); approach from the A429 via Yanworth or from the A436 via Withington

Opening
Mar–mid Nov Tue–Sun 10am–5pm, Mar & Nov 11am–4pm

Admission
Adult £3.90 Child £2

Contact
Yanworth,
Nr Cheltenham GL54 3LJ

t 01242 890256

267 Cheltenham

Cheltenham Art Gallery & Museum

1 hr   All year

This collection has been built up over the last 100 years by generous residents who have donated their collections. There is a nationally important Arts & Crafts collection and one room is dedicated to Edward Wilson who travelled with Scott to Antarctica.

* Started with donation of 43 important paintings in 1897
* Oriental gallery with Chinese pottery and costume

Location
Cheltenham town centre

Opening
Mon–Sat 10am–5.20pm; closed Bank hols

Admission
Free, donations appreciated

Contact
Clarence Street, Cheltenham GL50 3JT

t 01242 237431
w cheltenham.art.gallery.museum
e artgallery@cheltenhammuseum.gov.uk

268 Cheltenham

Holst Birthplace Museum

1 hr   Feb–Dec

This Regency terrace house is where Gustav Holst, composer of *The Planets Suite* was born in 1874. The story of the man and his music is told alongside a fascinating display of personal belongings, including his piano. The museum is also a fine period house.

* Working Victorian kitchen and laundry
* Regency drawing room and Edwardian nursery

Location
In the Pitville area of Cheltenham, opposite Pitville Park

Opening
Tue–Sat 10am–4pm (closed Jan)
Tours by appointment

Admission
Adult £2.50, Child £2, Concs £2

Contact
4 Clarence Road, Cheltenham GL52 2AY

t 01242 524 846
w holstmuseum.org.uk
e holstmuseum@btconnect.com

269 Chipping Campden

Hidcote Manor Gardens

2 hrs+   Mar–Oct

One of England's great gardens created early in the C20 by the horticulturist Major Lawrence Johnston. A series of small gardens separated by walls and hedges of different species. The varied style of the outdoor 'rooms' ensures an interesting visit at any time.

* Rare & unusual plants from around the world

Location
4 miles NE of Chipping Campden,
off B4081

Opening
19 Mar–30 Oct Sat–Wed 10.30am–6pm
(last entry 1 hr before close)
Shop & Restaurant open Nov–mid Dec
12noon–4pm Sat & Sun

Admission
Adult £6.60, Child £3.30

Contact
Hidcote Bartrim,
Chipping Campden GL55 6LR
t 01386 438333
w nationaltrust.org.uk/hidcote
e hidcote@nationaltrust.org.uk

270 Chipping Campden

Kiftsgate Court Garden

1 hr   Apr–Sep

A series of interconnecting gardens each with a distinct character, including a sheltered Mediterranean garden. There are many unusual plants that have been collected by the garden's creators – three generations of women.

* Newly-added water garden
* Views stretch to the Bredon & the Malvern Hills

Location
SE of Mickleton and 4 miles NE of
Chipping Campden off B4081

Opening
Apr, May, Aug & Sep Wed, Thu, Sun &
Bank Hol Mons 2pm–6pm
Jun–Jul Mon, Wed, Thu, Sat & Sun
12noon–6pm

Admission
Adult £5, Child £1.50

Contact
Chipping Campden GL55 6LN
t 01386 438777
w kiftsgate.co.uk
e info@kiftsgate.co.uk

271 Cinderford

Dean Heritage Centre

2 hrs+   All year

This is the museum of the Forest of Dean, situated by a mill pond in a wooded valley, with woodland walks, adventure playground and picnic site. There are exhibits reflecting the area's social and industrial history, including a beam engine and a water-wheel.

* Traditional charcoal burning demonstrations annually
* Various woodland craft workshops also at this site

Location
In the Forest of Dean on the B4227
at Soudley

Opening
Daily; Apr–Oct 10am–5.30pm
Nov–Mar 11am–4pm;
closed 24–26 Dec & 1 Jan

Admission
Adult £4.50, Child £2.50, Concs £3.50

Contact
Camp Mill, Soudley,
Cinderford GL14 2UB
t 01594 822170
w deanheritagemuseum.com
e deanmuse@btinternet.com

272 Gloucester

Gloucester City Museum & Art Gallery

1 hr   All year

This museum is nearly 150 years old and in that time it has acquired a fine collection of art, archaeological, geological and natural history items. Many local people have donated their collections and these include paintings by Rembrandt and Turner.

* Hands-on & interactive computer displays

Location
Gloucester city centre at junction with
Parliament Street

Opening
Tue–Sat 10am–5pm.
closed 25,26,31 Dec & 1 Jan

Admission
Free

Contact
Brunswick Road GL1 1HP
t 01452 396131
w glos-city.gov.uk
e culture@gloucester.gov.uk

273 Gloucester

Gloucester Folk Museum

1 hr+   All year

Housed in splendid Tudor and Jacobean buildings which date from the C16 and C17. Displays include local history, such as the Siege of Gloucester (1643), Severn fishing and farming and an attractive garden. Craft industries including pin-making, shoemaking and toys and games.

* Exhibition of domestic life – kitchen & laundry
* Displays of a dairy, ironmongers and carpenters

Location
Gloucester city centre, nr the docks

Opening
Tues–Sat 10am–5pm
Please phone for details

Admission
Free

Contact
99–103 Westgate Street GL1 2PG

t 01452 396868/ 396869
w livinggloucester.co.uk
e folk.musuem@glos.gov.uk

275 Gloucester

National Waterways Museum

2 hrs   All year

Housed in the historic Gloucester docks, the museum charts the story of Britain's canals with a nationally important collection. You enter through a replica lock complete with running water and the exhibits show what it was like to live and work on the waterways.

* See Gloucester's role as an important historical dock
* For boat trips please phone for availability

Location
Follow signs for 'Historic Docks'

Opening
Daily 10am–5pm; closed 25 Dec

Admission
Adult £5, Child £4, Concs £4

Contact
Llanthony Warehouse,
Gloucester Docks GL1 2EH

t 01452 318200
w nwm.org.uk
e bookingsnwml@thewater-
    waystrust.org

274 Gloucester

Clearwell Caves – Ancient Iron Mines

2 hrs   All year

Mining in the Forest of Dean is believed to have started over 7000 years ago as people migrated back into the area after the last Ice Age. Large scale iron ore mining continued until 1945. Visitors are allowed to walk into some of the oldest underground mines in Britain.

* See first hand how miners struggled to 'win' ore
* Nine caverns open, deep level visits by appointment.

Location
1½ miles S of Coleford

Opening
Mar–Oct 10am–5pm; Nov–Dec
Christmas Fantasy, phone for details;
Jan–Feb weekends only 10am–5pm

Admission
Adult £4, Child £2.50, Concs £3.50

Contact
Clearwell Caves & Ancient Iron Mines,
nr Coleford, Royal Forest of Dean,
Gloucester GL16 8JR

t 01594 832535
w clearwellcaves.com
e jw@clearwellcaves.com

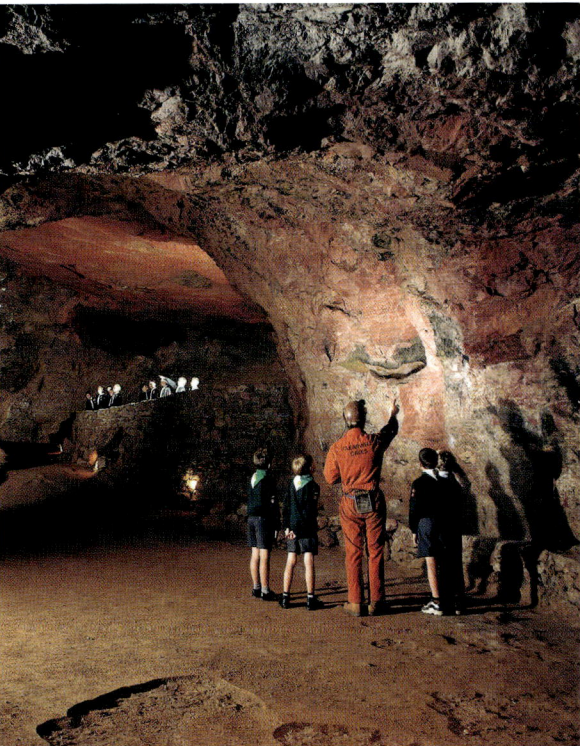

276 Gloucester

Soldiers of Gloucestershire Museum

1 hr+   All year

Housed in the Customs House in Gloucester's historic docks, the museum tells the story of how two regiments (one an infantry regiment of the regular Army, the other a territorial Yeomanry cavalry regiment) have brought honour to Gloucestershire.

* The Gloucestershire Regiment (regular Army)
* The Royal Gloucestershire Hussars (territorials)

Location
Follow signs to 'Historic Docks'

Opening
Daily 10am–5pm; closed winter Mons & Christmas (last entry 4.30pm)

Admission
Adult £4.25, Child £2.25, Concs £3.25

Contact
Gloucester Docks GL1 2HE

t 01452 522682
w glosters.org.uk
e rhqrgbw@milnet.uk

---

277 Lower Slaughter

Old Mill Museum

½ hr+   All year

A C19 flour mill on the banks of the River Eye is home to a museum and an organic ice cream parlour renowned for its handmade ice cream. Owned by jazz singer Gerald Harris, the mill has been extensively restored and has become a popular Cotswold attraction.

* Free ice cream tasting Apr–Oct
* Voted 'Most beautiful village in the Cotswolds'

Location
Off A429 between Stow-on-the-Wold and Bourton-on-the-Water

Opening
Daily 10am–6pm, when clocks change 10–dusk; closed 18–25 Dec

Admission
Adults £1.25, Child 50p

Contact
Mill Lane, Lower Slaughter GL54 2HX

t 01451 820052
w oldmill-lowerslaughter.com
e info@oldmill-lowerslaughter.com

---

278 Moreton-in-Marsh

Batsford Arboretum

2 hrs   All year

With over 1600 different trees and species from all over the world, Batsford Arboretum has colour throughout the year. There are winter snowdrops and daffodils, cherry blossom and magnolias, summer bamboo and a glorious display of golden autumnal colour.

* One of the largest private collections in the country
* Diverse range of birds & animals often seen

Location
Off A44 W of Moreton-in-Marsh

Opening
Mid Nov–Jan, weekends 10am–4pm; Feb–mid Nov daily 10am–5pm, 26 Dec & 1 Jan 11am–3pm

Admission
Adult £5, Child £1, Concs £4

Contact
Batsford Park, nr Moreton-in-Marsh GL56 9QB

t 01386 701441
w batsarb.co.uk
e batsarb@batsfound.freeserve.co.uk

---

279 Moreton-in-Marsh

Sezincote Gardens

1 hr+   Jan–Nov

Built in a Moghul architectural style, a mixture of Hindu and Muslim, Sezincote is a very unusual English house. The gardens are fascinating and include canals, Moghul paradise gardens and a small Indian-style pavilion. The water gardens contain many rare plants.

* Indian bridge decorated with Brahmin bulls
* Sezincote is from Cheisnecote, 'the home of the oaks'

Location
1½ miles W of Moreton-in-Marsh A44

Opening
House May–Jul & Sep Thu & Fri 2.30pm–6pm
Gardens Jan–Nov Thu, Fri & Bank Hol Mons 2pm–6pm or dusk if earlier

Admission
Gardens Adult £4, Child £1.50
House & Garden £6 (no children)

Contact
nr Moreton-in-Marsh GL56 9AW

t 01386 700444
w gloucestershire.gov.uk

280 Moreton-in-Marsh

Wellington Aviation Museum

1 hr   All year

Near a training school for Bomber Command during the Second World War, the museum now contains an extensive collection of artefacts from the war years including a Vickers-Armstrong Wellington bomber. A separate tail section shows the famous Barnes-Wallis structure.

* Thousands of documents to investigate
* Collection of aviation & military art

Location
On A44 NE of Cheltenham

Opening
Tue–Sun 10am–12.30pm & 2pm–5pm
Jan–Feb weekends only

Admission
Adult £2, Child £1

Contact
British School House,
Moreton-in-Marsh GL56 0BG
t 01608 650323
w wellingtonaviation.org

282 Painswick

Painswick Rococo Garden

2 hrs   Jan–Oct

The rococo style was a short but important design period more often associated with art or architecture. Few such gardens survive and its mixture of formal and informal creates a unique effect. Characterised by winding paths, the garden is full of fascinating features.

* Plunge pool, geometric kitchen garden & maze
* An interesting mixture of building styles

Location
Off A46, then B4073 ½ mile N
of Painswick

Opening
Daily; Jan–Oct 11am–5pm

Admission
Adult £4, Child £2, Concs £3.50

Contact
Painswick GL6 6TH
t 01452 813204
w rococogarden.co.uk
e info@rococogarden.co.uk

281 North Cerney

Cerney House Gardens

1 hr   Apr–Jul

This beautiful 'secret' garden sits high above the Churn Valley in the heart of the Cotswolds. It has many features including a lovely Cotswold walled garden with lots of old-fashioned roses, a well-labelled herb garden and kitchen garden, as well as plenty of scenic views.

* Next to Chedworth Roman Villa
* Walks available in surrounding woodland

Location
On A435 Cheltenham road. Turn left
opposite Bathurst Arms

Opening
Apr–Jul Tue–Thu & Sun 10am–5pm

Admission
Adult £3, Child £1

Contact
North Cerney GL7 7BX
t 01285 831205
w cerneygardens.com
e cerneygardens@hotmail.com

283   Tetbury

Chavenage House

1 hr+   Apr–Sep

This wonderful Elizabethan manor house, with Cromwellian connections, has changed little in 400 years. The house is noted for Cromwell's room, the main hall with its magnificent stained glass windows, the ballroom and the Oak Room.

* Set in beautiful gardens
* A favourite with filmmakers

Location	Contact
On B4014, 1½ miles NW of Tetbury	nr Tetbury GL8 8XP
Opening	t 01666 502329
Apr–Sep Thu, Sun & Bank Hols	w chavenage.com
2pm–5pm	e info@chavenage.com
Admission	
Please phone for details	

284   Tetbury

Tetbury Police Museum

½ hr   All year

This museum is housed in the town's original Police office and cells of a former magistrate's court. The building is Victorian with an interesting collection of artefacts from the Gloucestershire Constabulary. An under-court room display demonstrates what a trial would have been like.

* See early police batons, helmets & gas-masks
* Extensive photographic collection

Location	Contact
5 mins walk from town centre	The Old Court House, 63 Long Street, Tetbury GL8 8AA
Opening	
Mon–Fri 9am–3pm; closed Bank Hols	t 01666 504670
Admission	w tetbury.com/policemuseum
Free, donations appeciated	e tetburycouncil@virgin.net

285   Uley

Owlpen Manor House & Gardens

2 hrs+   Apr–Sep

This Tudor manor house (1450–1616) has a splendid great hall and stands at the centre of a clutch of medieval buildings. The terraced garden is a rare survival of an early formal garden with magnificent yew topiary, old roses and box parterres.

* Queen Margaret of Anjou is said to haunt the manor
* Contains a great collection of furniture, textiles & paintings

Location	Contact
1 mile E of Uley, off B4066	nr Uley, Dursley GL11 5BZ
Opening	t 01453 860261
Apr–Sep 2pm–5pm; closed Mon, open	w owlpen.com
Bank Hols	e sales@owlpen.com
Admission	
Adult £4.80, Child £2	
Garden only £2.80, £1	

286   Westbury-on-Severn

Westbury Court Garden

1 hr   Mar–Oct

Originally laid out at the turn of the C17, this is the only restored Dutch water garden in the country. It was also the National Trust's first garden restoration, completed in 1971, and is planted with species pre-dating 1700.

* Replica C17 panelling installed in pavilion
* Parterre & vegetable plots reinstated to C17 style

Location	Admission
9 miles SW of Gloucester on A48	Adult £3.50, Child £1.70
Opening	**Contact**
Mar–Jun Wed–Sun 10am–5pm	Westbury-on-Severn GL14 1PD
Jul–Aug daily 10am–5pm	t 01452 760461
Sep–Oct Wed–Sun 10am–5pm	w nationaltrust.org.uk
	e westburycourt@nationaltrust.org.uk

287 Tetbury

Westonbirt Arboretum

3 hrs+   All year

Westonbirt has one of the finest collections of trees in the world today with 18,000 trees and shrubs in 600 acres of landscaped countryside. There is also an extensive array of wild flowers, fungi, birds and animals throughout the year.

* International Festival of Gardens Jun-Sep
* Finest autumn & spring leaf colour display in Europe

Location
3 miles S of Tetbury on A433 to Bath

Opening
Daily; 10am–8pm or dusk if earlier

Admission
Adults £6, Child £1, Concs £5

Contact
Westonbirt,
nr Tetbury GL8 8QS
t 01666 880220
w forestry.gov.uk/westonbirt
e westonbirt@forestry.gsi.gov.uk

288 Winchcombe

Sudeley Castle & Gardens

2 hrs+   Mar–Oct

Sudeley Castle is steeped in history. With royal connections spanning a thousand years, it has played an important role in the turbulent and changing times of England's past. It has played host to Henry VIII, Elizabeth I and King Charles I – the latter during the Civil War.

* Home & tomb of Queen Katherine Parr.
* Spoiled in the Civil War, resoration began in 1837

Location
8 miles NE of Cheltenham on B4632

Opening
Castle Mar–Oct 11am–5pm
Gardens Mar–Oct 10.30am–5.30pm

Admission
Castle Adult £6.85, Child £3.85, Concs £5.85
Gardens £5.50, £3.25, £4.50

Contact
Winchcombe GL54 5JD
t 01242 602308
w sudeleycastle.co.uk
e marketing@sudeley.org.uk

289 Barrington

Barrington Court

2 hrs+   Mar–Oct

An enchanting formal garden laid out in a series of walled rooms, including the white garden, the rose and iris garden and the lily garden. The working kitchen garden has espaliered apple, pear and plum trees trained along high stone walls.

* Tudor manor house restored in the 1920s

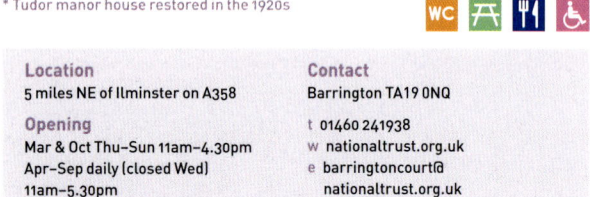

Location
5 miles NE of Ilminster on A358

Opening
Mar & Oct Thu–Sun 11am–4.30pm
Apr–Sep daily (closed Wed)
11am–5.30pm

Admission
Adult £6, Child £3

Contact
Barrington TA19 0NQ

t 01460 241938
w nationaltrust.org.uk
e barringtoncourt@
nationaltrust.org.uk

290 Bath

The American Museum & Gardens

2 hrs   Mar–Oct

Learn how Americans lived from the time of the early European settlers to the American Civil War. Rooms include a replica C18 tavern where all visitors are given a piece of home-cooked gingerbread. Wonderful collection of quilts, native American objects and folk art.

* Extensive gardens
* See website for exhibition programme

Location
Off A36 S of Bath at Claverton
(5 mins drive from city)

Opening
19 Mar–30 Oct, 12noon–5.30pm;
closed Mon, open Bank Hols

Admission
Adult £6.50, Child £4, Concs £6

Contact
Claverton Manor,
Bath BA2 7BD

t 01225 460503
w americanmuseum.org
e info@americanmuseum.org

291 Bath

Bath Aqua Theatre of Glass

1 hr   All year

In this living/working museum glass is produced for church windows, art projects and for private commissions. You can see the beautiful aquamarine glass being blown in the theatre during regular public demonstrations.

* Signed and dated pieces available in shop
* Exhibition of old and new stained glass

Location
5 mins walk W out of city centre

Opening
Daily 10am–1pm & 1.45pm–5pm
Preferred viewing times 10.15, 11.15,
12.15, 2.15, 3.15, last demo at 4pm.

Admission
Adults £3, Child £1.50, Concs £2

Contact
105–107 Walcot Street,
Bath BA1 5BW

t 01225 428146
w bathaquaglass.com
e bathaquaglass@hotmail.com

292 Bath

Holburne Museum of Art

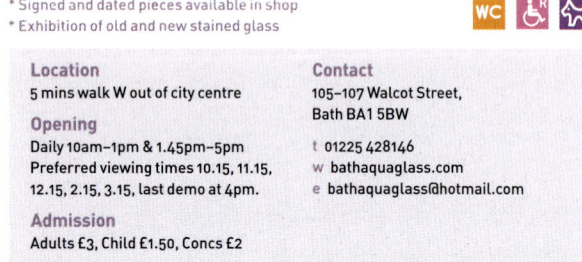

1 hr+   All year

This jewel among Bath's splendid array of museums and galleries displays the treasures collected by Sir William Holburne. Superb English and continental silver, porcelain, majolica, glass and Renaissance bronzes. Paintings include works by Turner and Gainsborough.

* Regular specialist exhibitions & lectures
* Book & gift shop open to the public free

Location
5 mins walk from Pulteney Bridge at
end of Great Pulteney Street

Opening
Tue–Sat 10am–5pm open Bank Hols
Sun 2.30pm–5.30pm

Admission
Adult £4, Child £1.50, Concs £3.50

Contact
Great Pulteney Street,
Bath BA2 4DB

t 01225 466669
w bath.ac.uk/holburne
e holburne@bath.ac.uk

293 Bath

Bath Abbey –
Heritage Vaults Museum

1 hr   All year

Situated on the south side of Bath's C15 abbey (itself built on the site of a Saxon abbey), the vaults have been beautifully restored. They provide an interesting setting for objects that have survived from the abbey's fascinating past.

Location
S side of abbey, city centre

Opening
Mon–Sat 10am–4pm
closed Sun, 25,26 Dec, 1 Jan & Good Friday (last entry 3.30pm)

Admission
Adults £2.50

Contact
Bath BA1 1LT

t 01225 422462
w bathabbey.org
e office@bathabbey.org

294 Bath

Bath Postal Museum

3 hrs+   All year

The first letter sent with a stamp (the Penny Black) was sent from this building in 1840. The former post office now illustrates 4000 years of communication, including Egyptian clay tablets, various writing implements and the story of the first air mail sent from Bath to London.

* Special exhibitions
* Pillar boxes through the ages

Location
In Broad Street, city centre

Opening
Mon–Sat 11am–5pm

Admission
Adults £2.90, Child £1.50, Concs £2.20

Contact
8 Broad Street, Bath BA1 5LJ

t 01225 460333
w bathpostalmuseum.org
e info@bathpostalmuseum.org

295 Bath

Bath Balloon Flights

3–4 hrs   Apr–Oct

Balloons launch from Royal Victoria Park, close to the city centre. Booking ahead is essential and all flights are subject to suitable weather conditions. Flight direction is wind dependent, but central start point ensures fantastic views of city and surroundings.

* Bookings available for singles, couples & groups
* Champagne served during flight

Location
Royal Victoria Park is 5 mins walk from the city centre

Opening
Apr–Oct (office open all year round)

Admission
Please phone for details

Contact
8 Lambridge, London Road, Bath BA1 6BJ

t 01225 466888
w bathballoons.co.uk
e bath@balnet.co.uk

296 Bath

The Jane Austen Centre

1 hr   All year

Jane Austen is perhaps the best loved of Bath's many famous residents and visitors. She spent two long periods here at the end of C18 and start of C19 and the city featured in her work. The Centre features period costumes and exhibits that explore Jane's life in Bath.

Location City centre N of Queen Square	**Contact** 40 Gay Street, Bath BA1 2NT
Opening Daily; Mon–Sat 10am–5.30pm Sun 10.30am–5.30pm	t 01225 443000 w janeausten.co.uk e info@janeausten.co.uk
Admission Adults £4.65, Child £2.50, Concs £3.95	

297 Bath

Museum of Costume & Assembly Rooms

2 hrs   All year

The story of fashion over the last 400 years is brought to life with one of the world's finest collections of fashionable dress. There are more than 150 dressed figures illustrating changing styles for both men and women. Each of the museum's 30,000 items is original.

* Free audio-guides in seven languages

Location City centre, just off The Circus	**Contact** Bennett Street, Bath BA1 2QH
Opening Daily; Nov–Jan 11am–4pm Mar–Oct 11am–5pm	t 01225 477789 w museumofcostume.co.uk e costume_bookings@bathnes.gov.uk
Admission Adult £6, Child £4, Concs £5	

298 Bath

Roman Baths & Pump Rooms

2 hrs   All year

This is Bath's most famous attraction. Britain's only natural hot spring flourished between C1 and C5 and the remains are among the finest in Europe. Walk where Romans walked on ancient stone pavements around the steamy pool.

* Taste the water in C18 Pump Room above the Temple
* Displays include sculpture, coins & jewellery

Location City centre near Abbey	**Admission** Adult £9, Child £5, Concs £8
Opening Jan–Feb Nov–Dec 9.30am–4.30pm Mar–June Sep–Oct 9am–5pm July–Aug 9am–9pm closed 25,26 Dec (Last exit 1 hr after close)	**Contact** Abbey Church Yard, Bath BA1 1LZ t 01225 477785 w romanbaths.co.uk e romanbath_bookings@bathsnes. gov.uk

299 Bath

Sally Lunn's Refreshment House & Museum

1 hr   All year

Sally Lunn's famous bun is still served from what is Bath's oldest building (c.1482). The museum shows remains of Roman, Saxon and medieval buildings on the site. The ancient kitchen used by Sally Lunn in the late C17 can also be seen.

* Three themed refreshment rooms
* Historic Trencher dinner is served from 6pm

Location
Between Abbey Green & North Parade

Opening
Daily; Mon–Sat 10am–10pm,
Sun 11am–10pm;
closed 24–26 Dec & 1 Jan

Admission
Adult 30p, Concs free, Child free

Contact
4 North Parade Passage,
Bath BA1 1NX

t 01225 461634
w sallylunns.co.uk
e info@sallylunns.co.uk

301 Bath

Thermae Bath Spa

2 hrs+   All year

Bath's newest and most spectacular attraction. A unique opportunity to bathe in natural thermal waters enjoyed by the Romans 2000 years ago. Thermae Bath Spa is a state-of-the-art building with four bathing pools, steam rooms and full range of spa treatments. Booking advised.

* No membership or joining fee required
* Free Spa visitor centre

Location
100 yards from historic Roman Baths

Opening
Daily 9am–10pm; closed 25,26,31 Dec
& 1 Jan. Opening 2005, please phone
for details

Admission
Please phone for details

Contact
The Hotlin Pump Room
Hot Bath Street, Bath BA1 1SJ

t 01225 331234
w thermaebathspa.com
e info@thermaebathspa.com

300 Bath

William Herschel Museum

1 hr+   Jan–Dec

The home of C18 astronomer and musician William Herschel from which he made important discoveries such as Uranus and infrared radiation. The museum is furnished in the style of the period and is representative of Bath's famous mid-Georgian townhouses.

* Attractive Georgian garden
* Education programmes available on request

Location
5 mins walk W of city centre

Opening
Daily; 16 Jan–16 Dec 1pm–5pm, closed
Wed; weekends 11am–5pm

Admission
Adult £3.50, Child £2, Concs £2.50

Contact
19 New King Street,
Bath BA1 2BL

t 01225 311342
w bath-preservation-trust.org.uk
e debbie@herschelbpt.fsnet.co.uk

302 Cheddar

Cheddar Gorge & Caves

3 hrs+   All year

The highest inland limestone cliffs in Britain and the famous cathedral-like caves form a 360-acre nature reserve owned by Lord Bath (of Longleat). The gorge walk is worth the effort for the fantastic views across Somerset from the top.

* New 'Cheddar Man & the Cannibals' attraction
* Open top bus tour runs through gorge Apr–Sept

Location
Follow signs from junction 22 on M5 & A38 or take B3135 from A37 and the E

Opening
Jul–Aug 10am–5pm
Sep–Jun 10.30am–4.30pm

Admission
Explorer ticket for all attractions
Adult £9.50, Child £6.50

Contact
Cheddar BS27 3QF

t 01934 742343
w cheddarcaves.co.uk
e info@cheddarcaves.co.uk

303 Chard

The Wildlife Park at Cricket St Thomas

3–5 hrs   All year

This park is home to over 600 animals, including lemur, monkeys, leopards, oryx, zebra, bison, wallabies, birds and wildfowl. Through its captive breeding programmes, the park plays an important part in the conservation of rare and endangered species.

* Licensed for civil marriages
* Safari train, crazy golf and mini car ride

Location
3 miles from Chard on A30. Signed from M5 junction 25 and A303

Opening
Mon–Sun 10am–6pm in summer;
10am–dusk in winter

Admission
Adults £7.95, Child £5.95, Concs £5.95

Contact
Chard, Somerset TA20 4DB

t 01460 30111
w wild.org.uk

304 Dunster

Dunster Castle

2 hrs   Mar–Nov

Dramatically sited on top of a wooded hill, there has been a castle here at least since Norman times. The present building was remodelled between 1868–72. A sheltered terrace to the south is home to the National Collection of strawberry trees.

* C13 gatehouse survives
* Surrounded by beautiful parkland for walking

Location
Off A39, 3 miles SE from Minehead

Opening
Castle Daily; 19 Mar–30 Oct 11am–5pm;
31 Oct–6 Nov 11am–4pm (closed Thu & Fri)
Garden & Park Daily; closed 25,26 Dec

Admission
Castle Adult £7.20, Child £3.60
Garden & Park £3.90, £1.70

Contact
Dunster, nr Minehead TA24 6SL

t 01643 821314
w nationaltrust.org.uk
e dunstercastle@nationaltrust.org.uk

305 Glastonbury

Glastonbury Abbey

2 hrs   All year

The abbey is set in 36 acres of peaceful parkland in the centre of this ancient market town. One of the oldest religious sites in Great Britain visited, so legend has it, by Joseph of Arimathea and St David and St Patrick. Believed by many to be the burial site of King Arthur.

* Visitor centre with award-winning museum
* Period-dressed guides in summer months

Location
Take A39 from junction 23 of M5, follow signs once in Glastonbury

Opening
Daily; Jun–Aug 9am–6pm (or dusk if earlier) Mar–May & Sep–Nov 9.30am–6pm; Dec–Feb 10am–dusk

Admission
Adults £4, Child £1.50, Concs £3.50

Contact
Abbey Gatehouse, Magdalene Street, Glastonbury BA6 9EL

t 01458 832267
w glastonburyabbey.com
e info@glastonburyabbey.com

306 Farleigh Hungerford

Farleigh Hungerford Castle

2 hrs   All year

The ruins of this C14 castle lie in the beautiful valley of the River Frome. A free audio guide tells the story of the castle, its sinister past and the occupants during the Middle Ages. The impressive castle has a chapel that contains wall paintings and stained glass.

* Important collection of death masks in chapel crypt
* Programme of living history throughout the year

Location
8 miles SE of Bath off A36

Opening
Daily; Apr–Jun 10am–5pm
Jul–Aug 10am–6pm
Sep 10am–5pm;
Oct–Mar Sat & Sun 10am–4pm

Admission
Adult £2.80, Child £1.40, Concs £2.10

Contact
Farleigh Hungerford,
nr Trowbridge BA2 7RS

t 01225 754026
w english-heritage.org.uk/southwest
e customers@english-heritage.org.uk

307 Highbridge

Alstone Wildlife Park

1 hr+   All year

A small, non-commercial family-run park and licensed zoo with camels, pigs, deer, ponies, emu, owls and llama. Special features include Theodore, the friendly camel, tame red deer, and a pets' corner.

Location
A38 Highbridge to Bridgwater road,
signed turning on the right 1/2 mile
from Highbridge

Opening
Daily 10am–5.30pm

Admission
Adults £4, Child £3, Concs £3.50

Contact
Alstone Road, Highbridge
Somerset TA9 3DT

t 01278 782405

© English Heritage Photographic Library

308 Sparkford

Haynes Motor Museum

3 hrs   All year

The museum contains a unique collection of hundreds of classic, veteran and vintage cars and motorcycles, all in full working order. Features the famous red collection of 1950s and 1960s sports cars.

* Fabulous collection of American sports cars
* 70-seater video theatre

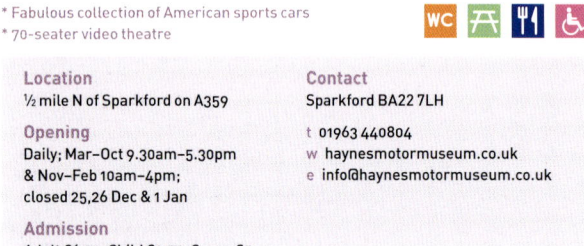

Location
½ mile N of Sparkford on A359

Opening
Daily; Mar–Oct 9.30am–5.30pm & Nov–Feb 10am–4pm; closed 25,26 Dec & 1 Jan

Admission
Adult £6.50, Child £3.50, Concs £5

Contact
Sparkford BA22 7LH

t 01963 440804
w haynesmotormuseum.co.uk
e info@haynesmotormuseum.co.uk

309 Taunton

Hestercombe Gardens

2 hrs+   All year

Hestercombe is a unique combination of a Georgian landscape created by Bampfylde in the 1750s, Victorian terraces and Edwardian gardens by Lutyens and Jekyll. The landscaped park (40 acres) has walks, lakes, temples, woods and stunning views.

* Jekyll's original planting faithfully restored

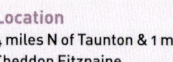

Location
4 miles N of Taunton & 1 mile NW of Cheddon Fitzpaine

Opening
Daily 10am–6pm

Admission
Adult £5.20, Child £1.30, Concs £4.90

Contact
Cheddon Fitzpaine, Taunton TA2 8LG

t 01823 413923
w hestercombegardens.com
e info@hestercombegardens.com

310 Weston–super–Mare

The Helicopter Museum

2 hrs   All year

The museum houses over 80 helicopters from Britain, Europe and the US. A team of conservationists restore the aircraft and prepare them for exhibition. The museum organises special events throughout the year, including open-cockpit days and air experience flights.

* The world's largest helicopter museum
* Weston-super-Mare's largest all-weather attraction

Location
On the A371, off M5 (junction 21)

Opening
Apr–Oct Wed–Sun 10am–5.30pm; Nov–Mar 10am–4.30pm; Easter & summer school hols daily 10am–5.30pm

Admission
Adult £4.95, Child £2.95

Contact
The Heliport, Locking Moor Road, Weston-super-Mare BS24 8PP

t 01931 635227
w helicoptermuseum.co.uk

311 Williton

The Bakelite Museum

1 hr+   Mar–Sep

Set in peaceful Somerset countryside, and housed within a historic watermill, this is the largest collection of vintage plastics in Britain. Exhibits from the inter-war period, stylish Art Deco plus hundreds of domestic items.

* Thousands of quirky & rare items on show
* 'Before Bakelite' – a display of Victorian plastics

Location
Williton is at the junction of the A39 & A358, NW of Taunton

Opening
Mar–Sept 10.30am–6pm
Only Thurs–Sun in school term

Admission
Adult £3.50, Child £2, Concs £3

Contact
Orchard Mill, Williton TA4 4NS

t 01984 632133
w bakelitemuseum.co.uk
e info@bakelitemuseum.co.uk

312 Wookey Hole

Wookey Hole Caves & Papermill

4 hrs   All year

One of Britain's most spectacular complex of caves cut into the Mendip Hills. The story of the famous Witch of Wookey is a highlight of the cave tour. The C19 papermill has demonstrations of papermaking with the opportunity for visitors to make their own.

* Magical mirror maze & penny arcade
* New Haunted Witches Ghost Train

Location
Junction 22 of M5 & follow signs
A39 from Bath to Wells

Opening
Daily; Mar–Oct 10am–5pm
Nov–Feb 10.30am–4.30pm;
closed 17–25 Dec

Admission
Adults £8.80, Child £5.50, Concs £5.50

Contact
Wookey Hole,
nr Wells BA5 1BB
t 01749 672243
w wookey.co.uk
e witch@wookey.co.uk

313 Yeovil

Fleet Airarm Museum

3 hrs+   All year

Now one of the largest aviation museums in the world, situated alongside an operational naval air station. Today the museum covers 6½ acres and has more than 40 aircraft on display including Concorde. The museum has an excellent simulated tour of HMS *Ark Royal*.

* 40 further aircraft in store or renovation
* Fly by simulated helicopter to flightdeck of *Ark Royal*

Location
1 mile off A303/A37 roundabout

Opening
Daily; Apr–Oct 10am–5.30pm
Nov–Mar 10am–4.30pm
closed 24–26 Dec

Admission
Adult £8.50, Child £5.75, Concs £6.75

Contact
PO Box D6, RNAS, Yeovilton,
Illchester BA22 8HT
t 01935 840565
w fleetairarm.com
e info@fleetairarm.com

314 Yeovil

Montacute House & Gardens

3 hrs+   Mar–Oct

A glittering Elizabethan house with splendid Renaissance features. The magnificent state rooms, including a long gallery (the largest of its type in England), are full of fine C17 and C18 furniture and period portraits from the National Portrait Gallery.

* Featured in the film *Sense and Sensibility*
* Parkland & gardens including historic rose garden

Location
On A30, 5 miles W of Yeovil

Opening
House 19 Mar–31 Oct Weds–Mon
11am–5pm
Garden Mar–Oct Weds–Mon
11am–6pm; Nov–Mar 11am–4pm
Wed–Sun

Admission
Adults £7.40, Child £3.70
Gardens only £3.70, £1.70

Contact
Montacute, nr Yeovil TA16 6XP
t 01935 823289
w nationaltrust.org.uk
e montacute@nationaltrust.org.uk

315 Yeovil

Tintinhull House & Gardens

1 hr   Mar–Sep

This small manor house (mainly C17 farmhouse with Queen Anne facade) stands in a beautiful formal garden created by Mrs Phyllis Reiss. The garden is divided into seven 'rooms' by clipped yew hedges and walls. Includes pool garden, fountain garden and kitchen garden.

* Striking mixed borders & colour schemes

Location
Tintinhull is just off A303 S of Yeovil,
follow signs from village

Opening
24 Mar–30 Sep Wed–Sun
12noon–6pm, open Bank Hols

Admission
Adult £4.20, Child £2.10

Contact
Farm Street,
Yeovil BA22 9PZ
t 01935 822545
w nationaltrust.org.uk
e tintinhull@nationaltrust.org.uk

©English Heritage Photographic Library

316   Amesbury

Stonehenge

1 hr   All year

Stonehenge is a ring of upright stones set in a circle – each stone towering about 19 feet (6m). Its original purpose is unclear, but theories range from a temple made to worship ancient deities to an astronomical observatory. Others claim it was a sacred burial site.

* World Heritage site
* Audio tours in nine languages

Location
2 miles W of Amesbury on junction of A303 & A360

Opening
Daily; 16 Mar–31 May 9.30am–6.00pm, Jun–Aug 9am–7pm, 1 Sep–15 Oct 9.30am–6pm 16 Oct–15 Mar 9.30am–4pm; closed 24–26 Dec & 1 Jan

Admission
Adult £5.20, Child £2.50, Concs £3.90

Contact
Stonehenge Information Line
t 01980 624715
w english-heritage.org.uk/stonehenge

---

317   Avebury

Avebury

2 hrs+   All year

One of the most important megalithic monuments in Europe dating back to *c.*3000BC. The great stone circle, encompassing part of the village of Avebury, is roughly a quarter of a mile across. It encloses an area of about 28 acres and has two smaller circles within it.

* World Heritage site
* World's biggest megalithic monument

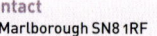

Location
6 miles W of Marlborough, 1 mile N of the Bath road (A4) on A4361 and B4003

Opening
Daily

Admission
Free

Contact
nr Marlborough SN8 1RF

t 01672 539250
w nationaltrust.org.uk
e avebury@nationaltrust.org.uk

318 Avebury

Silbury Hill

  ½ hr All year

Built around 2500BC, Silbury Hill stands 130 feet high. The base covers more than 5 acres and the top is about 100 feet across. More material was used in its construction than for the great pyramids of Egypt and it is estimated to have taken 500 men 15 years to complete.

* The largest purpose-built structure in Europe

Location
N of the A4 between Marlborough and Beckhampton

Opening
Daily dawn–dusk

Admission
Free

Contact
Kennet District Council, Devizes

w kennet.gov.uk

---

319 Corsham

Corsham Court

  1 hr+ All year

Corsham Court is based on an Elizabethan house dating from 1582. It was bought by Paul Methuen to house a collection of C16 and C17 paintings and, after alterations to the house in C19, more Italian Old Masters and works of art were added.

* Works by Van Dyck, Carlo Dolci & Reynolds
* Picture gallery boasts a rare ornate ceiling

Location
Signed 4 miles W of Chippenham from the A4 Bath road

Opening
20 Mar–30 Sep, closed Mon & Fri (open Bank Hols) 2pm–5.30pm
1 Oct–19 Mar Sat & Sun 2pm–4.30pm (last entry 30 mins before close)

Admission
House & Garden Adult £5, Child £2.50

Contact
Corsham SN13 0BZ

t 01249 701610
w corsham-court.co.uk
e staterooms@corsham-court.co.uk

---

320 Chippenham

Lacock Abbey & Fox Talbot Museum

  2 hrs+ Mar–Nov

Founded in 1232 and converted into a country house *c*.1540, the medieval cloisters, sacristy, chapter house and monastic rooms of the Abbey have survived largely intact. The museum commemorates the achievements of William Henry Fox Talbot, photographic pioneer.

* Harry Potter movies filmed here
* Beautiful Victorian woodland garden

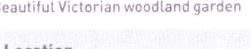   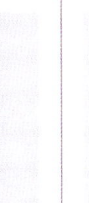

Location
3 miles S of Chippenham, just E of the A350

Opening
Abbey: Daily; Mar–early Nov 11am–5.30pm *Museum:* Mar–early Nov open 11am–5.30pm; winter open weekends only. Both closed Good Fri, 25,26 Dec & 1 Jan

Admission
Adult £6.50, Child £3.60

Contact
Chippenham SN15 2LG

w nationaltrust.org.uk

---

321 Devizes

Broadleas Gardens

  1 hr+ Apr–Oct

Lady Anne Cowdray's valley garden, bought in 1946, has been created and developed since the early 1960s. Treasures include a secret garden, winter garden, a woodland, a sunken rose garden and a silver border packed with plants which are unusual or rarely seen.

*Afternoon teas on Sundays

Location
A360 road to Salisbury, garden 1 mile S of Devizes

Opening
Apr–Oct Sun, Wed & Thu 2pm–6pm

Admission
Adult £4, Child £1.50

Contact
Broadleas Gardens Charitable Trust Limited, Broadleas, Devizes SN10 5JQ

t 01380 722035

322 Salisbury

Salisbury Cathedral

1 hr   All year

Salisbury Cathedral is one of the finest medieval cathedrals in Britain. Started in 1220 it was completed by 1258, with the spire, the tallest in England (404ft/123m) added a generation later. It also boasts the largest and best-preserved cathedral close in Britain.

* Voluntary guide tours of cathedral & Chapter House
* Chapter House contains rare original Magna Carta

Location	Contact
Centre of city	Visitor Services, 33 The Close, Salisbury SP1 2EJ
Opening	
Daily; 7.15am–6.15pm, times vary depending on services, please phone for details	t 01722 555120
	w salisburycathedral.org.uk
	e visitors@salcath.co.uk
Admission	
Recommended voluntary donation Adults £3.80, Child £2, Concs £3.30	

323 Salisbury

Larmer Tree Gardens

2 hrs   Apr–Oct

These gardens were created by General Pitt Rivers in 1880 and have been restored over the last 10 years. An open air theatre, Roman temple, Nepalese carved buildings and water features cover the land. Ornamental pheasants and peacocks also feature in the gardens.

* Larmer Tree Festival in July

Location	Contact
On the B3081 off A354 Salisbury to Blandford road.	Tollard Royal, Salisbury SP5 5PT
Opening	t 01725 516228
Apr–Oct Sun–Thurs 11am–4pm	w larmertreegardens.co.uk
Admission	e events@larmertreegardens.co.uk
Adult £3.75, Child £2.50	

324 Salisbury

Salisbury & South Wiltshire Museum

1 hr+   All year

The museum holds material from major archaeological sites in Salisbury and South Wiltshire. Exhibitions cover the entire range of the museum's interests which, in addition to archaeology, include fine and decorative arts, costume, and social history.

* Temporary exhibitions all year round & giftshop
* A collection of Turner watercolours

Location	Contact
In Cathedral Close, opposite the West Front	The King's House, 65 The Close, Salisbury SP1 2EN
Opening	t 01722 332151
Mon–Sat 10am–5pm	w salisburymuseum.org.uk
Jul & Aug open Sun 2pm–5pm	e museum@salisburymuseum.org.uk
Admission	
Adult £4, Child £1, Concs £3	

325 Stourhead

Stourhead Gardens

3 hrs+   All year

The garden was designed by Henry Hoare II. Classical temples, including the Pantheon and the Temple of Apollo, are set around the central lake. Vistas change as the visitor walks around the paths and through the magnificent mature woodland.

* Palladian mansion & gift shop
* King Alfred's Tower, a 50m red-brick folly

Location	Contact
Just off A303 at Mere	Stourhead Gardens, nr Warminster BA12 6QD
Opening	t 01747 842020
Gardens Daily	w national-trust.org.uk
House Apr–Oct; closed Wed, Thurs	e stourhead@nationaltrust.org.uk
Admission	
Gardens or House Adult £5.40, Child £3	
Both Adult £9.40, Child £4.50	

326 Swindon

STEAM – Museum of the Great Western Railway

2 hrs   All year

This museum tells the story of the men and women who built, operated and travelled on the Great Western Railway. The museum celebrates Isambard Kingdom Brunel and the thousands of ordinary people who made the GWR one of the world's greatest railways.

* Special events running throughout the year
* Featuring world famous GWR locomotives

Location
Follow signs from Swindon town centre

Opening
Daily 10am–5pm, closed 25,26 Dec
& 1 Jan

Admission
Adult £5.95, Child £3.80, Concs £3.90

Contact
Kemble Drive, Swindon SN2 2TA

t 01793 466 646
w steam-museum.org.uk
e steampostbox@swindon.gov.uk

327 Warminster

Longleat

4 hrs+   Feb–Nov

Longleat is set in more than 900 acres of Capability Brown landscaped parkland with further woodlands, lakes and farmland. Longleat House is one of the best examples of high Elizabethan architecture, and there's the safari park, mazes and murals.

* Longleat hedge maze
* Featured in TV's *Lion Country* and *Animal Park*

Location
Off the A36 between Bath & Salisbury
(A362 Warminster to Frome road)

Opening
Daily; 12 Feb–6 Nov.
Please phone for details

Admission
Please phone for details

Contact
The Estate Office, Longleat,
Warminster BA12 7NW

t 01985 844400
w longleat.co.uk
e enquiries@longleat.co.uk

328 Warminster

Shearwater Lake

2 hrs · All year

Surrounded by 38 acres of woodland, Shearwater Lake is one of the finest waterways in west Wiltshire. The lake, which is part of the Longleat Estate was designed in 1791 by Francis Drake of Bridgwater. It is known for its fishing and sailing.

* 20-mile cycleway to Salisbury begins here
* Regular fishing & sailing competitions

Location
1 mile off A350 at Crockerton

Opening
Daily dawn–dusk

Admission
Car park 50p

Contact
The Estate Office, Longleat
Warminster BA12 7NW
t 01985 844400
w longleat.co.uk
e enquires@longleat.co.uk

329 Westbury

Westbury White Horse & Bratton Camp

3 hrs+ · All year

This famous landmark in west Wiltshire has views of the Wiltshire and Somerset countryside. Cut into a chalk hillside in 1778, the white horse is thought to rest on the site of an older horse that commemorated the defeat of the Danes by King Alfred at Ethandun in AD 878.

*Neolithic barrow or burial mound

Location
Between Westbury and B3098

Opening
Daily

Admission
Free

Contact
Westbury Tourist Information Centre
t 01373 827158
w english-heritage.org.uk

330 Wilton

Wilton House

2 hrs · Mar–Oct

Wilton House contains many state rooms including the Double Cube room, which houses a world famous collection of Van Dyck paintings. Other attractions include the old riding school, Tudor kitchen, Victorian laundry and a new costume exhibition for 2004.

* Gardens and parkland bordered by the River Nadder

Location
3 miles W of Salisbury, situated on A30, off A36. 10 miles from A303

Opening
Grounds daily. House Mar 24–Oct 31, Sun–Fri 10.30am–5.30pm

Admission
House & Grounds Adult £9.75, Child

£5.50, Concs £8
Grounds only £4.50/£3.50

Contact
The Estate Office, Wilton,
Salisbury SP2 0BJ
t 01722 746720
w wiltonhouse.com
e tourism@wiltonhouse.com

Ludham, Norfolk

Eastern

Bedfordshire Cambridgeshire Essex
Hertfordshire Norfolk Suffolk

331 Bedford

Cecil Higgins Art Gallery

2 hrs+   All year

The gallery is housed in a Victorian mansion, once home to the Higgins family who were wealthy brewers. Adjoining this is a modern gallery housing an internationally renowned collection of watercolours, prints and drawings, ceramics, glass and lace.

* Rooms include items from the Handley-Read collection
* Furniture by Victorian architect William Burges

Location
Just off the Embankment
and High Street

Opening
Tue–Sat 11am–5pm
Sun & Bank Hols 2pm–5pm

Admission
Free

Contact
Castle Lane, Bedford MK40 3RP

t 01234 211222
w cecilhigginsartgallery.org
e chag@bedford.gov.uk

332 Biggleswade

Shuttleworth Collection

2 hrs+   All year

This world famous collection of aircraft, started by Richard Shuttleworth, depicts the history of flight from 1900–1940s and ranges from a 1909 Bleriot to a Second World War Spitfire. Cars, motorcycles and carriages are exhibited alongside the aircraft in eight hangars.

* Regular flying displays during the summer
* Clayton and Shuttleworth steam traction engine

Location
Shuttleworth Old Warden Aerodrome
is 2 miles W of A1 where it bypasses
Biggleswade

Opening
Daily; Apr–Oct 10am–5pm
Nov–Mar 10am–4pm

Admission
Adult £7.50, Child free, Concs £6

Contact
Old Warden Park, Biggleswade
SG18 9EP

t 01767 627288
w shuttleworth.org
e collection@shuttleworth.org

333 Biggleswade

The English School of Falconry

3 hrs+   All year

The family-run centre is sited at Shuttleworth Old Warden Park to create a woodland setting as near as possible to the birds' natural surroundings. The centre is home to over 300 birds of various species including falcons, hawks, eagles, vultures, and owls.

* Three flying displays daily
* Hands-on experience

Location
Old Warden is 2 miles W of A1 where it bypasses Biggleswade

Opening
Daily; Nov–Mar 10am–4pm
Apr–Oct 10am–5pm

Admission
Adult £6, Child £4

Contact
Old Warden Park, Biggleswade
SG18 9EA
t 01767 627527
w shuttleworth.org
e falconry.centre@virgin.net

334 Dunstable

Leighton Buzzard Railway

2 hrs   Mar–Oct

One of the few narrow-gauge light railways to survive in England. Built 85 years ago to transport sand, the line has carried a steam-hauled passenger train service since 1968, and passengers can now make a 70-minute round trip from Page's Park to Stonehenge Works.

* Children's play area
* Explore the Guntry terminus

Location
Off A4146 on the edge of Leighton Buzzard, close to the junction with A505, Dunstable–Aylesbury road

Opening
Early Mar–end Oct open Sun & extra holiday services
Please phone for details

Admission
2004; Adult £5.50, Child (2–15) £2.50, Concs £4.50

Contact
Billington Road,
Leighton Buzzard LU7 4TN
t 01525 373888
w buzzrail.co.uk
e info@buzzrail.co.uk

335 Henlow

Stondon Motor Museum

2 hrs   All year

This museum is one of the largest private collections in the country with over 400 exhibits. It includes veteran cars dating from 1890–1990, housed in eight different halls, some exhibits are for sale. An exclusive collection of Rolls Royce and Bentley vehicles is a feature of the museum.

* Full size replica of Captain Cook's HM Bark *Endeavour*
* Large free car park

Location
At Lower Stondon near Henlow off A600

Opening
Daily; 10am–5pm

Admission
Adult £6, Child £3, Concs £5

Contact
Station Road, Lower Stondon, Henlow
SG16 6JN
t 01462 850339
w transportmuseum.co.uk
e info@transportmuseum.co.uk

336 Kensworth

Dunstable Downs Countryside Centre & Whipsnade Estate

Fine   2 hrs+   All year

Whipsnade and Dunstable Downs comprise 510 acres of grassland and farmland, where the steep slopes are rich in flora and associated fauna. With outstanding views, it's a great place to walk, fly kites or watch paragliders. The centre has exhibits and kites for sale.

* Annual kite festival
* Designated area of outstanding natural beauty

Location
4miles NE of Ashridge between B4540 & B4541

Opening
Downs All year
Centre Daily; Apr–Oct 10am–5pm
Nov–Apr, Sat–Sun 10am–4pm

Admission
Free

Contact
Whipsnade Road, Kensworth,
Dunstable LU6 2TA
t 01582 608489
w nationaltrust.org.uk
e dunstabledowns@nationaltrust.org.uk

337 Leighton Buzzard

Ascott House

2 hrs+   Mar–Aug

Ascott is a black-and-white C19 house set in 30 acres of grounds. It houses Anthony de Rothschild's collection of art, French and English furniture and oriental porcelain. The garden has unusual trees, flower borders, topiary, a sundial, Italian garden and fountain statuary.

* Houses one of the foremost collections of Chinese three-colour wares ceramics in the world

Location
On A418 betweem Aylesbury and Leighton Buzzard, E of Wing

Opening
Daily; 15 Mar–30 Apr & 2–31 Aug except Monday 2pm–6pm
3 May–28 Jul Tue–Thurs 2–6pm

Admission
Adult £6, Child £3

Contact
Wing, Leighton Buzzard LU7 0PP

t 01296 688242
w ascottestate.co.uk
e info@ascottestate.co.uk

338 Luton

Stockwood Craft Museum & Gardens

1 hr+   All year

This award-winning museum covers nine centuries of garden history. There are displays on rural life and crafts, the Mossman Collection of horse-drawn vehicles, stunning period gardens and a programme of events which changes throughout the year.

* Sculpture garden with work by Hamilton Finlay
* Largest display of horse-drawn carriages in the UK

Location
2 miles S of Luton town centre, close to junction 10 of the M1

Opening
Apr- Oct, Tues–Sun 10am–5pm
Nov–Mar, Sat–Sun 10am–4pm

Admission
Free

Contact
Farley Hill, Luton LU1 4BH

t 01582 738714
w lutonline.gov.uk
e museum.gallery@luton.gov.uk

339 Marston Moretaine

Forest Centre & Marston Vale Country Park

3 hrs+   All year

Stretching over 600 acres, the park has a mosaic of habitats from wetlands to woodlands – lakes and lagoons. It is home to a wealth of wildlife – in particular wild birds. Discover some of the new inhabitants who can be viewed from paths, boardwalks and bird hides.

* Walkway and cycleway with stunning views
* Forest Centre hands-on exhibition

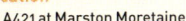 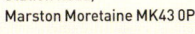

Location
Off A421 at Marston Moretaine

Opening
Daily; summer 10am–6pm
winter 10am–4pm

Admission
Free, *Wetlands* Adult £2.50, Child & Concs £1.75

Contact
Station Road,
Marston Moretaine MK43 0PR

t 01234 767037
w marstonvale.org
e info@marstonvale.org

340 Milton Keynes

Woburn Safari Park

6 hrs   All year

Situated in a 40-acre leisure park, the safari reserves allow you to experience wild animals roaming free at close quarters. During the hour-long drive you're likely to see rhino, eland, oryx, antelope, giraffe, zebra, elephants, tigers, wolves, bears, monkeys and hippos.

* Visitor Attraction of the Year 2000

Location
5 minutes off M1 (junction 13). Follow the signs

Opening
Daily; Mar–Oct 10am–5pm (last admission); Nov–Feb open weekends 11am–3pm

Admission
Please phone for details

Contact
Woburn MK17 9QN

t   01525 290407
w   woburnsafari.co.uk
e   enquires@woburnsafari.co.uk

341 Shefford

Hoo Hill Maze

1 hr+   All year

Set within an orchard, this hedge maze measures 300 square feet and 7 feet high (30m² x 2m). Visitors are invited to picnic in the orchard, where there is also an open area. An adult garden maze is currently being constructed.

* All three species of woodpecker present
* Abundance of daffodils in the Spring

Location
Off A507 and A600 close to Shefford

Opening
Daily; 10am–5pm

Admission
Adult £3, Child £2, Concs £2

Contact
Hoo Hill Maze, Hitchin Road, Shefford SG17 5JD

t   01462 813475

342 Woburn

Woburn Abbey

3 hrs+   Jan–Oct

A palatial C18 mansion founded in 1145 as a religious house for a group of Cistercian monks. In 1547 Edward VI gave Woburn Abbey to Sir John Russell who became the 1st Earl of Bedford. Tours include Queen Victoria's bedroom and the state dining room.

* Woburn's treasures are acknowledged worldwide
* Home to the Dukes of Bedfordshire for over 400 years

Location
Located on the edge of the village of Woburn

Opening
Daily; 14 Mar–31 Oct 11am–4pm
Sat & Sun only Jan–Mar

Admission
Adult £9, Child £4.50, Concs £8

Contact
Woburn MK17 9WA

t   01525 290666
w   woburnabbey.co.uk
e   enquiries@woburnabbey.co.uk

343 Cambridge

Cambridge University Botanic Garden

3 hrs   All year

This tranquil 40-acre garden offers year round interest to visitors. Over 10,000 labelled plant species in beautifully landscaped settings, including rock garden, lake, glasshouses, winter garden, woodland walk, and nine National Collections.

* Important collections of native English plants
* Founded by mentor of Charles Darwin

Location
1 mile S of city centre

Opening
Daily; Nov–Jan 10am–4 pm
Feb–Oct 10am–5pm
Mar–Sep 10am–6pm

Admission
Adult £2.50, Child £2, Concs £2

Contact
Cory Lodge, Bateman Street,
Cambridge CB2 1JF

t 01223 336265
w botanic.cam.ac.uk
e enquiries@botanic.cam.ac.uk

344 Cambridge

Fitzwilliam Museum

3 hrs+   All year

This is the art museum of the University of Cambridge with public access to its collection of international repute. Antiquities from ancient Egypt, rare printed books, Chinese jades and paintings by Titian, Canaletto, Rubens, Monet and Picasso. Fine collection of C20 art.

* Collection of Japanese ceramics
* Exhibition of medals since the Renaissance

Location
Approx 500 yards from city centre

Opening
Tue–Sat, 10am–5pm
Sunday, 2.15–5pm.
Closed Mon except Summer Bank
Hols

Admission
Free

Contact
Trumpington Street,
Cambridge CB2 1RB
t 01223 332900
w fitzmuseum.cam.ac.uk
e fitzmuseum-enquiries@lists.cam.
   ac.uk

345 Cambridge

King's College

½ hr+   All year

King's is one of the oldest colleges in Cambridge, founded in 1441 by Henry VI. It is also the premier tourist attraction primarily due to the stunning architecture of its perpendicular chapel and its impressive interior that includes the painting Adoration of the Magi by Rubens.

Location
Take junction 11 or 12 from M11 follow signs for centre parking or park+ride

Opening
Daily; Term time, Mon–Sat
9.30am–3.30pm
Sun 1.15–2.15pm & 5–5.30pm
Out of term, Mon–Sat 9.30am–4.30pm
Sun 10am–5pm (closed 24 Dec–3 Jan)

Admission
Adult £4, Child £3

Contact
King's College,
Cambridge CB2 1ST

t 01223 331212
w kings.cam.ac.uk/visitors

346 Cambridge

Museum of Archaeology & Anthropology

2 hrs+   All year

Established in 1884, the museum displays renowned archaeological and anthropological collections from around the world. Highlights include world prehistory and local archaeology; historical and geographical display of the social anthropology collection.

* Faculty's current research interests displayed
* Newly created photographic collection on-line

Location
City centre between Pembroke
Emmanuel College

Opening
Tue–Sat 2pm–4.30pm

Admission
Free

Contact
Downing Street, Cambridge CB2 3DZ

t 01223 333516
w museum-server.archanth.cam.
   ac.uk/museum.html
e cumaa@hermes.cam.ac.uk

347 Duxford

Imperial War Museum Duxford

3 hrs+   All year

This former Battle of Britain airfield is now home to 180 historic aircaft including biplanes, Spitfires, Concorde and Gulf War jets – many of which still regularly fly. The 7 acres of indoor exhibition space also house one of the country's finest collections of military vehicles.

* 'D-Day Experience' complete with video story
* Flying displays held throughout the summer

Location
Off junction 10 of M11

Opening
Daily; Summer Mar– Sep, 10am–6pm
Winter 10am–4pm

Admission
Adult £10, Child free, Concs £8

Contact
Duxford CB2 4QR

t 01223 835 000
w iwm.org.uk/duxford
e duxford@iwm.org.uk

348 Ely

Stained Glass Museum

1 hr All year

The museum offers a unique insight into the story of stained glass, an artform practised in Britain for at least 1,300 years. This Trust, set up in the 1970s to rescue and preserve stained glass, now houses a National Collection of British stained glass.

* Work by William Morris on display
* Opportunity to design your own pattern

Location
Inside Ely Cathedral

Opening
Mon–Fri, 10.30am–5pm Sat
10.30am–5.30pm (5pm in Winter) Sun
12noon–6pm (4.30pm Winter)
Closed 25/26 Dec & Good Friday

Admission
Adult £3.50, Child £2.50, Conc £2.50

Contact
Ely Cathedral, Ely CB7 4DL
t 01353 660347
w stainedglassmuseum.com
e Admin@stainedglassmuseum.com

349 Ely

Ely Cathedral

3 hrs+ All year

Begun by William the Conqueror, this magnificent cathedral stands on the site of a monastery founded in 673 by St Ethelreda. Essentially Romanesque, there is a blend of architectural styles complemented by many beautiful objects in stone, wood and glass.

* Extensive renovation completed in 2000

Location
Ely city centre

Opening
Daily; summer 7am–7pm
winter Mon–Sat 7.30am–6pm
Sun 7.30am–5pm

Admission
Adult £4.80, Concs £4.20, Free on Sun

Contact
Chapter House, The College,
Ely CB7 4DL
t 01353 667735
w cathedral.ely.anglican.org
e receptionist@cathedral.ely.
anglican.org

350 Lode

Anglesey Abbey

3 hrs All year

This site of a former Augustinian priory (many C12 stonework features remain) was brought to its current splendour by Lord Fairhaven in the first half of the C20, Fairhaven purchased the vast collection of paintings, planned the elaborate gardens and purchased the mill.

* Watermill can be seen working on 1st & 3rd Saturdays
* One of country's finest collections of historic statuary

Location
6 miles NE of Cambridge on B1102

Opening
Daily; summer, *Gardens* Apr–Nov
10.30am–5.30pm *Mill* 1pm–5pm
winter, *Gardens* 10.30am–4.30pm
Mill Sat–Sun 11am–3.30pm

Admission
Summer Adult £7, Child £3.50
Gardens only £4.30/ £2.15
Winter £3.40/£1.70

Contact
Lode CB5 9EJ
t 01223 810080
w nationaltrust.org.uk/angleseyabbey
e angleseyabbey@nationaltrust.org.uk

351 Peterborough

Peterborough Cathedral

1 hr All year

Today's cathedral is essentially the third abbey, founded in 1118 (the first dates from 655). It suffered badly at the hands of Oliver Cromwell, but many of its unique features remain to be admired today. The west front is a remarkable example of medieval architecture.

* The interior remains largely unchanged in 800 years
* Burial place for two queens

Location
Follow signs for city centre from
junction 16/17 of A1M

Opening
Daily; 8.30am–5.15pm, Sun
12noon–5pm
Closed 25/26 Dec

Admission
Free, donations encouraged

Contact
Little Prior's Gate, Minster Precincts,
Peterborough PE1 1XS
t 01733 560964
w peterborough-cathedral.org.uk
e a.watson@peterborough-cathedral.org.uk

352 Peterborough

Peterborough Museum & Art Gallery

2 hrs   All year

Built in 1816, this former hospital now houses over 220,000 objects, collected over 130 years, including Jurassic marine reptile (underwater dinosaur) fossils, crafts, finds from Roman Peterborough and the original manuscripts of the poet John Clare.

* Changing exhibitions, talks and workshops
* Gift shop with a range of books and souvenirs

Location
Peterborough town centre

Opening
Tue-Fri 12pm-5pm, Sat 10am-5pm, Sun 12pm-4pm

Admission
Free

Contact
Priestgate, Peterborough PE1 1LF
t   01733 343329
w www.peterboroughheritage.org.uk
e   museum@peterborough.gov.uk

353 Peterborough

Flag Fen Bronze Age Centre

4 hrs   All year

The museum is home to artefacts found on site, including Bronze Age timbers, reconstructed Iron Age roundhouses, primitive breeds of sheep, a mock archaeological sand dig and a real Roman road. Guided tours of excavations available in spring and summer.

* Featured on Channel 4's *Time Team*
* The oldest wheel in England discovered here

Location
NE of Peterborough, off A1139 or A605

Opening
Daily; 10am-5pm
Closed 25 Dec

Admission
Adults £4, Child £3, Concs £3/£3.50

Contact
The Droveway, Northey Road, Peterborough PE6 7QJ
t   01733 313414
w www.flagfen.com
e   office@flagfen.freeserve.co.uk

354 Peterborough

Nene Valley Railway

3 hrs+   All year

A 15-mile round trip through the beautiful Nene Park from Wansford to Peterborough. One of Britain's leading steam railways is home for a wide range of British and European engines and carriages, both steam and diesel.

* Train galas in March, June and September
* Talking Timetable 01780 784404

Location
Off the southbound A1 at Stibbington between A47 & A605 junctions

Opening
Daily; 9am-4.30pm
Closed 24 Dec-1 Jan

Admission
Adults £10, Child £5, Concs £7.50

Contact
Wansford Station, Stibbington, Peterborough PE8 6LR
t   01780 784444
w nvr.org.uk
e   nvrorg@aol.com

355 Royston

Wimpole Estate

3 hrs+   Mar-Nov

First built in 1643 and much altered by subsequent owners, Wimpole has developed into the largest country house in Cambridgeshire. The 360 acres of beautiful parkland is the product of four celebrated designers including Capability Brown.

* Parkland includes restored lakes and gothic tower
* Walks available through woodland & rolling hills

Location
8 miles SW of Cambridge
junction 12 off M11/junction 9 off A1(M)

Opening
Mar-Nov, Tue-Sun (not Fri ex during Aug & Good Friday) & Bank Hol Mons 1pm-5pm (Bank Hol Mons\ 11am-5pm)
Farm open weekends Nov-Mar

Admission
Adult £6.90, Child £3.40

Contact
Wimpole Hall, Arrington, Royston SG8 0BW
t   01223 206000
w wimpole.org
e   wimpolehall@nationaltrust.org.uk

356 Sawtry

Hamerton Zoo Park

2 hrs+   All year

Opened as a conservation sanctuary in 1990, Hamerton's 15 acres of parkland provide a safe home for a fascinating array of beautiful creatures from around the world, including many endangered species and some that are extinct in the wild.

* Spacious indoor-outdoor enclosures for monkeys
* Opportunity to handle many different animals

Location
On A14, turn off to B660 at junction 15 onto A1M follow signs

Opening
Daily; 10.30am–6pm (4pm in winter)
Closed 25 Dec

Admission
Please ring for details

Contact
Hamerton, nr Sawtry PE28 5RE

t 01832 293362
w hamertonzoopark.com
e office@hamertonzoopark.com

357 Wisbech

Peckover House & Gardens

3 hrs+   Mar–Oct

This outstanding Victorian garden includes an orangery, summer-houses, roses, herbaceous borders, fernery, croquet lawn and reed barn. The townhouse, built c.1722, is renowned for its very fine plaster and wood rococo decoration.

* Restored Victorian library
* One of the finest walled town gardens in England

Location
From A47 to Wisbech town centre, follow signs

Opening
Gardens 21 Mar–31 Oct, daily (ex Fri)
House 21 Mar–29 Apr, Wed–Sun &
Bank Hols, 1.30pm–4.30pm
May–Aug, Wed, Thur, Sat, Sun.
Sept–Oct, Wed, Sat, Sun

Admission
House Adult £4.25, Child £2
Gardens £2.75, £1.50

Contact
North Brink, Wisbech PE13 1JR

t 01945 583463
w peckoverhouse.com
e info@peckoverhouse.com

358 Wisbech

Fenland & West Norfolk Aviation Museum

1 hr+   Mar–Oct

Home to a range of aircraft and artefacts, including the cockpit from one of the MiG-29s which collided at RAF Fairford in 1995, a Boeing 747 simulator, uniforms and militaria, and weapons and armour. On a fine day, explore the cockpits of some of the aircraft on display.

Location
Follow the brown tourist signs from A47 Wisbech bypass; or take the old B198 to King's Lynn from Wisbech and the museum is ½ mile from the bypass

Opening
Mar–Oct weekends & Bank Holidays
9.30am–5pm (4pm in Mar & Oct)

Admission
Adult £1.50, Child 75p, Concs 75p

Contact
Old Lynn Road, West Walton,
Wisbech PE14 7DA

t 01945 461771
w fawnaps.co.uk
e bill@wwelbourne.freeserve.co.uk

359 Castle Hedingham

Colne Valley Railway

2 hrs+   Mar–Oct

Take a ride on a period country railway. A pretty line, relocated station buildings, signal boxes and bridges all lovingly restored and rebuilt. A large collection of vintage steam and diesel engines, carriages and wagons is available to explore.

* Seven steam engines and 40 carriages and wagons
* Colne Valley Farm Park

Location
Located on right hand side of A1017
1 mile from Castle Hedingham

Opening
Daily; Mar–Oct 11am–5pm
dates vary, phone for details

Admission
Adult £6, Child £3, Concs £5

Contact
Yeldham Road, Castle Hedingham
CO9 3DZ

t 01787 461174
w colnevalleyrailway.co.uk
e info@colnevalleyrailway.co.uk

360 Chelmsford

Chelmsford Museum & Essex Regiment Museum

1 hr+   All year

The museum is set in a Victorian mansion where visitors may follow the story of Chelmsford from the ice ages, via the Roman town, to the present day. See also the superb Essex regiment museum housing many military artefacts.

* Bright & colourful Victorian pottery from Hedingham
* Period dress and room settings

Location
In Oaklands Park, off Moulsham Street

Opening
Daily; Mon–Sat 10am–5pm
Sun 2pm–5pm
(Winter 1pm–4pm)

Admission
Free

Contact
Oaklands Park,
Chelmsford CM2 9AQ

t 01245 615100
w chelmsfordmuseums.co.uk
e oaklands@chelmsfordbc.gov.uk

361 Chelmsford

RHS Garden Hyde Hall

3 hrs   All year

40 years of work has transformed a windswept hill with just six mature trees, to the present day garden of 24 acres. It contains the National Collection of viburnum and an attractive garden of 8 acres including woodland and a large collection of modern roses.

* Rope walk of climbing and pillar roses
* Ornamental ponds with lilies and fish

Location
From Rettendon follow flower signs

Opening
Daily; 10am–dusk

Admission
Adult £4.50, Child £1

Contact
Rettendon,
Chelmsford CM3 8ET

t 01245 400256
w rhs.org.uk/gardens/hydehall
e hydehall@rhs.org.uk

362 Colchester

Beth Chatto Gardens

2 hrs+   All year

These gardens began in 1960 when the site was an overgrown wasteland between two farms. Faced with difficult conditions and with dry and damp soil in both sun and shade, the owners have put into practice what is now referred to as ecological gardening.

* Remarkable drought resistant garden
* Water garden and woodland

Location
Located on A133. Approx 4 miles E of Colchester and a ¼ mile E of Elmstead Market

Opening
Mar–Oct Mon–Sat 9am–5pm
Nov–Feb Mon–Fri 9am–4pm

Admission
Adult £4, Child free

Contact
Elmstead Market, Colchester CO7 7DB

t 01206 822007
w bethchatto.co.uk
e info@bethchatto.fsnet.co.uk

363 Colchester

High Woods Country Park

2hrs+   All year

This country park boasts areas of woodland, wetland, grassland and farmland. Numerous footpaths provide an opportunity to see a wide range of wildlife. A visitor centre houses exhibits of local history and natural history.

* Quality Assured Visitor Attraction

Location
Accessible from Mile End Road & Ipswich Road, travelling N from Colchester

Opening
Daily; *Visitor Centre:* 1 Apr–30 Sep open Mon–Sat 10am–4.30pm, Sun & Bank holidays 11am–5.30pm; 1 Oct–31 Mar open weekends only 10am–4pm

Admission
Free

Contact
Turner Road
Colchester CO4 5JR

t 01206 853588

---

365 Colchester

Colchester Castle Museum

2 hrs   All year

The museum covers 2,000 years of the most important events in British history. Once the capital of Roman Britain, Colchester has experienced devastation by Boudica, invasion by the Normans and a siege during the English Civil War.

* The castle has been a gaol for witches
* 2250 BC Dagenham idol

Location
Situated in Castle Park at the eastern end of the High Street

Opening
Daily; Mon–Sat 10am–5pm
Sun 11am–5pm

Admission
Adult £4.50, Concs £2.90

Contact
High Street, Castle Park, Colchester
CO1 1TJ

t 01206 282939
w colchestermuseums.org.uk
e marie.taylor@colchester.gov.uk

---

364 Colchester

Colchester Zoo

6 hrs   All year

Colchester Zoo has some of the best cat and primate collections in Europe. See a white tiger eye to eye in White Tiger Valley, or get closer to the zoo's chimpanzees at Chimp World. Other enclosures include Penguin Shores and Serengeti Plains for African lions.

* Playa Patagonia – sealion underwater experience
* Tiger campaign earned a Platinum Certificate

Location
Take A1124 exit from the A12

Opening
Daily; summer 9.30am–5.30pm
winter 9.30am–1 hr before dusk

Admission
Adult £12.49, Child £7.49, Concs £9.49
Disabled/Carers £4.99

Contact
Maldon Road, Stanway, Colchester
CO3 0SL

t 01206 331292
w colchester-zoo.co.uk
e enquiries@colchester-zoo.co.uk

366 East Mersea

Cudmore Grove Country Park

1 hr   All year

Cudmore Grove is at the eastern end of Mersea Island, with fine views across the Colne and Blackwater estuaries. Walk the sea wall, explore the shore and watch for wildlife. Behind the sandy beach is a tranquil area of cliff top and grassland.

* Wildside walk and bird hides
* Ranger-led guided walks available by request

Location
Take B1025 S of Colchester & Mersea Island. Take left hand fork to East Mersea – signed

Opening
Daily; 8am–dusk

Admission
£1 per hour per car, £2 per day per car

Contact
Bromans Lane, East Mersea CO5 8UE
t 01206 383868
w essexcc.gov.uk
e cudmoregrove@essexcc.gov.uk

367 Halstead

Hedingham Castle

½ hr+   Apr–Oct

This is one of the best preserved Norman keeps in England. Built in 1140, it possesses four floors including a magnificent banqueting hall with a minstrels' gallery and Norman arch. It is approached by a Tudor bridge, built in 1496 to replace the drawbridge.

* Woodlands and lake with a pretty C18 dovecote
* 1920s bog garden contains camellias and azaleas

Location
Situated in Castle Hedingham, ½ mile from A1017 between Cambridge & Colchester

Opening
Apr–Oct Thu, Fri & Sun 11am–4pm
Special school holiday opening 10am–5pm, phone for details

Admission
Adult £4, Child £3, Concs £3.50

Contact
Halstead CO9 3DJ
t 01787 460261
w hedinghamcastle.co.uk
e hedinghamcastle@aspects.net.co.uk

368 Pitsea

The Motorboat Museum

2 hrs+   Feb–Dec

This museum is devoted to the history and evolution of sports and leisure motorboats, with over 31 exhibits of motorboats from 1873 to present. From the state-of-the-art offshore powerboats to the early days of steamers, trace the history of these wonderful crafts.

* Collection of inboard and outboard motors
* Carstais collection

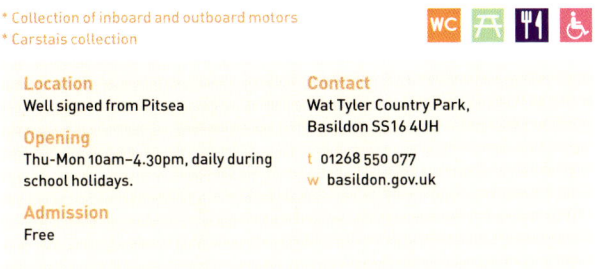

Location
Well signed from Pitsea

Opening
Thu-Mon 10am–4.30pm, daily during school holidays.

Admission
Free

Contact
Wat Tyler Country Park,
Basildon SS16 4UH

t 01268 550 077
w basildon.gov.uk

369 Saffron Walden

Mole Hall Wildlife Park

2 hrs   Easter–Oct

This family-owned wildlife park was first opened to the public in 1963 and has continued to grow. The collection of animals and birds contains many exotic species including otters, primates including chimpanzees, owls, birds and many more.

* Tropical butterfly pavilion
* Animal adoption scheme

Location
Signed from B1383 & junction 8
of M11

Opening
Daily; Easter–Oct 10.30am–dusk

Admission
Adult £5.50, Child £3.80, Concs £4

Contact
Widdington,
nr Saffron Walden CB11 3SS

t 01799 540400
w molehall.co.uk
e enquiries@molehall.co.uk

370 Stansted

Mountfitchet Castle & Norman Village

2 hrs   Mar–Nov

This is a Norman motte and bailey castle and village, re-constructed on its original ancient site. Vivid exhibition of village life at the time of the conquest includes houses, exhibition, seige tower and church. Computerised figures give historical information.

* Iron-Age fort, Roman, Saxon and Viking settlements

Location
2 miles from Junction 8 of M11

Opening
Daily; Mar-Nov 10am–5pm

Admission
Adult £6, Child £5, Concs £5.50

Contact
Stansted CM24 8SP

t 01279 813237
w mountfitchetcastle.com
e mountfitchetcastle1066@btinternet.com

371 Tilbury

Tilbury Fort

2 hrs   All year

The finest surviving example of C17 military engineering in England, Tilbury Fort remains largely unaltered. Today, exhibitions, the powder magazine and bunker-like 'casemates', demonstrate how the fort protected the city. Visitors can even fire an anti-aircraft gun.

* Regular military collectors fairs
* Designed by Charles II's chief engineer

Location
Located 5 miles E of Tilbury off A126

Opening
Daily; Apr-Sep 10am–6pm
Oct-Nov 10am–5pm
Dec-Apr Wed-Sun 10am–4pm

Admission
Adult £3.20, Child £1.60, Concs £2.40

Contact
Tilbury, RM18 7NR

t 01375 858489
w english-heritage.org.uk

372 Saffron Walden

Audley End House & Gardens

3 hrs+   Mar–Oct

The house was built by the first Earl of Suffolk, Lord Treasurer to James I, on the scale of a great royal palace. Parts of the house were demolished in the early C18 and what remains is one of the most significant Jacobean houses in England.

* Historic kitchen and dry laundry
* Landscaped garden walks

Location
1 mile W of Saffron Walden on B1383 (M11 exits 8 and 9, northbound only, and 10)

Opening
Mar–Oct Wed–Sun 10am–6pm

Admission
Adult £8.50, Child £4.30, Concs £6.40

Contact
Saffron Walden CB11 4JT

t 01799 522399
w english-heritage.org.uk

373 Waltham Abbey

Royal Gunpowder Mills

3 hrs+   All year

The world of explosives is uncovered with a range of interactive and static displays which follows the trail back to the C17. This unique museum traces the evolution of gunpowder technology and reveals the impact it had on the history of Great Britain.

* Muskets, rifles, pistols, machine guns
* Munitionettes – photo exhibits of women in Second World War

 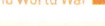

Location
1 mile from junction 26 of M25, A121

Opening
30 Apr–25 Sep Sat, Sun & Bank hols 11am–5pm (last entry 3.30pm)

Admission
Adult £5.50, Child £3, Concs £4.70

Contact
Beaulieu Drive, Waltham Abbey EN9 1JY

t 01992 707370
w royalgunpowdermills.com
e info@royalgunpowdermills.com

114   South Bank

Clink Prison Museum

1 hr   All year

On the site of the original Clink prison, this fascinating exhibition examines some of London's unsavoury past. From the C12 until its destruction in 1780 its inmates have ranged from priests to prostitutes.

* Possibly the oldest men's prison in London
* Whipping post, torture chair, foot crusher and more

Location
Underground London Bridge

Opening
Daily; 10am-6pm;
summer & Sat-Sun 10am-9pm

Admission
Adult £5, Child £3.50, Concs £3.50

Contact
1 Clink Street, South Bank,
London SE1 9DG

t 020 7378 1558
w clink.co.uk
e museum@clink.co.uk

115   South Bank

Globe Theatre

1–3 hrs   All year

The Globe Theatre is a reconstruction of the open-air playhouse, designed in 1599, where Shakespeare worked and for which he wrote many of his greatest plays. You can see a performance or visit the Globe Exhibition, for an introduction to the theatre of Shakespeare's time.

* Annual programme of Shakespeare's plays
* Permanent exhibition & theatre tours

Location
Mainline London Bridge, Waterloo
Underground Southwark

Opening
Daily; May–Sep, *Theatre* 10am–7.30pm
Exhibition 9am–5pm Oct–Apr *Exhibition*
10am–5pm (tours available)

Admission
Exhibition Adult £8.50, Child £6,
Concs £7

Contact
21 New Globe Walk, London SE1 9DT
t *Enquiries* 020 7902 1400
  Box office 020 7401 9919
w shakespeares-globe.org
e info@shakespearesglobe.com

116   South Bank

Tate Modern

2 hrs+   All year

This major gallery of modern and contemporary art is housed in the old Bankside Power Station on the south side of the Thames. This spectacular gallery is one of the world's most popular modern art galleries, featuring a permanent collection alongside temporary exhibits.

* Superb shop at gallery entrance
* Spectacular river views from restaurant on level seven

Location
Opposite St Paul's Cathedral
Underground Southwark, Blackfriars
Boat from Tate Britain to Tate Modern

Opening
Daily; Sun–Thu 10am–6pm;
Fri & Sat 10am–10pm

Admission
Free, donations welcome, exhibitions
may charge

Contact
Bankside, London SE1 9TG

t 020 7887 8000
w tate.org.uk
e info@1001daysout.com

112 Shepherd's Bush

BBC Television Centre Tours

2 hrs   All year

Tours of the most famous television centre in the world last up to two hours. You'll see behind the scenes, into studios, visit BBC News, play in our interactive studio and be shown around by well-informed, entertaining guides. No two tours are the same.

* Winner of the 2003 Group Travel Awards
* Winner of the 2002 Best Sightseeing Tour in London

Location
Underground White City

Opening
Tours run 6 times a day Mon–Sat.
Booking essential

Admission
Adult £7.95 Child £5.95

Contact
BBC Television Centre,
Wood Lane,
London W12 7RJ

t 0870 603 0304 (bookings)
w bbc.co.uk/tours
e bbctours@bbc.co.uk

113 South

Imperial War Museum

3 hrs+   All year

This is the national museum of C20 conflict. It illustrates and records all aspects of modern war and of the individual's experience of it, whether allied or enemy, service or civilian, military or political. Its role embraces the causes, course and consequences of conflict.

* Special Holocaust exhibition
* Cinema shows museum's collection of film & video

Location
Mainline Waterloo, Elephant and Castle
Underground Lambeth North 5 min walk

Opening
Daily; 10am–6pm

Admission
Free, exhibitions may charge

Contact
Lambeth Road, London SE1 6HZ

t 020 7416 5320
w iwm.org.uk
e mail@iwm.org.uk

108   Liverpool Street

Bank of England Museum

1 hr+   All year

This fascinating collection charts the history of the bank from its earliest days to the present. Discover how banknotes are made, take an audio tour, lift a genuine gold bar, and view bank notes (real and forged), coins, books, furniture and pictures.

Location
Underground Bank & Liverpool Street

Opening
Weekdays 10am–5pm; also open on the day of the Lord Mayor's Show; closed Sat, Sun & Bank holidays

Admission
Free

Contact
Threadneedle Street, London EC2R 8AH
t 020 7601 5491
w bankofengland.co.uk
e museum@bankofengland.co.uk

109   London Bridge

London Dungeon

1 hr+   All year

Deep in the heart of London, buried beneath the paving stones of historic Southwark, lies the world's most chillingly famous horror attraction. The London Dungeon brings more than 2000 years of gruesomely authentic history vividly back to life... and death.

* Great Plague exhibition & Judgement Day boat ride!
* The terrible truth about Jack the Ripper

Location
Underground London Bridge

Opening
Daily; Jul–Sep 9.30am–7.30pm; Oct–Mar 10.30am–5.30pm

Admission
Adults £13.95, Child £9.95, Concs £11.25

Contact
28–34 Tooley Street, London SE1 2SZ
t 020 7403 7221
w thedungeons.com
e londondungeon@ merlinentertainments.biz

110   Marylebone

Lord's Tour & MCC Museum

2 hrs   All year

The Lord's tour is an enjoyable and informative visit to the world famous home of cricket. The tour includes the Pavilion, Long Room, dressing room & the MCC museum, which houses cricketing memorabilia including bats, balls, paintings and much more.

* Don Bradman's cricket kit
* Home of the Ashes urn

Location
Underground St Johns Wood

Opening
Daily; Apr–Sep tours at 10am, 12 noon & 2pm; Oct–Mar 12 noon & 2pm;

Admission
Adult £7, Child £4.50, Concs £5.50

Contact
Lord's Cricket Ground, St John's Wood, London NW8 8QN
t 020 7616 8595 / 8596
w lords.org
e tours@mcc.org.uk

111   Regent's Park

London Zoo

4 hrs   All year

Come face to face with some of the hairiest, scariest, tallest and smallest animals on the planet. See our Animals in Action presentation and watch some of our finest flying, leaping and climbing animals showing off their skills. Don't miss a visit to B.U.G.S!

* Regular programme of feeding times & special shows
* New Komodo dragon a very impressive preditor

Location
At the NE corner of Regent's Park on the Outer Circle
Underground Camden Town

Opening
Daily; Mar–Oct daily 10am–5.30pm
Nov–Feb 10am–4pm

Admission
Adult £13, Child £9.75, Concs £11

Contact
Regent's Park, London NW1 4RY
t 020 7722 3333
w londonzoo.co.uk

106 Kensington

Science Museum

3 hrs+   All year

This museum presents a record of scientific, technological and medical change since the C18. Originally funded by profits from the Great Exhibition of 1851, the museum was intended to improve scientific and technical education, and has done so for 150 years.

* Range of interactive exhibits, including new Energy gallery
* IMAX cinema

Location
Underground **South Kensington**

Opening
Daily; 10am–6pm

Admission
Free, donations welcome, exhibitions may charge

Contact
Exhibition Road, South Kensington, London SW7 2DD
t 0870 870 4868
w sciencemuseum.org.uk
e sciencemuseum@nmsi.ac.uk

107 Kensington

Victoria & Albert Museum

2–6 hrs   All year

The V&A is widely regarded as the world's greatest museum of applied and decorative arts. Home to amazing artefacts from the world's richest cultures, the V&A's unsurpassable collection has inspired and informed for over 150 years.

* A wide choice of special events, exhibitions and activities
* Spend time wandering the seven miles of corridors

Location
Underground **South Kensington**

Opening
Daily; 10am–5.45pm; Weds 10am–10pm; last Fri of month 10am–10pm

Admission
Free, exhibitions may charge

Contact
Cromwell Road, South Kensington, London SW7 2RL
t 020 7942 2000
w vam.ac.uk
e vanda@vam.ac.uk

102 Green Park

Buckingham Palace

1 hr+   Aug–Sep

The official London residence of Her Majesty The Queen. The state rooms are used extensively to entertain guests on state, ceremonial and official occasions but are open to the public during August and September when the Queen makes her annual visit to Scotland.

* The state rooms form the heart of the working palace
* Furnished with treasures from the Royal Collection

Location
Mainline Victoria
Underground Victoria, Green Park & Hyde Park Corner

Opening
Aug–Sep daily 9.30am–6pm

Admission
Please phone for details

Contact
Ticket Sales and Information Office, The Official Residences of The Queen, London SW1A 1AA

t 020 7766 7300
w royal.gov.uk
e buckinghampalace@royalcollection.org.uk

103 Greenwich

National Maritime Museum

2 hrs+   All year

This is part of a World Heritage site comprising the National Maritime Museum, Royal Observatory and the Queen's House. It houses important items on the history of Britain at sea, including maritime art, ship models, plans, navigational instruments and time-keeping.

* Three marvellous museums in close proximity
* Planetarium shows at the Observatory, daily 2.30pm

Location
Mainline Greenwich or Maze Hill, *Docklands Light Railway* Cutty Sark station. Boat from Embankment or Westminster

Opening
Daily; summer 10am–6pm; winter 10am–5pm

Admission
Free, exhibitions may charge

Contact
Park Row, Greenwich SE10 9NF

t 020 8312 6565
   020 8858 4422
w nmm@ac.uk

104 Greenwich

The *Cutty Sark*

1 hr   All year

Built in 1869 to be the fastest ship in the annual race to collect the first of the season's tea from China, the clipper *Cutty Sark* was opened to the public in a specially-built dry dock in 1957. Take a tour of her decks and find out about the urgent need for conservation.

* One of the world's most beautiful ships
* Subject of a huge conservation appeal

Location
Mainline Docklands Light Railway Cutty Sark Station
Underground Canary Wharf
By boat from Westminster Pier

Opening
Daily 10am–5pm (last admission 4.30pm)

Admission
Adult £4.25, Child £2.95, Concs £3.25

Contact
King William Walk, Greenwich, London SE10 9HT

t 020 8858 3445
w cuttysark.org.uk
e info@cuttysark.org.uk

105 Holborn

Sir John Soane Museum

1 hr+   All year

The famous architect Sir John Soane (1753–1837) designed this house to live in, but also to exhibit his antiquities and works of art. Today the house remains as he wanted it – a museum to which amateurs and students should have access.

* Celebrating over 250 years of space, light and invention
* For students and lovers of architecture and sculpture

Location
Underground Holborn

Opening
Tue–Sat 10am–5pm

Admission
Free

Contact
13 Lincoln's Inn Fields, London WC2A 3BP

t 020 7405 2107
w soane.org
e jbrock@soane.org.uk

100 City

St Paul's Cathedral

1 hr+   All year

The distinctive dome of Sir Christopher Wren's magnificent cathedral is prominent in London's skyline. Its monumental interior, sacred tombs and atmospheric crypt ensure it remains one of London's major tourist attractions.

* Full range of musical performances & events
* Try out the Whispering Gallery

Location
The top of Ludgate Hill
Underground St Paul's

Opening
Mon–Sat 8.30am–4pm
Special services and events may close all or part of the Cathedral

Admission
Free *Guided tours* Adult £7, Child £3, Concs £6

Contact
The Chapter House, St Paul's Churchyard, London EC4M 8AD
t 020 7236 4128
w stpauls.co.uk
e chapter@stpaulscathedral.org.uk

101 County Hall

London Aquarium

2 hrs   All year

The London Aquarium is for everyone who appreciates the stunning and unusual natural world. Let your imagination take you on a voyage under the sea, from the beautiful coral reefs and Indian Ocean to the secret depths of the Pacific and Atlantic Oceans.

* Late night opening times in summer
* Themed activity weeks

Location
Inside County Hall on the south bank of the Thames by Westminster Bridge
Underground Westminster

Opening
All year 10am–6pm (7pm on selected summer evenings)

Admission
Please phone for details

Contact
County Hall, Westminster Bridge Road, London SE1 7PB

t 020 7967 8000
w londonaquarium.co.uk
e info@londonaquarium.co.uk

097 City

Museum of London

2 hrs   All year

The Museum of London is the world's largest urban museum and presents a quarter of a million years of history. Its collections include over a million items relating to one of the finest cities in the world.

* Covers the history of the city since it began
* Regular calendar of exhibitions & special events

Location
Underground **Barbican, St Paul's**

Opening
Mon-Sat 10am–5.50pm
Sun 12noon–5.50pm

Admission
Free

Contact
London Wall,
London EC2Y 5HN

t 0870 444 3852
w museumoflondon.org.uk
e info@museumoflondon.org.uk

098 City

Monument

½ hr   All year

Built in memory of the Great Fire of London in 1666 at a cost of £13,700, the monument stands exactly 202 feet from the fire's source in Pudding Lane. This is the tallest free-standing stone column in the world – 311 steps lead to the deck with a great view over London.

* Get a certificate of achievement for reaching the top
* Superb panoramic views of London from the top

Location
Underground **Monument**

Opening
Daily; 9.30am–5pm

Admission
Adult £2, Child £1

Contact
Monument Street,
London EC3R 8AH

t 020 7626 2717
w towerbridge.org.uk
e enquiries@towerbridge.org.uk

099 City

The Streets of London

2 hrs   All year

The Streets of London invite you to sample the many faces of this great and fascinating city. Journey through 2000 years of history on walks that will inform, excite and stimulate your curiosity.

* Programme of fascinating walks all over the city
* Each walk lasts approximately two hours

Location
Walks start at different tube stations every day of the week

Opening
Please phone for details

Admission
Adult £5, accompanied under 12s free

Contact
Please telephone for details

t 020 8906 8657
w thestreetsoflondon.co.uk
e contactstreetsol@hotmail.com

094 Bloomsbury

The Charles Dickens Museum

1 hr   All year

Charles Dickens lived in this house between 1837–39 and wrote several of his most famous novels during that time. The house is now the world's foremost repository of Dickens-related material and the headquarters of the Dickens Fellowship.

* Regular calendar of special Dickens events
* Collection of letters, first editions & portraits

Location
Underground **Russell Square**

Opening
Mon–Sat 10am–5pm
Sun 11am–5pm

Admission
Adult £5, Child £3, Concs £4

Contact
48 Doughty Street, London WC1N 2LX

t 020 7405 2127
w dickensmuseum.com
e info@dickensmuseum.com

095 Chelsea

Chelsea Physic Garden

2 hrs+   Apr–Oct

Founded in 1673 by the Worshipful Society of Apothecaries, this is one of Europe's oldest botanic gardens. Its 312 acres hold a garden showing the history of medicinal plants, a pharmaceutical garden, glasshouses and many rare plants.

* Historical walk
* One of the oldest rock gardens in Europe (1773)

Location
Underground **Sloane Square**

Opening
Apr–Oct Wed noon–5pm
Sun 2pm–6pm

Admission
Adult £5, Child £3, Concs £3

Contact
66 Royal Hospital Road, Chelsea,
London SW3 4HS

t 020 7352 5646
w chelseaphysicgarden.co.uk
e enquiries@chelseaphysicgarden.
co.uk

096 County Hall

London Eye

½ hr   All year

This is the most popular tourist attraction in London. The 443-foot (135m) big wheel provides the most spectacular views of one of the biggest cities in the world. On a clear day you can see 25 miles in every direction from a safe and comfortable capsule.

* Over 15,000 people a day travel on the Eye
* Views are spectacular in all conditions

Location
On the south bank by County Hall
Underground **Waterloo**

Opening
Daily; 9.30am–8pm
please phone for details

Admission
Adult £11.50, Child £5.75 (must be
accompanied by an adult) Concs £10

Contact
BA London Eye, Riverside Building,
County Hall, London SE1 7PB

t 0870 5000 600
w ba-londoneye.com
e customer.services@ba-londoneye.
com

092 Baker Street

Madame Tussaud's

2 hrs+   All year

This is the most famous waxworks collection in the world. It includes a whole range of interactive exhibits including Pop Idol, The Hulk, Chamber Live, the World Stage, the Spirit of London and more. The same building also houses the Planetarium.

* Updated and revamped chamber of horrors
* New online ticket booking allows timed ticketing

Location
Underground Baker Street

Opening
Weekdays 9.30am–5.30pm
Weekends 9am–6pm

Admission
9am–3pm: Adult £21.99, Child £16.99, Concs £17.99

3pm–5pm: £17.99, £13.99, £14.99
5pm–6pm: £13, £8; £11

Contact
Marylebone Road, London NW1 5LR

t 0870 400 3000
w madame-tussauds.com
e csc@madame-tussauds.com

093 Bloomsbury

The British Museum

2 hrs+   All year

The British Museum is home to a collection of art and antiquities from ancient and living cultures. Housed in one of Britain's architectural landmarks, the collection is one of the finest in existence, spanning two million years of human history.

* Spectacular covered courtyard

Location
Underground Tottenham Court Road

Opening
Daily, Sat–Wed 10am–5.30pm,
Thu–Fri 10am–8.30pm (selected galleries 5.30pm–8.30pm)

Admission
Free, exhibitions may charge

Contact
Great Russell Street,
London WC1B 3DG

t 020 7323 8299
w thebritishmuseum.ac.uk
e information@
thebritishmuseum.ac.uk

090 Tunbridge Wells

Groombridge Place Gardens & The Enchanted Forest

4 hrs+

Apr–Nov

Groombridge Place's history dates back to medieval times. Flanked by a deep moat, and with a classical C17 manor as its backdrop, the formal gardens boast a rich variety of lawns and flower displays. High above the walled gardens and vineyard lies the Enchanted Forest.

* Bird of prey Raptor Centre
* Maze

Location
A26 towards Tunbridge Wells, turn right onto B2176 towards Penshurst. 3 miles past Penshurst village, turn left at T junction with A264. Follow signs

Opening
Daily Apr–Nov 9.30am–6pm

Admission
Adult £8.50, Child £7, Concs £7.20

Contact
The Estate Office, Groombridge Place, Groombridge,
Royal Tunbridge Wells TN3 9QG

t 01892 863999 / 861444
w groombridge.co.uk
e office@groombridge.co.uk

091 Westerham

Chartwell

2 hrs+

Mar–Nov

The home of Winston Churchill for over 40 years, Chartwell remains as it was in his day. With many personal possessions and reminders of the man voted greatest Briton of all time the house captures the mood of a key period in British history.

* Exhibition of sound recordings
* Collection of Churchill's paintings

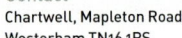

Location
2 miles S of Westerham, turn off A25 on to B2026, follow signs

Opening
18 Mar–7 Nov Wed–Sun 11am–5pm
July–Aug Tue as well

Admission
Adult £7, Child £3.50

Contact
Chartwell, Mapleton Road, Westerham TN16 1PS

t 01732 866368
w nationaltrust.org.uk/places/chartwell
e chartwell@nationaltrust.org.uk

087 Sevenoaks

Knole

2 hrs+   Apr–Oct

This great house is set in a magnificent deer park. The original C15 house was enlarged and embellished in 1603 and has remained largely unaltered since then. State rooms house a superb collection of furniture, tapestries and paintings.

* Virtual reality tour of state rooms
* Children's period costume events

Location
Sevenoaks town centre, off A225

Opening
Apr–Oct Wed–Sun 11am–4pm

Admission
House: Adult £6, Child £3
Gardens: £2, £1

Contact
Sevenoaks TN15 0RP

t 01732 462100
w nationaltrust.org.uk/places/knole
e knole@nationaltrust.org.uk

088 Sissinghurst

Sissinghurst Castle Garden

2 hrs+   Mar–Oct

This is one of the world's most celebrated gardens, created by Vita Sackville-West and her husband Sir Harold Nicholson, in the ruins of a large Elizabethan house. The library and tower, which are open to the public, include Vita's writing room.

* History of the house & the making of the garden
* Restaurant uses local recipes and produce

Location
1 mile E of Sissinghurst on A262

Opening
19 Mar–30 Oct Mon, Tue & Fri
11am–6.30pm, Sat & Sun 10am–6.30pm.
Woodland walks open all year

Admission
Phone for details. *Woodland* free

Contact
Sissinghurst, nr Cranbrook TN17 2AB

t 01580 710701
w nationaltrust.org.uk/places/
   sissinghurst
e sissinghurst@nationaltrust.org.uk

089 Tenterden

Tenterden Vineyard

2 hrs+   All year

This 15-acre vineyard is at the forefront of the English wine-making industry. Visitors are free to wander around the winery, vineyard, rural museum and plant centre. Guided tours explain the wine-making process in more detail. A free wine-tasting follows each tour.

* Café, wine & gift shop
* Guided tours available during the summer months

Location
From Tenterden (A28), turn onto
B2082 to Wittersham & Rye. Vineyard
is 2 miles on the right at Small Hythe

Opening
Daily; 10am–5pm

Admission
Free
Tours Adult £4, Child £2.50

Contact
Small Hythe, Tenterden TN30 7NG

t 01580 763033
w englishwinesgroup.com
e sales@englishwinesgroup.com

084 Maidstone

Leeds Castle

3 hrs   All year

This medieval castle, situated on two islands in a lake set in 500 acres of parkland is a popular attraction. Once a Norman stronghold, the castle has since been residence for six of England's medieval queens, a palace for Henry VIII, and a retreat for the powerful.

* Open-air concert programme
* Grand Firework spectacular

Location
Leave M20 at junction 8, castle is 7 miles E of Maidstone

Opening
Daily; Mar–Oct 10am–5.30pm
Nov–Mar 10am–3pm

Admission
Adult £12.50, Child £9.50, Concs £11.50
Gardens & attractions £10.50, £7, £9

Contact
Maidstone ME17 1PL

t 01622 765400
w leeds-castle.com
e enquiries@leeds-castle.co.uk

---

085 New Romney

Romney, Hythe & Dymchurch Railway

2 hrs   All year

This was the world's smallest public railway when it opened in July 1927. It now runs passenger services covering a distance of 13½ miles from the picturesque Cinque Port of Hythe, near the channel tunnel, to the fishermen's cottages and lighthouses at Dungeness.

* Thomas the Tank Engine & Santa specials
* Dining-train specials

Location
The stations at New Romney, Dungeness and Hythe are all on or near the A259 trunk road

Opening
Trains run daily Apr–Sep & weekends Oct–Mar. Please phone or see website for timetable

Admission
Adult £5.80–£9.60, Child half fare

Contact
New Romney TN28 8PL

t 01797 362353
w rhdr.org.uk
e info@rhdr.org.uk

---

086 Penshurst

Penshurst Place & Gardens

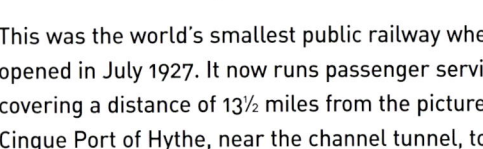

3 hrs+   Mar–Nov

This medieval manor house was built in 1341. The great hall, with its 60ft-high, chestnut-beamed roof and trestle tables, is regarded as one of the world's grandest rooms. Much of the house and the gardens remain unchanged since the days when Elizabeth I made her visits here.

* Includes a fabulous toy museum
* 'A Family Home for 450 Years' exhibition

Location
Leave M25 at junction 5 or M20/M26 at junction 2a, follow A21 to Hildenborough, then signposted

Opening
Daily; Mar–Nov *House* 12noon–5pm,
Gardens 10.30am–6pm

Admission
House & Gardens Adult £7, Child £5, Concs £6.50 *Gardens* £5.50, £4.50, £5

Contact
Penshurst TN11 8DG

t 01892 870307
w penshurstplace.com
e enquiries@penshurstplace.com

080 Goudhurst

Bedgebury Pinetum

3 hrs   All year

This wooded valley, with the finest collection of conifers in the world, will delight visitors who come to appreciate its beauty and tranquillity. This unique attraction nestles quietly among lakes and valleys in the Kentish countryside.

* Special events & tours
* Pinetum Pantry provides light refreshments

Location
On the B2079 from Goudhurst, signed from A21 before Flimwell

Opening
Daily; Apr–Oct 10am–5pm, Nov–Mar 10am–4pm

Admission
Adult £3.50, Child £1.50, Concs £3

Contact
Park Lane, Goudhurst TN17 2SL

t 01580 211044 / 211781
w bedgeburypinetum.org.uk
e bedgebury@forestry.gov.uk

081 Hamstreet

South of England Rare Breeds Centre

3 hrs   All year

Here's a chance to meet and pet all your favourite friendly farm animals as you wander around a farm trail. The centre is also home to many endangered and rare British animals. Set in acres of beautiful woodland there are plenty of places to picnic while the kids play.

* Woodland activity quiz trail
* Piglet racing in season & trailer rides all year

Location
Leave M20 at junction 10, follow signs to Brenzett and Hamstreet. Situated between Hamstreet & Woodchurch

Opening
Daily; Apr–Sep 10.30am–5.30pm; Oct–Mar Tue–Sun 10.30am–4.30pm

Admission
Adult £5.50, Child £5.50, Concs £4.50

Contact
Woodchurch, Ashford TN26 3RJ

t 01233 861493
w rarebreeds.org.uk
e visit@rarebreeds.org.uk

082 Lamberhurst

Bewl Water

1 hr+   All year

This reservoir is the largest area of open water in the south east. Set in an area of outstanding natural beauty, Bewl is home to a huge variety of wildlife. There are many exciting outdoor pursuits here, including windsurfing, fishing, cycling and walking.

* Water-efficient garden
* Interactive exhibition

Location
1 mile S of Lamberhurst, signed from A21

Opening
Daily; Mar–Oct 9am–sunset winter 9am–4pm

Admission
Apr–Oct car park £5, Nov–Mar £2.50

Contact
Bewl Water Reservoir, nr Lamberhurst TN3 8JH

t 01892 890661
w bewl.co.uk
e bewl@southernwater.co.uk

083 Maidstone

Museum of Kent Life

2 hrs+   Feb–Nov

A unique open-air living museum that celebrates 300 years of Kentish history. Traditional crafts are demonstrated on a working farm. One of the only places in England where hops are grown, harvested, dried and packed by hand, using time-honoured techniques.

* Calendar of events throughout the year
* Hop-picking festival in September

Location
Off M20 at junction 6, follow signs

Opening
Daily: Feb–Nov 10am–5.30pm

Admission
Adult £6.50, Child £4.50, Concs £5

Contact
Cobtree, Lock Lane, Sandling, Maidstone ME14 3AU

t 01622 763936
w museum–kentlife.co.uk
e enquiries@museum–kentlife.co.uk

077 Eynsford

Eagle Heights
Bird of Prey Centre

4 hrs+   All year

With over 100 birds in indoor and outdoor aviaries, the centre gives visitors the opportunity to see birds of prey in action during flying displays, promoting conservation through education. It also provides sanctuary for injured and unwanted animals.

* Five-day falconry courses available
* Now housing otters

Location
Off M25 at junction 3 onto A20, or M20 at junction 1

Opening
Daily Mar–Nov 10.30am–5pm,
Nov–Feb weekends 11am–4pm

Admission
Adult £6.60, Child £4.60, Concs £5.60

Contact
Lullingstone Lane,
Eynsford DA4 0JB

t 01322 866466
w eagleheights.co.uk
e office@eagleheights.co.uk

078 Edenbridge

Hever Castle & Gardens

4 hrs   Mar–Nov

This romantic C13 castle was the childhood home of Anne Boleyn. It is set in magnificent gardens, which include a formal Italian garden, a lake and a Sunday walk. There is a water maze on Sixteen Acre Island and the yew maze challenge.

* Costumed figure exhibition
* Historic instruments of execution & torture

   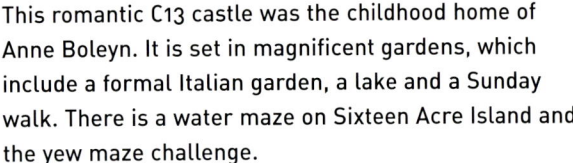

Location
3 miles SE of Edenbridge off B2026
between Sevenoaks & East Grinstead

Opening
Daily Mar–Nov
Gardens 11am–6pm,
Castle 12noon–6pm (last entry 5pm);
Mar & Nov 11am–4pm.

Admission
Castle & Gardens Adult £8.80,
Child £4.60, Concs £4.60,
Gardens £6.70, £5.70, £4.40

Contact
Edenbridge TN8 7NG

t 01732 865224
w hevercastle.co.uk
e ampedley@hevercastle.co.uk

079 Goudhurst

Finchcocks Living Museum of Music

3 hrs   Mar–Oct

This Georgian manor house in the Kent countryside houses a huge collection of historical keyboard musical instruments, and contains the world's largest collection of playing instruments. The house is noted for its dramatic brickwork and its beautiful and tranquil garden.

* Annual music festival & special events in Sep
* All openings include a demonstration concert

Location
Take A262, Goudhurst turning,
from A21, follow signs

Opening
Mar–Oct, Sun 2pm–6pm; Mon–Sat by appointment
Aug Wed & Thu 2pm–6pm
Bank Hols 2pm–6pm

Admission
House & Garden Adult £7.50;
Child £4 *Garden only* £2.50

Contact
Finchcocks, Goudhurst TN17 1HH

t 01580 211702
w finchcocks.co.uk
e Katrina@finchcocks.co.uk

074 Dover

Dover Castle

3 hrs+ All year

Commanding the shortest English sea crossing, this site has been the UK's most important defence against invasion since the Iron Age. It was built in the C12 and reinforced by Henry VIII in the 1530s. Underneath the nearby White Cliffs are a series of underground tunnels.

* Reconstruction of Henry VIII's visit in 1539
* Visit the Dunkirk command room

WC

Location
Clearly signed to the E of the city, on the white cliffs

Opening
Mar–Sep 10am–6pm, Oct 10am–5pm, Nov–Mar 10am–4pm

Admission
Adults £8, Child £4, Concs £6

Contact
Dover CT16 1HU

t 01304 201628
w english-heritage.org.uk

075 Dover

South Foreland Lighthouse

½ hr Mar–Oct

Built in 1843, this distinctive landmark on the White Cliffs was the first lighthouse to use electricity and the first to display an electrically-powered signal. It was used by Marconi for his first successful international radio transmission.

* Original 3500-watt lamp on display
* Leaflets on local walks available

WC

Location
2½ miles NE along coast from Dover
2 mile walk from NT car park

Opening
Guided tour Mar–Oct Thu–Mon 11am–5pm, school hols daily

Admission
Adult £2, Child £1

Contact
The Front, St Margaret's Bay, Dover CT15 6HP

t 01304 852463
w nationaltrust.org.uk
e southforeland@nationaltrust.org.uk

076 Eynsford

Lullingstone Roman Villa

1 hr+ All year

One of the best preserved Roman villas in England, Lullingstone was built in AD 75 and rediscovered in 1949. It is now housed in a modern two-storey building. Renowned for its mosaics, it also features a frescoe and a bathing complex.

* Free audio tour
* Gift shop

WC

Location
Off M25 at junction 3, just outside Eynsford on A225

Opening
Daily; Oct–Nov & Feb–Mar 10am–4pm
Apr–Sep 10am–6pm
Dec–Jan Wed–Sun 10am–4pm

Admission
Adult £3.50, Child £1.50, Concs £2.80

Contact
Lullingstone Lane, Eynsford DA4 0JA

t 01322 863467
w english-heritage.org.uk

070 Canterbury

Roman Museum

1 hr   All year

This underground museum is an exciting mix of excavated real objects, authentic reconstructions, and remains of a Roman town house with mosaics. Reconstructions include a Roman market place, with a shoemaker's workshop plus fruit and vegetable stall.

* Computer reconstruction shows the Roman house
* Touch-screen computer game on Roman technology

Location
Butchery Lane, close to the cathedral

Opening
Mon–Sat 10am–5pm (last admission 4pm). From Jun–Oct, also open Sun 1.30pm–5pm

Admission
Adult £2.80, Child £1.75, Concs £1.75

Contact
Longmarket, Butchery Lane, Canterbury CT1 2JE

t 01227 785575
w canterbury.gov.uk
e museums@canterbury.gov.uk

071 Canterbury

The Canterbury Tales

1 hr+   Mar–Jan

This fascinating audio-visual experience, sited in the centre of Canterbury, is one of the town's most popular visitor attractions. Step back in time to experience the sights, sounds and smells of the Middle Ages in this stunning reconstruction of C14 England.

* Uses headsets with earphones
* Recreates the pilgrimages of Chaucerian England

Location
City centre, off the High Street

Opening
Daily; Mar–Jun 10am–5pm, Jul to Aug 9.30am–5.30pm, Sep–Oct 10am–5pm, Nov–Jan 10am–4.30pm

Admission
Adults £6.95, Child £5.25, Concs £5.75

Contact
23 St Margaret's Street, Canterbury CT1 2TG

t 01227 479227
w canterburytales.org.uk
e info@canterburytales.org.uk

072 Chatham

The Historic Dockyard Chatham

4 hrs+   Feb–Nov

Housed in wonderful Victorian and Georgian buildings, the dockyard complex brings 400 years of naval history to life. Attractions include historic warships and the Wooden Walls exhibition which recreates the sights, sounds and smells of the dockyard in 1758.

* Royal dockyard from 1613 to 1984
* Nelson's flagship HMS *Victory* was built here

Location
Leave the M2 at junction 1, 3 or 4 & follow the signs

Opening
Feb–Oct 10am–6pm (last admission 4pm); weekends only in Nov 10am–6pm

Admission
Adult £10, Child £6.50, Concs £7.50

Contact
Chatham ME4 4TZ

t 01634 823800
w chdt.org.uk
e info@chdt.org.uk

073 Chislehurst

Chislehurst Caves

1 hr   All year

Over 20 miles of dark mysterious passageways form a labyrinth deep beneath Chislehurst. Dug over a period of 8000 years in search of flint and chalk, these handmade caves include a church, a druid's altar, a haunted pool and much more.

* Lamp-lit tours
* Original Second World War air-raid shelter

Location
Take the A222 between the A20 & A21. At the railway bridge turn into Station Road then right again to Caveside Close

Opening
School hols daily 10am–4pm (except Christmas). Rest of the year Wed–Sun 10am–4pm

Admission
Adults £4, Child £2, Concs £2

Contact
Old Hill, Chislehurst BR7 5NB

t 020 8467 3264
w chislehurstcaves.co.uk
e enquiries@chislehurstcaves.co.uk

Kent

067 Ashford

Godinton House & Gardens

1 hr+   Mar–Oct

Built in the C14, Godinton House is one of the most fascinating homes in Kent whose history, from its medieval origins to the present day, is revealed through the variety of its style, taste and furnishings. Set in glorious gardens.

* Collection of porcelain, pictures & furniture
* Three stunning delphinium borders best mid Jun–Jul

Location
Junction 9 off M20, for Maidstone A20.

Opening
Gardens 20 Mar–3 Oct Thu–Mon 2pm–5.30pm. *House* 9 Apr–3 Oct Fri–Sun 2pm–5.30pm (last tour at 4.30pm)

Admission
Gardens Adults £3, Child free
House & Gardens £6.

Contact
Godinton Lane, Ashford TN23 3BP

t 01233 620 773
w godinton–house–gardens.co.uk
e ghpt@godinton.fsnet.co.uk

068 Broadstairs

Dickens' House Museum

1 hr+   Easter–Oct

Once the home of Miss Mary Pearson Strong, on whom Charles Dickens based the character of Miss Betsey Trotwood in his novel *David Copperfield*, this building has been adapted as a museum to commemorate the novelist's association with the town of Broadstairs.

* Some of the author's own letters & memorabilia
* Collection of costumes & Victoriana

Location
On the main seafront at Broadstairs

Opening
Daily; Easter–Oct 2pm–5pm; Aug 11am–5pm

Admission
Adult £2.50, Child £1.20

Contact
2 Victoria Parade, Broadstairs CT10 1QS

t 01843 861232
w dickenshouse.co.uk
e aleeault@aol.com

069 Canterbury

Canterbury Cathedral

1 hr+   All year

Founded in 597 AD by St Augustine, a missionary from Rome, the cathedral has been the home of Christianity in England for 1400 years and has attracted thousands of pilgrims each year since the murder of Archbishop Thomas Becket in 1170.

* Site of the murder of Archbishop Thomas Becket
* Stained glass windows from the C12

Location
City centre, off the High Street

Opening
Daily; summer 9am–6.30pm; winter 9am–5.30pm.

Admission
Please phone for details

Contact
Cathedral House, 11 The Precinct, Canterbury CT1 2EH

t 01227 762862
w canterbury–cathedral.org
e enquiries@canterbury–cathedral.org

064 Wroxall

Appuldurcombe House Owl & Falconry Centre

2 hrs+   Feb–Dec

Visit the ruin of Appuldurcombe, designed by Capability Brown and once the grandest house on the Isle of Wight. A display of prints and photographs depicts the house and its history. The former servants' quarters now house the owl and falconry centre.

* Old brew house used for indoor bird flying
* C18 baroque mansion

Location
In Wroxall off the B3327 to Ventnor

Opening
Daily; Feb–Apr & Oct–Dec 10am–4pm;
May–Sep 10am–5pm

Admission
House Adult £2.50, Child £1.50,
Concs £2.25

House & Falconry Centre
£5.75, £3.25, £5.25

Contact
Wroxall, Isle of Wight PO38 3EW

t 01983 852484
w appuldurcombe.co.uk
e enquiries@appuldurcombe.co.uk

065 Winchester

Winchester Cathedral

1 hr+   All year

Visit this 900-year-old cathedral and see the memorials of Jane Austen and Isaac Walton, a unique collection of chantry chapels and hear the story of the diver, William Walker, who saved the cathedral in 1906. Visit the crypt with its renowned Anthony Gormley Sound II sculpture.

* The longest medieval cathedral
* The Winchester Bible – finest of the great C12 bibles

Location
Winchester town centre

Opening
Mon–Sat 8.30am–6pm ;
Sun 8.30am–5pm

Admission
Adult £3.50, Concs £2.50
Donations appreciated

Contact
Cathedral Office,
1 The Close,
Winchester SO23 9LS

t 01962 857200
w winchester–cathedral.org.uk
e cathedral.office@
    winchester–cathedral.org.uk

066 Winchester

INTECH–Hands-on Science & Technology Centre

2 hrs+   All year

This unique hands-on interactive science and technology centre houses over 100 exhibits designed to amuse and enthuse. Here you will understand how to bend light, create your own tornado and vortex and work out how much energy it takes to power a light bulb.

* Regularly changing exhibitions
* Gift-shop with unusual & educational items

Location
Junction 9 off the M3, take the B3404
towards Alton

Opening
Daily 10am–4pm; closed Christmas
Day, Boxing Day and New Year

Admission
Adult £5.95, Child £3.75, Concs £4

Contact
INTECH, Telegraph Way
Morn Hill, Winchester SO21 1HX

t 01962 86379
w intech-uk.com
e htct@intech-uk.com

060   Southampton

Southampton City Art Gallery

2 hrs+   All year

This gallery is internationally renowned for its impressive collection of contemporary works by British artists. A fine selection of works by the Camden Town Group, and paintings by Sir Stanley Spencer, Matthew Smith and Philip Wilson Steer are brought together.

* Studio potters' work from between the wars
* Regular exhibitions throughout the year

Location
Central Southampton

Opening
Tue–Sat 10am–5pm, Sun 1pm–4pm
Closed 21 Dec–2 Jan & Good Friday

Admission
Free

Contact
Civic Centre, Commercial Road,
Southampton SO14 7LP

t 02380 832277
w southampton.gov.uk/art
e art.gallery@southampton.gov.uk

061   Southsea

The D-Day Museum & Overlord Embroidery

1 hr+   All year

This museum was established in 1984 to tell the story of Operation Overlord from its origins in the dark days of 1940 to victory in Normandy in 1944. The museum's centrepiece is the Overlord embroidery.

* Audio-visual theatre
* Dawn-to-dusk reconstruction of the Allied landings

Location
On seafront, 2 miles from town centre

Opening
Daily; Apr–Sep 10am–5.30pm
Mar–Oct 10am–5pm
closed 24–26 Dec

Admission
Adults £5, Child £3, Concs £3.75

Contact
Clarence Esplanade, Southsea
PO5 3NT

t 023 9282 7261
w ddaymuseum.co.uk
e enquiries@ddaymuseum.co.uk

062   Stockbridge

Museum of Army Flying

2 hrs+   All year

Celebrating over 100 years of army aviation, this award-winning museum houses one of the country's finest collections of military kites, gliders, aeroplanes and helicopters. Trace the development of army flying from the Royal Flying Corps to the present day.

* Children's science & education centre
* Viewing gallery overlooking airfield

Location
A343 6 miles from Andover & 12 miles from Salisbury. Accessible from A30, A303 & M3

Opening
Daily 10am–4.30pm.
Closed 18 Dec–1 Jan

Admission
Adults £5, Child £3.50, Concs £4

Contact
Middle Wallop, Stockbridge SO20 8DY

t 01980 674421
w flying-museum.org.uk
e enquiries@flying-museum.org.uk

063   Ventnor

Ventnor Botanic Garden

2 hrs+   All year

This is one of the youngest botanic gardens in Britain. The southern edge of the garden comprises clifftop grassland and cliffs, and the eastern end is backed by a cliff face to the north. Enjoy the large number of British native flowers.

* Japanese plant collection & visitor centre
* Exhibition 'the greenhouse'

Location
The southern tip of the Isle of Wight

Opening
Daily; summer 10am–5pm, except July–Aug 10am–6pm;
winter weekends only 10am–6pm

Admission
Free

Contact
Undercliff Drive, Ventnor
Isle of Wight PO38 1UL

t 01983 855397
w botanic.co.uk
e simon.goodenough@iow.gov.uk

056 Romsey

Mottisfont Abbey

2 hrs+   Mar–Oct

This C12 Augustinian priory boasts sweeping lawns and magnificent old trees, set amid glorious countryside. Medieval monastic remains include a cellarium and original stonework revealed through cut-away sections of the building.

* Unusual *trompe-l'oeil* painting by Rex Whistler
* National Collection of old-fashioned roses

Location
4½ miles NW of Romsey,
1 mile W of A3057

Opening
Mar–Jun & Sep–Oct 11am–6pm
closed Thu & Fri
Jun–Aug 11am–6pm closed Fri

Admission
Adult £7, Child £3.50

Contact
Mottisfont, nr Romsey SO51 0LP

t 01794 340757
w nationaltrust.org.uk
e mottisfontabbey@nationaltrust.org.uk

057 Romsey

Sir Harold Hillier Gardens

3 hrs+   All year

These gardens, which were formerly known as the Hillier Arboretum, hold the greatest collection of hardy trees and shrubs in the world. Started by the late Sir Harold Hillier in 1953, the gardens now extend to 180 acres.

*Gurkha memorial garden
* Largest winter garden of its kind in Europe

Location
Between Ampfield & Braishfield,
3 miles NE of Romsey

Opening
Daily 10.30am–6pm

Admission
Adult £6, Child free, Concs £5.50

Contact
Jermyns House, Jermyns Lane,
Ampfield, Romsey SO51 0QA

t 01794 368787
w hilliergardens.org.uk
e info@hilliergardens.org.uk

058 Shanklin

Shanklin Chine

1 hr   Apr–Oct

This historic gorge has formed over the last 10,000 years and boasts a unique collection of flora and fauna, many extremely rare. There is a designated trail with numbered stopping places. The Chine drops 105ft to sea level and covers an area of approximately three acres.

* Over 150 varieties of wild plants
* 45-foot waterfall

Location
Enter via the old village, off the A3055
or through the Western end of
Shanklin Esplanade, off Chine Hill

Opening
Daily; 1 Apr–20 May & 27 Sep–31 Oct
10am–5pm;
21 May–26 Sep 10am–10pm

Admission
Adult £3.50, Child £2, Concs £2.50

Contact
12 Ponona Road, Shanklin
Isle of Wight PO37 6PF

t 01983 866432
w shanklinchine.co.uk
e jill@shanklinchine.co.uk

059 Southampton

Maritime Museum

1 hr+   All year

Originally a warehouse for Southampton's wool trade, this building was used to house hundreds of prisoners of war 200 years ago; more recently it was an aircraft factory. Now the museum tells the history of the port from the building of the first docks to the present day.

* Titanic Voices exhibition

Location
Between town centre & the waterfront

Opening
Tue–Fri 10am–5pm
Sat 10–4pm, Sun 2pm–5pm

Admission
Free

Contact
Wool House, Town Quay,
Southampton SO14 2AR

t 02380 635904
w southampton.gov.uk/heritage
e historic.sites@southampton.gov.uk

053 Portsmouth

Charles Dickens' Birthplace Museum

3 hrs+   Apr–Oct

The famous writer, Charles Dickens, was born in this modest house in Portsmouth in 1812. The house has survived and is now preserved as a museum furnished in the style of 1809, the year John and Elizabeth Dickens began their married life together.

* Regency–style furniture & household objects
* Charles Dickens & Portsmouth exhibition

Location
Just off the A3 heading S towards the city centre

Opening
Daily; Apr–Sep 10am–5.30pm
Oct 10am–5pm

Admission
Adult £2.50, Child £1.50, Concs £1.80

Contact
393 Old Commercial Road, Portsmouth PO1 4QL

t 02392 827261
w portsmouthmuseums.co.uk
e david.evans@portsmouthcc.gov.uk

054 Portsmouth

Royal Garrison Church

½ hr+   Apr–Sep

This church was constructed around 1212 as a hostel for pilgrims. It was also used as a store for weapons and ammunition before becoming a garrison church in the 1560s. The church was badly damaged in 1941 and modern windows tell the story of the building.

* Charles II married Catherine of Braganza here in 1662
* Once known as Cathedral Church of the British Army

Location
On Grand Parade S of Portsmouth High Street

Opening
Apr–Sep Mon–Sat 11am–4pm

Admission
Free

Contact
Grand Parade, Old Portsmouth

t 02392 823973/02392 735521
w english–heritage.org.uk

055 Portsmouth

Portsmouth Historic Dockyard

2 hrs+   All year

This is the home of the Tudor warship *Mary Rose*, Admiral Lord Nelson's flagship HMS *Victory*, the mighty iron-hulled HMS *Warrior* (1860), the Royal Naval Museum and the attraction Action Stations. Together they make Portsmouth Historic Dockyard an essential stopping place.

* Frigates, destroyers, mine warfare ships & more
* Harbour boat tour

Location
Follow Historic Waterfront & Historic Dockyard signs from junction 12 of M27

Opening
Daily; Apr–Oct 10am–5.30pm;
Nov–March 10am–5pm

Admission
Adult £15.50, Child £12.50,
Concs £12.50

Contact
Visitor Centre, College Road,
HM Naval Base. Portsmouth PO1 3LJ

t 02392 861533
w historicdockyard.co.uk
e enquiries@historicdockyard.co.uk

049 Lymington

Hurst Castle

3 hrs+   Apr–Oct

Hurst Castle was built by Henry VIII as one of a chain of coastal fortresses and it was completed in 1544. The location was perfect to defend the western approach to the Solent. Charles I was imprisoned here in 1648 before being taken to London for his trial and execution.

* Modernised during the Napoleonic wars
* Two huge 38 ton guns

Location
By ferry from Keyhaven or on foot from Milford-on-Sea

Opening
Daily; Apr–Sep 10am–5.30pm
Oct 10am–4pm

Admission
Adult £2.80, Child £1.60, Concs £2.50

Contact
Hurst Spit, Keyhaven, Lymington SO41 0QU
t 01590 642500
w hurst-castle.co.uk
e info@hurst-castle.co.uk

---

050 Newport

Carisbrooke Castle

1 hrs +   All year

Built over 1000 years ago, this castle has a rich and varied history. Since time immemorial, whoever controlled Carisbrooke controlled the Isle of Wight. The castle has been a feature of the island since its foundation as a Saxon camp during the C18.

* Remnants of a Saxon wall & a Norman keep
* Interactive museum

Location
1 mile SW of Newport on B3323

Opening
Daily; Apr–Sep 10am–6pm, Oct 10am–5pm
Nov–Mar 10am–4pm
Closed 24–26 Dec & 1 Jan

Admission
Adult £5, Child £2.50, Concs £3.80

Contact
Carisbrooke, Newport, Isle of Wight
t 01983 522107
w english–heritage.org.uk

---

051 Newport

Classic Boat Museum

2 hrs +   Mar–Nov

A great indoor collection of lovingly-restored sailing and motorised classic boats, dating back to C19. Highlights include the ultimate sailing classic, a Dragon, WWII airborne lifeboats, and a fragile folding canoe. Also on display are engines, equipment and memorabilia.

* Displays and boats change annually

Location
On the harbour, free parking

Opening
Daily; Mar–Nov, 10am–4.30pm

Admission
Adult £3, Child £1, Concs £2

Contact
The Quay, Newport Harbour, Newport, Isle of Wight PO30 2EF
t 01983 533493
w netguides.co.uk/wight/boatmus
e cbmiow@fsmail.net

---

052 Petersfield

Queen Elizabeth Country Park

3 hrs+   All year

This park forms part of the landscape of the South Downs and falls in the East Hampshire Area of Outstanding Natural Beauty. There are 1400 acres of open access woodland and downland. The site features trackways, barrows, lynchets and the remains of a Roman farmstead.

* Visitor centre
* National nature reserve

Location
Located in SE Hampshire, 4 miles S of Petersfield

Opening
Daily

Admission
Car park £1 per day Mon–Sat; £1.50 per day Sun & Bank Hols

Contact
Gravel Hill, Horndean Hampshire PO8 0QE
t 02392 595040
w hants.gov.uk/countryside
e info.centres@hants.gov.uk

046 Fareham

Titchfield Abbey

  ½ hr All year

An abbey was first founded at Titchfield in the C13 by the Bishop of Winchester. Its history was uneventful until the Dissolution when drastic alterations were made to convert the abbey into a mansion known as Place House. Now a ruin, the remains are magnificent.

* Residents were the Earls of Southampton
* The 3rd Earl was closely connected to Shakespeare

Location
½ mile N of Titchfield off A27

Opening
Daily; Apr–Sep 10am–6pm; Oct 10am–5pm; Nov–Mar 10am–4pm

Admission
Free

Contact
Mill Lane, Titchfield, Fareham PO15 5RA

t 01329 842133
w english-heritage.org.uk

047 Fordingbridge

Braemore House & Museum

  2½ hrs Apr–Sep

This is a large Elizabethan house, set in beautiful parkland, with a Saxon church nearby. Former kitchen gardens house a major countryside museum, village workshops and a reconstructed cottage. Pleasant walks lead to an ancient maze on the downs.

* Fine collection of pictures & C17 furniture
* Visitors go back to when a village was self sufficient

Location
3 miles N of Fordingbridge, off the A338

Opening
House Apr–Sep 2pm–5.30pm
Museum 1pm–5.30pm
Closed Mon & Fri (last tour 4.30pm)

Admission
Adult £6, Child £4, Concs £5

Contact
Nr Fordingbridge SP6 2DF

t 01725 512233
w braemorehouse.com
e braemore@ukonline.co.uk

048 Gosport

Explosion! The Museum of Naval Firepower

  2 hrs+ All year

An award-winning visitor experience on the shores of Portsmouth Harbour, Explosion! tells the story of naval warfare from the day of gunpowder to the Exocet. A hands-on, interactive museum set in the historic buildings of the Navy's former armaments depot.

* See Old Bill's Locker-supplying the Navy from C18-C20
* Dramatic audio-visual effects & scene-setting

Location
M27 to junction 11. Follow A32 to Gosport & brown tourist signs

Opening
Daily; Apr–Oct 10am–5.30pm; Nov–Mar Thu, Sat & Sun 10am–4.30pm

Admission
Adult £5.50, Child £3.50, Concs £4.50

Contact
Priddy's Hard, Gosport PO12 4LE

t 023 9250 5600
w explosion.org.uk
e info@explosion.org.uk

©English Heritage Photographic Library

045   East Cowes

Osborne House

3 hrs+   Apr–Sep

Queen Victoria's favourite country home captures the spirit of a world unchanged since the country's longest-reigning monarch died here 100 years ago. Queen Victoria and Prince Albert rebuilt the original Osborne House in 1845 as a 'modest country home'.

* Indian Durbar Room, Queen Victoria's gifts from India
* Glorious gardens & Swiss cottage

Location
1 mile SE of East Cowes

Opening
Daily; Apr–Sep 10am–5pm

Admission
Please phone for details

Contact
East Cowes PO32 6JY

t 01983 200022
w english-heritage.org.uk

Hampshire

041 Alton

The Allen Gallery

2 hrs+   All year

The gallery is housed in a group of C16 and C18 buildings and named after local artist William Herbert Allen. Its collection of decorative arts with ceramics, dating from 1250 to the present day, is considered to be one of the best in the south of England.

* Displays of WH Allen's watercolours & oil paintings
* Walled garden with outdoor sculptures

Location
Located in Church Street just off
Alton High Street

Opening
Tue–Sat 10am–5pm
closed 21 Dec–2 Jan & Good Friday

Admission
Free

Contact
Church Street,
Alton GU34 2BW

t 01420 82802
w hants.gov.uk/musuem/allen

042 Alton

Jane Austen's House

1 hr+   All year

Jane Austen's house is a pleasant C17 house in the pretty village of Chawton, not far from her birthplace of Steventon. The museum houses an attractive collection of items connected with Jane and her family including the table at which she wrote her novels.

* Pretty garden with varieties of C18 plants and herbs
* Examples of Austen's jewellery & needlework skills

Location
Situated in the village of Chawton,
2 miles SW of Alton

Opening
Daily; Mar–Nov 11am–4pm
Dec–Feb Sat & Sun only

Admission
Adult £4.50, Child £1, Concs £3.50

Contact
Chawton, Alton GU34 1SD

t 01420 83262
w janeaustenmuseum.org.uk
e enquiries@jahmusm.org.uk

043 Bishop's Waltham

Bishop's Waltham Palace

1 hr   Apr–Sep

The last Bishop of Winchester to live at Bishop's Waltham left in a dung cart, disguised as a farm labourer! He was escaping from Oliver Cromwell's troops after unsuccessfully defending his palace. Much of what can be seen today dates from the C12 and C14.

* Exhibition on the powerful bishops of Winchester
* Decorative & furnished Victorian farmhouse

Location
5 miles from junction 8 of M27

Opening
Apr–Sep closed Sat; 10am–6pm

Admission
Free Mon–Fri;
Sun exhibition Adult £2.50, Child
£1.30, Concs £1.90

Contact
Winchester Road,
Bishop's Waltham SO32 1DH

t 01489 892460
w english-heritage.org.uk

044 Brockenhurst

Beaulieu Abbey and National Motor Museum

3 hrs+   All year

Visit the C13 Beaulieu Abbey, Palace House and grounds, and the National Motor Museum. Few car museums in the world can match the unique collection here at Beaulieu, with legendary world record breakers like Bluebird and Golden Arrow.

* Exhibition of James Bond vehicles & props
* In 2004 the abbey celebrated its 800 year anniversary

Location
Going W on M27 take A326. Signed
Beaulieu or National Motor Museum

Opening
Daily; May–Sep 10am–6pm; Oct–Apr
10am–5pm; closed 25 Dec

Admission
Please phone for details

Contact
Brockenhurst SO42 7ZN

t 01590 612345
w beaulieu.co.uk
e info@beaulieu.co.uk

037 Exceat

Seven Sisters Country Park

4 hrs+   All year

Named after the famous Seven Sisters that form part of the Sussex chalk cliffs on Britain's heritage coastline. This site, situated in an Area of Outstanding Natural Beauty, is a popular location for outdoor activities including walking, cycling, canoeing and horse riding.

* Restaurant with beautiful walled garden
* Shop selling leaflets, maps & souvenirs

Location
Off the A259 between Eastbourne and Seaford or bus 712, 713 or 714 from Eastbourne

Opening
Daily

Admission
Free

Contact
Exceat,
Seaford BN25 4AD

t 01323 870280
w www.sevensisters.org.uk
e sevensisters@southdowns-aonb.gov.uk

038 Hailsham

Herstmonceux Castle

2–4 hrs   Easter–Oct

Herstmonceux is renowned for its magnificent moated castle, beautiful parkland and Elizabethan gardens. Built originally as a country home in the mid-C15, the castle embodies the history of medieval England and the romance of Renaissance Europe.

* Castle is only open to guided tour parties
* Tours last for approximately one hour

Location
Off A27 on the A22 toward Hailsham

Opening
Gardens Daily; Easter–Sep 10am–6pm; Sep–Oct 10am–5pm
Castle Easter–Oct Sun–Fri; only with guided tour, phone for details

Admission
Gardens Adult £4.50, Child £3, Concs £3.50 *Castle* £2.50, £1, £2.50

Contact
Hailsham BN27 1RN

t 01323 833816
w herstmonceux-castle.com
e c_dennett@isc.queensu.ac.uk

039 Pevensey

Pevensey Castle

1 hr   All year

The ruins of this medieval castle stand in one corner of a Roman fort, on what was once a peninsula surrounded by the sea and salt marshes. The Roman fort, named Anderida, was built in about AD 290. It is one of the largest surviving examples in Britain.

* 491 AD, Britons massacred here by Anglo-Saxons
* 1066, William the Conqueror landed his army here

Location
In Pevensey off A259

Opening
Daily; Apr–Sep 10am–6pm
Oct–Mar Sat & Sun 10am–4pm

Admission
Adult £3.50, Child £1.80, Concs £2.60

Contact
High Street,
Pevensey BN24 5LE

t 01323 762604
w english-heritage.org.uk

040 Sheffield Green

Bluebell Railway

1 hr+   All year

This is the UK's first preserved standard gauge railway, which runs along the Lewes to East Grinstead line of the old London Brighton and South Coast Railway. It serves to preserve this country branch line, its steam locomotives, coaches and signalling systems.

* Famous Terrier class engines, Stepney & Fenchurch
* Featured in the film *The Railway Children*

Location
Sheffield Park Station

Opening
Daily; May–Sep 11am–4pm;
Oct–Apr Sat & Sun 11am–4pm

Admission
Adult £9.00, Child £4.50

Contact
Sheffield Park Station TN22 3QL

t 01825 720800
w bluebell-railway.co.uk
e info@bluebell-railway.co.uk

Brighton Sea Life Centre

  2 hrs+ All year

Originally opened in 1872, the centre combines beautifully restored Victorian architecture with spectacular displays of marine life from shrimps to sharks. It is active in marine conservation projects and in raising awareness about threats to marine life.

* One of the longest underwater tunnels in England
* Over 30 modern marine & freshwater habitats

Location
Take the M23/A23 from London or the A27 from Portsmouth & Lewes

Opening
Daily from 10am;
please phone for details of winter opening times

Admission
Adult £8.50, Child £5.50, Concs £7.50

Contact
Marine Parade,
Brighton BN2 1TB
t 01273 604234
w sealifeeurope.com
e slcbrighton@merlinentertain-ment.biz

Ashdown Forest Llama Park

  2 hrs All year

See over a hundred llamas and alpacas! Watch them in the fields or get close to them in the barns. Enjoy farm walks, a museum, a picnic area, a coffee shop, an adventure play area and a lovely shop selling alpaca knitwear and South American crafts.

* 100–plus llamas & alpacas
* Angora & cashmere goats

Location
Located beside A22, 300 yards S of junction with A275

Opening
Daily 10am–5pm

Admission
Adult £4.00, Child & Concs £3.50

Contact
Wychross Forest Row RH18 5JN

t 01825 712040
w llamapark.co.uk
e info@llamapark.co.uk

033 Brighton

The Royal Pavilion

2 hrs+   All year

This former seaside residence of King George IV with its exotic Indian-style exterior boasts a myriad of domes and minarets. Admire magnificent decorations and furnishings in the Chinese style and gardens replanted to the original Regency scheme. Complete with a superb shop.

* Tactile/Sennheiser tours for partially sighted/hearing
* Wonderful Regency furniture & antiques

Location
Brighton town centre, 15 mins walk from Brighton station

Opening
Daily; Oct–Mar 10am–5.15pm (last admissions 4.30pm)
Apr–Sep daily 9.30am–5.45pm (last admissions 5.00pm)

Admission
Please phone for details

Contact
Brighton BN1 1EE

t 01273 603005
w royalpavilion.org.uk
e visitor.services@brighton-hove.gov.uk

034 Brighton

University of Brighton Gallery & Theatre

1 hr   All year

The presence of some of the country's most innovative artists and students makes this one of the most appealing gallery spaces in the south. The modern gallery presents exhibitions covering many aspects of the arts.

* A frequently changing exhibition programme
* Theatre has lectures & musical performances

Location
Grand Parade university campus, Central Brighton

Opening
Gallery Mon–Sat 10am–5pm
Theatre Many evenings, phone for details

Admission
Gallery Free
Theatre Please phone for details

Contact
Grand Parade, Brighton BN2 0JY

t 01273 643012
w brighton.ac.uk/gallery-theatre/
e c.l.matthews@brighton.ac.uk

17

031 Battle

Battle Abbey & Battlefield

1 hr+   All year

There is almost as much myth surrounding the Battle of Hastings as known fact. The two armies did not even fight at Hastings, but at a place south of the town now named Battle. Visit the ruins of the abbey that William the Conqueror built to commemorate his victory.

* Interactive audio tour recreates the sounds of battle
* Stand on the spot where defeated King Harold fell

Location
In Battle, at S end of High Street. Battle is reached by turning off A21 onto A2100 10 mins from Battle Station

Opening
Daily; Apr–Sep 10am–6pm
Oct–Oct 10am–5pm
Nov–Mar 10am–4pm

Admission
Adult £5, Child £2.50, Concs £3.80

Contact
High St, Battle TN3 30AD

t 01424 773792
w english-heritage.org.uk

032 Brighton

Brighton Museum & Art Gallery

2 hrs+   All year

The museum has a famous collection of Arts & Crafts, Art Nouveau and Art Deco; Salvador Dali's sofa in the shape of Mae West's lips and stunning gowns from Schiaparelli to Zandra Rhodes. Exhibits include intricate sculptures, decorated masks and beautiful textiles.

* Paintings by Duncan Grant & Edward Lear
* Regularly changing exhibits

Location
Brighton town centre

Opening
Tue 10am–7pm, Wed–Sat 10am–5pm, Sun 2pm–5pm, Bank holiday Mondays 10am–5pm; Christmas closed

Admission
Free

Contact
Royal Pavilion Gardens, Brighton
BN1 1EE

t 01273 290900
w virtualmuseum.info
e museums@brighton-hove.gov.uk

027 High Wycombe

Wycombe Summit Ski & Snowboard Centre

2 hrs   All Year

This world-class ski and snowboard school is suitable for experts and beginners. It has a 300m main slope, 100m trainer slope and several nursery areas with three lifts. Training available at all ability levels. The centre regularly hosts national race competitions.

* England's longest ski slope
* Alpine chalet bar & restaurant open all day

Location
Between junctions 3 & 4 of the M40, just ½ hour from London

Opening
Daily; summer Mon–Fri 10am–10pm, Sat & Sun 10am–6pm; winter 10am–10pm; closed 25 Dec
Please phone for details

Admission
Please phone for details

Contact
Abbey Barn Lane
High Wycombe HP10 9QQ
t 01494 474711/439099
w wycombesummit.com
e info@wycombesummit.com

028 Ivinghoe

Pitstone Windmill

½ hr   Jun–Aug

This post mill is believed to be one of the oldest in Britain, dating back to at least 1627. The mill was given to the National Trust in 1937. Restoration was started in 1963 and that work is now regarded as one of the forerunners of voluntary restoration work in the UK.

Location
Located S of Ivinghoe on B488 to Tring

Opening
Jun–Aug Sun 2.30pm–6pm

Admission
Adult £1, Child 30p

Contact
Holland Cottage, Whipsnade, Dunstable, Bedfordshire LU6 2LG
t 01582 872303
w nationaltrust.org.uk

029 Stoke Mandeville

Obsidian Art

½ hr+   All year

This large art gallery houses over 300 original paintings, drawings, sculptures and limited edition prints. The gallery exhibits a range of British art, from traditional to modern abstract.

* Regularly changing exhibitions & local artists
* Opportunity to purchase original artwork & gifts

Location
On A4010 S of Stoke Mandeville, follow signs for Goat Centre

Opening
Tue–Sun 10am–5pm
Closed 24 Dec–1 Jan

Admission
Free

Contact
The Bucks Goat Centre,
Old Risborough Road,
Stoke Mandeville HP22 5XJ
t 01296 612150
w obsidianart.co.uk
e info@obsidianart.co.uk

030 Wendover

The Chiltern Brewery

1 hr   All year

Opened in 1980, this family-run establishment is now Buckinghamshire's oldest working brewery. The site offers tours and tastings.

* Five bespoke, award-winning beers are produced here
* Tours on Sat only, booking necessary

Location
On the B4009, which joins the A413 1 mile from Wendover

Opening
Mon–Sat 9am–5pm

Admission
Free
Tours £3.50

Contact
Nash Lee Road, Terrick,
Aylesbury HP17 0TQ
t 01296 613647
w chilternbrewery.co.uk
e enquiries@chilternbrewery.co.uk

025 High Wycombe

Hughenden Manor

2 hrs+   Mar–Oct

The home of Victorian prime minister and statesman Benjamin Disraeli from 1848 until his death in 1881. Most of his furniture, books and pictures remain here – his private retreat from parliamentary life in London. There are beautiful walks through surrounding park.

* Certain rooms have low electric light – avoid dull days
* Events throughout the house & park

Location
1 mile N of High Wycombe W of the Great Missenden road (A4128)

Opening
House Mar Sat & Sun 1pm–5pm
Apr–Oct Wed–Sun 12noon–5pm
Garden Mar Sat & Sun
Apr–Oct Wed–Sun

Admission
House & Garden Adult £4.70, Child £2.30, *Garden only* £1.70, 80p

Contact
High Wycombe HP14 4LA

t 01497 755565/01494 755573
w nationaltrust.org.uk
e hughenden@nationaltrust.org.uk

026 High Wycombe

Wycombe Museum

1 hr+   All year

Trails and special activities combine with imaginative displays to make this a lively museum for visitors. Permanent exhibits, videos and sound recordings tell the story of High Wycombe and the local district.

* Superb collection of Windsor chairs
* Gardens include a Norman 'castle' mound

Location
Off A404 towards Amersham

Opening
Mon–Sat 10am–5pm, Sun 2pm–5pm
Closed Bank Hols

Admission
Free, donations appreciated

Contact
Priory Avenue,
High Wycombe HP13 6PX

t 01494 421895
w wycombe.gov.uk/museum
e museum@wycombe.gov.uk

Chalfont St Giles

Chiltern Open Air Museum

2 hrs+   Apr–Oct

This unusual museum contains over 30 historic buildings, including a 1940s, fully furnished prefab, a working Victorian farm and forge. Set in beautiful open parkland with a nature walk and seat-sculpture trail, the museum is a wonderful place for all ages to visit.

* Explore more than 30 rescued historic buildings
* Visit Skippings Barn, home to the Hawk and Owl Trust

Location
Signposted from A413 at Chalfont St Giles and Chalfont St Peter

Opening
Daily; Apr–Oct 10am–5pm

Admission
Adult £6, Child £3.50, Concs £5

Contact
Newland Park, Gorelands Lane, Chalfont St Giles HP8 4AB

t 01494 871117
w coam.org.uk
e coamuseum@netscape.net

---

022   Chalfont St Giles

John Milton's Cottage

1 hr+   Mar–Oct

This picturesque late C16 Grade I-listed cottage, set in an attractive garden, is the only surviving building in which the famous writer and parliamentarian lived. It was bought by public subscription in 1887 to celebrate Queen Victoria's jubilee and to preserve it for visitors.

* Milton came here in 1665 to escape the plague
* He completed *Paradise Lost* here

Location
On A40 to Chalfont St Giles, cottage in the centre of village

Opening
1 Mar–31 Oct 10am–1pm & 2pm–6pm (closed Mon, ex Bank Hol)

Admission
Adult £3, Child £1

Contact
Chalfont St Giles HP8 4JH

t 01494 872313
w miltonscottage.org
e info@miltonscottage.org

---

024   High Wycombe

Hellfire Caves

1 hr+   Mar–Oct

These caves were originally excavated in the 1750s by Sir Francis Dashwood on the site of an ancient quarry. It is thought that his inspiration for the design of the caves came from his grand tour of Europe and the Ottoman Empire.

* Sir Francis Dashwood founded the Hellfire Club
* The caves are haunted by Sir Paul Whitehead.

Location
Approx 3 miles from High Wycombe on the A40 towards Oxford

Opening
Daily; Mar–Oct 11am–5.30pm

Admission
Adults £4.00, Conc £3.00

Contact
High Wycombe HP14 3AJ

t 01494 533739
w hellfirecaves.com

Buckinghamshire

019 Brill

Boarstall Tower

1 hr   Mar–Sep

Visit the C14 gatehouse and gardens of Boarstall House (demolished 1778). Built by John de Haudlo in 1312, and updated in 1615 for use as a banqueting pavilion or hunting lodge, the tower has retained its medieval belfry, crossloops and crenellations.

* Many rooms remain virtually unchanged since 1615
* Handsome oriel windows

Location
Midway between Bicester and Thame, 2 miles W of Brill

Opening
27 Mar–30 Sep Wed 2pm–6pm & Sat 11am–4pm
Bank Hols by appointment

Admission
Adult £2.20, Child £1.10

Contact
Boarstall, Aylesbury HP18 9UX

t 01844 239339
w nationaltrust.org.uk
e rob.dixon@erros.co.uk

020 Buckingham

The Old Gaol

½ hr+   All year

The Old Gaol is the landmark building in Buckingham town centre. Restored by the Buckingham Heritage Trust, it houses a fascinating museum that reflects the building's history via audio-visual display and exhibits of Buckingham's past and military history.

* Regular themed exhibitions
* The ancient cells with their double doors still remain.

Location
Buckingham town centre

Opening
Mon–Sat 10am–4pm

Admission
Adult £2.00, Child & Concs £1.50

Contact
Market Hill, Buckingham MK18 1JX

t 01280 823020
w mkheritage.co.uk
e old.gaol@lineone.net

021 Buckingham

Stowe Landscape Gardens

2 hrs+   All year

This is one of the finest Georgian landscape gardens, comprising valleys, vistas, narrow lakes and rivers. You'll also find more than 30 temples and monuments designed by many of the leading architects of the C18. At the centre is Stowe House, now Stowe School.

* Audio-visual display about the evolution of Stowe
* Voted one of finest gardens in Britain in 2003

Location
3 miles NW of Buckingham via Stowe Avenue, off A422

Opening
Feb–Oct Wed–Sun 10am–5.30pm
Nov–Feb Sat &Sun 10am–4pm

Admission
Adult £5, Child £2.50

Contact
Buckingham MK18 5EH

t 01280 822850
w nationaltrust.org.uk
e stowegarden@nationaltrust.org.uk

016 Aylesbury

The King's Head

½ hr+   All year

Thought to be one of the oldest surviving courtyard inns in the country. Enclosed by the public area and the stable block, it provided services for the many horse-drawn carriages. Excavation has proved activity from the Bronze Age.

*Second-hand bookshop in courtyard open 11am-3pm
* Large mullioned window contains pieces of C15 glass

Location
At the NW corner of Market Square in Aylesbury

Opening
Mon–Thurs 11am-3pm 6pm-11pm
Fri & Sat 11am-11pm

Admission
Adult £2, Child free

Contact
King's Head Passage,
Market Square, Aylesbury HP20 2RW
t 01296 381501
w nationaltrust.org.uk
e kingshead@ntrust.org.uk

017 Aylesbury

Tiggywinkles, The Wildlife Hospital Trust

1½ hrs+   All year

Since opening its doors the Wildlife Hospital Trust has treated over 100,000 patients. Watch and learn about a remarkable number of patients including hedgehogs, badgers, rabbits, deer, wild birds, snakes. Virtually all species of British wildlife are featured here.

* Hedgehog museum and baby mammal viewing
* New children's play area & CCTV link to animal hospital

Location
Signed off the A418 from Aylesbury

Opening
Easter–Sep Mon–Sun 10am-4pm
Oct–Easter Mon– Fri 10am-4pm

Admission
Adult £3.80, Concs £2.80

Contact
Aston Road, Haddenham,
Aylesbury HP17 8AF
t 01844 292292
w sttiggywinkles.com
e mail@sttiggywinkles.org.uk

018 Aylesbury

Waddesdon Manor

2 hrs+   All year

Created by Baron Ferdinand de Rothschild, this Renaissance-style chateau was built in the 1870s for his house parties. The house contains a unique collection of French C18 objects. The landscape gardens are famous for their spectacular views.

* Meissen exhibition
* Good example of C19 needlework window dressings

Location
Via Waddesdon village, 6 miles NW of Aylesbury on A41

Opening
Grounds 3 Mar–31 Oct & 17 Nov–23 Dec
Wed–Sun 10am–5pm; call for Jan–Mar
House 23 Mar–30 Oct Wed–Sun & Bank Hols 11am–4pm; 17 Nov–23 Dec

Wed–Sun 10am–5pm

Admission
Grounds Adult £4, Child £2
House Adult £11, Child £8

Contact
Waddesdon, Aylesbury HP18 0JH
t 01296 653211/01296 653226
w waddesdon.org.uk

Berkshire

Buckinghamshire

013   Windsor

Windsor Castle

2 hrs+   All year

This is an official residence of the Queen and the largest occupied castle in the world. A fortress for over 900 years, the castle remains a working palace today. Visit the state apartments–extensive suites of rooms at the heart of the working palace.

* The magnificent & beautiful St George's Chapel
* Apr–Jun, the Changing of the Guard at 11am (not Sun)

Location
Follow brown signs to central Windsor

Opening
Daily; Mar–Oct 9.45am–5.15pm
Nov–Feb 9.45am–4.15pm
Closed 25, 26 Dec

Admission
Please phone for details

Contact
Ticket Sales and Information Office,
The Official Residences of The Queen,
London SW1A 1AA
t 0207 766 7304
w royal.gov.uk
e information@royalcollection.org.uk

014   Aylesbury

Buckinghamshire County Museum & Roald Dahl Gallery

1 hr+   All year

This award-winning museum is housed in beautifully restored buildings, some dating from the C15. It is a showcase for the county's heritage and runs a varied programme of exhibitions as well as interactive fun in the Roald Dahl Children's Gallery.

* Regular Roald Dahl activities & events
* Collections of British studio pottery, costume & lace

Location
Aylesbury town centre

Opening
Museum Mon–Sat 10am–5pm;
Sun 2pm–5pm
Roald Dahl Gallery Mon–Fri 3pm–5pm
(term time) 10am–5pm (hols);
Sat 10am–5pm, Sun 2pm–5pm

Admission
Museum **Free**
Roald Dahl Gallery Adult £3.50, Child £2.75

Contact
Church Street, Aylesbury HP20 2QP
t 01296 331441
w buckscc.gov.uk/museum
e museum@buckscc.gov.uk

015   Aylesbury

Buckinghamshire Railway Centre

2 hrs+   Apr–Oct

A working steam museum where you can experience the sights, sounds and smells of the golden age of steam. Ride behind a full-sized steam engine or aboard the miniature railway. The centre has a large collection of steam locomotives, carriages and wagons.

* See the Royal Train of 1901
* Santa Steaming the four weekends before Christmas

Location
Signed from A41 near Waddesdon &
A413 at Whitchurch

Opening
Apr–Oct Wed–Fri 10.30am–4.30pm;
Weekends 10.30am–5.30pm

Admission
Adult £6, Child £4, Concs £2

Contact
Quainton Road Station, Quainton
Aylesbury HP22 4BY
t 01296 655720
w bucksrailcentre.org
e abaker@bucksrailcentre.
   btopenworld.com

009 Reading

Basildon Park

1 hr+   Mar–Nov

Fascinating and beautiful, this C18 Palladian mansion has an extraordinary history. It was used as a hospital during World War I, and as a base for American servicemen during World War II when it was left a near ruin. It's been lovingly restored by Lord and Lady Iliffe.

* Studies for the tapestry 'Christ in Glory' on show
* Pleasure gardens & trails through woodland

Location
A329 between Pangbourne & Streatley

Opening
Mar–Nov Wed–Sun & Bank Hols
House 1pm–5.30pm
Grounds 11am–5.30pm

Admission
Adult £4.80, Child £2.40

Contact
Lower Basildon, Reading RG8 9NR

t 0118 9843040
w nationaltrust.org.uk
e basildonpark@nationaltrust.org.uk

010 Reading

Beale Park

4 hrs   Easter–Oct

This unique RBST-approved charity, is home to an amazing collection of birds including swans, owls, parrots and pheasants. It also boasts a narrow gauge railway. There are boat trips in summer, acres of lawns and gardens for picnics, sculpture, ponds and fountains.

* The Trust breeds & rears endangered species
* National collection of model boats

Location
6 miles from Reading on the A329 between Pangbourne & Streatley

Opening
Daily; Easter–Oct 10am–6pm

Admission
Adult £6.00, Child £4, Concs £5.00

Contact
Lower Basildon, Reading RG8 9NH

t 0118 9845172
w bealepark.co.uk
e administration@bealepark.co.uk

011 Reading

Museum of English Rural Life

1 hr   All year

Founded by the University of Reading in 1951, the museum reflects the changing face of farming and the countryside. It houses collections of national importance, including objects, archives, photographs, film and books.

* A programme of free fun family days
* Part of the University's Museum & Collections Service

Location
On the Whiteknights' campus of the University, 2 miles SE of Reading

Opening
Tue–Sat 10am–1pm & 2pm–4.30pm
closed Christmas, New Year & Easter

Admission
Adult £1, Child & Concs free

Contact
University of Reading, PO Box 229, Whiteknights, Reading RG6 6AG

t 0118 378 8660
w ruralhistory.org
e merl@reading.ac.uk

012 Thatcham

Thatcham Nature Discovery Centre

2 hrs+   All year

An exciting place to learn about local wildlife. The wide range of hands-on exhibits in Discovery Hall are set against a dramatic backdrop of giant insect models, colourful banners and wildlife quilts. Visitors can enjoy a walk around the lake and visit the reed-bed bird hide.

* Gallery with changing exhibitions
* Bird hide

Location
Between Thatcham & Newbury signed from A4

Opening
Nov–Feb Tues–Sun 1pm–4pm
Mar–Oct Tues–Sun 11am–5pm

Admission
Free, donations appreciated

Contact
Muddy Lane, Lower Way, Thatcham RG19 3FU

t 01635 874381
w westberks.gov.uk
e naturecentre@westberks.gov.uk

007 Newbury

Greenham & Crookham Common

2 hrs+   All year

After many years as a military site, the common has been restored and reopened to the public. Paths and marked walk routes allow you to explore the heathland and visit old bombsites and taxiways. Visitors can look across the cruise missile silo enclosure.

* The area is a Site of Special Scientific Interest (SSSI)
* Rare plant communities

Location
Car Park at Bury's Bank Road, Greenham

Opening
Daily; Summer 8am–8.30pm; Winter 8am–4pm

Admission
Free

Contact
West Berkshire Council, Countryside & Environment, Council Offices, Faraday Road, Newbury RG14 5AS

t 01635 519808
w westberks.gov.uk
e tourism@westberks.gov.uk

008 Newbury

The Living Rainforest

1 hr+   All year

Explore the rainforest and discover its wonders for yourself. This living rainforest aims to promote a sustainable future by providing education on the world's rainforests. The site features a tropical rainforest-inspired ecological garden with free-roaming animals.

* Endangered Goeldi's monkeys leap among branches
* Birds, butterflies, lizards roam freely as you explore

Location
Clearly signed from junction 13 of the M4

Opening
Daily; 10am–5.15pm (last admission 4.30pm) closed Dec 25/26

Admission
Phone for details or check website

Contact
Hampstead Norreys RG18 0TN

t 01635 202444
w livingrainforest.org
e enquiries@livingrainforest.org

004 Newbury

Highclere Castle

1 hr   Jul–Sep

Highclere is probably the finest Victorian house in existence. The three men who made Highclere what it is today were the 3rd Earl of Carnarvon who built the new house, Sir Charles Barry who designed it and the 4th Earl of Carnarvon who finished the interiors.

* Georgian pleasure grounds laid out by Robert Herbert
* 5th Earl of Carnarvon found the tomb of Tutankhamun

Location
Off A34, 4½ miles S of Newbury

Opening
Jul 6–Sep 5 Tues–Fri & Sun 11am–5pm
All Bank Hols (ex Mons)
last entry 1 hr before close

Admission
Adults £7, Child £3.50, Concs £5.50

Contact
Highclere, Newbury RG20 9RN
t 01635 253210
w highclerecastle.co.uk
e theoffice@highclerecastle.co.uk

005 Newbury

Desmoulin

½ hr+   All year

Desmoulin is housed in the granary on the wharf, in one of Newbury's finest old buildings. This contemporary gallery exhibits an ever-changing collection of quality art and artefacts – paintings, photographs, furniture, jewellery in silver and gold, glassware and ceramics.

* Café supplies light lunches, caters for vegetarians

Location
Town centre next to tourist information

Opening
Mon–Sat 10am–5pm
Sun by appointment

Admission
Free

Contact
The Granary, The Wharf,
Newbury RG14 5AS
t 01635 35001
w desmoulin.co.uk
e snail@desmoulin.co.uk

006 Newbury

Donnington Castle

½ hr+   All year

Constructed during the late C14, the striking twin-towered gatehouse of this castle survives amid some impressive earthworks. Originally built as a fortified residence, it was seized by Royalists at the beginning of the English Civil War.

* External viewing only

Location
1 mile N of Newbury off B4494

Opening
Dawn to dusk

Admission
Free

Contact
Newbury RG14 8LT
t 0845 3010008
w english-heritage.org.uk

Berkshire

001   Eton

Museum of Eton Life

1 hr   Apr–Oct

The museum tells the story of the foundation of Eton College in 1440 and provides a glimpse into the world of the Eton schoolboy, past and present. Find out about work, games, punishment, and some of the colourful customs of the past.

* Discover well-known Old Etonians, from poets to PMs
* Explore the College buildings

Location
Eton High Street

Opening
Daily; Apr–Oct 10.30am–4.30pm
school hols; 2.30pm–4.30pm term
time

Admission
Adult £3.80, Child £3, Concs £3

Contact
Visits Manager, Eton College, Eton,
Windsor SL4 6DW

t 01753 671177
w etoncollege.com
e r.hunkin@etoncollege.org.uk

---

002   Maidenhead

Cliveden

3 hrs   Mar–Oct

This spectacular estate overlooking the River Thames has a series of gardens, each with its own character, featuring topiary, statuary, water gardens, a formal parterre, informal vistas, woodland and riverside walks. It was once the home of Nancy, Lady Astor.

* Magnificent Italianate palace
* Winter parks & gardens

Location
2 miles N of Taplow, A404 to Marlow &
follow brown signs

Opening
Estate & Garden Daily; Mar–Oct
11am–6pm; Nov–Dec 11am–4pm
House Apr–Oct Thurs & Sun
3pm–5.30pm

Admission
Adult £6.50, Child £3.50

Contact
Taplow, nr Maidenhead SL6 0JA

t 01628 605069
w nationaltrust.org.uk
e cliveden@nationaltrust.org.uk

---

003   Newbury

Ashdown House

1 hr   Apr–Oct

An extraordinary Dutch-style C17 house, famous for its association with Elizabeth of Bohemia, Charles I's sister, to whom the house was consecrated. The interior has a great staircase rising from hall to attic, and important paintings contemporary to the house.

* Spectacular views from the roof over the gardens
* Beautiful walks in neighbouring Ashdown Woods

Location
2 miles S of Ashbury, 3 miles N of
Lambourn, on W side of B4000

Opening
House & Garden Apr–Oct Wed & Sat
2pm–5pm
Woodland All year closed on Fri.
Tours begin at 2.15pm, 3.15pm &
4.15pm

Admission
Adult £2.20, Child free

Contact
Lambourn, Newbury RG16 7RE

t 01488 72584
w nationaltrust.org.uk
e ashdownhouse@nationaltrust.org.uk

gleswade
Haverhill
Sudbury **409**
Ipswich **415**
Urford Ness

33 **355** **372**
Saffron **412**
Walden
407

369 **359**
Felixstowe

381
Baldock
ESSEX
Halstead **367**
Manningtree
Harwich

HFORDSHIRE **370** **STANSTED**
Braintree
362–365
Colchester
The Naze

Stevenage
Bishop's Stortford
Witham
West **366**
Mersea
Clacton-on-Sea

380 **360–361**
Hertford
Chelmsford
Maldon

385 **382**
Hatfield
M11 Harlow **377**
Burnham-
on-Crouch

8 Hoddesdon **373**
Foulness
Island

79 **M25**
Enfield
Chigwell
Brentwood
Rayleigh
Southend-on-Sea

net **092–128**
M11
368
Basildon
Canvey Island

NDON **CITY** **371**
Tilbury
Sheerness

chmond
Woolwich
Gravesend
Isle of Sheppey
Herne Bay
Margate

gston
Dartford
Rochester
Whitstable
068

n Thames
Swanley
Gillingham
Sittingbourne
Ramsgate

140 **073** **M25**
Chatham
Faversham
Canterbury
Sandwich

Croydon **M20** **072**
North Downs
069–071
Deal

076–077 **M26** **083–084**
M2
KENT
074–075

Caterham **091**
Sevenoaks
Maidstone
M20
Dover

Oxted **086**
Tonbridge
Ashford
CHANNEL TUNNEL TERMINAL

gate Redhill **078** **142**
067
Folkestone

M23
Tunbridge Wells
079–080 Cranbrook
M20
Hythe

ICK East **036** **090** **082** **088**
Tenterden
081

ey Grinstead **173**
089
New Romney

rsham
Crowborough
085
LYDD/ASHFORD

4–175 Haywards **040** Uckfield
Rye
Dungeness

Hea Heathfield

E. SUSSEX Battle
Hastings

032–035 Lewes **038** Hailsham **031**

Hove Brighton Newhaven **039** Bexhill-on-Sea

g Seaford **037** Eastbourne

South Downs
Beachy Head

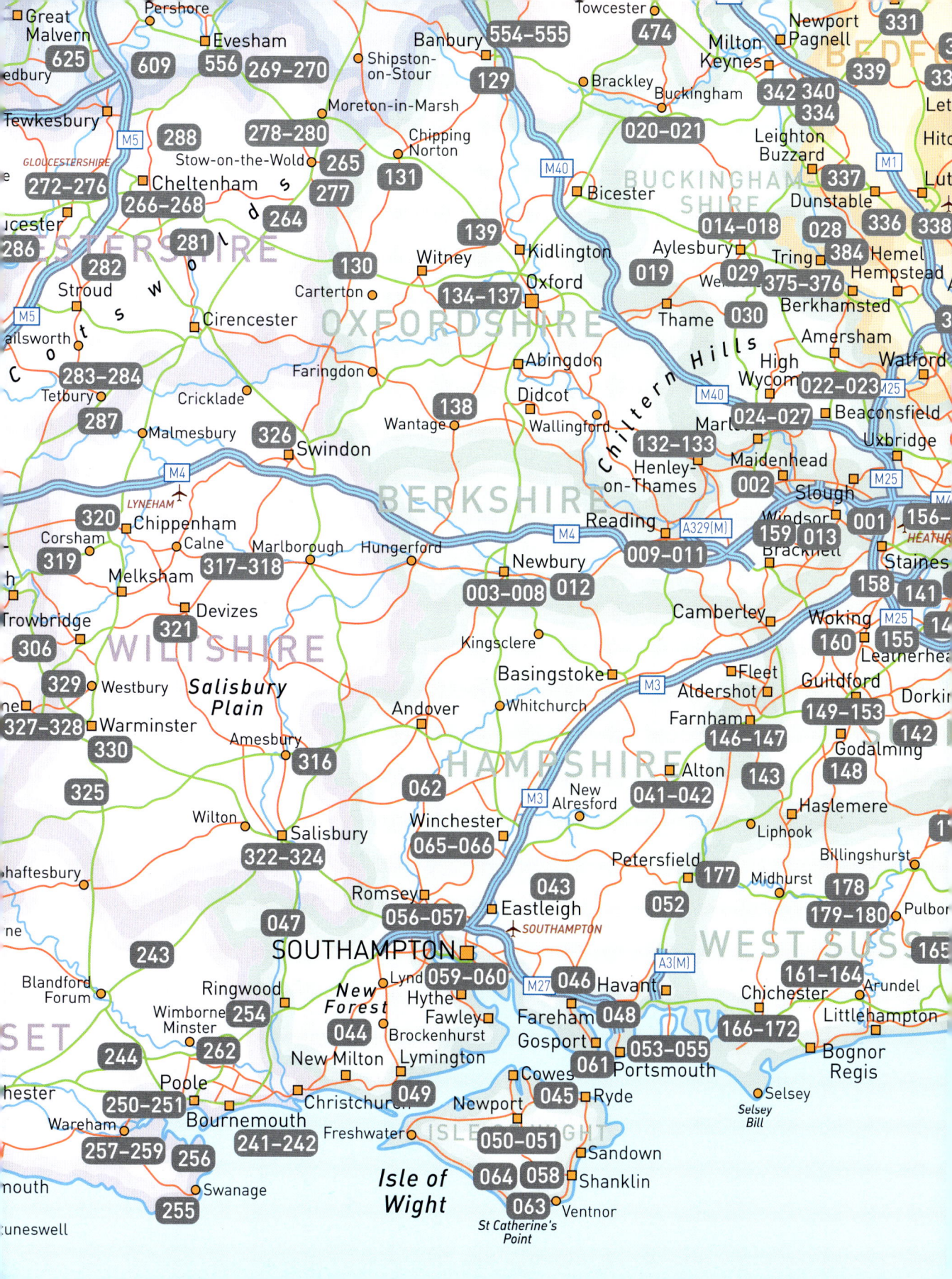

The Needles. Isle Of Wight

South East

Berkshire Buckinghamshire East Sussex
Hampshire and Isle of Wight Kent London
Oxfordshire Surrey West Sussex

Festivals & Events Calendar

www.steam-fair.co.uk
A hugely popular annual event drawing more than 200,000 visitors from all over the UK. The fair also features shire horses and rural crafts. Considered the finest of its kind in Europe.

3-4 September
Chatsworth Country Fair
Tel: 01246 565300
www.chatsworth-house.co.uk
Chatsworth House (home of the Duke and Duchess of Devonshire) hosts this annual autumn country fair. Local crafts and delicious foods available from over 200 stalls.

3-4 September
Bristol International Kite Festival
www.kite-festival.org.uk
Held in the grounds of the Ashton Court Estate, this event is an opportunity to see some of the most spectacular kites from around the world. A regular programme of displays takes place in the arena.

3 September
The Braemar Gathering, Aberdeenshire
Tel: 013397 55377
www.braemargathering.org
With a history going back over 900 years, the Braemar Gathering is still an important Highland event with international athletes taking part in 'heavy' and 'track' events. Braemar also hosts the Inter Services Tug of War Championship.

10-11 September
Riverside Festival, Leicester
Tel: 0116 299 5982
www.leicesterfestivals.co.uk
The city's Bede Park is the home to this annual event on and off the water. There are lots of things for children to do as well as boat rides, illuminated boat parades and live music.

11 September
Brick Lane Festival, London
www.bricklanefestival.com
An annual celebration that captures the flavour and excitement of an area that has welcomed new Londoners for over 2000 years. Entertainment includes a mix of top music acts, dance and Bollywood bands.

11-23 September
Techfest, Aberdeen
www.techfest.org.uk
An unusual event that celebrates technology and science. Events, which take place across Aberdeen including the exhibition and conference centre,

feature tours of local industries, workshops and activities for all ages.

17-18 September
The Mayor's Thames Festival, London
Tel: 020 7928 8998
www.thamesfestival.org
A riverside bazaar, fireworks and a huge lantern procession are the highlights of a series of activities centred on the River Thames. This free event also has numerous live bands throughout the day.

17-18 September
Royal Berkshire Show, Newbury
Tel: 01635 247111
www.newburyshow.co.uk
Camel racing and spectacular motorcycle displays complement the displays of show-jumping and heavy horses as well as the usual collection of farm animals. A great family day out.

17-18 September
Biggin Hill International Air Fair
Tel: 01959 572277
www.bigginhillairport.com
This international flying display involves military and civilian aircraft and teams performing aerial feats and stunts.

First week in October
Nottingham's Goose Fair
Tel: 0115 915 5330 or 0115 9156970
www.nottinghamgoosefair.co.uk
One of Europe's largest travelling fairs with over 150 rides and 450 games and exhibitions - including white knuckle rides, children's rides, a crafts marquee and food stalls at the Forest Recreation Ground.

7-9 October
MELA, NEC Birmingham
Tel: 020 8902 2270
www.mela2005.com
The UK's biggest Asian lifestyle show highlights the best of Asian culture. Experience the colours, aromas, sounds and tastes of the sub-continent.

9 October
World Conker Championship, Ashton, Northamptonshire
Tel: 01832 272735
www.enjoynorthamptonshire.co.uk
The 41st World Conker Championship takes places with the usual array of stalls and entertainments. Events for men, women, juniors and teams with all proceeds going to charity.

8-23 October
Canterbury Festival
Tel: 01227 452853
www.canterburyfestival.co.uk
Opera, dance, comedy, world music

and exhibitions. Canterbury Festival has something for every taste. The event climaxes with the spectacular choral concert in the magnificent cathedral.

29-30 October
Croxteth Hall Halloween Haunts, Liverpool
Tel: 0151 228 5311
www.croxteth.co.uk
Listen to haunting tales of ghosts and the supernatural by the light of a log fire then encounter the eerie atmosphere of the Hall by lamplight. (Adults only)

24 October 2005 – 10 April 2006
BG Wildlife Photographer of The Year
Tel: 0207 9425011
www.nhm.ac.uk
The Natural History Museum and BBC Wildlife Magazine organise this annual award. The winners and runners up are displayed in a show at the museum, which then tours the UK and the world.

Dates througout November
Somerset Carnivals
www.somersetcarnivals.co.uk
The Somerset Carnivals are highly regarded as some of the largest illuminated processions in the world. Starting in Bridgwater, they travel through the major towns of Somerset throughout the month.

Firework displays are held all over the country over the weekend of November 5/6. Check local press or council websites for exact details of an event near you.

6 November
Veteran Car Run (London to Brighton)
www.vccofgb.co.uk
Established in 1896 as the 'Emancipation Run' to celebrate the lifting of the speed limit from 4mph to 14mph and abolition of the need for a vehicle to be preceded by a man on foot. Open to all vehicles built before 1905.

4-13 November
Motor Cycle Show, NEC
www.motorcycleshow.co.uk
The annual event for motorcycle fans everywhere. All the new models will be on display as well as plenty of opportunity to buy the latest gear.

9-12 November
Bradford Animation Festival, National Museum of Photography, Film and Television
Tel: 01274 207688
www.baf.org.uk
This will be the twelfth festival of

animation with the usual mix of talks, demonstrations and workshops. Vote on-line for your favourite animation.

End November-late January
Somerset House Ice Rink, London
Tel: 0207 8454600
www.somerset-house.org.uk
Dominated by a 40ft Christmas Tree, this popular seasonal rink is a great destination for the whole family.

Throughout December
Edinburgh's Capital Christmas
Tel: 0845 2255121
www.edinburghscapitalchristmas.org
With Europe's largest outdoor ice rink in Princes Street Gardens, plus pony and trap rides, festive lights and a fairground, Edinburgh is the perfect place for a Christmas day out.

Christmas Tree in Trafalgar Square, London
www.norway.org.uk
Every year, the Norwegians give the British a giant Christmas tree as a token of appreciation of friendship during the Second World War. The magnificent Norwegian Spruce is bedecked with traditional white lights.

mid December-New Year
Medieval Frost Fair
Tel: 0870 442 2375
www.warwick-castle.co.uk
With snow, music and twinkling Christmas trees, the colours, sights and sensations of a Medieval Christmas are brought vividly to life. A host of entertainers add to this magical event.

29 December-1 January
Hogmanay, Edinburgh
www.edinburghshogmanay.org
See in the new year in Scotland where Edinburgh is said to host the world's best celebrations – fireworks, first-footing and a host of other Scottish traditions make these festivities something special.

Please note: Many of the dates listed are provisional at the time of going to press. We highly recommend that you use the contact details that we have provided to confirm event details before planning a trip.

Cornwall's major annual events. Primarily an agricultural event, it also boasts a fine selection of entertainment, a flower show and more.

12-17 June
World Town Crier Tournament, Chester
Tel: 01244 324324
www.chestercc.gov.uk/town-crier-tournament
The historic city of Chester hosts the Lord Mayor's World Town Crier Tournament when forty-eight of the world's extroverts, in period dress, descend on the city to compete for the title of world champion.

14-18 June
Royal Ascot at York
Tel: 01344 622211
www.royalascot.com
With Ascot's Berkshire home under redevelopment, the 2005 meeting will be staged at York Racecourse – the first time the meeting has been held away from Berkshire in its 300 year history.

19 June
World Nettle Eating Championships, Dorset
Tel: 01297 678254
www.thebottleinn.co.uk
The village of Marshwood hosts this extraordinary event where Champions munch through over 70 nettles re-enacting a dispute between two farmers. Plenty of entertainment adds to the fun.

25 June-10 July
Peterborough Festival
Tel: 01733 747474
www.peterboroughfestival.co.uk
This festival of music, theatre, art and sport starts with the Mayor's Carnival – a colourful parade. Central Park is the site of Party in the Park in the afternoon with local bands and some national stars.

June-July
Alnwick Medieval Fair, Northumberland
Tel: 01665 605004
www.northumberland.gov.uk
Alnwick Medieval Fair is a costumed re-enactment of a fair dating from the Middle Ages including craft stalls, courts, a ducking stall and entertainment.

Throughout July
Cardiff Festival
Tel: 029 2087 2087
www.cardiff-festival.gov.uk
The UK's largest free outdoor festival bringing colour and cultural vibrancy to the city and the waterfront of Cardiff Bay. Street theatre, music, drama and children's entertainment.

1-4 July
Winchester Hat Fair
Tel: 01962 849841
www.hatfair.co.uk
The city centre hosts Britain's longest-running festival of street theatre where spectators will be asked to dig into their pockets to fill the hats that are passed around.

9-10 July
Cotswold Show and Country Fair, Cirencester
Tel: 01285 652007
www.cotswoldshow.co.uk
Discover the gastronomic highlights of the Cotswolds along with crafts, live-stock shows, country pursuits and more.

16-18 July
Rothbury Traditional Music Festival, Northumberland
Tel: 01669 620419
www.rothbury-traditional-music.co.uk
This festival offers a mixture of local and international musicians who play and sing with a passion for traditional music.

18-22 July
Swan Upping on the River Thames, Berkshire
www.thamesweb.co.uk/windsor
Traditional boats and costumes add to the atmosphere of the annual swan-marking procession which dates back to medieval times.

5 July
Kent Beer Festival
Tel: 01227 463478
www.kentbeerfestival.co.uk
The home of Britain's hop production, Kent hosts the annual beer festival at Merton Farm which boasts brews from seven of the county's finest breweries.

8-10 July
National Adventure Sports Show, Shepton Mallet
Tel: 0845 1300670
www.national-adventuresports.com
The biggest event in the Freesports calendar, the show presents board and bike sports platforms and showcases music and sport from BMX and freestyle Moto X to mountain boarding and biking.

18-21 July
Royal Welsh Show, Builth Wells
Tel: 01982 553683
www.rwas.co.uk
The Royal Welsh Show is a window on the world of farming in wales. The show runs for four days and attracts over 200,000 visitors each year.

23 July
World Toe Wrestling Championships, Staffordshire
www.benjerry.co.uk/worldchampionships/toewrestling
Perhaps the oddest sport of all – the first World Toe-Wrestling Championships were held in 1994 and this year sees the latest search for the supreme winner.

24-25 July
Sunderland International Air Show
Tel: 0191 5109317
www.sunderland-airshow.co.uk
The Sunderland International Air Show showcases military and civilian aircraft, parachute teams, stunt flying, entertainment, trade stands, displays and more on the seafront at Seaburn.

30 July-6 August
Sidmouth International Festival
Tel: 01629 827010
www.sidmouthfestival.com
This Edwardian seaside town comes alive for Europe's largest celebration of folk dance and song.

31 July
Manchester Lord Mayor's Parade
Tel: 0161 234 4014
www.manchester.gov.uk
Manchester's Lord Mayor's Parade is one of the largest civic events of the year and celebrates everything that is great about the city.

31 July-1 August
Bristol Harbour Festival
Tel: 0117 9222000
www.bristol-city.gov.uk
The renovated Dockside and Canon's Marsh Amphitheatre hosts this maritime extravaganza. The two-day festival is a wealth of free entertainment including live bands, fireworks, crafts and more.

2-8 August
Robin Hood Festival
Tel: 01623 824490
www.robinhood.co.uk
This festival is held in honour of its most famous outlaw in Sherwood Forest, with events to interest the whole family including jousting, jesting and archery.

5-27 August
Edinburgh Military Tattoo
Tel: 08707 5551188
www.edinburgh-tattoo.co.uk
The Edinburgh Military Tattoo celebrates over fifty years of music and spectacle set against the world famous backdrop of Edinburgh Castle.

6 August
Leicester Caribbean Carnival
Tel: 0116 225 7770
www.lccarnival.org.uk
The carnival is a day of fun, live music and dance as well as a colourful parade through the town centre. It is Britain's second largest regional carnival, second only to London's Notting Hill.

6-8 August
King Arthur's Last Battle Reenactment, Cornwall
Tel: 01840 779084
www.tintagelweb.co.uk
Warriors recreate the final battle between King Arthur and his illegitimate son, Mordred, where both men lost their lives to the other's hand, at Tintagel.

7-29 August
Edinburgh Fringe Festival
Tel: 0131 2260026
www.edinburghfestivals.co.uk/fringe
Originally open-access for all performers, the Fringe showcases some of the best talent in live performance, ranging from stand-up comedy to music and performance art.

12-15 August
International Balloon Fiesta, Bristol
www.bristolfiesta.co.uk
Set in the Ashton Court Estate, the International Balloon Fiesta features over 150 hot air balloons and offers a wealth of family entertainment.

28-29 August
Notting Hill Carnival
Tel: 08700 591111
www.rbkc.gov.uk/nottinghill
This carnival began in the St Pancras area of London and moved around until it found its home in Notting Hill. Music, dance, food and fun are the order of the day at the largest carnival in Britain.

29 August
World Bog Snorkelling Championships, Llanwrtyd Wells
Tel: 01591 6100666
www.llanwrtyd-wells.powys.org.uk/bog
This international sporting event takes place in the dense Waen Rhydd Peat bog on the southern outskirts of the smallest town in Britain.

1-4 September
Great Dorset Steam Fair, nr Blandford

Some of the best days out can be at one of the myriad of festivals that have sprung up all over the British Isles. Some, such as Nottingham's Goose Fair, have taken place for hundreds of years, the Goose Fair is thought to be 700 years old. Others, such as the National Adventure Sports Show near Shepton Mallet, are exciting upstarts by comparison.

Today's festival line-up covers every conceivable taste: music and dance; comedy and drama; animals; transport of every description; food and drink... and so the list goes on. Here, we have selected a broad cross-section of events offering a 'taster' of what is available across the British Isles.

Please be warned, we strongly recommend that you check first before setting off in search of an event listed here! Where possible, we have given dates for 2005 - some events are not yet finalised and others liable to change or even cancellation, so please check with

the websites and phone numbers listed to ensure that the festival that you are planning to visit is actually taking place. If in doubt the local Tourist Information Centres will help.

An added bonus of many of these events is that you can find a whole day's entertainment either free or for a small one-off entrance fee. This is particularly true if you are already a member of The National Trust or English Heritage whose properties regularly have fantastic events for no additional fee beyond your annual membership.

Please note: Many of the dates listed are provisional at the time of going to press. We highly recommend that you use the contact details that we have provided to confirm event details before planning a trip.

---

5 February-6 March
Orchid Festival, Richmond
Tel: 0208 3325655
www.rbgkew.org.uk
Kew Gardens hosts its annual orchid festival and displays over 100,000 orchids from all over the globe.

9 February
Chinese New Year, Liverpool
Tel: 0151 7080204
www.visitliverpool.com
Join Liverpool's Chinese community to celebrate the Year of the Rooster. Enjoy the variety of traditional food and New Year celebrations in a city with one of the oldest Chinese communities in Europe.

13-22 February
Jorvik Viking Festival, York
Tel: 01904 543403
www.jorvik-viking-centre.co.uk
York was once ruled by the Vikings and every year, they are remembered through this annual festival which includes living history events, markets, battle re-enactments and boat races.

10-13 March
Crufts, Birmingham NEC
Tel: 0870 6066750
www.crufts.org.uk
The greatest dog show on earth with over 20,000 top pedigree dogs chasing the title of 'Best in Show'.

25-28 March
Lancaster Easter Maritime Festival, Lancaster
Tel: 01524 582394
www.lancashire.gov.uk
To celebrate Lancaster's golden age of maritime trade, St George's Quay

hosts this Easter Maritime Festival with shantymen and songsters and an array of other maritime entertainment.

March-April 05
Spring Gardens Week and Flower Festival, Kent
Tel: 01622 765400
www.leeds-castle.com
The grounds of Leeds Castle are brimming with thousands of daffodils, bluebells, anemones and other blooms in springtime.

17 April
The London Marathon
Tel: 0207 9020189
www.london-marathon.co.uk
More than a sporting event, this is the largest streetparty in the world. The route is marked by the sound of bands, cheering crowds, entertainment and of course 30,000 runners.

1-23 May
Brighton Festival
Tel: 01273 260810
www.brighton-festival.org.uk
Brighton becomes a festival city for three weeks when a range of entertainment from opera and street theatre to stand-up comedy and cabaret takes over this lively town.

2-3 May
Weymouth Beach Kite Festival
Tel: 0208 846 9000
www.weymouth.gov.uk
Aerial fanatics from around the world assemble in Weymouth each May for Britain's biggest kite festival.

8-23 May
Isle of Wight Walking Festival
Tel: 01983 813813

www.walkthewight.org.uk
The biggest walking festival in the UK. Walkers from all over the world join in over 120 walks, covering 72,000 miles.

19 May-28 August
Glyndebourne Festival
Tel: 01273 814686
www.glyndebourne.com
This festival takes place in one of the world's best known opera houses set in one of the country's most beautiful gardens.

29-30 May
Southend Air Show
Tel: 01702 390333
www.southendairshow.com
Europe's largest free air show takes place over the seafront at Southend. Impressive aerobatics and plenty of exciting entertainment on the ground.

1-7 June
Etruria Canal Festival, Stoke-on-Trent
Tel: 01782 235000
www.stoke.gov.uk
The Etruria Industrial Museum hosts a family-friendly sumer festival. This gathering of narrowboats, canal boats and the Princess steam engine takes place in a carnival atmosphere.

1-4 June
Royal Bath and West Show, Shepton Mallet
Tel: 01749 822200
www.bathandwest.co.uk
The southwest's foremost agricultural event features the best in livestock, as well as majoring in food and country produce.

2-3 June
Suffolk Show, Ipswich

Tel: 01473 707110
www.suffolkshow.co.uk
The Suffolk Show, held on its own showground outside Ipswich, features farm livestock, agricultural trade stands, flower shows, horticultural exhibits and displays including showjumping.

5 June
Strawberry Fair, Cambridge
Tel: 01223 560160
www.strawberry-fair.org.uk
Held at Midsummer Common and now into its third decade, the Strawberry Fair has become a highlight of the Cambridge calendar.

5 June
Man versus Horse Marathon, Llanwrtyd Wells
Tel: 01591 610666
www.man-v-horse.org.uk
The pitting of man and horse in a marathon appears to be unique to the annual event in Llanwrtyd Wells.

8-12 June
Festival of Science, Cheltenham
Tel: 01242 522878
www.cheltenhamfestivals.co.uk
Cheltenham's Science Festival includes a packed programme of talks, debates, family events, events for schools, an interactive exhibition and cinema. A great opportunity to learn and have fun.

9-11 June
Royal Cornwall Show, Wadebridge
Tel: 01208 812813
www.royalcornwall.co.uk
Every June, Wadebridge hosts a three-day country show that is one of

918 Edinburgh (p342)

Edinburgh Castle

Part of Edinburgh's World Heritage Site

Built on a great volcanic rock, Edinburgh Castle is the most visited ancient monument in Britain after the Tower of London. The battlements of the castle provide spectacular panoramic views over the city. A stronghold was recorded here before 600AD and by the Middle Ages it had become a mighty fortification and the royal residence of Scotland's kings and queens. It has witnessed much of the nation's rich history including the birth of James VI, Mary Queen of Scots' only child. The tiny St Margaret's Chapel is Edinburgh's oldest building and dates from the 1100s; Crown Square, the main courtyard, was developed in C15; the Great Hall was built by James IV, the Half Moon Battery was created in the late C16; and the Scottish National War Memorial was added after the WW1. Other attractions include the Honours of the Kingdom exhibition which tells the story of Scotland's crown jewels; the famous Stone of Destiny – taken to Westminster Abbey in 1296 and returned to Scotland 700 years later; the medieval siege cannon, Mons Meg; and the National War Museum of Scotland. Listen out for the One O'Clock gun, fired every day at 1pm, except Sunday. Since 1950 the castle esplanade has hosted the annual Edinburgh Military Tattoo which is attended by some 200,000 people from all over the world.

Directions

Edinburgh Castle is in Edinburgh city centre and easily accessible on foot

Car Parking available, max 2 hours, £3

878 Carlisle-Newcastle (p323)

Hadrian's Wall

World Heritage Site

Built over a period of six years, by order of Emperor Hadrian who came to Britain in AD122, Hadrian's Wall is the most important Roman structure in Britain and probably the best-known frontier in the Roman Empire. Its purpose was to separate the Romans from the 'Barbarians', which it did for over 250 years. The wall was 8-10 feet wide and 15 feet high, with a rampart walk and 6-foot-high parapet. It is estimated that more than a million cubic metres of stone were used in its construction. There were over 80 forts, at one-mile intervals, each with a kitchen and barracks for a small garrison. There were also 17 larger forts holding from 500-1000 troops. Travelling along the 73-mile wall today, visitors can explore forts, milecastles, temples and turrets, all brought to life by museums, reconstructions and visitor centres. The central sections of the wall remain in good condition and are well worth visiting. The forts of Chesters, Corbridge, and Housesteads offer particularly good vantage points.

Directions

Car Access from the W via the M6 or A74 (Glasgow-Carlisle); access from the E via the A1 to Newcastle or the A68 (Edinburgh-Darlington). The A69 (Newcastle-Carlisle) runs parallel to Hadrian's Wall & is the main access route

Train Regular services to Newcastle & Carlisle, the 2 main access points for the wall

Bus Route AD122 Bowness-on-Solway-Wallsend via Carlisle & Newcastle

Foot Good network of footpaths. For more information email info@Hadrians-wall.org

789 Windermere (p291)

Windermere Cruises

Winner of the 2003 Cumbria for Excellence Award – Large Tourist Attraction of the Year

What better way to explore the Lake District? Windermere Cruises offer a wide range of sailings to suit all tastes: freedom tickets are valid for 24 hours from the time of purchase and are valid on all scheduled sailings from Bowness, Lakeside and Ambleside. Why not stop off and enjoy the World of Beatrix Potter, the Steamboat Museum or the Fell Foot National Trust Park with its adventure playground, woodland trail and picnic area? Islands Cruises provide a 45-minute sightseeing tour from Bowness Bay. A special one-hour version of this cruise is also available for exclusive use by private parties. Sailings between Lakeside and Bowness and between Bowness and Ambleside take 40 minutes and 30 minutes respectively in each direction with the option of breaking the journey and returning on a later sailing. Sailings between Brockhole and Ambleside depart hourly and are by traditional launch. Sailings between Bowness and Ferry House provide access to the opposite side of the lake for walkers and sailings between Lakeside and Fell Foot take you to Fell Foot National Park. All the vessels can be chartered for private functions.

Directions

Car Leave the M6 at junction 36 and follow the brown signs on the A590 for Windermere Lake Cruises and the A591 for Bowness and Ambleside sailings.

There are 300 car-parking spaces close to the piers at Lakeside and 250 spaces close to the pier at Ambleside (Waterhead). At Bowness, follow Lake Road (The Glebe) to the long-stay car park at Braithwaite fold which has 600 spaces

703 York (p260)

Castle Howard

Set in the beautiful Howardian Hills, Castle Howard is one of the finest stately homes in Britain. It was built in 1699 by the architect Sir John Vanbrugh and has been the private home of the Howard family for over 300 years. It took over 100 years to complete and was tragically destroyed by fire in 1940 but subsequently painstakingly restored to its former glory by George Howard after WW2. The castle has an impressive art collection, including works by Canaletto, Holbein, Gainsborough and Reynolds. There is antique sculpture, superb porcelain, and a set of three embroidered panels by William Morris representing Lucretia, Hippolyte and Helen of Troy. Authentically costumed characters, based on historical personalities, offer a range of themed tours of the castle. The grounds contain temples, statues and monuments and the lakes, fountains and waterways have all recently been restored. There are boat trips on the lake and a new plant centre set in Vanbrugh's 18th Century walled garden. With three eating places to choose from all tastes are catered for. The castle is a regular venue for outdoor concerts and events, and is also a popular film and television location. Productions filmed here include *Barry Lyndon*, *Twelfth Night*, *Brideshead Revisited* and *The Buccaneers*.

Directions

Castle Howard is 15 miles NE of York, just off the A64

Car Follow the brown & white tourist signs from from the A1, M1 and M62

Train Services from York or Scarborough to Malton. Taxis available at the station (01653 696969)

Bus Services from Yorkshire Coastliner (01653 692556), the Moorbus Network (0870 608 2608), or Eddie Brown Tours (01904 640760)

641 Caernarfon (p237)

Caernarfon Castle

World Heritage Site

Part castle, part royal palace, Caernarfon Castle is the birthplace of Edward II and undoubtedly the mightiest and most majestic of a number of castles built by Edward I after his conquest of North Wales in 1283. It is an enormous fortress by the sea and one of the most important and strategic in Britain. It is a testament to Edward's military might and a powerful symbol of his ambition being not only a military stronghold but also a seat of government and a royal palace. In common with his other castles in Conwy & Harlech, Caernarfon boasts massive gatehouses, towers and crossbow loops and there is also evidence of piped water, glazed windows and en-suite toilets. Caernarfon, however, surpasses the others, with its polygonal towers and banded masonry, inspired by the walls of Constantinople. Today the castle runs a number of exhibitions, an audio-visual programme, and is home to the Welsh Fusiliers' regiment museum. The symbolic status attributed to the castle when Edward's son, the first English Prince of Wales, was born here in 1284, was echoed in 1969 when the castle was used as the setting for the Investiture of Prince Charles as Prince of Wales.

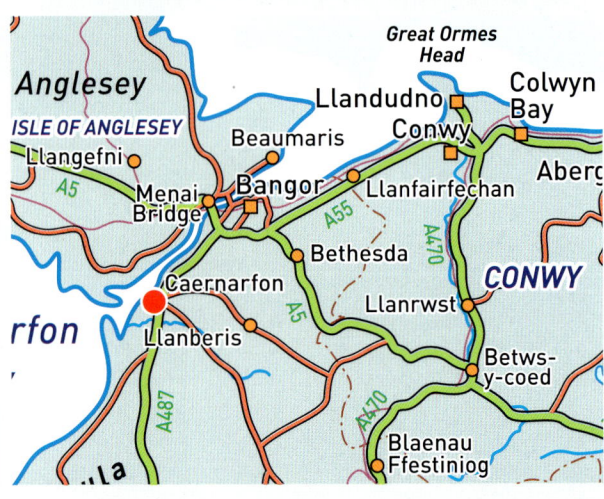

Directions

Caernarfon Castle is in the town of Caernarfon

Car Access to Caernarfon from the A405, A487(T) and B4366. There is a public car park with four wheelchair-user spaces close to the castle. Please note that there is a slope from the car park to the castle

Train 10 miles from Bangor on the Crewe-Bangor/ Holyhead route

Bus 220 yards from Caernarfon Penllyn, route No 5/5A/5B, Bangor-Caernarfon

532 Telford (p198)

Iron Bridge Gorge Museums

World Heritage Site

The Ironbridge Gorge has been described as 'the most extraordinary district in the world'. Today visitors can witness the furnaces, factories, workshops and canals that gave birth to the Industrial Revolution and made the area great. The first iron railway tracks, iron railway wheels and the first steam railway locomotive were all made here in the valley of the river Severn, which is spanned by the world's first iron bridge, cast in 1779 by Abraham Darby III. Within a six-mile radius are ten award-winning museums which represent various aspects of the area's rich industrial heritage. They are Broseley Pipeworks' Clay Tobacco Pipe Museum; The Tar Tunnel; Blists Hill Victorian Town; Coalbrookdale Museum of Iron; The Iron Bridge & Toll House; Museum of the Gorge; Darby Houses; Jackfield Tile Museum; Coalport China Museum & Enginuity. There are Sites of Special Scientific Interest along the valley where rich plant and animal life flourish.

Directions

The Ironbridge Gorge is on the River Severn, 5 miles S of Telford. There are 10 museums in the complex, within a six-mile radius, so transport is required to travel easily between them. There are car parks at or near all the sites

Car Take junction 4 from the M54, and follow the brown and white signs to Blists Hill Victorian town or follow the signs from Ironbridge. Pay-and-display car parking available

Train Telford train station is 5 miles N of Blists Hill Victorian town. For rail information call 08457 484950

Bus A regular shuttle bus service connects all 10 of the Ironbridge Gorge Museums on Sat, Sun & Bank Holidays, & has limited links to the train station. Call Telford Travelink on 01952 200005 for details

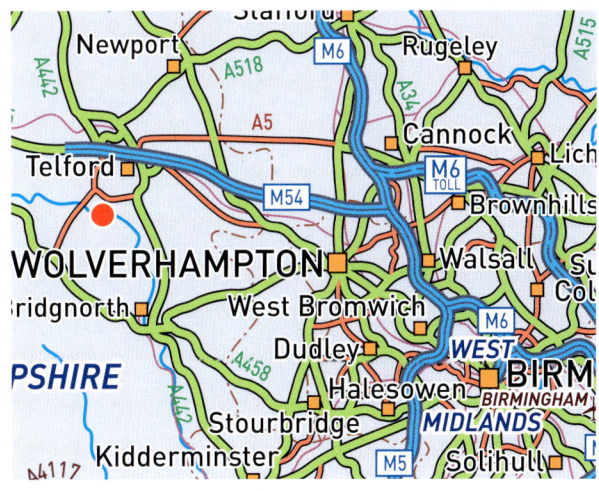

482 Nottingham (p179)

The Galleries of Justice

Visitor Attraction of the Year 2003

This award-winning visitor attraction is located in and around the magnificent Shire Hall. The grade-II listed site comprises two Victorian courtrooms, two prisons – one from 1800, one from 1833 – a prisoners' exercise yard, cave cells, a women's prison with bath house and laundry, a medieval cave system and an Edwardian police station. Costumed interpreters bring the whole experience to life, telling you how law and punishment has developed and changed over the years. The experience is very hands-on – whether you're having your fingerprints taken, doing laundry duty or spending a night in a police cell. The Crime & Punishment Galleries compare the splendour of the Victorian courtroom with the harshness of prison life, while the Transportation Gallery will give you an idea of how it felt to be a prisoner journeying to a new continent. The Police Galleries house an exciting and interactive exhibition, located in an original 1905 police station. Objects on display include forensic evidence from the Great Train Robbery and items from the museum's internationally-renowned collection of police memorabilia.

Directions

The Galleries of Justice are situated in Central Nottingham, near Broadmarsh Shopping Centre.

Car Follow brown & white tourist signs for the Galleries of Justice. Parking available in several nearby car parks, including the Broadmarsh Centre, Fletcher Gate & Stoney Street

Train Midland railway station is 10 mins' walk

Bus Victoria bus station is 10 mins' walk; Broadmarsh bus station is 5 mins' walk

345 Cambridge (p129)

King's College, Cambridge

Founded in 1441 by Henry VI as a college for 70 poor students from Eton College, today King's College is Cambridge's premier tourist attraction and home to over 600 students. The buildings were intended to be a spectacular display of Henry's power and unequalled in grandeur and style. He drew up elaborate plans for a great court but only the chapel, which took nearly a century to build, was ever completed (in 1547). One of the chapel's most famous features is the Rubens painting, *Adoration of the Magi.* The next major addition to the site was the Gibbs building, begun in 1724 and named after its architect. This was followed in the early C19 by the gatehouse and screen, the dining hall, library and old lodge. The most famous of these buildings is undoubtedly the magnificent perpendicular chapel, home to the King's College choir, whose carol renditions are broadcast live across the world on Christmas Eve. The college is set in beautiful grounds, known locally as The Backs, which sweep majestically down to the river Cam. In previous centuries these beautiful grounds have been home to a bowling green, a hop yard and a pigeon house.

Directions

King's College is situated on King's Parade in the heart of Cambridge

Car No parking at the college but there are several car parks in the city centre, all within walking distance of the college. Park and ride also available

Train Services run regularly from London King's Cross and take just under an hour. The college is a ¹/₂-hour walk or short bus/taxi ride from the station

Bus 5 mins' walk from Drummer Street, the main bus station

Bike Bicycle parking directly in front of the college. Cambridge is very bike-friendly and there are plenty of bike-hire shops

Highlight site **South West**

212 St Austell (p83)

The Eden Project

Travel to Cornwall and take a trip through the rainforests of the Oceanic Islands, Malaysia, West Africa and tropical South America to discover how the world relies on tropical plants and crops for survival. The Eden Project, a living rainforest, was built at a cost of £86 million and now attracts almost two million visitors a year. It aims to engage, educate and amuse visitors who want to learn more about man's relationship with the plant world. Its 35-acre site has over 100,000 plants representing 5000 species from many of the climatic zones of the world. Some of these (sunflowers, hemp and tea) grow outdoors in the mild English climate while others grow in one of Eden's two gigantic conservatories. The humid-tropics biome is home to rainforest plants – bananas, rubber, cocoa, coffee, teak and mahogany – while the warm-temperate biome has plants from South Africa, California and the Mediterranean. The humid-tropics biome is the largest conservatory in the world, weighing in at 240 m long, 110 m wide and 50 m high. Rainforests are hot places but there is a cool room and plenty of seats and water fountains if visitors need to cool off. The biomes transmit UV light, so remember to bring sun hats and protective suncream on sunny days.

Directions

4 miles E of St Austell

Car Signed from the A30, A390 & A391

Train Nearest station is St Austell. Buses connect with most mainline rail services. A combined train, bus & admission ticket is available for a small supplement. Call 08457 484950 for details

Bus Daily services from St Austell, Newquay, Helston, Falmouth & Truro – call Truronian on 01872 273453. Combined bus and Eden Project ticket available on the bus

Bike £3 discount for visitors arriving by bike – go straight to the fast-track desks

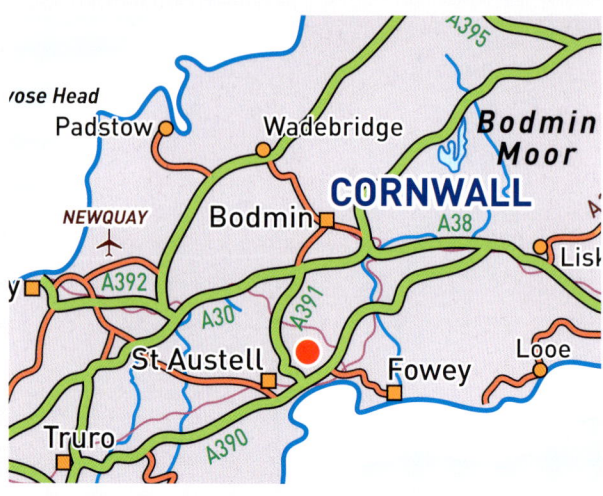

96 Central London (p37)

The London Eye

Designed by husband-and-wife architect team, David Marks and Julia Barfield, the British Airways London Eye is an amazing feat of design and construction. It is the largest observation wheel ever built, the only cantilevered structure of its kind in the world and the largest structure ever hoisted into a vertical position in one operation. Not surprising then that this multi-award winning attraction is one of the most spectacular and popular in the world. A flight on the Eye lasts 30 minutes and takes visitors 135 metres above the London skyline in a high-tech fully-enclosed capsule. Get a bird's-eye view of all the major London landmarks, from the British Museum to Tate Modern and the Houses of Parliament to Buckingham Palace. On a clear day it's possible to see Windsor Castle, 25 miles away. For an extra-special trip, visitors can book a guide who will point out all the major landmarks (in English, French, German or Spanish); have a champagne trip; travel in a private capsule; or be photographed with Big Ben in the background. For convenience, visitors are advised to book their preferred day and time well in advance.

'My favourite building? I'd pick the London Eye.'
Lord Foster, Architect

Directions

On the South Bank opposite Big Ben

Underground 5 mins' walk from Waterloo (follow signs for the South Bank) or Westminster (exit 1 & follow signs for Westminster pier)

Train 5 mins' walk from Waterloo. Take exit 6 & follow signs for the South Bank or 15 mins' walk from Charing Cross – access via Hungerford pedestrian bridge

Bus 211, 24 & 11, most London sightseeing buses & the RV1 route (London Eye-Tate Modern-Covent Garden)

Car Limited parking on the South Bank

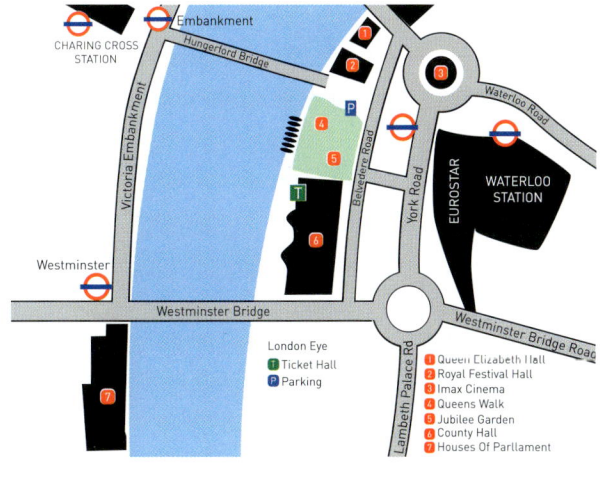

London Eye
T Ticket Hall
P Parking

1 Queen Elizabeth Hall
2 Royal Festival Hall
3 Imax Cinema
4 Queens Walk
5 Jubilee Garden
6 County Hall
7 Houses Of Parliament

could visit **www.5minutesaway.co.uk** for a useful list of services on and around the motorway network. Alternatively you may choose to take your own refreshments so a suitable picnic venue will be more important (see 'What to take with you').

Tourist Information Centres
If you are visiting an attraction as part of a longer stay in an area, or you just want to know more about where you are going to spend your day then one of the most useful places to find is the local Tourist Information Centre (TIC). TICs employ local staff that know the area intimately and can provide a personalised level of information.

There are nearly 1000 TICs in Great Britain so too many to list here. However, you can find a complete listing at **www.visitbritain.com** or by ringing one of the directory enquiry services. TICs can generally provide you with places to visit, places to eat and places to stay.

What to take with you
Planning what to take with you on your day out will depend on many things including the time of year and where you are planning to go. No two trips are the same and no two sets of people have the same feelings towards flasks, picnics, wet wipes, wellies, cameras or binoculars.

Once you have arrived at your destination, all you should have with you is a small rucksack with your

essentials: bottled water, tissues, money, a credit card and of course a camera – with film (or disk these days).

Picnic
Whether you take a picnic is definitely a matter of personal taste. For some it is an essential part of any day out while others will consider it an unnecessary hassle that is to be avoided at all costs.

As a minimum I would recommend that no trip be undertaken without a supply of bottled water and perhaps some fruit. Being stuck in traffic with no refreshments can make your journey miserable. Equally, arriving at your destination to find either there is no food that day, or the quality of what is available does not match your expectations can be frustrating.

Why not fill your picnic basket with a selection of delicious treats from the Marks & Spencer deli range? Watch out for special offers over the summer months.

Train travellers should use the National Rail Enquiries Online Journey Planner to find train times and fare information for any mainland UK train operator (**www.nationalrail.co.uk/planmyjourney**) or telephone 0870 484950. Local Tourist Information Centres (see below) should provide you with times of suitable bus connections or taxi details. Bus information can also be found at **www.timetables.showbus.co.uk** or the National Traveline 0870 608 2608.

Car health check

It does not take long to check petrol, oil, tyres and screen wash, so the day before your expedition take a little time for these essentials.

Have a quick look at the oil and top up if necessary. While the bonnet is up, fill the screen wash container and check your wiper blades are effective. Next make sure that tyres are all inflated to the correct pressures and that they have a legal amount of tread (1.6mm). You should also check that your jack is where it ought to be and that you are confident you know how it works. Faulty batteries are the single biggest reason for people calling the motoring rescue services, so it's always worth spending a little time on preventative maintenance.

Another simple check that can help protect you is to make sure all your lights and indicators are working. You should also ensure that the lenses are clean to maximise visibility.

This is a basic set of checks that may help prevent a frustrating day but should not be taken as a replacement for regular servicing by a qualified mechanic.

Breaking your journey

If your journey is more than two hours it is recommended that you have a break. The dangers of being tired at the wheel are now well documented and a 15-minute break can refresh you. When planning your journey think about where you can stop. Perhaps there is somewhere interesting en route and you can plan your day around two or more destinations – use the maps included in this book to see if there are places of interest that you could stop.

If your route is largely made up of motorway driving you

detail can then be found under the entry for each venue.

If you need further information you can try either *Microsoft AutoRoute* software or go to any of the major motoring support organisations' websites where you will find highly detailed route-planning facilities.

Before any day out it is always sensible to check the latest traffic and travel news. Try **www.theaa.com/travelwatch** which is a great source that also includes printable route plans and maps. Alternatively, telephone 09003 401100. The BBC also provides rolling reports of roadworks and accidents on **www.bbc.co.uk/travelnews**.

Preparing for a day out

by Sally Ferrier

AS ADVENTURERS David Hempleman-Adams, Sir Edmund Hillary, and even Richard Branson will tell you, the key to any successful expedition is planning, and a day out is no different.

Trust me, this is the voice of experience, as my husband and I suffered the very worst from bad planning. One bright morning in June, we decided we would take a trip to Arundel Castle. Fascinating architecture, beautiful grounds and an impressive collection of paintings... however, when we arrived after a two-hour drive, we found that Arundel Castle was actually shut that day!

It might seem an obvious thing to say but step one for any journey must be to check whether the attraction you are planning to visit is open. Even if this book and every other source you have consulted indicates it is open, circumstances can change without notice. The cost of a phone call might save a lot of wasted time – not to mention disappointment.

Once you have established that your destination is open there are all sorts of things to consider. How will you get there? How long will it take to get there? What are the opening hours? What will the weather be like? Should you take a picnic? Here we have tried to outline all the things you should think about and offer suggestions to help you plan your trip.

The weather

If the attraction you are planning to visit is open to the elements, then make sure you check the weather. Each entry has a weather symbol to indicate how important the weather is to your potential enjoyment. The radio, TV and newspapers will give you the bigger picture, and Ceefax and Teletext are also useful, but for a detailed weather forecast for the area you are planning to visit, try one of the weather websites. Sites such as **www.metoffice.com** will give regional and local forecasts over the whole of the UK as well as world and city forecasts. These are also available by phone and numbers are available from the website. If you would like an even more specific forecast then go to **www.bbc.co.uk/weather** and pinpoint your exact location by its postcode for a five-day forecast.

Plan your route

This book is divided into regions. At the start of each region is a map that shows the major roads and a rough indication of where the attractions are located. More

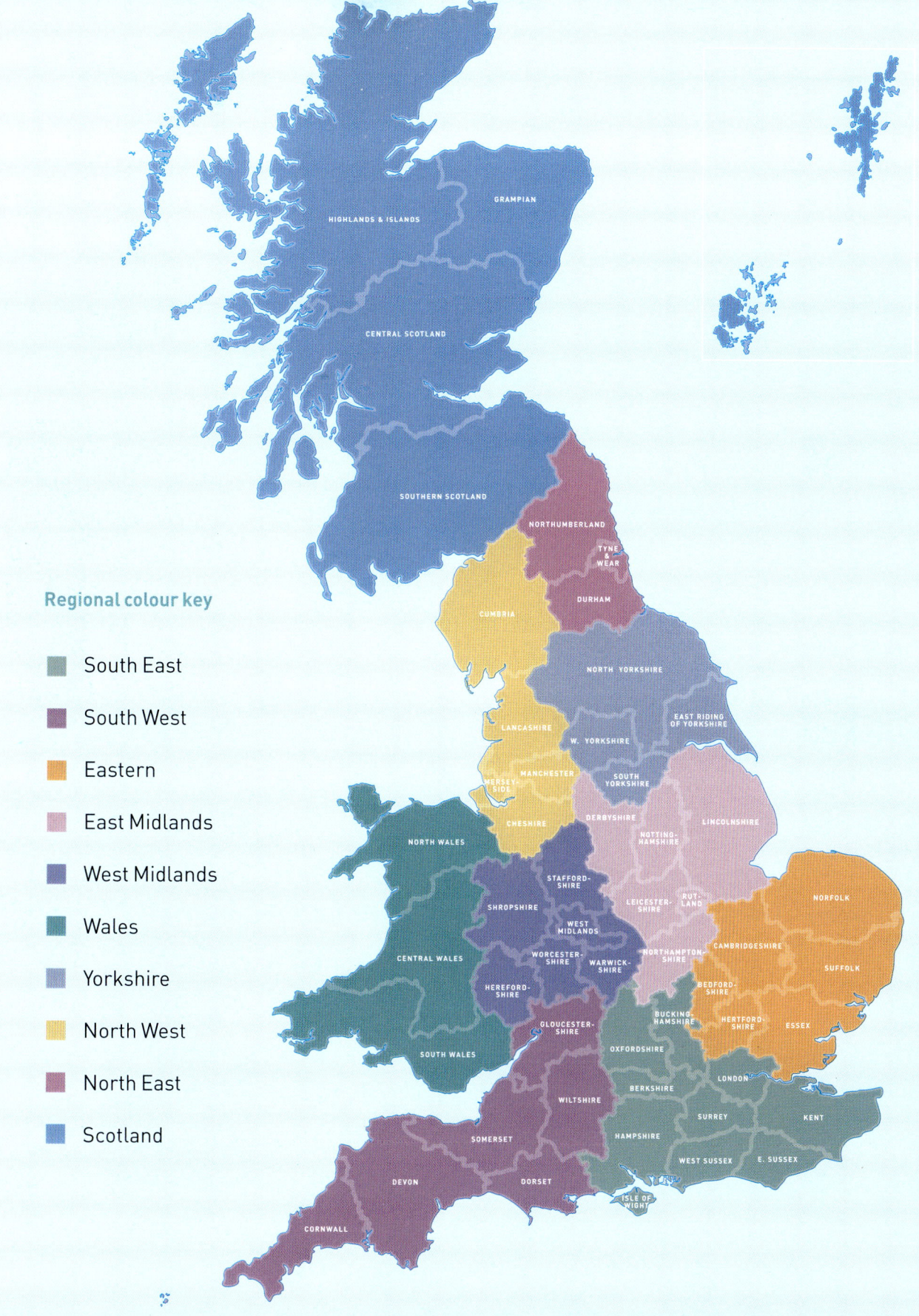

Regional colour key

- South East
- South West
- Eastern
- East Midlands
- West Midlands
- Wales
- Yorkshire
- North West
- North East
- Scotland

HIGHLANDS & ISLANDS

GRAMPIAN

CENTRAL SCOTLAND

SOUTHERN SCOTLAND

NORTHUMBERLAND

TYNE & WEAR

CUMBRIA

DURHAM

NORTH YORKSHIRE

EAST RIDING OF YORKSHIRE

LANCASHIRE

W. YORKSHIRE

MANCHESTER

MERSEY-SIDE

SOUTH YORKSHIRE

CHESHIRE

DERBYSHIRE

LINCOLNSHIRE

NORTH WALES

NOTTING-HAMSHIRE

STAFFORD-SHIRE

NORFOLK

SHROPSHIRE

LEICESTER-SHIRE

RUT-LAND

WEST MIDLANDS

CENTRAL WALES

WORCESTER-SHIRE

WARWICK-SHIRE

NORTHAMPTON-SHIRE

CAMBRIDGESHIRE

SUFFOLK

HEREFORD-SHIRE

BEDFORD-SHIRE

BUCKING-HAMSHIRE

HERTFORD-SHIRE

ESSEX

SOUTH WALES

GLOUCESTER-SHIRE

OXFORDSHIRE

LONDON

WILTSHIRE

BERKSHIRE

SURREY

KENT

SOMERSET

HAMPSHIRE

WEST SUSSEX

E. SUSSEX

DEVON

DORSET

ISLE OF WIGHT

CORNWALL

to toilets and refreshment facilities. Assistance dogs are usually accepted unless stated otherwise. For the hard of hearing, please check that hearing induction loops are available by contacting the attraction itself.

Location

These are simple directions, usually for motorists (although directions are given for those using the Underground in London) and have been provided by the attraction itself.

Opening times

These times are inclusive, e.g. Apr–Oct indicates that the attraction will be open from the beginning of April to the end of October. Where an attraction has varied opening times, these are indicated; and if it is open seven days a week, this is simply referred to as 'Daily'. Bank Holiday opening is indicated where provided by the attraction.
If you are travelling a long way please check with the attraction itself to ensure any unexpected circumstances are not going to prevent your entry.

Admission

Wherever possible the charges quoted are for the 2004–5 season, but please note that prices are subject to change and are only correct at the time of going to print. If no price is quoted, it does not mean that a charge will not be made. Many places that do not charge admission may ask for a voluntary donation. In some instances discounts may be available to families, groups, local residents or members of certain organisations such as English Heritage and the National Trust.

Contact details

We have given details of the administrative address and telephone number for each attraction. While this is usually the details of the attraction itself, some properties are administered by an area office, in which case these details are given (several English Heritage properties fall into this category).

Telephone numbers, email and website addresses are also included wherever possible.

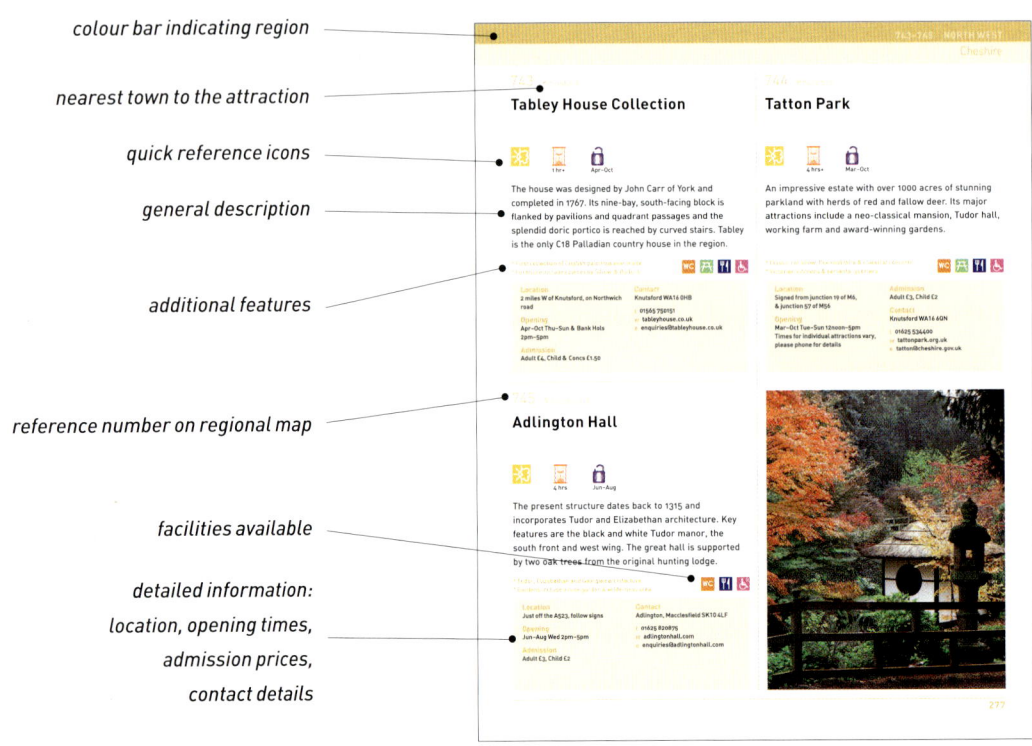

colour bar indicating region

nearest town to the attraction

quick reference icons

general description

additional features

reference number on regional map

facilities available

detailed information:
location, opening times,
admission prices,
contact details

Introduction

Britain is one of the most popular holiday destinations in the world. It's easy to see why. Major cities like London, Glasgow and York with their world-famous museums, palaces and stately architecture attract visitors all the year round. There are also areas of outstanding natural beauty like the Lake District and the Peak District, the Brecon Beacons and the Gower Peninsular in Wales and the Highlands in Scotland – all with their own natural history and wildlife. There are mountains and moors, industrial landscapes, castles, gardens... and all surrounded by at least 3000 miles of coastline. But with so many places to choose from, it's hard to know where to begin.

1001 Days Out will help you do just that. The book is packed with ideas to form the basis of a day out in Britain where you will discover the natural beauty, rich heritage and cultural attractions that England, Scotland and Wales have to offer. This practical guide offers a broad selection of attractions ranging from world famous castles, stately homes and gardens to carefully restored windmills, ancient ruins and rediscovered gardens. But also included are many small and more unusual places to visit. With 1001 entries, all tastes are catered for.

Of course, at any one time, many attractions are closed for renovation or refurbishment. For this reason, we have not included the Museum of the Moving Image on London's South Bank, or the Maritime Museum in Swansea for example. As this book is published annually, these attractions will be considered for inclusion next year.

About this guide

This guide covers England, Scotland (including the Northern and Western Islands) and Wales and is arranged in regions, shown on the national map on page viii. The counties within each region, the towns within each county and the attractions within each town are all, where possible, arranged alphabetically. Each attraction also has a reference number and this is used on the regional map at the beginning of each section.

Understanding the entries

Coloured bands at the top of each page indicate regions; the numbers in the top corners next to the regional name refer to the numbered range of attractions on the page. The nearest major town or village to the attraction is indicated above the name of the attraction.

Quick reference icons

an all-weather attraction

an attraction for sunny days only

the expected duration of your visit

when the attraction is open

Description

Each entry has a brief description of the attraction and a flavour of what visitors may expect to find. Additional features are also highlighted beneath the description.

Facilities

toilet facilities available

space available for you to eat your own food

restaurant, café or kiosk facilities available

good access for wheelchairs   restricted access

dogs allowed, but they may have to be kept on a lead

Disabled visitors

Visitors with mobility difficulties should look for the wheelchair symbol showing where all or most of the attraction is accessible to wheelchair bound visitors. We strongly recommend that visitors telephone in advance of a visit to check exact details, including access

Contents